# Also available at all good book stores

9781801500630

9781801500067

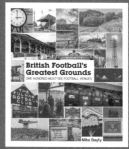

9781785316470

9781801500968

9781801500937

9781801500975

9781801501170

9781785317828

9781801501101

# WHEN ASIA WELCOMED THE WORLD

DANNY LEWIS

# WHEN ASIA WELCOMED THE WORLD

## THE 2002 WORLD CUP REVISITED

First published by Pitch Publishing, 2022

Pitch Publishing
9 Donnington Park,
85 Birdham Road,
Chichester,
West Sussex,
PO20 7AJ
www.pitchpublishing.co.uk
info@pitchpublishing.co.uk

ISBN 978 1 80150 125 5

Typesetting and origination by Pitch Publishing
Printed and bound in India by Replika Press Pvt. Ltd.

# Contents

# Introduction

FOR A six-year-old child who was only just getting into football, the 2002 World Cup felt truly magical. Every day there were games, I would do everything I could to catch a glimpse of the action, and there was even a television screen set up in my school where we could watch the England games.

Flags lining the streets, a pack of Panini stickers every time I went to the shops and *MATCH* magazine brought plenty of joy throughout the tournament. Even so, nothing at home – no matter how impressive – could compare to what was broadcast from South Korea and Japan.

There were so many incredible characters throughout the competition who couldn't possibly be ignored: Rüştü Reçber, the mad goalkeeper with lines drawn on his face; Oliver Kahn, who threw himself in front of everything; El Hadji Diouf, whose bleached hair was almost as eye-catching as his performances for Senegal; David Beckham, the star almost every England fan adored; Brazil's incredible trio of Ronaldo, Ronaldinho and Rivaldo who swept teams aside. Wherever I looked, there was a player ready to make me fall in love with football that little bit more.

Then there were all the major upsets, which showed me that anything is possible in football, and it is never guaranteed that one team will beat another. However not everybody shared my youthful naivety, and those upsets that had caught my attention became part of what is now a divisive legacy for the tournament.

Unbeknown to me, there were calls of corruption that had helped certain nations progress, while there is also the argument that scheduling put the stronger nations at a disadvantage – in turn, making the upsets that took place less impressive or noteworthy in the minds of some.

No matter the wider opinion about the World Cup's 2002 edition, this is a tournament that has maintained a strong place in the history books and is still being looked at and discussed 20 years later – whether that's reminiscing on moments of brilliance or questioning decisions. This edition will always be historic as it was the first to be hosted in Asia, as well as the first to be co-hosted by two nations.

So this book will delve into the first time Asia welcomed world football to its shores, reliving those incredible moments that captured my attention so emphatically, as well as the things that have stained the tournament in the minds of many others.

# 1

# Bringing the World Cup to Asia

SOUTH KOREA and Japan eventually became the first countries to co-host a World Cup, but that wasn't always the plan. The two Asian nations had initially gone up against each other (and Mexico) in a bid to host world football's biggest tournament. Both countries are said to have poured money into their publicity campaigns, partly fuelled by a historically poor relationship.

Eventually, the head of the Asian Football Confederation stepped in and the two nations were given an ultimatum: they would host the World Cup together or not at all. Mexico had always been deemed a long shot, so the pair had a straight run at co-hosting after the decision was made to partner up. There was even talk of some games being played in North Korea to help ease relations, but that was eventually ruled out.

There were complaints from some about the hosting situation. European fans were unhappy that they wouldn't be able to watch games at a time comfortable for them, while many questioned the logistical challenges of hosting a World Cup across two countries. The tournament's start date was also questioned, with the Asian climate playing a part in

9

the decision to play the first match just over two weeks after the Champions League Final and 20 days after the Premier League season ended.

Japan had never played in a World Cup when the hosting rights were awarded in 1996 – though they did in 1998 – which initially caused further questions to arise.

Queries even surrounded the Adidas Fevernova ball that was used throughout the tournament. Mick McCarthy said in *Ireland's World Cup 2002*, 'The ball is lively. It moves differently in the air, the bounce is unique and its unusual colour scheme deceives the eye as it comes up off the turf.' There were also issues with unused tickets being slow in being returned from the countries they were sent to.

There were positives as FIFA and the United Nations branded their partnership with a slogan reading 'Say Yes For Children'. The campaign was advertised at every game, aiming to encourage people to improve and protect the lives of children. Roger Milla was also brought in as an ambassador to help address AIDS during the tournament.

In addition, Japan and South Korea both heavily invested in their infrastructure to ensure they would be able to build and improve their venues so that they were up to the level required for football's biggest competition. In fact, eight of the ten arenas had 'World Cup Stadium' in their names.

No matter the questions that had arisen, there was a real buzz in the build-up as everyone waited to see who would be crowned world champions.

# Group Stage – Matchday One

*France 0 Senegal 1 (Group A, 31 May, Seoul)*

It seemed as though only one team could possibly win the opening game as it approached: France. Les Bleus were coming into the tournament off the back of their World Cup victory in 1998 and lifting the European Championship in 2000, so were seen as favourites to win in 2002. Meanwhile, Senegal were entering their first World Cup, having progressed through their CAF qualification group by outdoing Morocco on goal difference.

The Africans had also endured a tough time in the build-up: their pre-tournament friendlies resulted in a 0-0 draw at home to Guinea and a 3-2 defeat to Saudi Arabia. To make things even harder, Khalilou Fadiga was interrogated by South Korean police over the alleged theft of a $245 gold necklace from a jewellery shop in Daegu. The charges were dropped after the forward admitted he had taken it as part of a prank that had gone wrong and the store owner made peace by sending him a small golden pig as a good luck charm. Regardless of the happy ending, police interference days before a major tournament isn't ideal.

The individuals lining up for the two teams only seemed to accentuate the difference in quality. France had the top scorers from three of the world's most respected leagues at their disposal: Arsenal's Thierry Henry had notched 24 times in the Premier League, Juventus's David Trezeguet scored 24 goals in Serie A, while Auxerre's Djibril Cissé was the joint top scorer in Ligue 1 with 22 goals. The latter only made it to the bench for the opener. Their side also boasted Chelsea's leader Marcel Desailly, as well as big names including Patrick Vieira, Lilian Thuram and Frank Leboeuf. In comparison, all but two of Senegal's squad played their domestic football in France – with the others playing in Senegal and Morocco.

France were missing Zinedine Zidane, who was fresh from winning the Champions League for Real Madrid with his sensational volley against Bayer Leverkusen. The talismanic midfielder had gone off injured during a pre-tournament friendly against co-hosts South Korea, with it later being revealed that he had suffered a tear in the median third of the quadriceps. That wasn't enough for expectations in France to be dampened, though.

Even Vieira, who was actually born in Dakar, Senegal, seemed to dismiss the African side's chances. When speaking to *Le Parisien* days before the tournament, the midfielder's thoughts translated to, 'It will be hard for the Senegalese because they will discover the World Cup. In addition, we will be highly motivated because we know the importance of this match. It will condition all of our competition. Having said that, I really want an African team to be at least in the quarter-finals. It could be Cameroon. This selection gives off a nice impression of power. She progresses with each competition.'

Twenty-one-year-old El Hadji Diouf showed France that he posed a threat from the very beginning. Within a minute the winger had won a free kick off Desailly, then got his head on the delivery to force Fabien Barthez into the game's first save. If Diouf was showing that Senegal could attack, Aliou Cissé took it upon himself to remind France that the Africans would compete as the midfielder slid in on Henry moments later, conceding a free kick in the process.

There were also signs that France weren't at their imperial best, as Vieira and Leboeuf both gave the ball away cheaply. Still, this was a team packed with game-changing talent and despite having made a mess of two previous chances, Trezeguet offered a warning in the 23rd minute. Emmanuel Petit played the ball through to Henry, who slotted it to his strike partner. Trezeguet cut across the ball to send his effort out of goalkeeper Tony Sylva's reach, but it rebounded off the post and towards Omar Daf, who cleared the danger.

When Daf had the ball shortly after, he was doing much more than merely putting it into touch. The 25-year-old rushed in to steal it away from Youri Djorkaeff before releasing it to Diouf. Senegal's number 11 drew Leboeuf in before flying past the defender and reaching the byline. With Desailly approaching, Diouf was able to pick out Papa Bouba Diop in the six-yard box.

The midfielder came flying in to reach the ball ahead of Petit, but his initial effort was destined to go wide until it came off Barthez. Fortuitously, it came back to the Lens midfielder, who made no mistake despite being on the floor as he flicked out his left foot to tap the ball into the empty net. Diop ran off to the corner flag filled with jubilation, took off his shirt, placed it on the floor and proceeded to dance around it while instructing all of his team-mates to do the same. The vision of the team kicking their legs out before moving backwards and forwards in time is not only one of the most historic in Senegalese football, but also the entire nation.

As the first half drew to a close, Senegal struggled to keep any sustained possession. Despite this, Sylva was never truly stretched as Lamine Diatta and Pape Malick Diop were among those who got vital headers on deliveries into the box to clear for the Lions of Teranga. Diouf was also on hand to earn occasional respite for his team-mates by winning fouls with his trickery – a particularly cynical challenge earned Petit a yellow card from referee Ali Bujsaim, as well as an unimpressed glare from Daf. That actually turned out to be one of the final actions before the half-time whistle was blown.

Senegal captain Cissé had a fiery start to the second half, as having given away a foul on the edge of his own box – feeling the free kick should have been his – the number six was booked for bringing Desailly down when the Frenchman strode forward. It was only a couple of minutes after the latter incident that Vieira caught him with a robust challenge.

The Lions's first real scare of the second half came when Thuram picked up a loose pass before driving up the pitch with the ball. The right-back delivered a cross into the box that was begging for Trezeguet to head it in, but the 24-year-old could only direct it marginally wide with his shoulder. Just moments later, Sylvain Wiltord crossed to Henry, although with Ferdinand Coly for company the Arsenal star uncharacteristically made a complete mess of his header, sending it high and wide.

There was a period after this in which the ball was almost entirely France's. They moved it around and

Djorkaeff tested Sylva from range before being substituted for Christophe Dugarry, while Vieira's header forced another save from the man who had been playing backup at Monaco all season.

In the 65th minute Senegal offered an indication that they weren't going to merely sit back and attempt to keep hold of their one-goal lead. Fadiga picked up the ball near the halfway line and somehow managed to keep it despite pressure from Petit, Thuram and Wiltord. The number ten offloaded it to Papa Bouba Diop, who popped the ball off for Daf to immediately play it forward for Fadiga to run on to. He was off, and after throwing a step over and drop of the shoulder to earn a yard of space in the box, the winger unleashed an effort that went out off the top of the crossbar. Henry soon shared Fadiga's frustrations as his looped effort from outside the box also went off the bar and over.

France kept coming, but the men in white and green put their bodies on the line time and time again. Diatta provided the biggest example of this, as the centre-back slid in to dispossess Dugarry, despite the Bordeaux attacker diving in with his studs up. Diatta may have taken a knock to the ribs in the process, but the important thing was that he had done enough to deal with the danger.

In the 81st minute Roger Lemerre brought Cissé on for Wiltord in an attempt to earn France the goal they so desperately needed. The man wearing number nine on his back did bring a little bit of a spark, but it was once again Henry who came closest in the final stages. With injury time approaching, Daf struggled to deal with Barthez's long ball up the pitch, which allowed it to reach Henry. He got a shot off quickly, and while Sylva couldn't hold on to the ball at the first attempt, he gratefully clung on at the second.

Senegal weren't pretty at this point, but they were effective. Deep into injury time, Pape Malick Diop dived in front of Henry's attempted shot to send it wide. Just moments later, the full-time whistle was blown as Thuram tried to launch another attack, with disbelief ensuing.

This was the most remarkable result in Senegalese football history and it was clear to see from the celebrations just what it meant. Not only had they won their first World Cup game, but they had done it against the reigning World and European champions, who were also the nation that had colonised them. Back home in Dakar, President Abdoulaye Wade joined the party taking place outside the Presidential Palace and declared a national holiday. Senegal couldn't have asked for a better start.

### Republic of Ireland 1 Cameroon 1 (Group E, 1 June, Niigata)

The word Saipan will be enough to send shivers down Irish spines due to how terribly the Republic of Ireland's World Cup preparations went there. As Mick McCarthy recalled in his book, *Ireland's World Cup 2002*, the skips that had been sent over from Dublin with all of their equipment – 'from training gear to Nivea sun lotion, Lucozade and the official World Cup ball' – didn't arrive on time due to customs problems. Then, when McCarthy arrived at the training pitch he had been promised would be 'as good as the fairway at Coral Ocean Point', he found something that was 'more like a bone-hard fairway on your local pay and play'.

Roy Keane had seen McCarthy to complain about this, and then had an argument over the goalkeepers not partaking in a training match following a gruelling session for them. It was suggested that none of this played into the decision, but the Manchester United midfielder had come to the conclusion that he was going home, retiring from the World Cup and international football.

In the book, McCarthy recalls that he was in shock, asking, 'How could any football coach prepare for the day the best midfielder in the world tells you he wants to quit the Irish team on the eve of the World Cup finals?' The manager had made a series of phone calls in case Keane didn't change his mind, one of which went to Celtic's Colin Healy. He also sent Mick Byrne to talk to Keane in an attempt to bring him round. Byrne had managed to do just that, but upon hearing that Healy had been called, Keane insisted that the Celtic man should stay in the squad and was adamant that he was going home for his own personal reasons.

He then made a U-turn and decided to stay. However, that wasn't the end of it, as the midfielder did interviews with the *Irish Times* and *Irish Sunday Independent* slating the preparations and his team-mates. As quoted by *The Guardian*, the *Irish Times* interview included Keane saying, 'There's a lot of things I don't understand when we come away like this – barbecue with the media, say. I don't understand the purpose of things. Or some of the gear going missing. The barbecue. Training pitch being wrong. No balls. Only two goals. There's differences of opinions about different things. Maybe I just don't get it.'

In *Ireland's World Cup 2002*, McCarthy stated that a team meeting was called about the interviews, which left Keane furious as he didn't feel this should have been dealt with in a group situation. As McCarthy started reading extracts of the interviews, Keane 'explodes' and when McCarthy looked back, he said, 'I have never seen any human being act like this before, never mind a footballer.' The strength of

Keane's verbal assault meant things were now at the point of no return. A press conference was called and the man who was supposed to lead his country out was going home the day before they flew to Japan.

Looking back in conversation with the author, Matt Holland, a member of the Republic's 2002 squad, says, 'This was as big a thing that's ever occurred in my career that I can think of. If any other country was looking at taking one player out of our setup, I think pretty much all of them would have taken Roy. So, we were losing our best player which was a massive blow. But footballers are resilient and you have to get on with it.

'As much as it's a massive shock and a massive disappointment to lose Roy, the overriding feeling is that you've got to move on and you've got to carry on and do your job – which was trying to put in a performance and try to do well in the World Cup.'

When asked the one thing he would do again during the documentary *Keane and Vieira: Best of Enemies*, Keane responded, 'Play in the World Cup'. He continued, 'It would've been nice to play. I think a lot of people were disappointed, particularly my family. Mick did say to me, "Well, if you don't respect me, how can you play for me?" And what I should've said is I wasn't playing for him, I was playing for my country, but I think it had obviously gone then.'

Ireland had done brilliantly to get to the World Cup in the first place, finishing four points above the Netherlands in qualification and only coming behind Portugal on goal difference. They then beat Iran 2-1 on aggregate in the play-off to reach the finals. Despite all of this, the enduring Irish image pre-tournament was Keane at home walking his dog. Due to his departure coming after the squads were submitted, Keane was never replaced and remained named on official squad lists.

Cameroon's pre-tournament wasn't completely without incident, either. For the team seen as one of Africa's greatest hopes at this World Cup, this was to do with their kit. During the 2002 Africa Cup of Nations, which they won after beating Senegal on penalties in the final, the Cameroonians had been sporting Puma's sleeveless kits. However, FIFA banned them before the World Cup finals had begun. Eventually there was a compromise and the players wore black sleeves under the tops, in what would become an iconic look.

Nevertheless, when the game actually came around, all of that was forgotten. Cameroon boasted talents such as Arsenal's Lauren, Lyon's Marc-Vivien Foé, Real Madrid's Geremi and Real Mallorca's Samuel Eto'o. They had also won gold at the Olympic Games two years earlier. In addition, this was a Cameroonian side that was full of togetherness – the players walked with a hand on the shoulder of the man in front of them as they were led out by captain Rigobert Song. Ireland had star quality of their own, especially in the form of their strike duo of Leeds United's Robbie Keane and Blackburn Rovers' Damien Duff.

Both sides aimed to assert themselves early in the game, but it was the Irish who looked the strongest with their pre-match message being 'no regrets'. Not only were they getting on the ball a bit more than Cameroon, Holland had also displayed their combative side with a big tackle on Foé. Cameroon grew into the game quickly, though, and their confidence was displayed when Patrick M'Boma tried to score from just past the halfway line – even if his effort sailed high and wide.

M'Boma then played an integral part in creating the first clear-cut chance, in the 19th minute, as Eto'o played a one-two with him to break through the Irish defence. However the number nine was met by the onrushing Shay Given, who smothered him and allowed Gary Kelly to get back and put the ball out for a corner.

As Cameroon continued forward, Jason McAteer was the first booking on the half hour after he tripped Salomon Olembé while the Marseille man drifted past him. That was followed by a concerning moment for Cameroon, as defenders Bill Tchato and Raymond Kalla both rose to reach the ball ahead of Duff but ended up colliding heads. They were checked over thoroughly while substitutes began warming up with more vigour, eventually being deemed okay to carry on.

The men in white vests and black sleeves had been getting closer until they finally broke the deadlock in the 39th minute. Geremi played the ball down the line to Eto'o, who had made the sort of intelligent run into the channels he had been executing all game. This time he managed to shake Steve Staunton off by nutmegging the Ireland captain and leaving him on the floor while breaking into the box. The striker then showed selflessness as he was closed down by Given and Gary Breen, poking the ball to his strike partner M'Boma, who took a touch out of his feet and slotted his shot into the net while Kelly made a futile attempt to prevent the goal.

Having created the opener, Eto'o put his shirt on the floor for his team-mates to huddle around before sharing a dance with a couple of them. That vibrancy and party atmosphere was replicated off the pitch as the Cameroonian fans danced and sung while filling the stands with colour – even their

German coach, Winfried Schäfer, could be seen jumping around with his arms aloft.

That joy was almost halted just before half-time. Ian Harte's set pieces were notoriously difficult to deal with, and when the left-back crossed from a wide free kick, Song came close to deflecting the ball into his own net. The defender's blushes were spared as Alioum Boukar was able to get across quickly and hold on to it.

McCarthy made one change at half-time as Steve Finnan was brought on for McAteer – who had done well to play at all, as he was an injury doubt. The Fulham man got involved immediately, striding forward and putting balls in towards the edge of the box. Ireland's number two was also booked in the 51st minute for fouling M'Boma and throwing the ball away. Despite this, his intensity was indicative of how the Boys in Green had started the second period, as they were the ones applying pressure.

This was all almost completely undone just a minute later, when Harte couldn't sort his feet out on the edge of his own box and gifted the ball to Geremi. He was lucky as the Cameroonian opted to hit the loose ball first-time and sent his effort wide of the post.

It was a massive let-off that Ireland immediately capitalised on. From the ensuing goal kick, Given swung the ball to the left wing and picked out Kevin Kilbane. He controlled it masterfully on the turn with his chest and drove forward before attempting a cross that was headed away by Song. There wasn't much distance on the clearance, though, and as Holland met the ball outside the box, he hit it instantly with a brilliantly controlled half volley that was destined for the bottom corner from the moment it left his boot. The midfielder ran off with his arms in the air to celebrate in front of his wife, dad and two sons before being mobbed by his team-mates; Ireland were back on level terms after just seven second-half minutes.

'To walk out at a World Cup was special and a great feeling; to score just times that by 100,' Holland reminisces. 'It was really special, particularly because of the nature of how the game had gone as well.

'If I hit that shot 100 times, I might score ten. It's not one you're going to score every time but, fortunately, at that moment I caught it as sweetly as I could and it flew in. When it went in, crikey, you sort of lose yourself for three, four or five seconds before you realise the enormity of it.'

Perhaps feeling that he needed to atone for his costly miss, Geremi attempted an audacious chip from outside of the box soon after but Given was more than equal to it. A miss-hit cross from Lauren also looked like dropping below the bar until the Ireland goalkeeper got back to tip it over.

The Newcastle United stopper required treatment shortly after, having hit the floor hard while dealing with the ensuing corner, but was able to continue. Boukar had his own problems collecting a corner ball as he dropped it – thankfully for him a defender was first to react and cleared.

Ireland were inches away from taking the lead shortly after the hour. Harte's initial effort was blocked after a free kick was rolled short, but the ball quickly found itself being crossed in from the left wing. Breen managed to head it back across goal but Song got his chest to it before Keane could get there and Boukar dived across to prevent the own goal. While the Republic put their arms in the air in hope, referee Toru Kamikawa was not to be swayed.

Both teams were living slightly on the edge defensively, with Eto'o getting behind once again but dragging his shot wide. Perhaps spotting this, Schäfer made his first and only change of the game, bringing goalscorer M'Boma off for Patrick Suffo. The forward was certainly getting in the right positions after his introduction but sent an effort wide.

Harte went down injured in the 74th minute and was eventually replaced by Steven Reid despite trying to carry on. The substitute played a part in Keane almost getting in as Tchato failed to control a rushed pass that had been caused by Reid's pressing, but the Cameroonian managed to wrap his legs around the striker to put the ball out for a corner.

Both teams had their chances in the final ten minutes. Keane came closest with a shot that curled on to the post and stayed out. There were signs that both sides were also doing absolutely anything to avoid going behind – whether legal or not – as Reid was given a yellow before Kalla joined him in the book for pulling Duff down in the 89th minute.

That was followed by a venomous strike from Reid being tipped over. Song had an effort from range of his own but it flew harmlessly over the crossbar and was shortly followed by the full-time whistle, which confirmed that both teams had secured a well-earned point to start off their respective campaigns.

In *Ireland's World Cup 2002*, McCarthy declared, 'To manage a team that played like that, to lead a team that turned the game around in that manner, is a matter of enormous pride for me'.

### Uruguay 1 Denmark 2 (Group A, 1 June, Ulsan)

A decade after shocking the world and captaining Denmark to European Championship glory in 1992, Morten Olsen was looking to take the Nordic nation far in a World Cup once again after they had reached the quarter-final in 1998. The

Laudrup brothers, Michael and Brian, were no longer pulling on the red jersey but there was still talent at the manager's disposal. This included Chelsea's Jesper Grønkjær, PSV Eindhoven's Dennis Rommedahl, Feyenoord's Jon Dahl Tomasson and Schalke's Ebbe Sand – who had been the Bundesliga's joint top scorer in 2000/01.

In Uruguay, the Danes faced the last team to secure their place at the World Cup. La Celeste have a rich history in the competition after winning it in 1930 and 1950 but faced a plethora of issues in qualification. On top of financial problems, they had to contend with manager Daniel Passarella quitting over disputes with Club Atlético Peñarol and Nacional about players being released for the national team. Meanwhile, a bribes scandal rocked the domestic game in Uruguay, while their star man, Internazionale's Álvaro Recoba, was found guilty of passport fraud and banned for a year – reduced to four months upon appeal.

With all of that chaos acting as the backdrop for their campaign, it took a 1-0 victory over Brazil and 1-1 draw against Argentina for Uruguay to reach the play-off, pipping Colombia on goal difference by one goal. They met Australia and – as was typical of their campaign – didn't make things easy by losing the first leg 1-0 in Melbourne, but came out winners thanks to a 3-0 victory in Montevideo.

Despite the problems during qualification, the Uruguayans were expectant now that Victor Púa's team was at the finals. The South Americans started strongly and could have had a goal within 30 seconds, but the ball through to Darío Silva marginally evaded the attacker and was cleared. Gonzalo Sorondo had a good chance moments later after Sebastián Abreu had done well to win a corner, though the centre-back came close to hitting the corner flag with his header.

It was an end-to-end start to the game, and Rommedahl drove at his full-back before cutting inside and swinging an effort just wide of the post with his left boot. Recoba then responded by sending a free kick inches wide. Despite it only being 12 minutes into proceedings, it was difficult to believe that neither side had scored. That feeling was only accentuated when Sand leapt forward to get on the end of Thomas Helveg's cross, eventually sending his header bouncing off the ground, on to the crossbar and over.

Neither team was able to take full control, meaning that the chances kept coming, especially as the policy from both sides was seemingly shoot on sight – though that did produce a couple of ugly efforts, such as Thomas Gravesen's daisy cutter from a free kick. While Recoba got his curling effort from a dead ball on target, it was pretty comfortable for Thomas Sørensen to deal with.

One man who had struggled in the early stages was Gustavo Méndez, as Grønkjær managed to get behind him with relative ease a few times. As the right-back fought to keep up with the Dane in the 25th minute, he ended up tripping him and getting the game's first yellow card. Stig Tøfting soon left the referee, Saad Mane, looking scared and confused in equal measure by shouting at him – so much so that the menacing-looking midfielder escaped any repercussions. It wasn't long until Denmark got their first booking, though, as captain Jan Heintze was cautioned for clattering Gustavo Varela when he slid in and completely missed the ball.

While Denmark hadn't been able to test Uruguayan goalkeeper Fabián Carini too often throughout the first half, the patience of the men in Hummel strips meant they had far more of the ball than their opponents. It took desperate defending from Méndez to deny Tomasson in the 42nd minute after he'd been played through, but there was nothing that could be done to stop Denmark's number nine as half-time loomed. He played a one-two with Grønkjær, and upon receiving the return in the box, opened up his right boot and clinically finished before letting out a celebratory roar.

After all of Denmark's work to get ahead, it took just over a minute of the second half for Darío Rodríguez to restore parity with one outstanding swipe of his left foot. Denmark's clearance from a corner had only got as far as Pablo García, who kept the ball in the air before flicking it to Rodríguez. The left-back watched the ball all the way on to his boot and sent it spinning into the top corner, leaving Sørensen on the floor looking perplexed after producing a dive that was always doomed to be futile.

That goal momentarily put Denmark on the ropes as they looked to recover, and Martin Laursen earned himself a booking after finding Abreu's knee with his studs while attempting a tackle. Perhaps due to his earlier booking, Heintze was brought off for Niclas Jensen soon after – looking far from happy about it as he trudged off across the pitch. Even so, Púa was surely tempted to do the same with Méndez as the right-back took Grønkjær out again and was lucky to avoid a second yellow.

It looked like he would take off Rodríguez, who was struggling with an injury, but the goalscorer remained on the pitch. There would have been fear in Danish eyes as the ball fell to him on the edge of the box after a corner again – even if he wasn't 100 per cent – but this time Helveg rushed out quickly enough to block the shot. Grønkjær had put in an impressive shift but made way for Martin Jørgensen in the 70th minute, meaning Denmark had a fresher pair of legs to exploit Uruguay's weaknesses down the wings.

As time went on, Rodríguez looked as though he was struggling more and more – which isn't the sort of state you want to be in when going into a big collision with Helveg. Things weren't looking much better for Méndez on the other side of Uruguay's defence, as Jórgensen twisted and turned his way around the right-back with little resistance at all but eventually ran out of space and gave away a goal kick. Denmark even came close to breaking through the middle, but Gravesen couldn't quite get Sand's flicked ball under control.

It felt as though Uruguay were hanging on, which was reflected in Púa's 80th-minute substitution, as he brought off Recoba – the man who had been La Celeste's greatest creative spark – and replaced him with Mario Regueiro.

Despite this, Danish pressure eventually paid off in the 83rd minute. Rommedahl's initial cross into the box was headed away, but Varela was dispossessed by Jensen while attempting to carry the ball out and he quickly offloaded to fellow substitute Jørgensen. The Udinese man cut inside and placed a peach of a cross on to Tomasson's head; with the number nine being given far too much space in the box, there was never going to be any other outcome than his effort nestling in the back of the net. This one kissed the bar on its way in to make it even more aesthetically pleasing, and the composure stretched to the Feyenoord man's calm celebration.

Both teams made late changes as Rodríguez got his rest about 25 minutes later than he should have done, being joined in exiting by Abreu to be replaced by Federico Magallanes and Richard Morales. Sand was brought off for Christian Poulsen as the clock wound down.

Uruguay tried to restore parity but never truly looked like having enough to break Denmark down. That wasn't helped by Gravesen proving that there was a prime engine beneath his puffed-out chest and bald head as he chased down pretty much every ball until the very end. The referee's whistle soon came to put Uruguay out of their misery and confirm Denmark's first three points of the tournament. There was a nice touch at the end as the Danes all went over to applaud their fans who had made the trip to Ulsan.

*Germany 8 Saudi Arabia 0 (Group E, 1 June, Sapporo)*
As a nation, Germany is imperious when it comes to football. However, that reputation had seemingly slipped slightly in the build-up to this World Cup, with *The Official ITV Sport World Cup 2002 Fact File* stating that they were 'in rebuilding mode'. This came after embarrassment in the qualifying round when a goalless draw against Finland in their final match prevented them from going through automatically. Die Mannschaft beat Ukraine in the play-off, though, so star names such as Bayern Munich's Oliver Kahn and Bayer Leverkusen's Michael Ballack had the opportunity to show that Germany were still to be feared on the international stage.

Their first match came against Saudi Arabia, whose ranks included 2000 Asian Player of the Year Nawaf Al-Temyat and Mohamed Al-Deayea, who was named the all-time greatest goalkeeper from Asia and Oceania by specialist goalkeeping website Between the Sticks in 2020.

Germany took control from the very beginning and Carsten Jancker sent an effort in from a tight angle that went marginally wide within two minutes. The Europeans looked quicker, stronger and better technically from the off, which was also highlighted by Thomas Linke's challenge on Sami Al-Jaber, which left Saudi Arabia's captain needing treatment on the sideline. Jancker actually had the ball in the net eight minutes in after running behind Abdullah Zubromawi, but referee Ubaldo Aquino adjudged that there had been a foul when he slid in between the centre-back and goalkeeper to get the ball.

German pressure kept coming and the men in green eventually succumbed to it in the 20th minute when Miroslav Klose headed in Ballack's header after Jancker had missed his attempt at an overhead kick. The number 11's celebration was indicative of a man used to hitting the back of the net, and that was with good reason as the Kaiserslautern striker was coming into the World Cup off the back of a hat-trick in a friendly against Austria.

It took just five minutes for another goal to be scored, which was almost identical to the first. Again it was created by a Ballack cross into the box; again, Klose converted with a well-executed header. This time, the goalscorer brought out his trademark front flip celebration.

Exactly a quarter of an hour after delivering his second goal-assisting cross, Ballack was the man getting on the end of one. He had been afforded so much space in the Saudi Arabian box after running off the shoulder, and utilised it to confidently redirect Christian Ziege's peach of a cross into the bottom corner.

Saudi Arabia weren't giving up, as Al-Jaber made a burst into the German box before being dispossessed. Germany weren't taking their foot off the gas either and Ziege was booked for a late sliding tackle on Ahmed Dukhi Al-Dosari. Due to that attitude from the Germans, there was time for one more goal before half-time: Torsten Frings sent the ball into the box from deep, Klose got a little flick on it and Jancker sent it through Al-Deayea's legs before taking his shirt off in celebration.

The game was out of sight by the break, but Nasser Al-Johar tried to impact things anyway, bringing Ibrahim Al-Shahrani and Abdulaziz Al-Khathran on for Khamis Al-Dosari and Al-Temyat. Meanwhile, Rudi Völler replaced Carsten Ramelow – who had picked up a slight injury – with Jens Jeremies.

Despite the changes in personnel, there were plenty of similarities between the starts of the first and second halves as Germany were on top for large periods but unable to beat Al-Deayea. There were some slight improvements from Saudi Arabia, who had the odd burst forward but could not trouble Kahn much at all.

Whether it was to inject some fresh legs into the game or rest a starter, Völler brought Oliver Bierhoff on for Jancker in the 67th minute. In the same minute, Saudi Arabia's resolve was shown as Redha Tukar got up well to head a cross away, before carrying on despite struggling with back pain after hitting the floor.

It wasn't long until that resolve was broken, though, as Klose scored yet another header to secure his hat-trick. Bernd Schneider was the creator this time, racing down the line and skipping past Hussein Sulimani before getting his cross into the box. There was never any doubt from Germany's number 11, and this time he opted to head the ball into the ground on its way into the net.

Following their fifth goal of the game, it took Germany less than four minutes to get their sixth – once again scoring with a header. Ziege earned his second assist, curling the ball just past the front post from a corner where Linke rose between Tukar and Abdullah Al-Waked before simply nodding home.

Klose soon came close to getting his fourth but was taken off for Oliver Neuville in the 76th minute to a deservedly loud round of applause. Al-Johar used his last change at the same time to replace Al Hasan Al-Yami with Abdullah Jumaan Al-Dosari.

The Saudis were still going and Al-Deayea made a great save with his legs to deny Ballack his second of the game in the 80th minute, then Al-Jaber drew a foul from Dietmar Hamann that earned the German a yellow card. However they conceded yet again moments later when Bierhoff caught the goalkeeper out by sliding in to reach Schneider's dinked pass and hit a strike from range.

As the game entered injury time and the final whistle edged closer Saudi Arabia probably thought the pain was over, but there was still time for salt to be added to their proverbial wounds. Mohammed Noor was booked for fouling Schneider on the edge of the box, and having won the free kick, Germany's number 19 jumped to the front of the queue to take it and effortlessly stuck the ball into the top corner.

It wasn't long until Aquino finally put an end to an affair that hadn't proven much of a match-up at all. It may have been against one of the tournament's minnows, but after all of the uncertainties around Germany pre-tournament, handing out such a humbling defeat proved they had the devastating efficiency so many of their teams gone by have been known for. The 8-0 scoreline was an unmistakable signal of intent.

*Argentina 1 Nigeria 0 (Group F, 2 June, Ibaraki)*
Group F was deemed the Group of Death prior to the tournament, pitting Argentina, England, Sweden and

Nigeria against each other. Argentina went to Asia as one of the favourites to win the World Cup, especially after topping CONMEBOL qualifying by 12 points. Marcelo Bielsa's side was absolutely brimming with attacking talent, such as Gabriel Batistuta, Juan Sebastián Verón and Ariel Ortega – so much so that there wasn't room for Juan Román Riquelme, despite the midfielder collecting the South American Footballer of the Year award for 2001 and signing for Barcelona less than a month after the World Cup's culmination.

Ahead of the draw, Nigeria was arguably the African nation with the highest expectations – though Cameroon and now Senegal also had high hopes. That was down to the Super Eagles having both talent and recent history on their side as Festus Onigbinde's team boasted the likes of Paris Saint-Germain's Jay-Jay Okocha, Chelsea's Celestin Babayaro, former Internazionale centre-back Taribo West and Arsenal's Nwankwo Kanu. Nigeria had previously won the Olympic Games in 1996, the FIFA World Under-17 Cup in 1985 and 1993, and the Africa Cup of Nations in 1994 and 2000. Their qualification hadn't been completely straight-forward, though, as hinted at by coach Jo Bonfrere leaving after poor performances provoked by internal bickering.

In the clash of South America's and Africa's greatest hopes, Nigeria surrendered possession almost immediately. Claudio López couldn't punish them, getting too much on his cross to find Batistuta. Nigeria delivered a dangerous ball in of their own moments later but Diego Placente did well to deny Okocha a chance at the back post.

As is probably expected of a side managed by the man nicknamed 'El Loco', it was an all-action start from Argentina and the only real break in play came when Kanu went down injured around the tenth minute, although after being stretchered off he was able to come back on with a wince on his face and limp in his step.

After a momentary drop-off, the Argentines slowly increased their level of pressure without managing to test goalkeeper Ike Shorunmu – though Javier Zanetti's strike from range certainly caused concern before going over and wide. The goalkeeper actually handed La Albiceleste their best chance so far when his ensuing goal kick went straight to Batistuta, but the Roma star couldn't capitalise as Shorunmu made a fairly routine save – even so, he was off goal kicks for the rest of the half. 'Batigol' was released once again moments later before being denied by the outrushing goalkeeper who swiped the ball away with his legs.

Nigeria created their own chances and a superb ball into the box from deep came inches away from finding 17-year-old forward Bartholomew Ogbeche – who was Nigeria's youngest ever player at a World Cup. Bielsa was prowling around his technical area while Ortega did the same on the pitch, waiting for opportunities. When the ball fell to the number ten outside the box, he fizzed off a strike that Shorunmu did well to tip over the crossbar. Not one to be outdone, Okocha let off his own shot from range that had everyone concerned, but similarly to Shorunmu, Pablo Cavallero did brilliantly to dive and tip it over. The policy for both teams was seemingly shoot on sight, as Joseph Yobo tried his luck seconds later.

With half-time edging closer, Batistuta did well to get up above West at the back post when a corner delivery came into the packed box. Frustration ensued as he should have done more to get his header on target. Bielsa clearly wasn't happy with what he was seeing as Kily González was stripped off and lurking in a manner that indicated he was ready to be brought on.

In a microcosm of the first half, Julius Aghahowa struck a bicycle kick that looked fantastic at first but did very little to test the goalkeeper – eventually going out for a throw. There wasn't to be much more telling action before the break, but Mauricio Pochettino got an arm to the face from Kanu as the pair jumped for a header.

With Bielsa having waited, González was eventually introduced in place of López, and while Kanu had played on through the pain in the first half he went down and then limped off just 30 seconds into the second period. The 25-year-old was replaced by Pius Ikedia after a slight delay in getting him ready. Batistuta should have scored before Nigeria got back to full numbers, sliding in to latch on to a corner at the back post but somehow missing the target.

Nigeria's awkward start to the half continued when Shorunmu came rushing out to catch the ball under pressure but had to drop it for a corner to stop himself carrying it out of his box. Another great opportunity was headed wide from the ensuing corner, this time from Juan Pablo Sorín.

The game was end-to-end with both sides getting plenty of chances. In the 51st minute, seconds after Batistuta smashed his free kick attempt marginally over the bar, Walter Samuel was handed the first booking for committing a foul on the edge of his own box.

As the hour approached, Pochettino was the latest Argentine to miss a sitter when the centre-back sent his header wide despite no Nigerian coming close to adequately marking him. The longer this went on, the more agitated Bielsa looked and Sorín having a shot saved from point-blank range wouldn't have helped.

Bielsa may not have looked any more relaxed after it, but Argentina were finally given their relief as Batigol eventually lived up to his nickname and reputation in the 63rd minute. Verón sent a corner towards the back post, where the striker had attacked most corners, and this was no different as he raced in to bravely head the ball towards goal and over the line. Efe Sodje scrambled across to try to keep it out, but could only send the ball into the roof of the net as Batistuta and his team-mates ran off to give each other a celebratory embrace.

Argentina didn't let up and Verón tested Shorunmu with a free kick moments later, with the Lucerne goalkeeper tipping it over. The men in luminous green were struggling now, as they were being swarmed from all angles in true El Loco style. Still, there were occasional moments of slight concern as Nigeria tried to carve out an equaliser.

In trying to block off Diego Placente, Crewe Alexandra's Sodje went over the ball and stamped down on the defender's ankle, getting himself a yellow card. The defender also hurt himself and was substituted for Justice Christopher straight away. Argentina followed that up with quickfire changes as Pablo Aimar and Hernán Crespo came on within three minutes of each other, replacing Verón and Batistuta respectively – the latter's final act was to strike a venomous free kick that was well saved. The striker was also given an expectedly warm reception as he left the field of play.

Things were beginning to open up even more for the Argentines as Nigeria began stepping up their pursuit of an equaliser. This allowed Crespo to get behind a couple of minutes after his introduction, but the Lazio striker was unable to keep his effort down while attempting to curl it into the far corner. It also took some desperate defending from West to deny Sorín from having a clear-cut chance.

Diego Simeone got a yellow card in the 90th minute for clumsily sticking one on Okocha, but Argentina's defence – which had been seen as their weak point pre-tournament – wasn't stretched at all in the latter stages. In fact, González really should have doubled the lead in the dying moments, going for power and failing to get his effort in the corner which allowed Shorunmu to make a save that was impressive nonetheless.

With that said, Cavallero wasn't looking too comfortable in goal, and sloppily parried Okocha's shot from range wide when he really should have held it. He was let off as the referee blew the whistle as soon as Nigeria played it short – not even giving them time to take a touch – and the party atmosphere among the Argentines in the stands ramped up even further. They'd got off to a winning start, while Nigeria now had everything to do if they were to progress.

## Paraguay 2 South Africa 2 (Group B, 2 June, Busan)

Paraguay would have, of course, been looking forward to entering the World Cup, but there was one very obvious void in their team for the opener: José Luis Chilavert, their star name. Aside from preventing opposition goals, the Strasbourg stopper was known the world over for scoring from free kicks and penalties. He had even got on the scoresheet against Colombia and Peru in qualifying. However, he still had one game left on a four-match suspension incurred after spitting at Brazil's Roberto Carlos, so would have to sit out their opening group match.

In South Africa, Paraguay faced a side that had been very much in the ascendancy; having never reached the World Cup finals before 1998, Bafana Bafana were now in their second in a row. This had been achieved despite the long-term absence of Leeds United's Lucas Radebe, though thankfully the veteran was available now.

The preparations hadn't been seamless for South Africa, however, as they had changed coach. Carlos Queiroz had got them to the World Cup but after a poor showing at the Africa Cup of Nations, Jomo Sono was appointed as a technical director. This made Queiroz feel that his position was being undermined and the Portuguese tactician resigned, with Sono taking over the role.

There was almost trouble for Sono's side just 20 seconds in as Roque Santa Cruz had a shout for a penalty after being put through on goal and going down under pressure from goalkeeper Andre Arendse. Referee Ľuboš Micheľ showed no interest, though, giving a goal kick and telling the Bayern Munich striker to get up.

There were other signs that South Africa were struggling defensively in the early stages, with Aaron Mokoena being booked for a late lunge on Jorge Campos just three minutes in, while there was an almost identical situation for Pierre Issa just six minutes later. MacBeth Sibaya also showed that they could carry a threat of their own in that time as he struck an effort from range that worried Ricardo Tavarelli before whistling past the post.

Any questions over South Africa's defending momentarily dissipated in the 20th minute when Radebe miraculously hooked away the cross that was destined for Santa Cruz's head in front of goal. There were soon to be more problems though, as Issa picked up an injury while battling with Santa Cruz to stop him getting a clean pass across goal – which worked, as the number nine couldn't find the runner.

There was a goalmouth scramble in the centre-back's absence following a corner delivered to the near post, but

Arendse was eventually able to collect the ball despite Carlos Gamarra swinging his legs all over the place in an attempt to reach it. Once play stopped again, MacDonald Mukasi was brought on to replace the injured man.

There was yet another warning of Santa Cruz's threat in the box when he met Campos's cross and unleashed a header – easily the best effort of the game so far. That was soon followed by Julio César Cáceres preventing Manchester United midfielder Quinton Fortune's run down the left by pulling him down and earning a yellow card for his trouble.

Benni McCarthy received a booking of his own for kicking Roberto Acuña while trying to reach a high ball in a dangerous area. Facing Santa Cruz after the striker had already had a couple of chances made this situation even more threatening. Francisco Arce put in a free kick that curled away from Arendse's approaching fist, with Santa Cruz able to dive far enough forward to plant his head on it at the back post and convert the game's opening goal in the 39th minute.

South Africa's defence simply couldn't deal with Paraguay's number nine and were soon out-jumped by Santa Cruz once again. It was a second big save from Arendse rather than another goal for the striker, as the goalkeeper got a fingertip on the ball to tip it over the crossbar. It had been a frustrating first half for Bafana Bafana, and the ending showed that as Sibusio Zuma was booked for tripping Cáceres.

Despite this, it was South Africa who had a quick start to the second half. Tavarelli was forced into a save by Zuma's acrobatic effort almost immediately after the restart, initially patting the ball into the air before diving and catching it. Paraguay replied quickly with an effort of their own as Gamarra broke through before letting off a shot that went just wide, indicating that this could be an action-packed second period.

When Paraguay were awarded a free kick in the 55th minute, it seemed inevitable that Arce would cross it in for the likes of Santa Cruz and Celso Ayala to attack. The right wing-back fooled everybody – most importantly Arendse. After initially running up to the ball and stepping back again, he snapped his foot around it, sending it in off the underside of the crossbar. Arce was off immediately as he went to hug his manager Cesare Maldini before being mobbed by his jubilant team-mates, while the original free kick master Chilavert looked on with pride.

It was imperative that South Africa responded to this setback quickly and that was exactly what they did, playing plenty of attacking football that made Paraguay resort to last-ditch defending and deploying a deep back line. While that tactic worked in saving themselves in dangerous situations, it was to be the South Americans' downfall just eight minutes after they had gone two up.

When Acuña failed to convincingly clear a cross into the box, the ball fell to Teboho Mokoena. The midfielder took a touch out of his feet and hit a shot that deflected off Estanislao Struway's desperately outstretched leg. The unfortunate connection left Tavarelli attempting to contort his body in a way that would allow him to reach the ball but instead he watched it trickle past him and into the net.

There was a clear mixture of frustration and disbelief felt within Paraguay's ranks and written across Struway's face. Denis Caniza offered an example when he was booked for going through the back of Fortune just moments after the restart. Paraguay were firmly on the back foot now, relying on counter attacks and hoping that Santa Cruz could reach balls that were either hopeful or too ambitious depending on how you looked at things. In an effort to change this, Diego Gavilán was brought on for Guido Alvarenga.

On a rare occasion that Campos forayed forward, Cyril Nzama tracked the Paraguayan all the way. In a display of the confidence South Africa were now enjoying, he even took the ball around his own goalkeeper and Ocampos before passing it away. Paraguay's cause wasn't helped by Campos then limping off in the 73rd minute and being replaced by Gustavo Morínigo.

All of South Africa's positive momentum was almost quashed by a loose back pass from Bradley Carnell, but Arendse rushed out of his goal ahead of Santa Cruz, who was sliding in, to smash the ball off the Paraguayan and out for a goal kick. The left-back's blushes were spared and South Africa's chances of a comeback remained.

As the game approached its final ten minutes, the South Americans were taking every opportunity they got to slow down proceedings, and Acuña did just that after a collision with Carnell. Bafana Bafana used the break in play to replace McCarthy with George Koumantarakis, the striker who was born in Greece but grew up in Durban, South Africa, and played his club football for Basel.

While Fortune was able to get a header on target that was easily saved, there was seemingly a very clear pattern at this point. South Africa won the ball and passed it to work space, they played forward to spring an attack, Paraguay put their bodies on the line to make a tackle or block, they cleared and surrendered possession to Bafana Bafana. Repeat. Struway was brought off for the defender Juan Carlos Franco as the men in red and white did all they could to hang on and secure three points.

It looked as though they would do just that until South Africa cut them open in the 90th minute. When Zuma was played into the penalty area down the left, Tavarelli came flying out to try and reach the ball before the winger got there. Zuma was absolutely tearing towards it, though, and all the goalkeeper did was take him out, giving away a penalty and earning himself a yellow card.

Fortune confidently stepped up to take the spot-kick, and despite the Paraguayans' tactic of delaying it by staying in the box for as long as they could the midfielder struck across his body into the top-right corner, giving Tavarelli no chance. The Bafana Bafana shirt came off quickly as he ran off to passionately celebrate with the supporters and was joined by his ecstatic team-mates.

There was clear frustration for Paraguay, as shown by Franco getting himself booked for a high elbow. Having initially made things hard for themselves, South Africa were fully deserving of the point that was confirmed when Michel blew the full-time whistle. This may not have been the biggest game of the tournament in terms of stature, as was indicated by visible empty seats, but those who did attend certainly got their money's worth.

### England 1 Sweden 1 (Group F, 2 June, Saitama)
England's qualification for this World Cup had started with a 1-0 defeat to Germany and Kevin Keegan's resignation as manager. All of that was now in the past, with that very campaign providing two iconic moments: the 5-1 thrashing of the same eternal enemies in their own back yard, and the iconic David Beckham free kick that secured a 2-2 draw against Greece and top spot thanks to Die Mannschaft failing to beat Finland.

This meant that there was plenty of expectation on the side managed by their first foreign manager, Sven-Göran Eriksson. This was also elevated by the team including the likes of Rio Ferdinand, Sol Campbell and Ashley Cole at the back, Manchester United pair David Beckham and Paul Scholes in midfield, as well as 2001 Ballon d'Or winner Michael Owen up front.

Fellow Europeans Sweden had reason for excitement of their own, having gone unbeaten in qualifying, winning eight of their ten matches. They also had players recognisable to British audiences, including Celtic striker Henrik Larsson – who was Sweden's top scorer in qualifying with eight goals – Arsenal winger Freddie Ljungberg and Aston Villa defender Olof Mellberg. However they were without captain Patrik Andersson, who had picked up an injury during training the day before this game, ruling the Barcelona defender out of the tournament.

England looked in control during the opening minutes. The first moment of real excitement, which inspired a roar from the Saitama Stadium crowd, arrived when Owen picked up the ball and danced through the defence but just overcooked his final touch, allowing Magnus Hedman to come out and collect.

Neither side were able to create a clear opportunity for themselves early on. Larsson still worried Campbell enough to force the Arsenal centre-back into a late lunge on the edge of his own box, picking up the game's first yellow card. The Three Lions looked the strongest but were struggling to show enough cutting edge in the final third to break down Sweden's resolute defence. In fact, the first awkward moment for any goalkeeper came for David Seaman as he was forced to come out through the crowd to catch Campbell's misdirected header.

It seemed like Darius Vassell would also have a problem after clashing heads with Mellberg, but England's number 20 clearly wasn't too concerned as he rushed into a collision with Hedman moments later.

England supporters had been in full voice for pretty much the whole game and got their reward in the 24th minute. Their team won a corner when Cole got behind the defence and his attempted cross was blocked and then put behind by Mellberg.

Beckham proceeded to display why he was known as one of the game's greatest set-piece takers with a wonderfully inviting cross that Campbell fearlessly attacked, powering his header into the net that Hedman had left vacant as he tried to gather the ball. As Becks dropped to his knees and faced the fans to celebrate, Campbell sprinted off to do the same before his centre-back partner Ferdinand jumped on his shoulders to join in.

England had their tails up and Danny Mills came close to creating a chance when he smashed a low ball into the box, but Sweden dealt with it well. There weren't too many shots being hit at Hedman as England seemingly had spells where they were happy to merely control possession, but Cole let off a venomous strike from range that the stopper only just managed to keep hold of.

Sweden had been poor in the first period, to the point that England fans sarcastically chanted 'Are you Scotland in disguise?' The Scandinavians' first shot of any note came from Marcus Allbäck in the 39th minute, but it never looked like beating Seaman and was easily gathered. The striker, who joined Aston Villa from Heerenveen shortly before the tournament, had another go before the break, but while the second attempt was far more threatening it went wide. He then ended the half by getting booked for throwing the ball away after being caught offside.

Both teams had an opportunity within a couple of minutes of the restart, as Mills sent a weak left-footed shot straight at the goalkeeper while Allbäck hit his first-time effort comfortably over Seaman's crossbar.

There was a light-hearted moment of entertainment as Mills pulled out the corner flag before Carlos Simon ordered him to put it back in – with the Leeds United defender gesturing to make sure Sweden didn't take their throw while he was doing it.

There was no amusement for Mills or England in what soon followed. A couple of minutes after Anders Svensson replaced Magnus Svensson, Sweden got their equaliser. Mills had tried to chest down a long pass forward but gave it straight to Larsson before diving in to get the ball away from the striker. While successful, all the right-back did was give it to Niclas Alexandersson on the edge of the box. Mills tried to drop in as the Everton man shifted the ball, but the shot went between England's number two and Seaman to bring Sweden level in the 59th minute. Mills was left shaking his fist in frustration while Alexandersson's was raised defiantly.

Teddy Lučić came close to putting the Swedes ahead moments later but was denied by a good stop from Seaman. With Beckham beginning to struggle physically due to not being fully match fit – the second metatarsal on his left foot had been injured in April, initially causing doubts around whether he would make the World Cup – England's captain was replaced by Kieron Dyer in the 63rd minute as Eriksson tried to regain control from his country of birth. Owen took the armband.

Almost immediately afterwards, England's defence was dissected by Larsson's ball through to Lučić, who couldn't muster a convincing finish and saw his shot blocked by Seaman. England were in real danger of going behind after all their first-half dominance, and Tobias Linderoth was left furious with himself after smashing a shot over the crossbar when Cole's unconvincing header bobbled invitingly towards him.

Owen – along with pretty much anyone in a white shirt – had gone very quiet, but the Liverpool frontman momentarily burst into life in the 70th minute. He shifted the ball inside Andreas Jakobsson and hit an effort that first appeared destined for the bottom corner but went wide by the finest of margins, with it feeling unlikely that Hedman would have reached it. Ljungberg – still sporting the red hair he wore as an Arsenal player – had a weak shot denied by Gunners team-mate Seaman moments later.

With both teams having enjoyed a period on top, this felt like a genuine end-to-end game as it entered the final quarter of an hour and Vassell was cynically brought down by Jakobsson. Joe Cole replaced Vassell moments after that incident, going on to the wing while Emile Heskey went up top alongside Owen. It wasn't long until the West Ham United academy graduate was running at Sweden's defence, but he couldn't get the connection on his final attempt. The change also benefited Heskey, who had been quiet on the left but in his more natural position turned dynamically, drove into the box and fired just wide of the far post.

Sweden also showed their intent by bringing AIK striker Andreas Andersson on for Allbäck. Soon after that, Svensson's poor corner somehow found Jakobsson in the box but the centre-back got his shot all wrong and sent it harmlessly wide.

Hedman soon had a heart-in-mouth moment as Joe Cole swung in a cross that was unconvincingly cleared by a defender. With the ball sitting on the right, Mills would have had the freedom of Saitama if he had reached it with everybody else having been dragged inside. The goalkeeper sprinted to prevent that happening and eventually got in just ahead of the England man to spoon the ball out of play. Then Heskey rose highest to meet a lofted cross from Mills but couldn't quite find the target with his header.

It was Ashley Cole's turn to be scared after the game went into injury time when he made a complete mess of his clearance, allowing Svensson's long ball to wriggle underneath his foot and through to the danger man Larsson. The Celtic star's touch let him down too, forcing him to go wide and fire off target.

The final whistle was eventually blown, confirming the draw that both teams would have felt could have been a victory considering the game's flow. While it wasn't the perfect start, England and Sweden knew that the result would put them in a brilliant position with a win in the second round of fixtures.

### Spain 3 Slovenia 1 (Group B, 2 June, Gwangju)

Spain came into this tournament with the tag of serial underachievers. Their fourth-place finish in 1950 was the nation's best World Cup campaign despite a rich history at club level. Still, this didn't stop José Antonio Camacho's side also being dubbed one of the favourites. For a team that included Real Madrid trio Raúl, Fernando Hierro and Iker Casillas, Barcelona duo Carles Puyol and Luis Enrique, plus plenty of other talented players, that sort of expectation is only natural.

Slovenia were on the complete opposite side of the spectrum: they had only played their first game in 1992 – a year after breaking away from Yugoslavia – while their first qualifiers came in 1994. Slovenia's qualification campaigns for Euro '96 and World Cup '98 were pretty disastrous, culminating in second-from-bottom and bottom finishes respectively.

Yet, having also made Euro 2000, here they were on the biggest stage of all after outdoing Yugoslavia to finish second in their qualification group and reach the play-offs, where they beat Romania 3-2 on aggregate.

Before they even stepped on the pitch, one thing that would have caught the eye was their kit, which gave a nod to Mount Triglav, the highest peak of the Julian Alps – which also takes its place on Slovenia's flag.

To the surprise of many, Slovenia started strongly and Željko Milinovič got his head on Zlatko Zahovič's early corner to force a save from Casillas. While the stopper couldn't hold on to it, Aleksandar Knavs's follow-up went harmlessly wide.

Knavs would have another frustrating moment about quarter of an hour in, as referee Mohamed Guezzaz told him to go to the side for treatment on a cut to the eye following a clash of heads with Raúl. Thankfully for Slovenia their defence was able to stay strong while the medical team frantically worked to clean him up.

One of his first assignments after being reintroduced was to stand in the wall for Javier de Pedro's free kick, but while the defender had no chance of getting in the ball's way he didn't need to as it sailed narrowly over Marko Simeunović's crossbar. The fouls were beginning to build up for Slovenia, and De Pedro came even closer soon afterwards.

Slovenia were still getting the best chances despite Spain's domination, with Zahovič hitting an outswinging effort that was tipped wide by Casillas. Camacho was visibly annoyed with how the game was unfolding, which wouldn't have been helped by Željko Milinovič winning the header from the last of three ensuing corners – even if it went over the crossbar.

While Spain were largely being limited to efforts from range, there were signs that their quality was close to breaking Slovenia's defence down. The biggest example came when De Pedro played a one-two with Enrique before putting a cross in with the outside of his boot. Raúl was able to get between the Slovenian wall to head it towards goal but harmlessly sent the ball straight into Simeunovič's arms.

Juan Carlos Valerón picked up the game's first yellow card soon after the attempt, having tripped up Džoni Novak, with the referee indicating that it was for an accumulation of fouls from the Deportivo La Coruña midfielder. It felt like a natural progression for a game that had been full of fouls.

Even so, as the half-time break drew nearer, Spain were getting ever closer to breaking through, with brilliant pieces of individual defending all that was keeping out the men in red. Knavs would have thought that he had produced another of those goal-saving moments when he slid in to block Enrique's path in the 44th minute. Unfortunately for Slovenia the ball fell to Raúl, who had the composure and skill to evade two challenges with his first touch then stroked a shot through Milinovič's legs and past Simeunovič with his second.

Whether it was out of frustration or an eagerness to get back on top before the break, Amir Karić earned himself a yellow card for going over the ball while attempting a tackle on Valerón.

The second half started with nearly moments, instead of the brilliance that Camacho would have wanted – which was perhaps why he was working up the sort of sweat that left patches on his shirt. De Pedro came close to playing Enrique through but Novak did just enough to block him off, while some good work down the left from Juanfran set Raúl up for a volley the striker couldn't get on target.

With Slovenia struggling to make any real impact of their own, Srečko Katanec made the first change when replacing striker Milan Osterc with Sebastjan Cimirotič. This did little to alter the game's flow, though, as it was the Spanish who did most of the attacking – even if Diego Tristan's effort that bounced back off Simeunovič was the closest they were coming to scoring.

Zahovič's overcooked free kick summarised how things were going for the Slovenians. Whether or not that played into Katanec's decision-making, the number ten was brought off for Milenko Ačimovič just after the hour. There was a showing of frustration from the Benfica man as he kicked a bottle when coming off – something seemingly innocuous that would have larger ramifications.

Cimirotič was trying to get Slovenia back into the game after being introduced from the bench, and for a second the Lecce forward probably thought he had done just that in the 65th minute. With four Spaniards surrounding him in the opposition box, the 27-year-old shifted the ball and went to ground. Guezzaz blew his whistle but not in Cimirotič's favour and he was given a yellow card for diving, to the visible delight of Puyol and the other Spaniards who had been momentarily protesting.

Even if the decision didn't go their way, Slovenia seemed to gain hope from that incident. Meanwhile, Tristán had a problem with his ankle, so Camacho brought his number ten off for Fernando Morientes. The Real Madrid man could have made his mark within seconds as the ball fell to his feet just inside the box, but the ensuing shot was denied by Simeunovič's legs. Spain were almost made to pay for this lack of a clinical edge when Cimirotič's effort from range deflected off Rubén Baraja and on to the roof of the net.

The shots were raining in now as De Pedro forced a good save from Simeunovič, Ačimovič sent a shot from range wide, before De Pedro saw an attempt from just past the halfway line fly marginally wide. Perhaps looking to ensure the game's nature didn't cost Spain their lead, Camacho brought Iván Helguera on for Enrique.

The number four's introduction inadvertently contributed to Spain getting on the scoresheet again. As he rushed in to make sure there wasn't a hole in the midfield, Helguera made a big tackle to get the ball away from his box. A poor Slovenian pass handed the ball to Morientes, who flicked it over his head to De Pedro. The winger played a sublime pass into the box that curled its way perfectly towards Valerón so the midfielder could nonchalantly plant it into the bottom corner without breaking his stride. Even the goalscorer gave De Pedro the credit, pointing to his assister while wearing a massive grin.

With 25 minutes left on the clock, this put Spain firmly in control. In his final attempt to turn things around, Katanec threw Saša Gajser on for Novak. There was another break in play as Juanfran received treatment for his ankle, having gone over on it after catching Ačimovič's foot while trying to intercept his pass.

Spain were momentarily playing with ten men as they hadn't been allowed to make their substitution straight away, and Slovenia took full advantage. They moved the ball around well in the hope of exploiting the space playing with one extra man can create. A chance eventually presented itself on the edge of Spain's box as Ačimovič and Cimirotič played one-touch passes between themselves. The latter eventually took a precise touch and wrong-footed Casillas with a composed finish. It was brilliant play from the pair of substitutes, who shared a deserved embrace having got their team right back into the game – seemingly out of nowhere.

Finally, both teams had their full numbers out on the pitch, as Enrique Romero came on. He had a massive scare almost immediately when Ačimovič went to ground under pressure from the substitute claiming for a penalty, but the referee wasn't interested. The Slovenian frustration surrounding this would have only intensified when a penalty was given at the other end moments later, as Gajser caught Morientes after the Spaniard reached the dropping ball from the defender's poor touch before he did.

It took a while for the men in white to move as they protested to the referee, but when they did it was Hierro placing the ball on the spot. The captain was made to wait further but the delay didn't put him off at all. He sent Simeunovič the wrong way and slotted the ball home before jumping in the air, pumping his fist then being hugged by the man who had won the spot-kick before their team-mates joined in. Slovenia didn't give up but they never looked like restoring parity – if anything, Spain should have got their fourth as Raúl uncharacteristically wasted a good chance.

The final whistle should have marked the end of this game's drama, but there was plenty more to come for Slovenia. When Zahovič was substituted in the 63rd minute, somewhere between high-fiving Ačimovič, kicking a bottle and sitting down, events unfolded that would prove costly for both Zahovič and Katanec.

Speaking to Slovenian television after the game, Katanec said, 'We have two more games and then the cycle finishes'. His words were delivered in a strangely defeatist tone, and he followed up with, 'Certain players haven't done anything in attack'. When asked what was happening in the changing room – likely a generic question about the team's reaction – Katanec responded, 'I will not be talking about that, but in the next few days I will tell you what happened behind the dressing room doors after the game'.

It was revealed two days later that the player and manager had clashed. They were about as different as two men could be: both as a player and manager, Katanec was all about discipline and doing what was best for the team; Zahovič was a gifted maverick who wore his individualism like a badge of honour. Katanec was from Ljubljana, the capital city; Zahovič was from Maribor, the main city of what was formerly known as Styria. Those from Maribor had often felt that the national team was too geared towards Ljubljana, from the players selected to the inclusion of the colour green on kits.

During a press conference, Katanec began to weep as he spoke of how the Benfica man had claimed he was only subbing off Styrians, as well as saying, 'He could buy me, my house and my family and Smarna Gora,' referencing the mountain near Ljubljana where Katanec owned a house and had taken the team for pre-tournament training.

After announcing that he would step down as manager, Katanec added, 'I'm terrified of Slovenia being so small and still dividing itself into I don't know what. I'm proud to be Slovenian, and I'm proud my parents were Croatian, my father and my mother,' but with that, more tears came and he left.

Despite players being told not to speak to the media, Zahovič did just that in a press conference outside their training base. He said, 'Things were happening and I didn't want to react, even though I was having to listen to somebody putting me down every day. It wasn't only about me, but also about other players.'

Things got a bit more personal after that when he added, 'He [Katanec] should stop competing with me and the 32 goals I've scored. He should stop competing with my fame and he should stop competing with the other players because we've been hugely important in getting him where he is today. Nobody wants to take this away from him. Yesterday there was a meeting, and I wanted to hear what the rest of the players thought. They were very honest. They said that my reaction was not appropriate and they didn't agree with it, but they think I deserve more respect from my coach. They wanted me to stay. That's what he was crying about, he wasn't crying because he felt insulted.'

The midfielder finished by saying, 'I'm apologising in public to return the ball to his court'. In speaking to the press, he'd done the complete opposite, as it went directly against orders from the Football Association of Slovenia. Zahovič was supposed to be Slovenia's star man but this pushed through the decision to send him home immediately. The debacle surrendered far more of Slovenia's hope for the tournament than losing to one of the World Cup's favourites could ever have done.

### Croatia 0 Mexico 1 (Group G, 3 June, Niigata)

In their first World Cup as an independent nation, just four years before this one, Croatia had announced themselves in style by coming third in France. Finishing second in a group containing Argentina, Jamaica and Japan, they then beat Romania and Germany before succumbing to eventual champions France in the semi-final, then beating the Netherlands in the third-place play-off. On top of that, Davor Šuker had won the Golden Boot. There was still plenty of debate around whether the presence of various ageing stars from that impressive run was a positive sign or not after they failed to even reach Euro 2000.

The view of Croatia manager Mirko Jozić, who also took Yugoslavia's Under-20s to World Youth Championship glory in 1987, was, 'We are not going to renounce the gold, even if its shine has waned a little'. Mexico boss Javier Aguirre certainly didn't mind that ahead of their opener, saying, 'I've seen Croatia and now they don't scare me at all. They are very orderly but they have a hard time scoring'.

El Tri hadn't been too imposing themselves until Aguirre came along, as disappointing tenures from Manuel Lapuente and Enrique Meza left them fifth in their six-team qualifying group – the latter even oversaw Mexico suffering a first home World Cup qualifier defeat for 20 years. Still, a turnaround in form that culminated in a 3-0 win against Honduras saw Mexico pip them to third to progress alongside the United States of America and Costa Rica. Most of the world's attention was on their 23-year-old captain Rafael Márquez, the AS Monaco centre-back already being watched by Real Madrid and Barcelona.

After the national anthems, for which Mexico's players and fans did their salute with a straight hand covering their chest, the game started with both teams doing their utmost to get on top. The first opportunity went Croatia's way after Niko Kovač was fouled just outside Mexico's box, but Robert Prosinečki blazed the ensuing free kick over the crossbar.

They had a far more dangerous attempt from a free kick in the sixth minute when Josip Šimunić rose highest to meet Robert Jani's delivery, forcing a sprawling save from Óscar Pérez. Croatia's set pieces remained the main threat in the early stages and a knockdown from a corner resulted in Zvonimir Soldo sending his effort over the crossbar.

Mexico began to get on top after the first 15 minutes but Croatia's defence stood strong – with their two goals conceded being the lowest total in European World Cup qualifying. They also came close at the other end, forcing Pérez to rush out so he could reach a through ball ahead of Kovač.

Mexico's first real chance came in the 31st minute. When Ramón Morales's attempted short corner routine resulted in his cross deflecting behind off the first man, he resorted to causing danger the old-fashioned way. He whipped in a surging cross that went straight on to Cuauhtémoc Blanco's head, but the striker's effort was comfortably saved by Stipe Pletikosa. A scuffed Morales shot saw the ball travel to Jared Borgetti in the six-yard box moments later, but the Santos Laguna man somehow diverted his tap-in wide with the goal at his mercy.

Gerardo Torrado hit a tame shot from outside the box in the 40th minute, and Blanco's corner had to be punched away, but the half ended with plenty of sparring and a lack of real opportunities. In an effort to get Croatia going offensively, Jozić brought off Prosinečki and replaced him with Fenerbahçe's Milan Rapaić.

Rapaić was involved immediately, winning and taking a free kick that resulted in Soldo's bullet header being tipped over the crossbar within a minute of the restart. After that, the second half continued where the first had left off, with Mexico having some good moments but struggling to break down the opposition's back line – Rapaić's free kick was the closest Croatia came.

That all changed in the 59th minute when Borgetti's intelligent flick into the box lured Boris Živković to commit to clearing it before Blanco stole the ball away from him while going for goal. Having completely taken out the striker's legs, the Bayer Leverkusen defender conceded a penalty and was given a straight red card. Croatia's number six went off as slowly as possible, but Blanco held his nerve with an unusually long run-up culminating in him sending Pletikosa the wrong way and comfortably converting the penalty. As Blanco pointed to the sky, his team-mates jumped on him in appreciation.

With Mexico looking energised by their lead, Šuker was soon sacrificed by Jozić to bring on Daniel Šarić so that Croatia's back three could be restored. Despite the setbacks, the men in red and white almost equalised when Soldo's speculative effort from range was fumbled by Pérez and squirmed wide of the post.

After being part of a clash of heads, Alen Bokšić was then replaced by Chelsea's Mario Stanić in Croatia's final change three minutes later, which was swiftly followed by Aguirre taking Borgetti off for 33-year-old Luis Hernández.

Croatia wilted further in an attacking sense, partly due to their depleted numbers, but did remain resolute defensively. Still, Morales had a half chance in the 79th minute but the ball spun off his boot and harmlessly wide. After that effort, whether it was to go for a second goal or use up time to retain the lead they already had, Mexico's Aguirre brought the goalscorer Blanco off for Francisco Palencia.

The Balkan nation rarely looked like scoring after this point, with Morales having a shot well saved and some

Mexican passages of play even earning shouts of 'olé'. However, in the 90th minute, Jarni delivered a long throw that was flicked on to Šimunić in the box. With noises of anticipation rising in Niigata Stadium, the centre-back could only smash his effort off the goalkeeper and into the side netting.

The ensuing corner was well dealt with and amid a background of Mexican chanting and whistles, El Tri were able to comfortably see out the final minutes. It hadn't been a World Cup classic, but after Aguirre had spoken before the game his side had come good during it. Meanwhile, Croatia went into their match against group favourites Italy without any points to their name and one of their starting defenders suspended.

### Brazil 2 Turkey 1 (Group C, 3 June, Ulsan)

Brazil have a long and proud history in the World Cup, having played in every tournament since the inaugural edition in 1930, while also holding the record for victories – having lifted the trophy four times prior to the start of the 2002 finals. However they had stumbled through their qualifying campaign, only progressing due to a 3-0 win over Venezuela in their final game, while Luiz Felipe Scolari was the fourth manager to take charge during that term. They had also lost to Honduras in the Copa América and Australia in the Confederations Cup.

There was a further layer of chaos as Roma midfielder and supposed national team captain Emerson's shoulder popped out while he was mucking around in goal the day before Brazil faced Turkey. This meant his tournament was over, Cafu replaced him as skipper and Corinthians' Ricardinho came into the squad. In addition, Atlético Mineiro's Gilberto

Silva and Juninho Paulista became their midfield partnership – the former had never played a competitive game for Brazil and the latter came into this off the back of finishing 18th on loan at Flamengo.

However, this was still a side brimming with exciting talent – even if Scolari had resisted shouts to recall 36-year-old Romário. It boasted two of the world's best full-backs in Roberto Carlos and Cafu, a terrifyingly brilliant front three of Rivaldo, Ronaldo and Ronaldinho, with plenty of quality in other areas. As Alex Bellos told *FourFourTwo* for their preview, 'On paper they should be brilliant, but they have been playing appallingly'.

Turkey, on the other hand, had only ever played at a World Cup in 1954. Their place in the finals was indicative of their rise; 2000 had proven a significant year as Galatasaray beat Arsenal in the UEFA Cup Final to win Turkey's first European trophy before the national team made it to the quarter-finals of the European Championship. To reach Japan and South Korea, the team managed by former schoolteacher Şenol Güneş won their play-off with a resounding 6-0 aggregate win over Austria. The goal now was to get to the quarter-finals.

The side reflected the fact that other countries had started recognising Turkish talent, as it included Internazionale's Emre Belözoğlu, AC Milan's Ümit Davala, Bayer Leverkusen's Yıldıray Baştürk and Aston Villa's Alpay Özalan. Despite this, the man many had their eye on was Rüştü Reçber, the goalkeeper who had never played outside of his homeland. This wasn't just for his distinctive look that included painting black lines on to his face, but also because the Fenerbahçe stopper had conceded just eight goals in ten qualifying matches. As club and country team-mate Fatih

Akyel declared, 'God should give every team a goalkeeper like Rüştü'.

The Turks certainly weren't about to sit back and watch the Seleção play as they went out on the offensive with some tough challenges that saw them concede early free kicks. That commitment also served them well in dangerous positions, as Blackburn Rovers' Tugay Kerimoğlu made a great challenge to prevent Juninho slipping Ronaldo through. Still, Ronaldinho had a chance when Rüştü's poor clearance fell to his feet around 35 yards out, but he couldn't find the target with his quick effort.

Brazil continued to largely dominate the ball in an impressive fashion while being limited to shots from outside the box, with Rivaldo blazing an effort well over the crossbar while Ronaldinho's free kick was blocked by the wall. At the other end, Hakan Şükür almost got through after dispossessing Lúcio, but the Bayer Leverkusen centre-back retrieved the ball with a perfectly timed tackle.

Turkey fought their way back into the game well and it took brave goalkeeping from Marcos to prevent Hasan Şaş's cross from reaching Şükür in the six-yard box. While their free-kick routine on the edge of the box seemingly went horribly wrong, it resulted in a Tugay shot deflecting off Gilberto and behind off the top of the crossbar. There was more concern for Marcos from the ensuing corner, as the goalkeeper had to awkwardly tip it over with the ball seemingly headed for the top corner.

Fatih Akyel was given the game's first yellow card in the 21st minute after he protested that Roberto Carlos should have received one for diving in the Turkish box – Kim Young-joo didn't give a penalty, so must have at least half agreed. There was a real scare for Güneş as the game was stopped due to captain and main goalscorer Şükür going down holding his back soon after, but he was able to continue without receiving treatment. Hakan Ünsal soon joined Fatih in the book for pulling Ronaldinho's shirt.

Brazil had their best chance of the game so far just before the half-hour mark. Having already looked a threat with his bursts up the right flank, Cafu received Gilberto's pinpoint pass before delivering a cross that Rivaldo headed down to Ronaldo. 'O Fenômeno' held the ball up brilliantly with three men in red surrounding him, eventually laying off to Juninho for a first-time strike. The Flamengo loanee couldn't keep his shot on target. There were signs that Brazil were really beginning to turn it on as Ronaldinho produced a moment of trickery to get the fans excited, but Turkey stood resolute.

If there had been a Brazilian weak link so far, it was Edmílson. The Lyon defender sloppily conceded possession and allowed Tugay to get a shot off in the 36th minute, but Marcos was able to save it with relative comfort. Rüştü was given a far greater test a few moments later as Ronaldo's cross was headed goalward by Rivaldo. The goalkeeper somehow stopped as he raced back across goal before bending down to get a hand to the ball and then gratefully grabbing it. The Fenerbahçe man had left Rivaldo in disbelief, but Brazil's number ten should have ensured he didn't have the slightest chance. Rivaldo tested Rüştü again with a swerving strike from range, but he was equal to it.

A lapse of concentration from Bülent Korkmaz allowed Juninho to nip in and steal Tugay's pass before attempting to slip Ronaldo through on goal in the 44th minute. The ball never reached him, though, as Brazil's number nine was cynically tripped by Alpay. The South Americans pleaded for a red card but Ümit Özat's slightly deeper position saved the Aston Villa man, who walked away with just a yellow. Roberto Carlos smashed the ball straight at Rüştü from the resulting free kick and it was held impressively.

Ronaldinho then had a great chance to open the scoring after Marcos's long ball was flicked towards him, but the attacker couldn't get enough on his flick to lift it over the goalkeeper.

For all their scintillating play, Brazil hadn't scored and they were punished right on the stroke of half-time. Hasan Şaş latched on to Baştürk's wonderfully dinked ball behind the Brazilian defence, let it bounce and smashed his shot past Marcos at the near post. It was impossible to tell the goal's significance from the Galatasaray winger's celebration as he was the coolest man on the pitch while his team-mates jubilantly joined him. Scolari was anything but calm, desperately gesticulating to nobody in particular before putting his head in his hands.

Following what were probably harsh words from Scolari during the break, Brazil continued to show intent as Ronaldo hit an effort from range that was easily saved. The Seleção would have been wondering how on earth they still weren't on the scoresheet as Edmílson sprinted up the pitch with the ball before offloading it to Rivaldo, who tapped the ball round the goalkeeper only for Ronaldo to see his shot miraculously blocked in the 50th minute. It was a matter of seconds later that their goal finally came, however, when Ronaldo ran off the defender's shoulder and clinically converted Rivaldo's cross. As he celebrated with his line of supply, it seemed as though there was as much relief as joy.

Ronaldo thought he had scored a second within a couple of minutes of the equaliser after dancing through the Turkey defence, but Rüştü read his shot well. There was still no chance of Turkey retreating and the game became an end-to-end affair with both sides searching for a winner.

Şaş was also showing that Brazil weren't the only ones who could produce skills, finding himself fouled after pirouetting on the ball twice. Ünsal hit a thunderbolt of a shot from the ensuing free kick but Marcos got his body behind the ball and gathered it at the second attempt.

As the hour came and went, a Brazil corner resulted in Lúcio poking the ball towards goal to be saved by Rüştü, Juninho was also denied by the goalkeeper and when Rivaldo finally beat him with a header, the celebrations were shortlived as the attacker was offside by the finest of margins.

Turkey were still very much in the game, as Lúcio was reminded when he was pickpocketed by Fatih just outside his own box and ended up bringing down the Fenerbahçe man. Turkey manager Güneş showed further intent in the 66th minute, bringing İlhan Mansız and Ümit Davala on for Baştürk and Korkmaz. Scolari responded moments later by replacing Ronaldinho with Real Betis's Denílson – while the Paris Saint-Germain star showed flashes of brilliance, it wasn't quite the start he had wanted.

There was a farcical moment where Brazil kept running too early or standing far too close as Turkey tried their free-kick routine of touching the ball off before somebody struck it. In the end, the referee seemingly gave up and the shot was blocked just a yard or so away from where it was hit. With just under 20 minutes left Scolari made his last two changes in a bid to earn all three points, as Vampeta and Luizão replaced Juninho and Ronaldo, with Denílson getting himself booked in the few seconds of play between the changes.

The substitutions were initially perceived as negative, but Brazil looked anything but that on the pitch with Rivaldo's effort from range whistling over the crossbar. Turkey weren't sitting back either, and they made wholehearted forays forward at every opportunity – even though the South Americans were undoubtedly on top as the game entered its final ten minutes.

Denílson was proving an effective substitute, and his ball into the box came inches away from finding an attacker, before the 24-year-old won a free kick in a dangerous area. Roberto Carlos's initial effort from the dead ball was blocked and sat up nicely for him, though the left-back's right boot generated plenty of power but little accuracy.

Having made some terrific saves, Rüştü put his side in deep trouble in the 86th minute by miskicking his clearance and giving it straight to Luizão, who ran through on goal before being dragged down on the edge of the box by Alpay in a desperate attempt to keep the scores level. The referee didn't even bother reaching for a second yellow, as the defender was given a straight red for denying a goalscoring opportunity.

Even worse for Turkey, Kim decided to give a penalty, although it seemed Luizão had been fouled outside the box and fallen into it. The men in red used every trick in the book in their attempts to delay and distract Rivaldo as the forward stood with the ball in his hands. He still had to wait after putting it on the spot, but that didn't bother the Barcelona man at all and he stuck the ball past Rüştü despite the goalkeeper diving the right way before going to celebrate in a big huddle with his team-mates.

There were only a couple of minutes left but Turkey still weren't giving up, and İlhan Mansız won a free kick within seconds of the restart having completed a rainbow flick over Roberto Carlos's head. There was also a change when Galatasaray forward Arif Erdem replaced Tugay. The substitute's first action was to stick his free kick straight on Şaş's head, but Turkey's goalscorer couldn't keep his effort down this time.

With the Crescent-Stars going for it, more spaces were opening up for Brazil and Luizão had a great opportunity, eventually scuffing his effort harmlessly into Rüştü's arms. Seconds later, and with the game going into its two minutes of added time, the referee gave Erdem a free kick on the edge of Brazil's box for a blatant dive. He then let Brazil get away with rushing out of the wall to block it again and within seconds, the ball was up the other end with havoc playing out in the Turkey box.

Rüştü completely misjudged Roque Júnior's delivery into the box, allowing Rivaldo to steal it near the byline. The Brazilian then flicked the ball on to the goalkeeper's head before it bounced onto his yellow shirt and back into play, while Rüştü grabbed Rivaldo but not enough to let the referee award a penalty. The comedy sketch was eventually ended by the linesman's flag signalling a corner.

This is when the infamous incident that has earned millions of views on YouTube materialised. With Rivaldo time wasting, Ünsal kicked the ball at the Brazilian's thigh. That didn't stop Rivaldo rolling around on the floor holding his face, and somehow he got what he desired as Ünsal was given a second yellow card just seconds before the final whistle was blown.

Brazil had just overcome their toughest test in the group, while Turkey had displayed that they could compete with the very best. However a lot of the talk post-match revolved around what had happened in the final seconds, as Rivaldo was fined £4,500 by FIFA and forced to pay £680 in costs for his simulation.

There was no regret from the man himself, though. 'My experience counts. I think he deserved to be sent off, but of course he didn't get me in a place where I could be hurt,' Rivaldo said. 'The ball touched my leg, but the other player was wrong to kick the ball at me. I said sorry to him, but that's football.

'It may not have hit my face but the Turkish player should not have done that in the first place. I was glad to see the red card. Creative players must be able to express themselves if football is to stay a beautiful game. There's too much foul play and violence in football. It doesn't matter where the ball hit me. It was only the intent that mattered. In soccer, you have to be sly. It happens a lot and it will happen a lot in this World Cup.'

Rivaldo may not have cared, but he was a divisive figure in Brazil and now the rest of the world. In *The Guardian*'s World Cup review, Paul Wilson named the forward as his least favourite player of the tournament, adding, 'Some so-called superstars are grossly overrated. Could almost forgive this one his selfishness, wastefulness and complete lack of awareness of the rest of his team were he not also a blatant cheat and serial simulator'.

Aside from that moment of madness, this had been one of the World Cup's best games so far.

### Italy 2 Ecuador 0 (Group G, 3 June, Sapporo)

Having painfully finished as runners up at Euro 2000, Italy came into this tournament as one of the favourites to win what would have been their fourth World Cup – and with good reason. Giovanni Trapattoni had an embarrassment of riches at his disposal: Gianluigi Buffon overcame Francesco Toldo for a place between the sticks; their defence included

captain Paolo Maldini, Fabio Cannavaro and Alessandro
Nesta; there was incredible depth in midfield; then there
were the likes of Alessandro Del Piero, Filippo Inzaghi and
Christian Vieri – who scored five times at the 1998 World
Cup – to pick from in attack. However, the man Trapattoni
trusted above all was Francesco Totti. 'I have asked him to
take Gli Azzurri in his hands because this is the right moment
for him to do so,' said the veteran boss pre-tournament.

On the other hand, Ecuador were entering their first
World Cup finals, under the tutelage of the Colombian
Hernán Darío Gómez. They had got through in style,
though, with only Argentina finishing ahead of them in
CONMEBOL qualifying, thanks in large part to their form
while playing at altitude in Quito.

Gómez almost didn't make it to the World Cup, as he
intended to walk away after being beaten up and shot in
the leg by a fan disgruntled by his team selection. However,
having quit his job and flown back to Colombia after being
discharged from hospital, 'El Bolillo' (The Baton) came back
after encouragement from his mother, players threatening
to quit and a personal plea from Iván Hurtado and captain
Álex Aguinaga.

Italy have historically been seen as notoriously slow
starters before gaining momentum later in tournaments, but
they were made to wait while Ecuador had a team huddle
pre-kick off. However, Gli Azzurri dispelled that theory
once the game got going. Divine first-time passing that
had been started with a wonderful Totti flick released Vieri
but José Cevallos rushed out brilliantly to deny the striker's
dinked effort. Within seconds, Totti latched on to Christian
Ponucci's perfectly weighted pass behind the defence and
pulled the ball back for Vieri to calmly slot into the top corner

with a first-time finish. The game was just under seven minutes old but the Italians were already looking imperious.

Despite not having played for two months due to a thigh injury, Totti was certainly in the mood. Soon after his first assist of the tournament, the Roma legend took the ball on his chest while turning 25 yards out and smashed the ball as it rose back off the ground. However, Cevallos was able to scramble across his goal quickly enough to keep the audacious effort out. Any side would be struggling in the face of such opposition, and in the 14th minute Augusto Parozo got Ecuador's first yellow card after going through the back of Vieri.

Ecuador's heavy-handed disruption tactics seemed to have worked for now, as they got a slight foothold on the game and Édison Méndez had their best chance of the game so far but couldn't get it on target under pressure.

Gli Azzurri were always going to be a threat, though, and after Totti produced another delightful flick to keep the ball in play, Gianluca Zambrotta raced in to reach it before delivering a pinpoint cross to Vieri. Uncharacteristically, the Internazionale frontman was unable to find the target on the stretch.

Just as had been the case with the opener, Vieri made up for a squandered opportunity by taking another with 27 minutes on the clock. This time he became a one-man counter attack by latching on to Luigi Di Biagio's ball over the top and nudging Porozo out of the way. Cevallos got to the first attempt, but the goalkeeper's efforts were futile as Italy's number 21 smashed the ball over the line while it was bouncing towards it anyway.

Ecuador weren't giving up and Méndez's latest effort was deflected on to the side netting moments after the restart, while Edwin Tenorio had another attempt blocked following the ensuing corner. Not to have his limelight stolen, Totti hit a venomous strike from range that Cevallos couldn't keep hold of, requiring the goalkeeper to sprint forward and reclaim the ball before Vieri reached it.

Italy largely looked comfortable in the half's final ten minutes, with a tame shot from Cléver Chalá after he had been slipped in by Southampton's Agustín Delgado being the best Ecuador could muster. Totti came close once more just before the break, smashing a free kick from range that skimmed past the post.

Gómez was the only manager to make a change during the interval, taking Aguinaga off for Carlos Tenorio. That made no difference in the short term, though, as Italy looked incredibly comfortable defensively. Nesta made a tackle then produced a back-heel to retain possession, while Maldini smashed into two consecutive challenges before Hibernian's Ulisese de la Cruz was booked in the aftermath.

Zambrotta skipped down the line marvellously in the 51st minute before picking out Totti with a cross, but the man wearing number ten saw his volley blocked well. Chalá was booked three minutes after that for bringing down Cristiano Doni as the winger looked to start an Italian break. Damiano Tommasi successfully broke through the middle of the pitch soon after, but hit his strike straight at Cevallos for the goalkeeper to tip over. From the resulting corner, Doni flew in ahead of Cevallos to toe poke the ball goalward but it eventually went off the crossbar and behind.

After Carlos Tenorio hit an effort over the bar, his namesake Edwin was brought off for Marlon Ayoví. More impressive Italian play followed and a Totti back-heel saw Vieri hit a thunderous strike from outside the box that was parried away. With Ecuador having some bright moments, starting in the 64th minute Italy made all three of their changes in a ten-minute period as Angelo Di Livio and Gennaro Gattuso replaced Doni and Di Biagio respectively, before the culmination of Del Piero replacing Totti – the mere sight of the Juventus talisman on the sideline had been enough to earn applause from a largely muted crowd.

There wasn't much else to shout about as Vieri gunned for his hat-trick without being able to break through the Ecuadorian defences again, while Cannavaro was booked for grabbing the ball on the floor, feeling that he had been fouled by Chalá. As expected, Italy cleared the ensuing free kick with great conviction.

Ecuador made their final change in the 85th minute with Nicolás Asencio replacing Chalá as everyone had seemingly accepted the scoreline (well, aside from Vieri) and the game crawled to a close. Vieri did get one more chance with a header from Panucci's free kick, but the effort was blocked. Del Piero also came agonisingly close to playing Zambrotta through but there was just too much on his looped pass for his Juventus team-mate to control it convincingly.

In the final minutes, Delgado had his moment to put his Southampton struggles behind him and score against one of world football's tightest defences. The Italians had shown an uncharacteristic lack of awareness and completely stopped to call for offside when Alfonso Obregón's wayward shot fell to Delgado. However, after turning well, he tried to power the ball past Buffon at the near post and the stopper was equal to it, tipping the ball wide.

While this caused some excitement for the South Americans, they weren't able to hit the back of Italy's net as Brian Hall's whistle ended the game shortly afterwards. This wasn't a classic game for the neutral but Italy would have been satisfied after doing all their hard work in the opening half an hour before comfortably seeing the game out. Meanwhile, Ecuador could take positives from their first World Cup finals fixture.

*China 0 Costa Rica 2 (Group C, 3 June, Gwangju)*
Even at this early stage, both teams would have seen this game as a key one to win considering they were underdogs in a group containing Brazil and Turkey. Aside from that, it was a fixture for China boss Bora Milutinović to look forward to as he had managed a record number of nations in the World Cup finals, doing so with Mexico in 1986, Costa Rica in 1990, USA in 1994 and Nigeria in 1998 – reaching the second round with all of them.

This was the Serbian's first time taking a nation through qualifying, and it was also the first time China had reached a World Cup. It was a massive step up for a side who had faced Cambodia, the Maldives, UAE, Uzbekistan, Oman and Qatar to get to the finals. Their star man, Manchester City's Sun Jihai, had faced a year-long suspension for 'attacking a referee' during the previous qualifying tournament for the Olympics – their only other players abroad at club level were Dundee's Fan Zhiyi and St. Pauli's Yang Chen.

Meanwhile, Costa Rica were playing in their second World Cup following the aforementioned campaign in 1990 under Milutinović. Getting out of the group stages again would be an incredible achievement for Alexandre Guimarães's side. The feeling was that this would depend on their strike duo of Manchester City's Paulo Wanchope and Alajuelense's Rolando Fonseca getting on the scoresheet.

As was to be expected, there was a large Chinese presence in the stands, while the players also showed their togetherness by putting their arms around each other during the national anthem. Costa Rica were certainly making their own presence known.

Once the game had got going, China had the higher volume of early attacks but were unable to work Erick Lonnis in the Costa Rica goal. Gilberto Martínez ended up having the game's first shot in the fifth minute, but it trickled through to Jiang Jin. Wanchope showed the first moment of real quality soon afterwards, touching the ball down masterfully in a wide area before delivering an inviting cross that nobody in red could quite reach.

Costa Rica came close to releasing Fonseca shortly before the quarter-hour mark but Li Weifing went desperately flying through the air to prevent him getting through on goal, eventually kicking the Costa Rican in the face while doing so. There was no foul given for a moment that summarised the pragmatic approach the Chinese were taking. Seconds later, Hao Haidong went down after minimal contact with Lonnis, who gave the Dalian Shide striker a shake of the head as he threw the ball out of play.

Luis Marín received the game's first card after 15 minutes for preventing Yang from spinning behind. Mauricio Solís joined him just two minutes later after taking out Sun with a poor sliding tackle. China had got themselves on top as the 20th minute arrived, but Costa Rica's balls over the top were creating problems and Solís managed to break forward to get on the end of one only to send his effort straight at Jiang. His tackle on Sun had a more lasting impact than that run as China's number seven struggled afterwards and eventually came off in the 26th minute to be replaced by Qu Bo.

It was a first half that saw both teams seemingly focusing on disrupting the other rather than displaying quality of their own. Even Wanchope sent a header horribly wide, while Rónald Gómez trumped him with an attempt that spun off his boot and nowhere near the goal. Gómez did well to create space for himself inside the box a few minutes after that failed effort but opted to pass instead of shoot and picked out a space full of men in white. China's best chance of the half came five minutes before the break when a quick counter attack ended with Yang's eventual effort trickling into the goalkeeper's arms.

Lonnis was the first goalkeeper brought into serious action in the second half when, four minutes after the break, Hao's cross left him desperately sprawling over his own defenders to reach the ball. He eventually conceded a corner after flying into Martínez – who had his sleeves rolled up like an American football player.

There were signs that China were beginning to get on top in the second period as Yang smashed a first-time effort wide after being found by Wu Chengying's low cross flashing across the box – though the eventual shot was a bit of a mess. Guimarães responded by bringing Hernán Medford on for Fonseca in the 57th minute.

The tide was definitely turning, and Wanchope had a penalty claim turned down following a clumsy challenge from Wu just moments after the change. That was then followed by Li Tie earning China's first yellow card on the hour for a foul on the substitute Medford. From the resulting free kick, play was switched before a pass found Gómez just outside the box. He produced a brilliant flick to find Wanchope, and when the striker was dispossessed Gómez pounced on the loose ball and sent a first-time effort flying past the flailing goalkeeper before sprinting off to celebrate with the bench.

Emboldened by his goal, Costa Rica's number 11 danced around the Chinese defenders before going down the line and fizzing a ball into the box that Li Weifeng uncomfortably deflected over his own crossbar. The ball was played short to Gómez, who held his defender off and swivelled before delivering a cross that was glanced in by the head of centre-back Mauricio Wright, who jubilantly tore off his shirt while running to celebrate. China had equalled or even bettered Costa Rica for most of the game's opening hour but Gómez had produced two moments in four minutes that put them in a precarious position. Su Maozhen was brought on for Yang in an effort to change that.

The men in white came close to pulling a goal back in the 69th minute but a scramble in the box, with pretty much every Costa Rican taking part, saw the ball fall to Xu Yunlong who couldn't find the target with his rushed effort. Guimarães used the subsequent break in play to bring Harold Wallace off for Steven Bryce. Moments after his missed opportunity, Xu earned a yellow card for bringing down Martínez.

Milutinović decided to go for it in the 74th minute, taking centre-back Fan off for midfielder Yu Genwel. Gómez was soon booked for pulling Wu back as the left-back tried to start an attack, and Wanchope was then preserved and brought off for midfielder Wilmer López as Costa Rica looked to maintain their clean sheet.

A lack of creativity was widely cited as China's big concern pre-tournament, and that showed in the final minutes as they tried to find a glimmer of hope that they could earn a point. Substitute López had the best chance after more dazzling work from Gómez. Yu threatened to burst forward at one point but Walter Centeno ended the run by pulling the Tianjin TEDA man's shirt, earning himself a yellow card in the process.

Gómez had one final effort after being played through on goal. However, having twisted and turned to get away from the goalkeeper twice, he eventually saw his shot cleared off the line. Ma Mingyu then speculatively had a go of his own from almost 40 yards out moments before Kyros Vassaras blew up for full time.

Sections of the Chinese press had shown plenty of excitement before the tournament, but the team's opener made it evident that they were going to struggle in this group. Meanwhile, this wasn't Costa Rica's finest performance but they had got the result they needed ahead of their key match against Turkey.

## Japan 2 Belgium 2 (Group H, 4 June, Saitama)

1998 had seen Japan reach their first World Cup, in which they lost all three of their games, but things were expected to be different this time around – not just because they had won co-hosting rights. Philippe Troussier's side was seen as Asia's biggest hope as they had won the 2000 Asian Cup before reaching the Confederations Cup Final the following year.

They were also armed with Shinji Ono of Feyenoord, and Hidetoshi Nakata, who had made his impact in Italy and represented Parma at the time. There were also reasons for concern, though. Many players had flocked from the J.League to Europe with Troussier hoping that they would toughen up. This didn't do much to instil confidence in the side: Junichi Inamoto didn't start a Premier League game for Arsenal, Portsmouth's Yoshikatsu Kawaguchi was dropped for a 42-year-old Dave Beasant and consequentially lost his national team place to Seigo Narazaki, while Akinori Nishizawa played just three times for Bolton Wanderers and then returned to Cerezo Osaka before missing out on a starting spot against Belgium.

The Europeans were one of just six nations from their continent to reach every World Cup since 1982, though like Japan, they hadn't made it out of the group stages in the last edition. Robert Wasiege was hoping to take them deep into the tournament like their 1986 semi-finalists, with help from Schalke 04 forward Marc Wilmots. However, he wouldn't be able to call upon the captain's club team-mate Émile Mpenza, who missed out on a trip to Asia with a persistent groin injury after *FourFourTwo* had dubbed this as his 'opportunity to prove that comparisons with Michael Owen are deserved'.

There was a very clear sense of excitement in Saitama Stadium as the game kicked off, but it mustn't have come from the action itself as the opening exchanges were fairly bitty. After Japanese captain Ryuzo Morioka had gone through the back of Gert Verheyen for Belgium's second free kick up the pitch in the first four minutes, the Red Devils wasted the opportunity with two low strikes into the crowd. Nakata looked to spring a counter attack, but Atsushi Yanagisawa had strayed offside by the time the ball had been offloaded to him.

There were two very distinct styles on the pitch; Belgium often used brute force and the most direct route forward, while Japan attempted to conjure up enough guile to slip through the cracks. In the 13th minute, Timmy Simons encapsulated much of the game's attacking play until that point, smashing a shot against his own team-mate.

After Daniel Van Buyten had gone through Takayuki Suzuki, the resultant free kick was squared to the fiery-haired

Kazuyuki who struck the ball from outrageously far out, although his effort eventually floated harmlessly over the crossbar. Moments later, Belgium's failure to capitalise on a Japanese mistake resulted in a Daisuke Ichikawa-led counter attack down the right, but he was taken out by Peter Van Der Heyden, seeing the Club Brugge full-back earn the game's first yellow card after 21 minutes.

Verheyen produced the game's first real effort soon after, rising well in the box to meet Jacky Peeters's cross. The striker couldn't quite find the target with his eventual header despite looking to have controlled it well at first glance. There had already been 15 fouls by the 25th minute, offering an indication of why the game had been so stop-start.

Narazaki was the first goalkeeper brought into any notable action, palming away Verheyen's header just before the half-hour mark. Bart Goor attempted to clip the ball back into the mix but it was deflected out for a corner that came to nothing.

Toda soon took his place in the book after hitting Verheyen with a big challenge. While Belgium still weren't testing Narazaki in the Japanese goal, they were certainly in the ascendancy. Even so, Japan offered a reminder that they could create chances after Yanagisawa brilliantly cushioned the ball down for Nakata to hit a half-volley from outside the box – even if it went over the crossbar.

Goor had a far better opportunity moments later when Wilmots's blocked shot fell kindly to him. The Hertha BSC winger snatched at his attempt and sent it wide, leaving himself visibly frustrated while relief flowed through the Japanese team. It had seemed as though the game was livening up, but it quickly returned to its previously disjointed nature when Yves Vanderhaeghe momentarily went down with a back injury. Nakata ended the lull by producing an eye-catching piece of skill to beat his man on the left wing and cross for Yanagisawa, but he couldn't get a clean connection on the header and it trickled away from goal. By the time William Mattus blew up for half-time, a fair amount of the energy had been sucked out of a crowd that was hoping for more action in the second period.

Belgium had their first opportunity of the second half just two minutes in as Wilmots latched on to a header that put the ball behind Japan's defence following an unconvincing clearance. The Schalke midfielder couldn't get his prodded effort on target, though. The second period was starting where the first had left off as the foul count rose and potential opportunities were spurned – though Ryuzo Morioka did impressively recover from a team-mate's mistake to dispossess Verheyen. There was another yellow card in the 54th minute when Inamoto was adjudged to have fouled the same attacker while aiming to steal the ball from him.

The breakthrough finally came in the 57th minute, and did so fittingly for this game, starting with a free kick when Johan Walem was fouled by Toda. The Standard Liége midfielder took it himself, but this was all about Wilmots. Japan couldn't convincingly clear their lines and when Eric Van Meir lofted the ball back into the box, Belgium's captain produced an outstanding overhead kick to momentarily silence the Saitama Stadium.

The Red Devils's lead lasted just two minutes as their static defence allowed Suzuki to sneak in and toe poke Ono's long ball past Geert De Vlieger before the goalkeeper could get there. Japan's number 11 let out a roar that was seemingly matched by every fan in attendance, with the jubilation clear to see as parity was restored.

Belgium immediately went on the attack, but having just scored the equaliser Suzuki did well to block off Verheyen and stop him reaching a lofted ball into the box. Of course the fouls kept coming and Verheyen was booked after swiping Inamoto's legs in the 62nd minute. Moments later, Ono shot directly from another free kick despite it being at an incredibly tight angle and forced De Vlieger to awkwardly tip the ball over his crossbar. That was to be the Feyenoord man's final action, as he was substituted for Shimizu S-Pulse's Brazilian-born midfielder Alessandro Santos, who was often known as Alex and had gained Japanese citizenship in 2001.

There was a slight break in play as Morioka took a moment after picking up a knock but was still clearly struggling as the game continued. Even he would have been overcome with joy soon as Inamoto nipped in to steal a wayward Belgium pass and after getting the ball back from Alex, the Arsenal man burst through despite efforts to take him out. Breaking into the box, he smashed the ball into the back of the net. The stadium absolutely erupted as Japan's number five ran off to celebrate with the dugout. Just ten minutes after conceding the game's opener, the Samurai Blue were now 2-1 up.

Suzuki was replaced by Hiroaki Morishima straight afterwards, while Belgium's Walem was brought off for Genk striker Wesley Sonck. In a period of changes, Morioka's injury finally got the better of him and the centre-back went down before being stretchered off and replaced by Tsuneyasu Miyamoto – who certainly stood out with his protective mask and the retrieved captain's armband.

Belgium had been very much on the back foot before all of these disruptions, but the stoppages seemingly gave them a chance to regroup and Waseige's side were back on level terms in the 75th minute. Van Meir lofted a through ball over the Japanese defence after they failed to convincingly clear and Van Der Heyden ran on to it before coolly looping the ball over Narazaki's flailing arms, with the goalkeeper getting the slightest of futile touches. It wasn't the finish of a man scoring his first national team goal, but that's exactly what the left-back had done.

The game remained full-blooded with far more big tackles flying in than efforts soaring towards goal in the following minutes. The first half-chance after Van Der Heyden's goal came to Yanagisawa when he chested down a ball fizzed towards him, eventually failing to find the target from outside the box. Van Meir was then harshly booked in the 82nd minute after taking player and ball while attempting to dispossess Yanagisawa, before Verheyen was then brought off for Derby County's Branko Strupar.

In the 85th minute it momentarily seemed as though Inamoto had put Japan ahead after a herculean effort to keep the ball in Belgium's box with a touch of finesse and then an intelligent finish. However, disbelief was soon drawn across the midfielder's face as it was ruled out for what seemed a soft foul.

Strupar made a big shout for a penalty as the clock ticked past 90 but referee Mattus showed no interest. Both teams defended resolutely when required in the dying moments and a scintillating second half resulted in a point apiece. While both nations had reason for encouragement, this was especially significant for Japan, who had earned their first point at the World Cup finals. The aim was now to follow that up with a first victory.

### *South Korea 2 Poland 0 (Group D, 4 June, Busan)*
Having seen their co-hosts draw against Belgium, it was now time for South Korea to kick off their own World Cup

campaign on home soil. This was also a nation looking to get out of the group stages for the first time in their history, despite qualifying for the last four editions. Their first test was Poland, who were partaking in their first major tournament since 1986, as a lack of young players coming through is said to have been exacerbated by the financial crisis that followed the break-up of the Communist system that had been in place there.

Having scored eight goals in ten qualifying games, Emmanuel Olisadebe was looking to continue his fine form and fire the Poles into the knockout stages. The Nigerian-born forward created the game's first notable chance. He slid the ball through to Jacek Krzynówek, but Poland's number 18 sliced his shot wide. South Korea's influence on the game grew rapidly as they put the pressure on, with captain Hong Myung-bo striking an effort from range that was deflected behind. Poland could still pose a threat and Olisadebe came close to creating an opportunity for himself after running behind the defence, with the Koreans being saved by a last-ditch tackle from Choi Jin-cheul.

Kim Nam-il could feel lucky not to have given a penalty away while dealing with the ensuing corner. The Korean midfielder chested it down but failed to reach the ball ahead of Maciej Żurawski, taking the forward out as he touched it to Radosław Kałużny. Poland's number ten couldn't control his effort at all, and while Lee Woon-jae could have been facing an effort from the spot he was only tasked with taking a goal kick.

The Koreans responded with Song Chong-gug showing moments of trickery and flair down the right, while Yoo Sang-chul came close to finding the bottom corner with a strike from range.

The deadlock was broken in the 26th minute and it was the thousands of Koreans in the Busan Asiad Main Stadium who were overcome with jubilation. Poland had actually dealt with a threatening free kick well but completely fell asleep after clearing their lines to concede a throw. Lee Eul-yong was alert and threw the ball to Seol Ki-hyeon before getting it back. The Bucheon SK winger got his head up and crossed the ball to Hwang Sun-hong, who had the freedom of Poland's box having easily lost Michał Żewłakow and Tomasz Wałdoch. Even if he had been marked tighter, there was no stopping Hwang as he calmly slotted the ball past Jerzy Dudek with a first-time effort before running off to celebrate with those in the dugout.

Following the goal, singing filled the stadium and even small moments inspired an anticipatory outburst from fans. There was a slight break in that momentum in the 31st minute when Krzynówek was booked for a poor challenge on Yoo that left the midfielder writhing in pain on the floor. After coming back on, Yoo had the ball in the back of the net but the goal didn't count following a marginal offside call. This was the last big moment of a well-contested first half.

It didn't take much time for South Korea to test Dudek again after the break as Park Ji-sung hit a venomous volley when a corner was flicked to him by Seol. Despite the quick start, Hiddink felt the need to make a change in the 50th minute and brought the goalscorer Hwang off for Ahn Jung-hwan.

Just three minutes later some quick thinking from Ahn allowed South Korea to double their lead. When they were awarded a free kick inside Poland's half, Ahn's run across the defence encouraged Kim Nam-il to play a quick pass to him. Tomasz Hajto actually got to the ball ahead of him, but the Schalke defender couldn't clear convincingly and it fell to Yoo, who set himself and struck an effort from outside the box that was too hot for Dudek to handle – despite the Liverpool man getting both hands to it.

Hajto would have been feeling frustrated after being so close to denying a goal. If he was looking to use that for his strike, all it ended up doing was inflicting pain on Lee who blocked it with the most painful area possible. Pain was felt elsewhere in the Korean ranks when their second scorer in the game, Yoo, was stretchered off just eight minutes after his goal, being replaced by Lee Chun-soo. Poland had struggled with the home side's pace all game, and the substitute almost took advantage of that immediately as he ran behind before eventually hitting the side netting.

With 26 minutes left to find two goals, Jerzy Engel opted to use his last substitution to bring on forward Marcin Żewłakow for midfielder Kałużny, having made like-for-like changes earlier in the game. Despite the manager's attacking intent, Poland didn't seem to have the quality or a plan to work their way past the Korean back line, with Lee Woon-jae rarely being tested at all – this was arguably best shown when Olisadebe and Marek Koźmiński got in each other's way as they attempted to latch on to a cross. If anything the Koreans looked more likely to extend their lead, with Ahn pulling a shot wide after showing brilliant footwork to create space for himself.

The Poles weren't giving up but couldn't reach South Korea's level, as was shown by the challenges from Hajto and Piotr Świerczewski that saw the pair pick up yellow cards late on. By the time Seol was brought off for Cha Du-ri in the 89th minute, there was a party atmosphere among the South Koreans filling the stands. The substitute almost gave them something else to shout about as he reached the ball after Dudek had failed to hold Ahn's shot, but he could only strike it against the Poland stopper.

Park came inches away from adding another, but it didn't matter as Óscar Ruiz blew the final whistle just seconds later to confirm South Korea's victory. There was a massive roar from the stands, players and dugout at not just starting a home World Cup with a win, but also securing their nation's first victory at a World Cup finals.

## Russia 2 Tunisia 0 (Group H, 5 June, Kobe)

In their tenth year as an independent nation Russia hardly boasted a star-studded side, but there were definitely expectations for them to progress from what was deemed a kind group draw. That came from both outside and within the squad. 'Russia must qualify for the round of 16 from such a group, otherwise [Oleg] Romantsev and myself will resign,' declared assistant coach Mikhail Gershkovich pre-tournament. 'If we don't qualify, we just don't belong at the helm of the national team.'

No pressure, then, especially with the nation looking to regain their confidence on the footballing stage after the Soviet Union's collapse and failure to make the 1998 World Cup. Any nerves wouldn't have been helped by their performances in the LG Cup a few weeks earlier, where they had drawn against Belarus and Yugoslavia before losing both matches on penalties. They were also hindered by Celta Vigo playmaker Aleksandr Mostovoi being injured, while Bordeaux's Alexey Smertin also missed the opener.

Meanwhile, there was very little made of Tunisia, especially after head coach Henri Michel – whose World

Cup experience included a third-place finish with his native France in 1986 – walked out 67 days before their tournament started. Their side, the only African team to be dominated by players who played domestic football in their homeland, would now be led by Ammar Souyar and Khemais Labidi as they looked to get out of the group stages for the first time – having already made history by reaching back-to-back finals tournaments. The pair made a surprise decision for the opener, benching captain and star man Zoubeir Baya with striker Adel Sellimi taking the armband.

Valery Karpin had the game's first effort after Vladimir Beschastnykh had won a free kick on the edge of Tunisia's box within a couple of minutes. Karpin's powerful strike went straight at Ali Boumnijel, who was able to punch it away. At the other end, Tunisia were trying to get around Russia's ageing defence and Sellimi was inches away from reaching an early ball into the box.

Having had pretty much nothing to do all game, Ruslan Nigmatullin made a brilliant stop to prevent an own goal as Tunisia had broken well and two Russian defenders cut out Selim Ben Achour's through ball for Hassen Gabsi. In doing so, Yuri Nikiforov had knocked the ball on to Yuri Kovtun, with the left-back almost sending it into the bottom corner of his own net. In the end it dribbled past the post and Nigmatullin comfortably punched the ensuing corner clear. Russia were soon attacking the correct goal and the prodigal Marat Izmailov had an effort from range saved despite it swerving away from the goalkeeper.

The game saw its first yellow card in the 27th minute when Igor Semshov lunged into a tackle on Ziad Jaziri, leaving the forward in pain on the floor. As the action restarted, it did so with the backdrop of a Mexican wave that indicated

GROUP STAGE – MATCHDAY ONE

the fans weren't completely enthralled by events on the pitch. Trabelsi had been one of Tunisia's brighter players and he made a good break forward after intercepting a pass, only to eventually be blocked off by veteran defender Viktor Onopko – one of those who had played in the Commonwealth of International States (CIS) side that replaced the Soviet Union at Euro 1992.

They say that goalkeepers are a protected species and Boumnijel showed that in the first half's latter stages as he took exception to Pimenov's presence once again. The striker had done hardly anything, yet Tunisia's number one was outraged at contact being made and shoved the Russian in the back of the head while shouting at him. Raouf Bouzaiene was clattered by Karpin soon afterwards as they went up for an aerial challenge.

Still, Tunisia almost made the breakthrough before half-time. Khaled Badra couldn't quite reach a clipped pass ahead of Nigmatullin, while Yegor Titov hit a shot that whistled past the post with the half's last kick. Romantsev and his staff had looked surprisingly muted on the bench throughout the first half, but he took action during the break by substituting the booked Semshov for Real Sociedad's Dmitri Khokhlov.

The second half started as the first had done with a Karpin free kick posing questions. This time he crossed the ball from deep within 30 seconds of the restart and Khokhlov tamely headed wide. In an equally similar fashion to the opening 45 minutes, Tunisia didn't enjoy much of the ball but almost made a breakthrough, though Ben Achour couldn't quite get Sellimi's ambitious pass under control. Gabsi earned the African side's first yellow of the game soon afterwards having not retreated from a free kick quickly enough for referee Peter Prendergast's liking.

Ben Achour was looking the man in red most likely to breach Nigmatullin's defences, and it wasn't long until he smashed a loose ball from just outside the box inches away from the post. With Tunisian momentum building it took a superb last-ditch header from Karpin to deny Sellimi a near-certain goal at the back post.

Romantsev took action again in the 55th minute, bringing Beschastnykh off for Dmitri Sytchev. PSV Eindhoven defender Nikiforov was also looking to change the game's flow, as having already taken a few shots from range the man who had refused to play for his country for three years fired marginally wide. Moments later, Pimenov stabbed wide from inside the six-yard box.

Russia finally made the breakthrough just before the hour. Boumnijel dealt with a corner well but then proceeded to concede possession with his throw and was then unable to keep out Titov's strike despite getting a hand to it.

The Tunisian self-sabotage continued just a few minutes later as having assisted Titov for the opener, Sytchev ran inside the box at Radhi Jaïdi, who responded by clumsily sticking out a leg for the Spartak Moscow man to trip over. Karpin stepped up to take the penalty and confidently converted by sending the goalkeeper the wrong way. While Karpin's team-mates excitedly celebrated, he only afforded himself a celebratory shake of the fist and a thankful hug for Sytchev – the youngest player in Russia's squad at 18 years old, who had completely changed the game in just his fourth international match.

The men in red immediately attempted to get back into the game but an acrobatic Jaziri effort was easily collected by Nigmatullin. There was also action from the bench when Baya and Imed Mhedhebi replaced Gabsi and Sellimi. It was initially difficult for the pair to make an impact as Russia slowed down the game and whenever Tunisia did get forward, there were various men in white putting their bodies on the line to nullify the threat.

That didn't stop them from trying with Trabelsi doing particularly well from right-back. Jaziri went about things the wrong way and was booked for a blatant dive in the Russian box with a quarter of an hour remaining. Jaïdi delivered a great cross to Baya soon afterwards but the ball wouldn't drop quickly enough after the Beşiktaş man's first touch, and he eventually smashed his shot straight at Nikiforov's face. Jaziri fired wide as the game continued and the defender eventually picked himself up when Izmailov was brought off for Dmitri Alenichev.

Mhedhebi almost let Russia in after passing to an area completely devoid of red, but Sytchev's header eventually looped over the crossbar and on to the roof of the net. Souayah made his final change with six minutes remaining, Ali Zitouni replacing Badra. Despite the Espérance Sportive de Tunis forward attempting to add extra energy for his team, it was Russia who had the next chance as Boumnijel failed to catch the ball after coming out to grab it and Sytchev was unable to hit the target with his shot.

Jaziri went down in the box again after a mazy run, and while Prendergast didn't award a penalty he saved Tunisia's number five the embarrassment of being sent off after two dives and let play continue. A tired back-heel almost gifted Russia a third, but a goal evaded Sytchev, who slipped when the first opportunity to shoot came before eventually sending off a weak effort.

Alenichev was booked for kicking the ball away to waste time in the 88th minute. This felt needless because the Tunisians never looked like scoring – even if they did get more chances. Ben Achour shot well wide with what should have been a fairly simple finish, while their corner was headed away with the game's final touch.

This comfortable victory saw Russia top the group and likely settled any nerves from their disappointing pre-tournament results. Meanwhile, Tunisia had some bright moments and positives to take into their other group games, even if they left Kobe without a point to their name.

## USA 3 Portugal 2 (Group D, 5 June, Suwon)

Going into the tournament, Portugal had been the favourites to win Group D with imperious talents such as AC Milan's Rui Costa, Real Madrid's Luís Figo and Bordeaux's Pauleta among their ranks – the latter had just finished as the joint top scorer in Ligue 1 alongside Djibril Cissé. Meanwhile, there wasn't too much expected of the United States of America team. After all, their progression out of the groups in their home tournament of 1994 was the first time they had managed such an achievement since reaching the semi-finals in the inaugural World Cup of 1930.

However it was the Americans who were the game's early aggressors. When they were awarded a free kick in a deep position, it would have been easy for captain Earnie Stewart to float a ball into the box. Instead he fired off a strike from range that resulted in a corner. The midfielder then went over to provide a brilliant delivery, inviting Brian McBride to attack it.

The midfielder then obliged and climbed above Jorge Costa to fire a header towards goal. Vítor Baía got his hands to it but could only pat the ball down for John O'Brien to smash it into the back of the net from close range. It was just four minutes into the game but the USA were threatening to cause a major upset.

It could have easily been 2-0 just moments later when Petit fouled DaMarcus Beasley dangerously close to the box. Stewart delivered once again and Baía completely flapped at the ball this time, sending it bouncing off the crowd and into Eddie Pope's path, but the defender could only find the side netting. Portugal's box wasn't the only place where confusion took hold as Brad Friedel was left looking for a ball to take a free kick with, only to comically end up with three.

While that was dealt with fairly quickly, Portugal still looked shaky at the back. In the 14th minute a long ball forward that should have been easy for Beto to deal with saw the right-back undercook his back pass. Baía was forced to rush out of his goal and managed to clear, before Beasley reached it.

Portugal grew into the game but were still showing signs of severe sloppiness and that cost them in the 29th minute. Sérgio Conceição conceded a cheap free kick near the halfway line, which Jeff Agoos launched forward. It didn't connect with anyone, and while Costa should have been able to easily clear the defender passed to Figo, who slipped. After a 50-50 challenge left the ball at Landon Donovan's feet, the 20-year-old attempted a cross. By this time Costa had got himself in a position to block the forward's attempt, but as he flung his head at it the man who had spent the season on loan at Charlton Athletic sent the ball flying towards his own goal. Baía scrambled across as he tried to keep it out but could only push it into the net. As Donovan's team-mates came over to congratulate him, the number 21 looked more apologetic than anything else.

There was a slight break in play on the half-hour mark when Pope went down injured. While Portugal did give

USA the ball back after Friedel had kicked it into touch, they did so reluctantly. The Portuguese mood worsened further just six minutes later when USA had another goal to their name. After a loose ball came into their possession, it was played forward for Tony Sanneh to run on to. Once he had it, the Nürnberg defender lifted his head, seeing McBride in space. The ensuing cross into the box was an absolute peach and McBride dived to power his head through it, giving Baía no chance before letting out a celebratory roar. The USA were in dreamland; they had come into this game as the underdogs so it was simply incredible for them to be 3-0 up.

The Americans were given a slight dose of reality just three minutes later, though. They had dealt with a couple of Figo corners well but Beto won a header when Portugal's talisman floated another ball in. O'Brien couldn't clear convincingly and as the ball came back to Beto, Portugal's right-back instinctively struck it past Friedel.

Judging by the ferocity behind the Sporting CP defender's celebration, this was just the boost Portugal needed to finally get going. That was confirmed within moments of the restart as Pablo Mastroeni found himself under pressure on the edge of his own box, while Costa almost broke into their area.

That pressure continued into injury time as Rui Costa touched the ball down on the edge of the box and sent an effort agonisingly wide of the post. Sérgio Conceição would have also had a chance if his touch was better. Byron Moreno blew the whistle just seconds after that last opening, offering the USA the respite they needed.

The ball may have been flat at the beginning of the second half – as it had to be changed shortly after the restart – but the play wasn't. Even though neither goalkeeper was tested in the opening exchanges, the USA were playing aggressively while Figo was beginning to get on the ball and show his flair.

Petit soon had the game's second yellow card for hacking down Donovan as the American tried to break up the pitch. Rather naïvely, Portugal captain Fernando Couto pushed McBride over on the edge of the box when defending the ensuing free kick. The USA now had another chance but Agoos smashed his effort high and wide. Portugal soon had a great opportunity of their own after the ball was flicked towards Costa from a corner kick. The centre-back made a mess of his shot on the turn under pressure from Friedel, though. Encapsulating how end-to-end the game was at times, Donovan came a whisker away from scoring from a tight angle just seconds later.

Pauleta had his best chance of the game shortly after the hour mark, getting his head on Beto's cross. However, under pressure from Sanneh, Pauleta couldn't direct the ball anywhere near the goal. Another chance came his way when Agoos misplaced his pass and gave possession straight to Figo. The 29-year-old clipped a lovely ball with the outside of his boot for Pauleta to run on to but the striker sent his shot flying over the bar.

Portugal eventually received some help in their quest to get a second goal of the game. They worked the ball around well with Figo and Rui Costa central figures in the play. The latter passed to Pauleta, who had drifted out to the left flank and immediately crossed into the box. Agoos swung his foot in an attempt to clear the ball but in doing so the San Jose Earthquakes defender sent it flying off his shin and into the top corner. Things had looked so comfortable for the USA but with 19 minutes left their lead had been halved.

The Portuguese were now largely in control, but the USA took every opportunity they could to get forward with Beasley proving especially useful when he carried the ball up the pitch to relieve pressure. The real break came when Pope went down injured, before eventually being replaced by Carlos Llamosa.

Portugal also brought Nuno Gomes on for Rui Costa, a sign that they were taking a more direct approach for the final ten minutes. This didn't work though, as the United States defence dealt with any aerial threat well and the attackers did a good job of helping to run down the clock while also keeping Portugal honest.

Moreno left Beasley bemused in the 92nd minute after the winger was booked following an incident with Conceição. However, confusion was replaced by jubilation within seconds as the referee blew the final whistle, confirming that the USA had pulled off a magnificent upset, while condemning Portugal to defeat.

## 3

# Group Stage – Matchday Two

*Germany 1 Republic of Ireland 1 (Group E, 5 June, Ibaraki)*

There would have been plenty of expectation around Germany going into this game considering they opened their World Cup campaign with a commanding 8-0 victory – regardless of the opposition. However, as he stated in *Ireland's World Cup 2002*, Mick McCarthy wasn't fearful, saying, 'Circumstance dictated that the Cameroon match [the Republic's 1-1 draw in their opening game] was the toughest game of my life. If I could survive that, I can survive anything'.

Looking back, Matt Holland adds, 'The bigger they are the harder they fall is the saying, so I really enjoyed coming up against the big names and testing myself against them'.

Understandably, Rudi Völler opted to field the same team that had demolished Saudi Arabia, with Carsten Ramelow deemed fit enough to play. Meanwhile, Steve Finnan replaced Jason McAteer in the Republic of Ireland's only alteration. This meant that captain Steve Staunton became the nation's first player to reach 100 caps.

The Irish fans in Ibaraki didn't need any encouragement to make noise – as they were in full voice from the very beginning – but Damien Duff gave them some anyway. The Blackburn Rovers man raced through the heart of Germany's defence, and even though he was eventually dispossessed, it did offer an early warning that the Boys in Green could cause Germany problems.

There was also a battle that became prominent at the other end: Staunton against Miroslav Klose. The two had some collisions early in the game, with the Aston Villa centre-back likely looking to make his mark on the man who had caught the headlines with an opening-day hat-trick. Klose was also doing whatever he could to get the breakthrough, though Staunton was far from impressed when Germany's number 11 dived in an attempt to win a penalty. In addition to that, Gary Breen was competing in a physical match-up with Carsten Jancker.

These battles meant this game was a very different proposition for Germany than the one Saudi Arabia had offered. Still, there was a sense of familiarity in their opener as Michael Ballack put a pinpoint ball into the box – from deep this time – and Klose got in ahead of Ian Harte to clinically convert his header.

The Kashima Soccer Stadium instantly became considerably quieter as the Kaiserslautern frontman pulled out his trademark front flip, even if the Irish didn't stay silent for too long. As McCarthy put it in his book, 'The Germans will consider this as a great goal but our defending was poor. We should never concede a goal like that. It is time to sink or swim now'.

The early signs were that the Irish would swim, as some decisive goalkeeping from Oliver Kahn was all that stopped Duff from going through on goal within a minute of the restart. Holland came even closer soon afterwards with his effort from the edge of the box coming a matter of inches away from the post.

There were times that Germany had almost their whole team back heading into the latter stages of the first half. Ireland were still able to get some dangerous balls into the box – especially from Kevin Kilbane's left boot. One cross from Finnan almost led to a spectacular overhead kick from Robbie Keane, but after being flicked by a German head the ball didn't come down quickly enough for the striker to get a clean connection.

Duff could have had a strike destined for the top corner just before the break but Thomas Linke took the ball to his face. This happened moments before Kim Milton Nielsen's whistle and offered an indication of the way Germany had maintained their one-goal lead without always doing it in the most convincing of ways.

The Ireland team had been told not to go out in the second half and play nice football without getting a goal. However they could have conceded within two minutes of the kick-off if it hadn't been for Jancker missing the ball when a chance came his way. While Germany looked fairly happy for Ireland to have the majority of possession, there were flashes as Keane and Christoph Metzelder squared up after a coming together as the Leeds United man tried to get behind the German defence.

Völler's side were offered a reminder that they shouldn't get too comfortable in the 56th minute. Finnan's initial free kick had been far from his best, but the right-back took his second chance to get a quality delivery into the box. The ball was flicked on and suddenly Duff found himself with just Kahn between him and the goal, but that was all Germany needed as the stopper pulled off a great save to deny the 23-year-old.

In the 68th minute Jancker had another chance to make it 2-0, but Shay Given forced him into a chip attempt by rushing out at the striker. Thankfully for everyone associated with the Green Army, the effort eventually trickled its way wide of the post. There was another scare moments later, when Ireland failed to convincingly deal with Bernd Schneider's corner, though the ball bounced its way into Given's grateful arms.

McCarthy's half-time plan was to 'throw caution to the wind' if he hadn't seen a goal 20 minutes into the second period. He eventually played his hand in the 73rd minute, bringing Niall Quinn and Steven Reid on for Gary Kelly and Harte, switching to a 3-4-3 in the process. Völler took Jancker off for Oliver Bierhoff moments later.

The tactic of having Keane and Duff playing off Quinn caused Germany problems immediately, but it was Die Mannschaft who had another massive chance – uncharacteristically, Klose headed the ball over from just outside the six-yard box. The game was quicker than ever going into the final ten minutes, and a knockdown from Quinn would have released Keane if Kahn hadn't come out so quickly and authoritatively.

Perhaps in an effort to slow down proceedings, Völler made two separate stoppages to bring Marco Bode and Jens Jeremies on for Klose and Schneider, while Kenny Cunningham replaced Staunton for Ireland between them. Bode had a chance seconds after coming on when Given completely missed his kick, eventually failing to take advantage.

As the game edged into its three minutes of extra time, some minds might have strayed towards goal difference between Cameroon and Ireland in a bid to come second, but that wasn't the case for the men who mattered. Instead they continued pushing forward in a bid to grab a late equaliser and in the 92nd minute, Ireland finally got their breakthrough.

When the ball was smashed up the pitch from deep, Quinn had the physical prowess to out-jump Metzelder and culture to touch his header towards Keane. Running on to the ball perfectly, the striker touched it down and even though Kahn got a touch on his strike, the German's efforts were futile as the ball went off him, on to the post and into the back of the net. As Keane brought out a trademark celebration of his own before being mobbed by his team-mates, absolute pandemonium rang out among the Irish. The stands went mad while McCarthy ran around and hugged his coaching team.

It was just a matter of seconds after the Irish celebrations on the pitch subsided that they rejoiced once more as the final whistle was blown. It may not have been a victory, but it sure felt like one, and the result meant that Ireland now had a real chance of getting through to the knockout stages. In his book, McCarthy went as far as to call it 'the best 1-1 win in world football history' and there aren't many Irish people who would disagree. Plenty would have felt the players deserved the couple of drinks they had afterwards to celebrate. On the other hand, Germany now had to get a result against Cameroon, while a win against Ireland would have meant that they would go through regardless.

### Denmark 1 Senegal 1 (Group A, 5 June, Daegu)

Both teams came into this game off the high of opening-day victories: Denmark had overcome Uruguay thanks to an 83rd-minute winner, while Senegal shocked France. That was reflected in the starting line-ups, as the only change between the two sides was Pape Sarr replacing Aliou Cissé in the Senegalese midfield. It wasn't all joy for Denmark ahead of kick-off, as they had requested that their game was played at a different time due to the Daegu heat at 3.30pm – FIFA didn't budge at all.

Whether or not the conditions played a part, there wasn't much action in the first couple of minutes, with the first moment of entertainment coming from Senegal goalkeeper Tony Sylva. Rushing towards the edge of his box, the Monaco man patted the ball down to himself instead of catching it before fooling Ebbe Sand with a cut-back, eventually clearing his lines with a ball that forced Martin Laursen to concede a throw near his own corner flag.

Sand was beaten again soon afterwards, this time by Salif Diao, but there was to be no clearance as the striker slid right through his man while getting nowhere near the ball. It was a pretty simple decision for referee Carlos Batres to book him.

Thomas Helveg and Khalilou Fadiga had already developed a rivalry, and their second coming together – which only took ten minutes to arrive – resulted in the latter getting a yellow after kicking out, with there being a fair argument that it could have been a red. Pretty much everybody on the pitch got involved – with El Hadji Diouf and Stig Tøfting at the forefront – after the Dane pushed men in white back as they protested right next to his team-mate who was still on the floor.

The first opportunity arrived after a quarter of an hour and came in the only way expected of a game that had started so scrappily. When Jesper Grønkjær took a quick throw-in to release Jon Dahl Tomasson, Diao jumped straight into his back and conceded a penalty. The embodiment of calm amid the chaos, Tomasson stroked the ball into the bottom corner despite Sylva going the right way.

Senegal would have been left wondering how they hadn't quickly equalised when Thomas Sørensen's hand and Jan Heintze's boot denied Diao's header, before a follow-up effort hit Diouf in an offside position. Tomasson had the ball in Senegal's net again seconds later but this time he was booked for handball, even though it appeared to come off his chest. The decision resulted in the Dane kicking the advertising boards in frustration.

There were very few real chances as the first half progressed; Thomas Gravesen and Dennis Rommedahl forced Sylva into saves he would be expected to make, while last-ditch defending foiled some threatening Senegal deliveries. Fadiga forged the best opportunity for himself with a flick over Helveg's head that was so wonderfully disguised it fooled the cameraman, but eventually dragged his shot wide.

Both of Senegal's Camaras, Henri and Souleymane, came on after the break, with Moussa N'Diaye and Sarr making way. It didn't even take a minute for the second half's first big challenge as Diao hit Grønkjær hard enough to give away a free kick despite getting the ball. There were also chances for Senegal, as Henri Camara took the ball off Papa Bouba Diop's head a couple of minutes after coming on and couldn't find the target, which left anguish written across the midfielder's face. Looking like he was struggling a little bit, Grønkjær was replaced by Martin Jørgensen in the 50th minute.

Senegal had been the stronger starters in the second period and that paid dividends just two minutes later thanks to a blistering counter attack. Henri Camara won the ball back near his own corner flag before finding Diouf, who gave the ball to Diao with a first-time flick. The midfielder swept the ball left into Fadiga's stride before continuing to sprint up the pitch and getting it back inside the opposition box. He then took a touch before slotting past Sørensen, who, like the rest of his team-mates, was left helplessly watching on. The precision and speed of the move was simply breathtaking.

Senegal weren't about to let up now they had got themselves back on level terms, and Fadiga looked especially dangerous as he showed moments of skill and forced a save from Sørensen. The Danes began to get their foot on the ball a bit more after the hour, though, and Diao ended up going into the referee's book after making one reckless tackle too many, with his latest hitting Tomasson long after he had played the ball. As that happened, Gravesen was substituted for Christian Poulsen.

It wasn't long until there was more arguing, with the cause being that Helveg felt Fadiga had gone down too easily in the box – even though there was no chance of the referee giving a penalty. Whether it was a form of retaliation or coincidence, the AC Milan defender was on the receiving end of a tough tackle from Senegal's number ten moments later. Fadiga probably wondered why he was getting so much attention, as there was a strange moment in which the linesman insisted the forward tucked his shirt in before taking a corner.

There wasn't enough attention being paid to Souleymane Camara as he was afforded so much time upon receiving the ball from Diouf in Denmark's box. The substitute still completely wasted the opportunity, finding the side netting before sheepishly walking back to get into position while Bruno Metsu scratched his head in bewilderment. It seemed as though Senegal were coming out on top in every battle now, and Lamine Diatta easily beat Helveg in the air but couldn't get his header on target.

There was a moment of concern for the African side in the 75th minute when Sylva injured his thumb while dealing with a corner. Thankfully for the goalkeeper, it was nothing that a bit of magic spray couldn't handle and he was soon ready to get back between the sticks.

The stopper may have been able to continue but Diao's match was over five minutes later. He had got away with various poor challenges but one that went over the ball and into René Henriksen's shin earned his second yellow card. The midfielder was furious and kicked the bottles on his way down the tunnel after completing the rare set of conceding a penalty, scoring a wonderful goal and getting sent off. His frustrations would have been reciprocated throughout his nation as Senegal would now face Uruguay for a place in the knockout rounds without him.

The bad blood continued and Helveg finally received a booking for a late challenge in the 82nd minute on Souleymane Camara, who had the displeasure of being a substituted substitute as he was replaced by Habib Beye. Diouf kicked out at the right-back moments later and the two had to be separated with Senegal's number 11 squaring up to the Dane. The game was stopped again seconds later so Poulsen could be booked for fouling Papa Bouba Diop.

Players could be seen having a drink at every opportunity with the contest – as heated as the Daegu weather – approaching its culmination. Peter Løvenkrands was introduced in the 89th minute as Morten Olsen made his last bid for all three points. However, neither side was able to create a meaningful opportunity before Batres's whistle confirmed the draw. It had been a combative affair, with a point putting both sides in a strong position ahead of the final round of group fixtures.

## Cameroon 1 Saudi Arabia 0 (Group E, 6 June, Saitama)

Not only did Robbie Keane's equaliser against Germany help the Republic of Ireland's cause as they aimed to get out of Group E, but it also made the game between Cameroon and Saudi Arabia a lot more interesting. A victory would take Winfried Schäfer's side joint top of the group ahead of their meeting with the manager's home nation, while Saudi Arabia needed to hope that they could recover from the brutal defeat they had suffered in their opener.

Cameroon's only change from their own draw against the Irish saw Daniel N'Gom Kome replace Salomon Olembé. Understandably, Nasser Al-Johar didn't keep much continuity in his team, changing his formation so there were five at the back, while also making five changes in personnel including captain Sami Al-Jaber coming out of the team and Mohammed Al-Deayea taking the armband.

The Cameroonians could have easily had a penalty inside half a minute as N'Gom Kome went down when he was clipped in the box by Mohammed Al-Jahani. To the winger's disbelief, referee Terje Hauge showed no interest in awarding a spot-kick.

Despite this scare and enduring some early pressure, Saudi Arabia were looking far stronger than they had done against the Germans. Some intelligent play down the right even created a chance for Obeid Al-Dosari when he pulled off the defender to meet Abdullah Al-Waked's cross, but the Al-Ahli man couldn't keep his header under the crossbar. Just moments after that incident, Cameroon's left wing-back

Pierre Womé was given more problems, seeing yellow for bringing down Al-Jahani in the tenth minute.

In a game that was proving to be very open in its early stages, Patrick M'Boma thought he had scored the opener in the 12th minute after rounding Al-Deayea and placing the ball into the net, but the Cameroon striker was rightfully called offside.

The early flurry of activity was followed by a period in which neither goalkeeper was truly tested. Marc-Vivien Foé was proving particularly adept at winning the ball back from any loose Saudi touches – though Nawaf Al-Temyat was enjoying himself with some neat play. In this period, Geremi's cross from deep was the main moment of quality but M'Boma was unable to find the target with his header.

Al-Dosari had shown moments of promise in his first start of the tournament. This time, the Saudi Arabia number 11's game came to an abrupt end in the 32nd minute when he caught his studs in the turf while turning to press Raymond Kalla. Despite the medical team's best efforts, he was eventually replaced by Al Hasam Al-Yami.

N'Gom Kome managed to nutmeg Redha Tukur with a lovely moment of skill but Al-Jahani recovered to dispossess the winger. Just moments after that, Al-Deayea almost gifted Cameroon a goal when he made a mess of catching Womé's long throw before somehow managing to stretch out his leg quickly enough to smash the ball clear.

In the 43rd minute, Lauren scored what should have been the game's first goal when he clinically headed Geremi's cross into the net. He was deemed to be offside – even though the Arsenal man clearly wasn't upon further inspection. This would have left a bitter taste, but things could have been even worse going into the break as Al-Temyat's side-footed effort from outside the box came agonisingly close to nestling in the bottom corner.

N'Gom Kome had definitely caused some problems for Saudi Arabia in the first period, but he was the one who made way for Olembé – the man he had originally come into the side to replace.

Cameroon re-emerged with plenty of intent, immediately putting the men in white under pressure and Samuel Eto'o posing a particularly large threat. He did waste a decent chance after a blistering run forward from Olembé, though. The number nine turned and blazed his effort high and wide, while a poor touch allowed Al-Deayea to reach the ball ahead of the striker – even if he did get clattered while collecting it.

Al-Temyat had Saudi Arabia's best moment when he tore through the middle of the pitch before getting a strike off from just outside the box. Alioum Boukar made a bit of a mess of the save, spilling it to Al-Yami, but the substitute only managed to get himself a yellow card for a terribly disguised dive after the slightest of clips from the scrambling goalkeeper. There was an unorthodox piece of goalkeeping at the other end shortly after, when Al-Deayea found himself hanging from the crossbar after tipping a misplaced cross on to the roof of the net.

After all of the work that had been put in by both sides, it was a simple move that eventually broke the deadlock in the 66th minute. Geremi was given plenty of time near the halfway line and used it to clip the ball behind Saudi Arabia's defence for Eto'o to run on to. The striker made no mistake, taking his time and letting the ball bounce a couple of times before calmly poking it past the goalkeeper. The unbridled joy was clear to see as the Real Mallorca man took off his top, threw it to the side and ran to hug his manager before gesturing to the supporters.

Given what had happened against the Germans, the question on plenty of people's lips was whether or not Saudi Arabia would capitulate after going behind. While Foé should have done better with a headed chance inside the box, there was far from a meltdown from the men in white.

In fact there was a real scare for Olembé when he fouled Abdulaziz Al-Khathran on the edge of the box, but it was just outside penalty territory. Saudi Arabia showed their intent with an attacking change when midfielder Abdullah Jumaan Al-Dosari replaced centre-back Abdullah Zubromawi – Al-Dosari's first action was to fire the ensuing free kick into the wall.

Cameroon responded with a change of their own, taking M'Boma off for Pius N'Diefi. The substitute almost managed to force his way through to goal just moments after his introduction before being stopped by persistent defending from Fouzi Al-Shehri.

This was as big a sign as any that the Saudis weren't giving up. Al-Temyat continued to be their bright spark and the Al-Hilal man almost marked his promising performance with a sensational strike, his effort from range missing the target by a matter of inches. It felt like it wouldn't be his or Saudi Arabia's day when he got a half volley all wrong, then took a big blow from Kalla moments later.

Looking to ensure his side saw out the game, Schäfer opted to take left wing-back Womé off for Pierre Njanka. Meanwhile, with Saudi Arabia's World Cup hopes rapidly fading, Al-Johar took Al-Khathran off for Mohammed Noor in the 86th minute. Both teams were able to create half chances without really testing the goalkeeper before Hauge blew the full-time whistle.

This brought the realisation that Saudi Arabia were mathematically out of the World Cup. As Rigobert Song defiantly shook his hands in the air towards the Cameroon supporters in the stands, it was clear the Africans were still very much in it. A win against Germany would confirm their place in the knockout rounds but they would otherwise need the side they had just dumped out to get something against Ireland. The technicalities could wait for now, as the important thing was that they were still in with a chance.

## France 0 Uruguay 0 (Group A, 6 June, Busan)

The draw between Denmark and Senegal meant both sides came into this game knowing that a loss would condemn them to an early exit, regardless of what happened on the final day. Despite being far from their best in the opener France were expected to win, and Roger Lemerre put his trust in most of his players with Johan Micoud replacing Youri Djorkaeff in his only change. Having struggled against Denmark in Uruguay's first match, Gustavo Méndez was replaced by Alejandro Lembo, while Gianni Guigou came out for Marcelo Romero.

Les Bleus started like a team looking to prove a point. They moved the ball precisely and purposefully with Uruguay hardly getting a touch, and whenever the South Americans did there was always a meaty challenge coming sooner rather than later. David Trezeguet had the ball in the back of the net seven minutes in but was caught offside.

Pablo García was fronting the Uruguayan fightback with a shot from range that could have caused Fabien Barthez trouble but travelled through the bodies and into his arms.

La Celeste's number five also got the game's first booking for a late challenge on Patrick Vieira.

After quarter of an hour Thierry Henry shaped up to strike a volley in the box after cushioning the ball nicely with his thigh, though Paolo Montero flew across to clear just before the Arsenal talisman hit it. That wasn't the only reason for French frustrations, as Frank Leboeuf limped off to be replaced by Vincent Candela after the ball went out – the Roma defender went to right-back with Lilian Thuram going into the middle.

Álvaro Recoba's first effort of the match soon followed, flicking off Thuram's boot and forcing an awkward save from Barthez. The Internazionale man was beginning to look in the mood and nutmegged Vieira while starting another move, making the trick look far easier than it should.

His skill wasn't the only thing that left the French stunned. They went down to ten men in the 25th minute after Henry had tried to launch a counter attack to punish Uruguay's sloppy free kick. Henry over-ran the ball in getting past García and when he tried to reach it ahead of Romero, he lunged, studs up, straight into the winger's ankle, coming in too late to get the ball. Henry and everyone in Busan associated with France looked perplexed, perhaps thinking of the fact they would now have to find a way of beating Uruguay while playing with ten men for over an hour, then overcome Denmark in their final match without one of their biggest stars.

The man disadvantage didn't seem to impact the French too much at first and the men in white still had their chances – even if Uruguay grew into the game a bit more. Emmanuel Petit came closest, clipping the post with a free kick after Vieira had been brought down just outside the box.

The hostilities continued with Vieira and Recoba having words after the Frenchman seemed to manhandle the Uruguayan. Gonzalo Sorondo then ran into Barthez when the goalkeeper collected a loose ball – proceeding to comically say he had held on to the ball too long as the pair squared up. This soon led to the game becoming a scrappy affair, Darío Silva wasting every second he could after picking up a slight knock, while all the fouls made it very stop-start. Vieira was the next man down following a nasty challenge from Silva, who was lucky to escape punishment.

As was typical of the way the match had developed, the half ended with Petit and Sebastián Abreu getting booked after the Uruguayan tugged on the shirt of the Frenchman, who retaliated by swinging an arm out and then pushing the forward. Even though that had happened in the second minute of added time, there was still time for Romero to get his name in the book for planting his studs into Micoud's calf.

Uruguay had done everything possible to knock their more talented opponents off their stride and France were taking the bait. The players' frustration was evidently reflected by their manager, as Lemerre put his hand up to block the camera while walking back to the changing room at the break.

It looked like everyone was focused on playing football for the first couple of second-half minutes. That was until Silva came along and blatantly tripped Bixente Lizarazu, earning a yellow card that realistically should have come earlier. France didn't allow this to get to them and moved the ball around in one of their best spells to that point. A long ball forward almost resulted in a goal, releasing Sylvain Wiltord who couldn't get quite enough on his lob to get it over Fabián

Carini. Candela also attempted to chip the goalkeeper, but his effort was tipped over.

It was now an end-to-end game and Recoba soon had the opportunity to create an opening with Abreu in acres of space. He decided to go on his own, eventually seeing both of his shots saved by Barthez. The Uruguayan then had an open goal after rounding the goalkeeper but could only find the side netting from a tight angle – leaving himself visibly disappointed. The number 20 seemingly had a magnetic pull on the ball as he whipped a cross in for Abreu a matter of seconds later, but the striker's header went wide to add to a flurry of missed opportunities.

It was soon Carini's turn to be the denier after the ball fortuitously broke to Trezeguet, whose first-time effort was brilliantly palmed away by the Uruguayan. There was a slight break in the blistering play as Silva was substituted to a backdrop of boos and jeers moments after making another dangerous tackle – he was replaced by Federico Magallanes.

Trezeguet was putting a real shift in up top on his own. In the space of a couple of minutes he was tackled by one of the flood of blue shirts approaching him after getting into the box, had an acrobatic effort cleared off the line and won a free kick on the edge of Uruguay's box. Micoud then saw an effort palmed away well by the goalkeeper.

Púa made his second change with 70 minutes on the clock, taking Romero off for Valencia's Gonzalo de los Santos, despite Romero putting up some sort of argument that he shouldn't be coming off as France went ahead and put in a corner that Marcel Desailly headed over. That change was soon followed by Darío Rodríguez making way for Guigou – without any fuss this time.

Lemerre made his move in the 81st minute, taking Trezeguet off for Djibril Cissé as the possibility of the game ending 0-0 despite all its action became increasingly prominent. Cissé immediately got down the right and put in a dangerous ball that Montero almost turned into his own net. France had to wait until the 91st minute for their next chance as Wiltord was played in by Lizarazu. Sorondo spectacularly sprinted across the box and dived to get a block in, eventually deflecting the ball on to the roof of the net.

Uruguay immediately went up the other end after the corner was dealt with and Magallanes found himself with just Barthez standing between him and the goal. The Manchester United stopper came out on top, getting his legs in the way of the striker's first-time effort.

France made their final change in the 93rd minute, Cristophe Dugarry replacing Wiltord. However, it proved pointless as he didn't touch the ball and the final whistle blew 30 seconds later to confirm that the 2002 finals' 20th match had provided the first 0-0 draw. It also put both sides in a precarious position in terms of qualifying for the knockout rounds, as could be seen in the desperate expression on Desailly's face after full time. It was now imperative for each team that they won their final game.

### Sweden 2 Nigeria 1 (Group F, 7 June, Kobe)

Clearly feeling satisfied with the performance during Sweden's draw against England, the only change from joint head coaches Lars Lagerbäck and Tommy Söderberg reflected their first substitution in the opener, with Anders Svensson replacing Magnus Svensson in midfield. Festus Onigbinde made three alterations with Efe Sodje, Nwankwo

Kanu and Garbal Lawal losing their places to Ifeanyi Udeze, Justice Christopher and John Utaka.

Despite kicking off, Nigeria required last-ditch defending to prevent Sweden from going through on goal within 45 seconds. Within two minutes Henrik Larsson latched on to a ball played behind the Nigerian defence, but was held up and played it to Marcus Allbäck whose shot deflected off Taribo West and spun wide. As the African side's awkward start continued, Olof Mellberg hit a venomous strike marginally over the crossbar after a corner bounced to him near the back post – having never scored a goal for any club or his country.

While things calmed down considerably after that, Sweden still posed problems for Nigeria and Svensson produced a neat piece of skill before firing an effort from range wide. The Africans' first chance fell to Celestine Babayaro in the 12th minute after Jay-Jay Okocha got down the right wing and delivered a peach of a cross. The Chelsea man attempted to control the ball instead of hitting a first-time volley, which only left it rolling harmlessly into Magnus Hedman's grateful grasp.

Despite the lack of a clinical finish, the move was a sign of growing Nigerian confidence after getting through the early Swedish storm and it wasn't long before the Europeans were struggling to get a touch of the ball. Naturally, any Nigerian vibrancy on the pitch was also being matched by their supporters in the stands.

The Super Eagles kept coming, with Okocha smashing a free kick that rose just a bit too much before playing a couple of spectacular passes, while even West stepped out from centre-back to deliver a threatening ball into the box.

Sweden could pose questions of their own and Christopher was forced into a last-ditch sliding tackle in the box, which he made with aplomb. Freddie Ljungberg then came dancing around defenders and his team-mate, who was still on the floor, before being denied a sensational goal by an intervention near the goal line. Christopher cleared Johan Mjällby's header from the ensuing corner off the line to save his team once again.

This had been a game full of attacking flair and scintillating play, and it got its first goal in the 27th minute. Joseph Yobo received the ball on the right flank before taking a couple of touches and delivering a truly wonderful cross. Julius Aghahowa was on hand to ensure it was a telling contribution, sneaking between two Swedish centre-backs and reaching the ball ahead of the onrushing goalkeeper. Having got there first the Shakhtar Donetsk forward directed his header perfectly to find the top corner. The celebration was just as eye-catching – seven somersaults followed by a massive flip.

Mjällby was booked for diving moments later after going down in the opposition box under pressure from Yobo, though it seemed a bit harsh as the Celtic centre-back appeared to stumble over. Sweden kept coming forward in an attempt to restore parity, with a good block from Yobo being required to stop Svensson after a lung-bursting run forward. That attacking approach paid dividends just eight minutes after they had fallen behind when Ljungberg found Larsson on the break, allowing the striker to jink past Isaac Okoronkwo and poke the ball out of Ike Shorunmu's reach.

Sweden may have drawn level but Okocha was still causing havoc for their defence. The Paris Saint-Germain midfielder went on a mazy run into the box in which even one of his own players tried and failed to take the ball off him. The 28-year-old couldn't generate much power on his ensuing shot, but even that caused issues. Lučić panicked and smashed the ball on to Mjällby, sending it cannoning off the post before being cleared. Utaka also came close to scoring soon afterwards but his effort sailed over the crossbar.

The game slowed down a little bit as the break drew closer, but when referee René Ortubé blew his whistle the Bolivian was putting an end to a truly scintillating half of football.

Both teams continued to play good football as the second period got under way but there wasn't quite the same edge at first. This was epitomised when Udeze gave the ball away near the halfway line, as Larsson and Ljungberg took too long once the ball reached the penalty box's edge to get a shot off and capitalise. Even so, some of the trickery being displayed by Nigeria was brilliant to watch.

The Super Eagles were momentarily reduced to ten men while West received treatment for a cut just above his eye, but Sweden still weren't able to break down their resolute defence. West was beginning to look frustrated as five minutes passed without him stepping back on to the pitch, especially when a FIFA official demanded that bandages were put over the stitches and plaster that had already been applied.

Nigeria's number six was applauded as he was finally reintroduced, but their fans wouldn't have been in the mood to clap mere seconds later as Larsson was brought down by Udeze with a penalty being awarded. Shorunmu was decisive and went the right way to get the slightest of touches on Larsson's spot-kick but its power and height meant the goalkeeper's efforts were futile, leaving the Celtic man to celebrate putting his side ahead for the first time in either game this tournament.

West went over to get a fresh shirt before play resumed, with his blood-spattered top seemingly adding to his annoyance. Sweden also made their first change as Allbäck came off for Andreas Andersson. It wasn't long until Onigbinde responded by replacing Babayaro with Kanu, who had not started due to a stomach strain and ankle injury.

Svensson had a great opportunity to add some comfort to the scoreline for Sweden after making a great run forward and being slipped through, but the Southampton midfielder hit his effort straight at Shorunmu. Niclas Alexandersson was booked for time-wasting while taking the ensuing throw despite there being 20 minutes left. There was no chance of the Sweden fans slowing down, though, as they were now in full voice.

Nigeria were trying to find ways to change that and Pius Ikedia came on for the teenager Bartholomew Ogbeche. The Ajax winger won a corner within seconds of his introduction and while it was initially dealt with, Okocha's ensuing ball in was planted straight on to West's head. The Kaiserslautern defender couldn't make the most of it, sending his effort wide of the mark before lying face down in disbelief.

As the game became an end-to-end affair once again, Larsson seemingly had a great opportunity to bare down on goal after being played through; Okoronkwo did a brilliant job of forcing him wide before eventually winning possession back. His centre-back partner West was having an increasingly frustrating time, which was compounded when he was booked for a foul on Ljungberg in the 80th minute – not long after the Arsenal man had received treatment for a knee issue.

Nigeria were still going and almost drew level just over a minute later when Utaka did superbly to get behind Mellberg and even round the goalkeeper, but running at speed he couldn't get enough on his effort to turn it into the gaping net as Mjällby got back to clear off the line. Yobo then struck a left-footed shot from range against the post that landed at the feet of Kanu, who couldn't get a clean connection and sent the ball bobbling towards Hedman – though the Arsenal man was eventually pulled up for offside anyway.

Perhaps in an effort to calm things down, Lagerbäck and Söderberg opted to bring Anders Svensson off for Magnus Svensson. This seemed to work as neither side managed to create a clear-cut chance, with the best opportunity falling to Kanu when a deflected shot came to him on the edge of the box. He attempted a chip under pressure but Hedman was able to comfortably reach up and catch it.

In the end Nigeria were condemned to their second one-goal loss in as many games, making it mathematically impossible for them to get out of the group despite having a game against England to come. Meanwhile, Sweden were now in a superb position to reach the knockout stages, going above Argentina ahead of the South Americans' match against the Three Lions later that day.

### Spain 3 Paraguay 1 (Group B, 7 June, Jeonju)

With Juanfran having recovered from his ankle injury, José Antonio Camacho stuck with the same team that had beaten Slovenia. Meanwhile, Paraguay's Italian manager Cesare Maldini reinstated José Luis Chilavert at the first opportunity, while he also brought Diego Gavilán, Carlos Paredes and José Cardozo in for Estanislao Struway, Guido Alvarenga and Jorge Campos.

Paraguay came into this as the underdogs, especially after they had let their lead against South Africa slip in the final moments, but it became apparent early on that they weren't there to just sit back. The South Americans were pressing Spain at every opportunity and trying to get in behind their defence. This approach led to both Carles Puyol and Miguel Ángel Nadal being dispossessed inside their own half within the opening five minutes.

Perhaps trying to match that intensity, Rubén Baraja went in hard on Paredes, but ended up taking out the midfielder and earning a yellow card instead of the ball. That free kick resulted in Paraguay getting their deserved, albeit unorthodox, opener. Chilavert may not have been in a position to score directly, but the goalkeeper launched the ball forward in a way that caused unrest in the Spanish penalty box. An unconvincing header meant the ball dropped to Francisco Arce just inside the area and the wing-back took a touch out of his feet before firing in an effort on goal. Iker Casillas dived to parry it away but could only push it on to Puyol, whom the ball bounced off before careering into the back of the net. It didn't matter how it had happened; Paraguay were visibly delighted to be ahead after just ten minutes as they celebrated near the dugout.

Spain came back strongly. Raúl replied immediately with an attempted chip but Chilavert was equal to it, tipping the ball over the bar. By the 20th minute Puyol had come inches away from finding Juan Carlos Valerón in a position that surely would have resulted in a goal, while Raúl blazed another chance over the bar.

The South Americans had the odd foray forward but were struggling to regain their hold on the match, as wave after wave of Spanish attacks kept coming. In the next quarter of an hour both Raúl and Luis Enrique failed to make the most of Javier de Pedro's dangerous crosses, Diego Tristán couldn't grow quite enough to get a convincing header on goal, while an acrobatic effort from Raúl went wide.

A Spanish mistake meant that Paraguay got a long-awaited chance but Cardozo made a mess of it and dragged his shot wide. Just moments later, Casillas had a nightmare as he couldn't decide whether to stay or go when Paraguay hit a long ball forward. This left the Real Madrid stopper scrambling to get back as the ball was knocked down to Roque Santa Cruz. Luckily for Spain's number one, Puyol was in position to get a block in. Roberto Acuña also managed to get a shot away, but it was a wild effort in the end.

There was a level of desperation from Paraguay after the goal as they aimed to hang on, something that was evident when Arce was booked for not taking a free kick quickly enough in the 44th minute – even if it did seem a little bit harsh. Still, many would argue that it had worked as Maldini's men went into half-time with the lead.

Recognising that a change was needed to break down Paraguay's defence, Camacho brought Tristán and Enrique off for Fernando Morientes and Iván Helguera ahead of the second half. It didn't take long for those replacements to have the desired impact as just eight minutes after his introduction – and following a goal-line scramble that was interrupted by the offside flag – Morientes got La Roja back on level terms.

De Pedro's first corner delivery had failed to get past the first man, but the Real Sociedad winger's second went straight on to Morientes's head. Having seen so many opportunities wasted from the bench, the substitute powered his head through the ball and sent it flying into the back of the net, leaving Chilavert unable to do anything but watch on. Morientes ripped his shirt off and let out a massive roar in celebration.

Juanfran had picked up a genuine injury in the previous game, but when he lay on the floor holding his face it seemed as though this was more antics to get the opposition in trouble than anything else. There was also an insight into Chilavert's eccentric nature as he could have simply kicked the ball out of his hands after collecting it, but instead decided to roll it out for himself under pressure before shanking the ball out for a throw-in. Another quirk with Chilavert was the way that he would take free kicks from the halfway line and send them straight into Casillas's arms, only for the Real Madrid stopper to attempt to pick out the one Spaniard left up the pitch and give the ball back to Paraguay.

It wasn't all fun and games, though, and Spain continued stretching Paraguay – as reflected by the fact Gavilán got himself booked for pulling Juanfran back while the left-back was running down the line. Campos may not have been able to start after limping off in the opener, but Maldini hoped the Universidad Católica man could get Paraguay back into the lead, bringing him on for Cardozo in the 63rd minute.

It was moments after that Santa Cruz – who had been far quieter here than against South Africa – got behind Hierro, but partly due to the tight angle his effort was smothered by Casillas. Morientes had a chance at the other end within seconds, attempting a chip that was overcooked and flew over the crossbar.

Both teams continued to have their chances but it was Spain who took the lead in the 69th minute. It was far from pretty as Chilavert completely missed De Pedro's cross and it hit Morientes's midriff before rolling over the line. There wasn't a care to be had about that from the men in red, though, as Morientes went off jumping in the air before being congratulated by his team-mates.

With time a dwindling commodity, Paraguay were pushing everything at Spain in an attempt to get back into the game, which included Julio César Cáceres throwing his whole body through Baraja while trying to get the ball. He managed to escape a yellow card despite missing the targeted object, while the midfielder required treatment. Fitting in with the theme of Paraguay going for it, midfielder Struway replaced defender Denis Caniza.

There was one thing that everyone wanted to see when Paraguay needed a goal though: Chilavert taking a free kick, which was exactly what the world got when Campos was brought down about 25 yards out. Arce looked like he wanted it but when the goalkeeper had trudged up most of the pitch there was only one man taking charge. Before the tournament, Chilavert had told Radio Nanduti, 'I've got Canizares in my sights, because I'm going to score against him from a free kick in the World Cup'. He didn't get the opponent or result he had predicted, however, as Casillas was able to reach his low effort with relative ease and keep hold of the ball. Realising that Chilavert would struggle to reach his goal before Spain's counter attack, Santa Cruz blocked Casillas from releasing the ball and received a yellow card for his troubles.

It wasn't long until the spotlight was back on Chilavert, who was tasked with saving a penalty. Raúl had masterfully received De Pedro's long throw on the turn but was pulled down by Paredes while attempting to get a shot off. As had been the case against Slovenia, Hierro was the man to step up and take the spot-kick; as was the case against Slovenia, he sent the goalkeeper the wrong way and slotted his shot into the back of the net before jumping in the air and celebrating with his team-mates.

With less than ten minutes left and a two-goal lead, Camacho took his opportunity to replace Valerón with a 22-year-old by the name of Xavi, who had only represented Spain three times before this point – though he had also played at the 2000 Olympic Games.

There was a chance for Santa Cruz to give Paraguay a slice of hope when he intelligently placed himself between Hierro and Puyol, but the striker's header was uncharacteristically poor and went harmlessly wide.

Paraguay kept going but the final whistle was eventually blown, confirming Spain's victory and their status as the first nation to reach the round of 16. Meanwhile, it was imperative that Paraguay got all three points in their final game against Slovenia.

*Argentina 0 England 1 (Group F, 7 June, Sapporo)*
This was arguably the biggest match-up of the entire group stage, not just because Argentina and England were two of the biggest names in football but also due to the tangled history between the two nations both on and off the pitch. The Falklands War is the biggest example off it, but it is not the only one, as their intertwined history stretches over 200 years into Argentina's colonial past.

Aside from the fact an English schoolteacher is said to have brought football to Argentina, there have been various high-profile matches between the footballing greats throughout history. The most obvious came in 1986 when Diego Maradona scored with the 'Hand of God' before adding a wonder goal as La Albiceleste went on their way to lifting the World Cup. Looking back in conversation with *The Guardian*, former national team captain Roberto Perfumo said, 'In 1986, winning that game against England was enough. Winning the World Cup was secondary for us. Beating England was our real aim'. England also enjoyed victory over their eternal rivals on the way to lifting world football's most prestigious trophy after Geoff Hurst's goal proved the difference in a 1966 quarter-final – which was actually the Three Lions' most recent win in this fixture at a World Cup.

Marcelo Bielsa made just one change going into their latest meeting, mirroring his half-time substitution against Nigeria by taking Claudio López out for Kily González. There was also one change of personnel made by Sven-Göran Eriksson as Nicky Butt came in for Darius Vassell, but this also meant Paul Scholes went from the centre to the left and Emile Heskey was moved from the wing to his more natural position up front.

The bitter rivalry was only stoked further when, during the national anthems, Argentina's was met by booing and chants of 'England', while the favour was returned with England's being whistled at. The handshake also offered a reminder of a heated past with David Beckham's last handshake being with Diego Simeone, the man who had provoked him to get sent off in the 1998 World Cup before the Argentines eventually won their round of 16 match on penalties. Simeone had a slight grin on his face as hands were shaken on the day he earned his 106th cap, an Argentine record at the time.

Gabriel Batistuta had a combative start to the game, going into Sol Campbell late a couple of times and blocking a pass within the opening two minutes. Heskey was having a positive start at the other end, winning his first two headers and producing a nice flick. However Owen Hargreaves wasn't enjoying this scintillating start, requiring treatment off the pitch within four minutes after being on the receiving end of a challenge from Mauricio Pochettino.

Javier Zanetti was clearly in the mood for the spectacular, as in the couple of minutes it took Hargreaves to gingerly get back on to the pitch the Internazionale man had put a couple of crosses into the box and tried his luck from range – David Seaman was able to gather all three attempts. It wasn't long until González had a chance after a back-heel from Juan Pablo Sorín, but the winger blasted his shot just wide of the far post.

Pierluigi Collina handed Batistuta the game's first yellow card in the 13th minute, for taking Ashley Cole out after he had cleared the ball before claiming that the left-back had dived. Batistuta gave away another foul moments later for leading with his elbow while jumping with Beckham but avoided a second booking.

Rio Ferdinand came close to scoring as he attacked Beckham's corner delivery in the 19th minute but ended up jumping into Pablo Cavallero as the goalkeeper punched the ball away. Amid all of the action, Hargreaves had been doing his best despite visibly struggling from the earlier injury. Making a run to help earn that corner was the final straw as the Bayern Munich midfielder had to be replaced by Trevor Sinclair – meaning Scholes went back into the middle again. Sinclair had initially been on standby and even flew home in the build-up, only to travel back due to a Danny Murphy injury; he was now coming into what was shaping up to be one of this World Cup's most intense matches.

There would have been more positive English flashbacks to 1998 when Owen broke forward with Argentine defenders surrounding him – having scored a wonderful goal in that match – but the Liverpool man could only find the far post when he let a shot off and the ball was put behind for a corner. Batistuta had Argentina's best opportunity so far almost immediately, but González's great cross was headed straight at Seaman.

Sinclair had settled into the game brilliantly and jinked past two Albiceleste defenders before scuffing a shot that was eventually cleared for a throw. He also received a big blow from Pochettino but got back up. Cole joined Batistuta in Collina's book just before the half-hour mark having made a second poor challenge in quick succession.

As well as the fouls, chances kept coming in this scintillatingly tight affair, with González unleashing a strike that came agonisingly close to finding the target. The Valencia man was soon on the end of a foul and required treatment after Beckham's flailing arm caught him in the face, which led to blood pouring out of his nose. The Argentine medical staff and Bielsa were trying to convince the officials to let him back on despite the blood not being stopped, but the American fourth official Brian Hall was having none of it, causing some debate in the dugout until González was finally reintroduced.

There was more debate to come just seconds later as Pochettino brought Owen down in the box. The Englishman's footwork had proven too quick for the Paris Saint-Germain centre-back, who dangled out a leg as Owen went past him. Collina was unwavering and walked off with his hand pointing to the spot as a massive roar was let out by the English fans in the Sapporo Dome.

Simeone was at the front of the queue of Argentines trying to get into Beckham's head as the England captain stepped up to take the penalty. Waiting for the whistle, Golden Balls stood with his eyes fixated on the ball and slowed down his breathing. As soon as it went, Beckham ran up to the ball and smashed it just off-centre and past Cavallero's outstretched leg before bringing out one of the most iconic celebrations of his entire lifetime. The man with the mohican could be seen kissing the badge and pulling at his shirt while shouting 'YES' with all of his might before being joined in those celebrations by his team-mates.

Beckham had been sent death threats and had effigies of him burned having been vilified after the events of 1998. This was the ultimate form of redemption. The captain was already a national hero after scoring the free kick against Greece that got England to the finals in the first place; this felt as much for him as anybody else.

England had the lead with one minute to go until the break. Their commitment to defending went up yet another notch, ensuring they got into half-time with the lead intact as Campbell and Scholes flew in to make challenges. Argentina had one last corner but Ferdinand got a massive head on it to clear any danger, with the whistle following soon after. There was a nice touch from Simeone as the teams walked off with the Argentine shaking Beckham's hand.

Bielsa used the break to make his first substitution, bringing Juan Sebastián Verón off for Pablo Aimar. It took the curly haired number 16 less than a minute to have his first shot after good build-up play from Argentina, but it went straight at Seaman. Soon afterwards, Owen had his best chance of the tournament so far as Seaman's long kick reached him to turn Diego Placente brilliantly. England's number ten eventually dragged his shot wide of the far post. More chances were forthcoming and Heskey's blocked first-time effort came back to Scholes, who smashed a shot of his own that Cavallero could only awkwardly palm away.

Heskey picked up a yellow card in the 50th minute, seemingly for kicking the ball away and time-wasting. England weren't just sitting back, though, as some beautifully intricate passing saw Sinclair release Beckham behind the Argentine defence. Having got the better of Placente, the captain couldn't quite wrap his foot around the ball enough to get the resulting shot on target.

Heskey wasn't looking completely comfortable so was taken off for 36-year-old Teddy Sheringham in the 56th minute. The Tottenham Hotspur striker was involved immediately with some intelligent touches and passes, then almost scored a wonder goal a minute after his introduction, getting the cleanest of strikes on a volley after Scholes's pass forward, but it was saved well.

With half an hour remaining Batistuta was brought off for Hernán Crespo, with González being replaced by López four minutes later. Despite Bielsa's intent Argentina were struggling to break down a very resolute England side, with Butt doing a particularly good job of breaking up their play. The Three Lions also made their own charges forward, as shown by Sinclair collecting Seaman's throw and sprinting up the pitch before getting his shot off. When Aimar had La Albiceleste's first half-chance for a while, he smashed it well over the crossbar.

Having previously conceded the penalty, Pochettino hit Cole with a robust challenge after being beaten to the ball, conceding a 70th-minute free kick in a dangerous area. Beckham took it and swung the ball towards Sheringham. The striker did well to get his head on it but could only glance the ball narrowly wide.

Soon after that, England were facing a minute's worth of sustained Argentine pressure as the South Americans showed a plethora of ways to get the ball into the box. England were equal to each one, with Ferdinand proving particularly indomitable in the air until Seaman was able to come out and catch Ariel Ortega's attempt.

It wasn't long until Aimar's free kick found an Argentine head after all those previous efforts had failed to, but Pochettino could only guide the ball wide – much to his clear frustration. The centre-back might have thought that he had equalised when he hit the target with another header minutes later, but Seaman once again did well to get his legs in the way.

England were under real pressure going into the final ten minutes so Eriksson responded by taking Owen off and replacing him with Wayne Bridge – the left-back was used on the left of a five-man midfield. There was still one moment of terror to endure as Butt overplayed slightly on the edge of his own box and Ferdinand failed to reach the pass, but Mills took control of the situation to collect the ball and run away with it before giving away a corner by smashing the ball off López and back on to himself. Campbell did brilliantly to head the ensuing cross clear and Aimar relieved the pressure with a shot that was closer to leaving the stadium than finding the goal.

All 11 of England's players were camped out in their own box for pretty much the whole two minutes of injury time, and Argentina simply could not break them down. As the final whistle was blown, a massive celebratory roar was let out while Beckham was embraced by his team-mates. Argentina had enjoyed an 18-game unbeaten run going into this match yet it was the Three Lions who had come out on top.

This result wasn't only important for bragging rights, as it meant that England only needed to draw against an already eliminated Nigeria to qualify, while Argentina had to defeat Sweden.

*South Africa 1 Slovenia 0 (Group B, 8 June, Daegu)*

The two teams will have come into this game in very different states of mind: South Africa on a high after their 91st-minute equaliser against Paraguay; Slovenia in disarray with their star man Zlato Zahovič sent home and their manager Srečko Katanec already deciding that he would resign after the tournament.

This was reflected in the line-ups as South Africa's only change was to replace defender Pierre Issa with Udinese forward Siyabonga Nomvethe. As well as the omission of Zahovič, Marinko Galič and Milan Osterc came out of Slovenia's team with Milenko Ačimovič, Muamer Vugdalič and Sebastjan Cimirotič taking their places. There was also an obvious difference between the sets of players in the tunnel as some of the South Africans were clapping their hands, singing and dancing, while almost every Slovenian stood motionless.

It took just four minutes for Jomo Sono's change to be vindicated. Quinton Fortune won a free kick on the left wing, close to the penalty area, and whipped a ball just outside the six-yard box. As the Manchester United midfielder was setting himself, Nomvethe was the liveliest player in the box and was constantly changing direction in an effort to lose Vugdalič. The number 14's plan worked when the defender fell asleep and as the ball approached him, the South African was completely free to glance the ball into the bottom corner – even if it went in off his thigh rather than the head as intended. The delight was still there for all to see as the 24-year-old hurdled the boards behind the goal and revealed a t-shirt with a picture of a loved one before being joined by his team-mates.

This was the last thing Slovenia needed in their position, but they didn't give up. However neither side was showing too much quality, which led to various fouls, possession switching hands regularly and little goalmouth action. Lucas Radebe picked up the game's first caution for mistiming a challenge on Cimirotič and treading on his foot.

Fortune was at the heart of another good move when he played quick passes with Benni McCarthy before slipping the striker through on goal. However, the Porto loanee – who joined the Portuguese giants permanently after the World Cup – took himself wide with a poor first touch, which left him unable to test Marko Simeunovič.

Slovenia's best chance of the half came as a result of some neat work by Džoni Novak, but while Ačimovič got plenty of power on his first-time shot, the midfielder couldn't get the direction and it soared wide. Defender Vugdalič was on hand to offer a reminder of the lack of quality Slovenia were showing, dawdling on the ball and allowing McCarthy to pickpocket him before pulling the striker down to earn himself a yellow card. Katanec made his first change on 41 minutes, bringing Cimirotič off for Osterc after he had picked up a knock from Radebe.

Despite the change, South Africa remained on top before the half-time whistle and Sibusiso Zuma showed a couple of moments of flair while a short corner routine got Fortune into a good position in Slovenia's box, only for a poor touch to let him down.

It was more of the same as the second half got under way, with neither side showing the quality required to break down the opposition's defence. Nomvethe went down in the box only for referee Ángel Sánchez to show no interest whatsoever, while McCarthy unleashed a powerful shot from range that was straight at Simeunovič, who palmed it behind.

Off the pitch, a difficult week for Katanec got even worse as he was banished to the stands by the fourth official after persistently complaining to and about everyone. The Slovenian players may not have had their manager within earshot but they were still struggling, and it took Simeunovič's desperately outstretched hand to prevent Fortune's cross from finding McCarthy's head.

The lack of polish extended to the tackles being put in with Teboho Mokoena booked for a clumsy lunge, while Ales Čeh saw yellow with Slovenia's players gathering around the referee in protest. Nastja Čeh and Spasoje Bulajič replaced Alexander Knavs and Ačimovič between these incidents, with the latter showing that they weren't happy about it – though clearly not to the extent Zahovič had done in the first match. These two incidents within the space of a minute indicated that Slovenia were losing their heads, with Miran Pavlin among the worst offenders, and the crowd let the Europeans know they weren't impressed.

While this was happening, South Africa kept on moving in pursuit of a second goal and McCarthy's header in the 65th minute cannoned off the outside of the post. It was a matter of seconds until the striker had another shot, this time smashing it straight at the goalkeeper. There was still a reminder that Bafana Bafana didn't have their victory sealed just yet, though, as Nastja Čeh's header forced a good save from Andre Arendse.

Sono made the decision to bring his goalscorer Nomvethe off and replace him with Delron Buckley in the 71st minute. Slovenia's Pavlin then got a yellow card for pulling back an opposing player, but he wasn't the only one feeling frustrated as it was becoming clear this wouldn't be McCarthy's day in goalscoring terms, with the striker either straying offside or struggling to test Simeunovič. He was eventually stretchered off to be replaced by George Koumantarakis, having caught his foot on Željko Milinovič's studs while taking a shot.

Slovenia were definitely still part of the game as it entered the final ten minutes, which was abundantly clear when Amir Karič took a shot from the edge of the box that curled marginally over the crossbar.

There was a break in play as Bradley Carnell retrieved his boot after it had come off, while Sono replaced Fortune with Jabu Pule in his final change. Another substitute, Buckley, had the chance to wrap things up when Bafana Bafana hit Slovenia on the counter attack, but his effort was blocked by the goalkeeper's legs and spun behind for a corner.

South Africa opting to go for a second goal, as opposed to merely hanging on to their lead, meant the ending was one of this game's most entertaining periods as MacBeth Sibaya hit shots from range, Zuma brought out his favoured flick and Slovenia hit Osterc at every opportunity.

There wasn't to be another goal, though, and while the game wasn't a classic it did provide a piece of history: South Africa recorded their first win at a World Cup and just their second against European opposition. Not only that, they went into the final round of group games with a chance of reaching the knockout stages. Slovenia, on the other hand, went into their last match with nothing but the chance of restoring a bit of pride to play for.

*Italy 1 Croatia 2 (Group G, 8 June, Ibaraki)*

Off the back of a convincing performance, Giovanni Trapattoni understandably only made one change ahead of the Croatia clash as Luigi Di Biagio was replaced by his Internazionale team-mate Cristiano Zanetti. Aside from the forced exclusion of Boris Živković after his sending off against Mexico, Robert Prosinečki and Davor Šuker made way for Croatia with Daniel Šarić, Davor Vugrinec and Milan Rapaić coming into the side.

Croatia showed early intent and earned a corner in the opening minute, but the short routine didn't come off and the pressure was immediately alleviated. Gli Azzurri soon had their own set piece in a dangerous area after Stjepan Tomas pulled Francesco Totti down on the edge of the box – the number ten ended up smashing his effort against the wall.

With Italy having now settled into the game, Stipe Pletikosa faced his first test in the fourth minute. Gianluca Zambrotta hit a left-footed strike from range that would have found the top corner were it not for the goalkeeper's intervention.

By far the best early chance came on 15 minutes when Cristiano Doni bundled his way through the Croatia defence after some poor play from Robert Kovač, but the Atalanta man hit his effort straight at the goalkeeper. There was a stoppage soon afterwards as Niko Kovač's nose was bloodied after being caught by Tommasi's elbow when the pair competed for a header. After going off, Croatia's number ten was soon back on the pitch with a cotton wool ball up each nostril, though they quickly came out.

In the 22nd minute, what had become a bitty game only providing quality in flashes brought a moment for Croatia fans to shout about. Vugrinec hit an ambitious effort from outside Italy's box but Gianluigi Buffon was able to securely hold on to it. Soon after, having been hobbling around for some time after making a block tackle, Alessandro Nesta was forced off to be replaced by Marco Materazzi.

Croatia soon had a great chance to make the breakthrough after their quick passing cut through the Italian defence but Vugrinec's unconvincing shot was met by Buffon. While the goalkeeper couldn't hold on to the ball, Materazzi came across well to clear with Alen Bokšić desperately sliding in on him in an effort to get the ball over the line. Within seconds, a last-ditch intervention on the stretch was required from Materazzi to deny a dangerous cross into the box. Croatia were firmly on top at this point but Rapaić couldn't capitalise as his effort from range was a weak one.

There had been plenty of fouls throughout the first half, but the first yellow card only came in the 39th minute after Robert Kovač went through the back of Totti having initially given the ball away. There was another break in play shortly before half-time as Doni went down injured, and it was Croatia who almost scored in the aftermath after breaking well but Rapaić was once again unable to get enough on his shot to truly test Buffon.

Italy's final ball had been off for the majority of the first half, but Christian Panucci showed real quality with his crossing twice in injury time. Croatia's defence was up to the challenge on both occasions and beat Christian Vieri in the air to clear.

Croatia thought they had got a free kick before the break but Graham Poll blew for half-time and indicated that they weren't taking it quickly enough. While that was an annoyance for the Balkans, Trapattoni and his men would be more frustrated with the first period. Still, that wasn't enough for any change of personnel.

The second half's opening exchanges suggested that things would continue where they had left off and Vieri thought he had opened the scoring in the 50th minute, having been quiet in the first period. A short-corner routine hadn't quite come off but as the ball returned to Doni, he dinked it over the Croatian defence for Zambrotta to flick towards the back post where Vieri was on hand to head in. An offside was given much to the striker's understandable annoyance, as replays showed that both he and Zambrotta were comfortably onside. That didn't change the fact that all the Internazionale star received was a booking for his protests.

Rapaić had a strong effort from range saved well by Buffon moments later but it was Italy who hit the back of the net again five minutes after first doing so – and it wasn't ruled out this time. Paolo Maldini had picked out Vieri well, with the striker holding the ball up and releasing it to Totti. His pass found Doni despite not being the best, and the ball was dinked to the edge of the six-yard box for Vieri to attack and loop a wonderful header out of Pletikosa's reach. Angelo Di Livio had been preparing to come on but was soon sent back to the bench – after a quiet first 45, Italy were finally stepping up a gear.

Mirko Jozić responded immediately, replacing Vugrinec with Ivica Olić. The 22-year-old, who was widely regarded as the most exciting talent playing in Croatia, immediately got involved as his team let off shots in an effort to restore parity. As the hour came and went Di Livio was still warming up next to Trapattoni, as was Francesco Coco, but the manager wasn't making the change yet. Meanwhile,

Croatia's Jurica Vrangeš replaced Zvonimir Soldo, who had picked up a knock.

Italy still looked on top and Doni's pass at the end of a scintillating move narrowly evaded the runners in blue. In the 71st minute a fortuitous ball saw Vieri played through on goal, but he hit a wild effort under pressure from Tomas and couldn't find the target. Within a minute, Jarni played a superb cross that found Olić behind Materazzi, where he latched on to the ball to send it past Buffon. Having built up a reputation within Croatia, he had now announced himself on the world stage and celebrated the equaliser by revealing a t-shirt with a picture of his newborn baby.

The striker was struggling to get his top back on, but Italy weren't about to wait for him to finish fiddling with it as they launched an attack that ended in Maldini shooting high and wide. After that, as Olić went to the sideline to get a coach to cut the shirt as he continued trying to get it on, Croatia launched their own attack and Rapaić came within inches of latching on to Bokšić's delivery.

With Olić finally back on the pitch, Croatia were firmly on top and going for the jugular. In the 76th minute their pressure paid off when Rapaić beat Materazzi and delivered a cross that Cannavaro could only clear as far as Niko Kovač. The midfielder headed back to Rapaić who controlled and, despite being off balance and having the ball deflected on to his boot, left Buffon helpless as the ball looped over his head and nestled in the back of the net. Italy had been in such control just four minutes earlier but now found themselves behind.

Both managers responded quickly to the changing scoreline with Filippo Inzaghi replacing Doni and defender Dario Šimić coming on for goalscorer Rapaić, who looked exhausted as he trudged off before being kissed and congratulated by those in the dugout.

Inzaghi took a while to make any sort of impact, but when he won a free kick in a dangerous area Totti certainly looked capable of producing something special while the substitute jostled with the Croatian wall. With a steely look in his eyes, Totti smashed the ball and sent it curling against the post, but instead of crossing the line it trickled teasingly along it before rolling away to safety. Totti could do little more than look to the heavens with his hands covering his face.

It wasn't long until Zambrotta smashed an effort goalward, but Pletikosa was able to palm it away before the ball was desperately flicked clear. As the final moments approached, Panucci fearlessly flung himself at a corner delivery but couldn't keep his header down.

Four minutes of added time gave Italy a glimpse of hope and the men in blue thought they had equalised two minutes into that period. Materazzi's long ball from inside his own half sailed over Croatian heads and past Pletikosa, rolling all the way into the net after everybody – including Inzaghi – had somehow missed it. However Inzaghi's celebrations were cut short as the referee's assistant gave a foul against him for pulling his defender down, leaving Trapattoni furious on the sideline. Many others, especially those of an Italian persuasion, saw this as very harsh and their sense of injustice intensified after Vieri's earlier goal was disallowed.

Josip Šimunić tried to slow the game down after picking up a knock, but after he was forced off by Poll the final moments were played out and despite further time being added on, Croatia were resolute enough to see the result out.

The final whistle didn't mark the end for Poll as frustrated Italians looked for an explanation. There was nothing Italy could do now, though, aside from ensuring they went out and got a result against Mexico in their final group game. Meanwhile, Croatia would have been far more hopeful of getting through than they had been going into this match.

## Brazil 4 China 0 (Group C, 8 June, Seogwipo)

Despite being fined for his play-acting against Turkey, Rivaldo wasn't banned so Luiz Felipe Scolari's only change from the opening win saw Grêmio's Ânderson Polga replace Edmílson in the back three. Sun Jihai's injury forced Bora Milutinović to leave him out of the China line-up, and the Manchester City man was joined by Fan Zhiyi and Chen Yang in making way for Du Wei, Zhao Junzhe and Qi Hong.

There wouldn't have been much expected of China from the watching world, but the Asian outfit actually had the opening chances even if their best effort was deflected and comfortably saved by Marcos. There were still signs of Brazilian brilliance, such as a Ronaldinho flick to Ronaldo and O Fenômeno returning the favour with masterful skill that saw him nutmeg Du while pressured by three men in red.

China initially stood strong, though, defending deep and impressively in numbers. They could have even hit the South Americans with a dangerous counter attack ten minutes in if Hao Haidong had been able to control the ball played to him near the edge of the box.

Due to this display, Jiang Jin had hardly been worked by the time Ronaldinho was fouled about 25 yards from goal. However there was nothing he could do to stop Roberto Carlos's thunderous strike sailing past him and into the back of the net – even with the shot aimed at the side of the net unprotected by China's wall. After a quarter of an hour of matching Brazil at the very least, China found themselves behind.

The goalkeeper faced a powerful strike from Cafu moments later after the wing-back had burst up the pitch and broke any Chinese resistance with ease, but Jiang was equal to the shot this time. Brazil were very much on top now, with this match perfectly illustrating how a goal can completely change a game's complexion, although in fairness to China, that didn't stop them trying to come out and play whenever possible.

The men in yellow were turning it on with their trickery, but Ronaldinho was given a card to match his top after diving following a little tug of the shirt from Du on the edge of China's box. It wasn't long until Brazil were back, with Roberto Carlos delivering a threatening cross that Wu Chengying did well to put out for a throw rather than a corner.

Brazil's pressure eventually told in the 32nd minute when China's attempts at clearing Cafu's cross only went as far as Ronaldinho, who put the ball back in to provide Rivaldo with a simple finish at the back post. There were plenty of people who hadn't forgiven Brazil's number ten for the incident against Turkey but the massive smile on his face after scoring indicated that he didn't care in the slightest.

China were relentless in their dedication and carved out a good move almost immediately after conceding. However, as was indicative of their game so far, this came to nothing as Li Xiaopeng's cross was cleared with ease. They did have a couple of corners that Marcos struggled to take in, but the Palmeiras stopper got away with it both times.

Despite China's best efforts, Brazil were able to create another opportunity on the stroke of half-time. On this occasion Wu was pickpocketed by Juninho Paulista who passed inside to Ronaldo. The striker played a one-two with

Ronaldinho before driving into the box and eventually being wrestled to the floor by Li Weifeng and Du, only going down when both of them were pulling at him. Ronaldinho stepped up and sent Jiang the wrong way, slotting the ball into the bottom corner before dancing by the corner flag.

As Anders Frisk blew the whistle for half-time, China were unfortunate to find themselves three goals down and the game pretty much out of sight. They were simply coming up against a superior team who were clinically taking their chances. Perhaps due to his yellow card and Brazil's comfortable position, Scolari opted to replace Ronaldinho with Denílson during the break.

China continued to play with bravery but still had little bite as Ma Mingyu sent an effort from range dribbling wide. On the other hand, Brazil had taken a fairly relaxed approach to the second half and were biding their time, with Ronaldo only being denied a clear opportunity by the offside flag in the 54th minute after being played through by Juninho.

It only took another minute for Ronaldo to join his partners in the original front three on the scoresheet. Cafu chested down Rivaldo's long ball, drove past two Chinese defenders and hit a low cross towards the striker, who arrived for the simplest of tap-ins.

Cafu came close to getting a goal of his own after bursting forward and touching the ball past the goalkeeper, but Du did well to get back and scramble it behind before the Roma star could tap into the gaping net. China then finally carved out another chance on the counter attack only for Ma to be quelled.

Zhao went closer on the hour than any Chinese player had done during the game, skipping inside Lúcio and smashing an effort from the edge of the box. Marcos was getting nowhere near it but the ball went the wrong side of the post and out for a goal kick, leaving the midfielder with his head in his hands in disbelief. The captain, Ma, was brought off for Yang Pu in the immediate aftermath of that strike, while Qi was replaced by Shao Jiayi four minutes later.

Roque Júnior was given Brazil's second yellow card of the game in the 69th minute after sliding in on Xu to block his shot. The centre-back was left confused despite seemingly missing the ball, while substitute Shao stepped up and saw his effort tipped wide of the post by Marcos's fingertips. After the ensuing corner was wasted, Scolari brought Juninho off for Corinthians' Ricardinho. Having just been denied by a magnificent double save from Jiang, Ronaldo followed Juninho off the pitch to be replaced by Flamengo's Edílson two minutes later.

Brazil continued to show flair, as had been the case throughout the game, and Gilberto Silva hit a first-time strike that the goalkeeper gathered at the second attempt. With quarter of an hour remaining China made the match's final substitution by bringing Qu Bo on for Hao. Qu made an attempt to dash through the middle of the pitch and while the substitute made it into Brazil's box, he was eventually blocked off by Roberto Carlos and tackled by Roque Júnior.

Qu was proving to be the biggest threat from either team in the final stages as Brazil wound down. His one-two and burst into the penalty area forced Marcos into an awkward intervention before the goalkeeper scrambled to reach the loose ball ahead of the red shirts, eventually kicking it out of play. Fellow substitute Jiayi also brought out a lovely turn, though it came to nothing.

In the final moments Cafu tried to round Jiang for a second time in the match while pursuing his first goal of the tournament, but the Chinese custodian came to the very edge of his box and stopped him with an outstretched arm. Just before the whistle came, Denílson kicked the ball away in a fashion that hinted he may have been frustrated to not have had more of an impact on the game to show Scolari what he could do.

It was still a game that had proven very comfortable for the South Americans as they continued to assert their dominance on Group C. Meanwhile, China could leave with their heads held high after a performance that was better than the 4-0 scoreline suggested.

*Mexico 2 Ecuador 1 (Group G, 9 June, Miyagi)*
Having overcome Croatia in their opening game, Mexico knew that beating Ecuador would put them in a brilliant position for their group-closing meeting with Italy. Javier Aguirre made two changes as Jesús Arellano and Johan Rodríguez replaced Sigifredo Mercado and Gabriel Caballero. Meanwhile, Ecuador were looking for their first World Cup goal and point having been on the receiving end of Gli Azzurri's masterclass. Hernán Gómez's only alteration was to take captain Álex Aguinaga out of the starting line-up for Iván Kaviedes.

Mexico enjoyed more of the ball during the opening exchanges but found themselves behind after just five minutes when Édison Méndez and Ulises de la Cruz combined well to create enough space for the latter to whip in a left-footed cross that picked out Agustín Delgado, who produced a marvellous header. Óscar Pérez couldn't keep the ball out despite managing to stretch enough to tip it on to the underside of the crossbar and the post. The scenes were understandably joyous as Delgado was congratulated by his team-mates, knowing that he would forever be Ecuador's first goalscorer at a World Cup finals.

There was still a game to play, though, and Mexico immediately looked to restore parity as Arellano drove forward, eventually scuffing his effort wide. The men in green continued to control the ball and looked for a route to goal but a resolute Ecuadorian defence meant they were struggling to truly test José Cevallos. While the mullet-wearing Alfonso Obregón escaped a booking for a lunging tackle, Kaviedes wasn't so lucky when he tripped Salvador Carmona deep in Mexico's half after 15 minutes.

Soon afterwards, Raúl Guerrón went down theatrically holding his face after Rodríguez swung an elbow in the aftermath of a free kick being given. Referee Mourad Daami didn't take any action and Ramón Morales's effort was comfortably saved.

A clear pattern emerged as the game progressed: Mexico moved the ball around and tried to carve out an attack; Ecuador repelled it any way they could before struggling to maintain possession and gave the ball away; cycle repeats. The South Americans had now dropped deep and their goalkeeper Cevallos was even booked for time-wasting in the 26th minute.

This tactic didn't prove as effective as would have been hoped as Mexico equalised within two minutes of that booking. Following an Ecuadorian tackle, Gerardo Torrado stepped in to steal the loose ball and spread it wide to Morales, who took strides forward and crossed into the box for Jared Borgetti to get ahead of his marker and slot a neat first-time finish past Cevallos.

Ecuador attempted to impose themselves in an attacking sense but were struggling to do so having sat back for so long, and Rodríguez was almost played through for Mexico. Obregón did have a shot from range but it eventually skewed harmlessly wide of Pérez's goal. With this in mind, it took Gómez just 35 minutes to make his first substitution, taking Edwin Tenorio off for Marlon Ayoví.

Following some heated exchanges and Mexican half chances, Cuauhtémoc Blanco had a glorious opportunity towards the end of the first half. Rodríguez found him on the edge of the box after initially slipping, but the striker could only muster a weak effort that was gathered by Cevallos with ease.

Luis Hernández received a warm reception as he emerged from the changing rooms after the break, but he returned to the bench for now as neither manager made a change, and the second half started where the first had left off with Mexico controlling the ball. Guerrón was booked for pulling down Arellano as he threatened to sprint into the box – despite being in a good position, the ensuing set piece was wasted.

It wasn't too long until Ecuador made their second change as Carlos Tenorio replaced the booked Kaviedes, but Mexico maintained control. It still took a moment of magic for El Tri to get ahead and – having played his part in the opener – Torrado provided just that. After passing the ball to Rodríguez and getting it back, the midfielder stepped forward and rifled an effort past the goalkeeper from 20 yards out. Joy and relief were clear to see as Torrado started jumping about before being joined by his team-mates.

Seconds later, Obregón tried his luck from range again, but this effort sailed over and hit the roof of the net. That was to be the midfielder's last action as he was taken off for Aguinaga, who was tasked with getting his team back on level terms. All that followed quickly was another Ecuadorian yellow card for substitute Tenorio, who lunged into a tackle on Rodríguez just after the hour.

Ecuador had their strongest period for some time after this, with Tenorio doing more of what his manager would have asked for. The LDU Quito man went on a lung-bursting run down the left before attempting to cut the ball back for Delgado but his attempt was well blocked by Rafael Márquez, who conceded what was surprisingly the game's first corner. That came to nothing, but after Ecuador picked up the cleared ball Torrado was booked for a reckless challenge on De la Cruz.

Mexico were refusing to sit back and some great work down the left saw the ball fall kindly in the box to Rodríguez, whose first-time effort soared disappointingly high and wide. Borgetti had three half-chances moments later but couldn't get a proper connection on the first, smashed the second wide, then saw the third go behind off the far post – which was enough to have him looking around in disbelief.

This was a sign that Mexico were back on top but Borgetti eventually made way for Luis Hernández in the 77th minute, with the former golden boy of Mexican football getting another warm round of applause. He almost broke through after receiving a quick throw-in but his attempted pass to Blanco was intercepted.

Moments later, Tenorio thought he was about to get Ecuador back on level terms after some swift link-up play. His effort was deflected wide by Pérez, who was far from impressed with his defence for allowing the opportunity to materialise. Méndez then tried his luck only to see his attempt comfortably saved.

With the game approaching its final five minutes, Mexico were beginning to sit back and protect what they had while Ecuador pursued the goal required to give them any sort of chance of reaching the knockout stages. Méndez came a whisker away from finding that equaliser after Aguinaga showed the quality and composure to control the ball in the box and lay it off to him on the edge. However, the winger's first-time strike went agonisingly wide. Immediately after that scare, Rodríguez was brought off for Caballero.

Hernández did well to get Mexico some much-needed respite, dinking a cross towards the back post that forced Guerrón to head the ball behind for a corner. While Morales took as long as he could with it, there was soon another Ecuadorian attack with Manuel Vidrio making a superb last-ditch challenge to clear the ball just as Tenorio shaped to shoot from a dangerous position.

Blanco almost wrapped the game up in the 92nd minute with a curling effort from outside the box, but Cevallos was able to palm it wide. The ball may not have hit the back of the net, but getting a corner helped run down the final minute of injury time – as did substituting the striker off for Mercado.

In the end Mexico were able to see out the game, their perfect start to the tournament and a prime position to get out of the group. Meanwhile, Ecuador may not have been mathematically out of the running but there was very little hope of them getting through. Still, this was a historic game for the nation, and especially Delgado, thanks to that first World Cup goal.

## Costa Rica 1 Turkey 1 (Group C, 9 June, Incheon)

With Turkey expecting to beat China and Costa Rica likely to lose against Brazil in the final round of Group C fixtures, this was the big match for both teams in terms of their ambitions of reaching the knockout stage. Costa Rica even had a guaranteed place in the round of 16 if they won.

Şenol Güneş was without Alpay Özalan and Hakan Ünsal after their dismissals against Brazil, while Bülent Korkmaz also came out, with Emre Aşık, Ergün Penbe and Ümit Davala entering the Turks' line-up. Meanwhile, Alexandre Guimarães brought Wilmer López in for Rolando Fonseca in Costa Rica's only change of personnel.

The game got off to a false start after Hakan Şükür had been a bit too keen to close Costa Rica down from the kick-off. There was another comedic moment once things got going as referee Coffi Codjia almost tackled López. Once that was over, the match was played at an incredibly high pace in the early stages with both sides desperate to get on top.

There were big tackles, lung-bursting runs, aggressive passing choices and plenty of commitment, but few real opportunities. The game's first half-chance fell to Paulo Wanchope nine minutes in, though he couldn't find the target with a first-time strike on the swivel under pressure from Ümit Özat. Turkey's first opportunity came after Hasan Şaş was fouled about 25 yards from goal, but Özat's effort was always curling wide.

Turkey threatened to get on top as the game progressed – and a flat ball was disposed of – with Hasan Şaş and Yıldıray Baştürk looking particularly dangerous, while Emre Belözoğlu was drawing plenty of fouls.

There was a slight break in play in the 18th minute as Gilberto Martínez received treatment for a cut to the eye after a kick in the face from Ümit Davala went widely unnoticed. He was stretchered off to get it sorted while the game continued. Turkey didn't make a lot of their temporary man advantage and Aşık was booked for stopping Wanchope from starting a break by blocking him off.

A couple of minutes after returning to the action, Martínez picked up a booking of his own for flying through the back of Şaş. Moments later, Emre won a free kick after nutmegging Gómez. The midfielder then played a short pass, starting an intelligent routine that resulted in Turkey's number 11 having the ball in Costa Rica's box. Martínez was back again to ensure nothing came of it, though.

Costa Rica had by far the biggest opening of the game so far in the 33rd minute. López neatly shifted the ball and passed it forward to Gómez, who drew out the defender and passed inside to Walter Centeno. However, after he had taken a brilliant touch forward to set himself up, Costa Rica's number ten put his eventual effort over the crossbar.

Rüştü Reçber may not have been forced into a save but he still looked furious that the Turkey defence had afforded their opposition such a clear opportunity. The goalkeeper had another uncomfortable moment a couple of minutes later as he injured himself after coming to the edge of his penalty area to deny Centeno. Rüştü had to try to slow his momentum and eventually let go of the ball to stop himself carrying it out of the box. The Fenerbahçe man did well to kick it clear but went down holding his hamstring. To the relief of Güneş and everybody associated with Turkey, the man wearing a ponytail and black smudges on his face was able to continue.

Seemingly buoyed by coming close to opening the scoring, Costa Rica continued driving forward as they aimed to stay on top going into the break. Carlos Castro went a bit overboard with a challenge on Ümit Davala and got a yellow card in the 43rd minute. The final stages of the half turned into a bitty affair, and Centeno was lucky to escape a card having clearly elbowed Aşık in the face. Not long after getting away with another poor challenge, Tugay Kerimoğlu was booked for taking out Mauricio Solís to prevent him breaking forward.

An undercooked back-pass from Penbe forced Rüştü to fly out and smash the ball away – and limp back to his goal after – while Wanchope ran into traffic after some lovely touches in the Turkey box. The scores remained level as Codjia blew for half-time, ending 45 minutes that had been more entertaining than the goalless scoreboard suggested, with underdogs Costa Rica arguably being the better side.

Turkey began the second period on the front foot. Şükür came close to turning that positive start into a lead, eventually proving unable to get quite enough on his header from a corner to find the target. The Parma striker had another chance just moments later after he had been released behind Costa Rica's defence by a beautifully dinked pass, only to send his effort high and wide.

Costa Rica had a great chance of their own six minutes after the break when Castro dashed down the wing and offloaded the ball to Martínez, who eventually found Gómez on the edge of the box. The OFI Crete man showed great composure to shift the ball and open up space but then blazed his strike well off target.

The game had turned into an end-to-end affair as it had been for large periods of the first half. Wanchope came agonisingly close to a breakthrough a couple of minutes later, latching on to a through ball but having it touched away by Rüştü and being wrongly met by the offside flag as he tried to retrieve it.

Emre put Turkey ahead just a couple of minute later. He collected the ball cushioned down by Şaş's chest and saw his initial shot blocked by Martínez before turning away and scuffing the ball into the bottom corner. It was far from the best finish this World Cup would see, but Turkey didn't care as they went off to celebrate.

Costa Rica immediately went about trying to get back into the game, and Gómez forced a decent stop from Rüştü with a strike from range. Still, it wasn't all pretty play and ambitious efforts, as Mauricio Wright got away with sneakily stepping on the back of Şaş's leg after making a pass.

Guimarães's side had another great opportunity on the hour after Wanchope pickpocketed Özat in Turkey's half. The striker started a blistering attack that resulted in López getting a strike off from inside the box and spooning it over the bar. Another one followed within seconds after two Turkish players were completely sold by Castro's fake, with this move ending with Solís skying his shot despite the opportunity being perfectly set up for him on the edge of the box.

When López did force Rüştü to take action moments later, the goalkeeper was up for the challenge and denied him with his legs. Guimarães made the game's first change in the 66th minute, taking Centeno off for Hernán Medford in an effort to turn their chances into an equaliser.

There was a slight break in play as Tugay received treatment for a knock to the head after a collision with Wright. That was soon followed by more disruption, this time for various substitutions: İlhan Mansız replaced Şükür in the 75th minute, Winston Parks and Steven Bryce came on for Harold Wallace and López two minutes later, then Nihat Kahveci was brought on for Baştürk two minutes after that. There was enough time between the latter substitutions for the over-excited linesman to make a terrible call for offside after Martínez's long ball threatened to find Parks in a dangerous position moments after his introduction.

With the game now flowing, both teams continued to attack in the final ten minutes as Parks looked a real threat and Wright often managed to get himself into the thick of the action. He was bundled over by Rüştü after tussling with him, trying to get on the end of a corner delivery that hadn't been convincingly cleared.

When Costa Rica got a free kick about 40 yards from goal, it didn't look like their most threatening opportunity of the game. However, Castro lofted a ball towards the back post that Wanchope jumped highest to head down for it to be hooked back across goal. As Medford occupied the defender in the middle, Parks popped up to emphatically smash home from six yards out before jumping with joy. He had to make sure his nasal strip was still on after being joined in his celebrations.

With just three minutes of normal time remaining, Güneş responded immediately by taking Tugay off for Galatasaray forward Arif Erdem. Another stoppage followed as there was a massive coming together between the two sides after Emre had pushed one of the Costa Rican coaches who was holding on to the ball. The midfielder then threw the ball at a player while standing behind his team-mates. Once the commotion died down, Emre was handed a yellow card.

With that heat still lingering in the air, Emre could have had an assist moments later after playing a lovely dinked pass to Erdem but the substitute couldn't get a clean connection on his strike and the ball floated harmlessly into Erick Lonnis's gloves. From the resulting goal kick Parks went straight at Turkey's heart and rounded Rüştü, but having been forced fairly wide the substitute missed the eternal glory of guaranteeing his nation a place in the knockout rounds by spooning his shot high and wide. The angle wasn't the easiest, but there was no excuse for missing so terribly on such a big stage.

Costa Rica almost got through again but Gómez was denied by an instinctive flick from Fatih Akyel turning the ball behind for a corner. It was cleared with ease and the follow-up effort sailed well over the crossbar. Turkey had a corner of their own with the final kick of the game, but Erdem's delivery was punched away by Lonnis and the referee blew for full time.

There were some words exchanged by players from both teams after the whistle. The important thing was that this result left the group wide open. Turkey only had one point to their name but would now face China, while Costa Rica had four and had to come up against the already qualified Brazil. It promised to be an intriguing watch.

## *Japan 1 Russia 0 (Group H, 9 June, Yokohama)*

With Russia top and Japan having drawn with Belgium after a scintillating game, this match looked an intriguing one. There was a blow for the tournament's co-hosts, however, as captain Ryuzo Morioka was ruled out through injury. Daisuke Ichikawa didn't make the starting line-up either, with Tsuneyasu Miyamoto and Tomokazu Myojin coming in. On the other hand, Russia were boosted by the return of Alexey Smertin which saw them switch formation as he replaced frontman Vladimir Beschastnykh.

Russia didn't have the best of starts as a lazy pass back from the kick off was charged down and Japan ended up winning a throw deep in the opposition half. The Europeans recovered by nipping in and smashing the ball up the pitch so the game could get going properly. Not completely settled, Ruslan Pimerov gave a foul away for catching Miyamoto in the head with a forearm while jumping despite having no chance of getting the ball.

With Japan on top in the opening exchanges, Junichi Inamoto had the game's first real effort four minutes in when he smashed a bouncing ball from around 30 yards out but sent it swerving marginally wide. The Asians were also getting to every loose ball first and making Russia look lumbered, so while Smertin got an effort off that skewed wide, it wasn't much of a surprise when Pimenov got the game's first booking for a late challenge on Naoki Matsuda.

Still, 19-year-old Marat Izmailov gave Japan a scare with some nice footwork and a looping effort from range that whistled past the post having left Seigo Narazaki clutching at air. In the 16th minute, in what was already promising to be an intriguing personal battle, Miyamoto was booked for pulling Pimenov's arm as the striker tried to get in behind. Yuri Nikiforov blasted the ensuing free kick wildly off target, as he had done numerous times against Tunisia.

Hidetoshi Nakata hadn't quite reached his best at the tournament yet, and with Russia's defence – especially Viktor Onopko – standing strong, Japan's number seven sent an effort well over the crossbar in the 24th minute. The Parma midfielder had the game's best chance so far soon afterwards when Onopko was uncharacteristically indecisive with his clearance from Kōji Nakata's cross, but the defender's namesake sent the ball flying over once again.

Pimenov certainly wasn't holding back, and when Narazaki came to collect an intelligent Yegor Titov through ball that trickled just too close to the goalkeeper he jumped into a tackle that left the Nagoya Grampus man on the floor.

The game was regularly stopping and starting, and Andrei Solomatin got an obvious yellow card in the 38th minute for a poor foul on Atsushi Yanagisawa.

The right-back came close to creating Russia's best opportunity of the game so far mere seconds later after bursting up the pitch and getting to the byline. However, Pimenov couldn't get to the pass and Igor Semshov went down after being tugged by Kazuyuki Toda, allowing the midfielder to turn the ball behind for a corner that came to nothing. Semshov looked perplexed that he hadn't been given a penalty and Kōji Nakata then got himself booked for sliding into Valery Karpin from behind – giving an apologetic hand of acknowledgement to referee Markus Merk.

As the whistle was blown for half-time, the game seemed finely poised for somebody to step up and take all three points for their nation. As had been the case against Tunisia, Oleg Romantsev was the only manager to make a change during the break. This time he took off Pimenov – perhaps doing so before he was sent off – and replaced him with Dimitri Sytchev, the teenager who had proven to be the bright spark in their opening-day win.

There was a scare for Japan within a minute of the second half starting when Izmailov got a touch on to Karpin's cut-back, but the Lokomotiv Moscow midfielder couldn't turn it goalward, eventually winning a corner that was caught by Narazaki.

However it was the men in blue shirts who opened the scoring in the 51st minute. After Yuri Kovtun was adjudged to have fouled Takayuki Suzuki, Japan played the ball short and worked it out to the left where Kōji Nakata was waiting to deliver a precise pass to Yanagisawa in the Russian box. He intelligently offloaded the ball to Inamoto with a cushioned first-time pass, allowing the Arsenal midfielder to take a touch and coolly pass the ball into the top corner before being mobbed by his jubilant team-mates.

Those joyous scenes in Yokohama were juxtaposed by crowds that had gathered by a large screen that had been erected outside the Kremlin in Moscow so that fans could watch the game. The goal led to trouble among those watching in Russia as people started hurling bottles and acting aggressively. Back in Yokohama, clearly not one to hang around, Romantsev immediately took Izmailov off for Dmitri Khokhlov.

Japan were never going to sit back and protect what they had, so with the backdrop of an incredibly vocal crowd the game's frantic edge remained. This was accentuated by Russia stepping things up in an attempt to restore parity, bringing Beschastnykh on for Smertin in the 57th minute, getting an extra attacker on with their final change. Russia's number 11 had a glorious chance just moments after being introduced as he rounded the goalkeeper, and while Köji Nakata desperately scrambled back on to the line, he wasn't needed as Beschastnykh somehow only hit the side netting.

Despite there being around half an hour remaining, Russia already looked desperate and Khokhlov was booked after fouling Inamoto with a rash challenge on the edge of his own box. He was let off as Hidetoshi Nakata still hadn't found his range, while the men in white were given even greater relief when Yanagisawa blazed over having done brilliantly to work space in the box. Russia were still very much in the contest and Sytchev came close with an ambitious effort of his own moments later.

The game had become a blistering affair, and seconds after Onopko stopped Yanagisawa from bursting through,

Suzuki marginally missed the target from the edge of Russia's box. While Russia had their own attacks it was Hidetoshi Nakata who came close again, smashing the crossbar with a venomous strike from range in the 71st minute. Just after that there was a massive roar as Masahi Nakayama replaced Suzuki, while Ono soon came off to be replaced by Toshihiro Hattori.

Japan were giving everything they had but Russia managed to create an opening as the game went into its final quarter of an hour. Karpin – who had seemingly been growing increasingly frustrated – showed the presence of mind to cut inside and find Khokhlov in the box. However, having done well to work space away from Köji Nakata, the Real Sociedad man's shot went straight at Narazaki, who patted it down before holding on to the ball.

Just as Sytchev thought he was the latest Russian to get an opening moments later, the masked Miyamoto came flying in to block the teenager's shot. The resultant corner saw the ball bounce towards Titov just outside the box but he couldn't keep his shot down. In a sign of Russia's growing desperation in the final ten minutes, Nikiforov sent a first-time shot into row Z from about 30 yards out.

Meanwhile, Japanese fans' building hope could be felt as they cheered on their team. There was also a thankful outpouring when Narazaki held on to Sytchev's effort from range, then another as Titov failed to hit the target again. With five minutes left, Inamoto was able to feel their adoration as he was replaced by Takashi Fukunishi in Philippe Troussier's final change.

As Japan fought to keep hold of their lead, they even had a penalty shout turned down in the 89th minute when Yanagisawa went down under pressure from Nikiforov.

Nakayama was then booked for a reckless challenge on the halfway line two minutes later. With the pressure building, Japan were offered relief by Khokhlov's foul throw. Japanese bodies flew into every challenge and just as Karpin was about to take a free kick, Mark blew the sweetest of final whistles the nation would have heard for some time, sending Yokohama into rapture.

It was a very different scene in Moscow, where riots broke out and dozens of cars were overturned, a Japanese restaurant was attacked, shop windows were smashed and many people of Asian heritage were forced to take refuge in a McDonald's. There was also a heavy police presence outside the Japanese embassy. The riots resulted in two deaths and 60 football hooligans being detained. 'Our public is not ready for this. I'm ashamed,' said Andrei Norkin, head of an independent Moscow television company whose outdoor broadcast facilities were attacked. 'If we're not good at football, we should behave like human beings and support our players properly.'

In terms of the World Cup, Russia now had to prove that they were at least good enough to get through the group with Belgium yet to come. Meanwhile, Japan were in a strong position ahead of their final group game against Tunisia.

### South Korea 1 USA 1 (Group D, 10 June, Daegu)

Both of these sides came into the game in high spirits after winning their respective openers. Guus Hiddink kept the same South Korea team that had secured victory over Poland, while Bruce Arena took out Earnie Stewart and Pablo Mastroeni for Claudio Reyna and Clint Mathis.

It was the USA who kicked off proceedings and they went straight for the jugular immediately, hitting the ball long before winning a throw-in and then a free kick in the space of 20 seconds. This gave Reyna his first opportunity of the World Cup to make an impact, and while his deflected delivery caused confusion in the box, South Korea were able to clear convincingly.

The intensity of the start didn't dim down at all and the Asians carved out a great chance in the fifth minute. The move started with Park Ji-sung's persistence getting the better of Frankie Hejduk down the right, before the 21-year-old offloaded the ball to Hwang Sun-hong, who clipped a well-weighted pass towards Seol Ki-hyeon at the back post. The Anderlecht forward couldn't control his effort as he came steaming in and lifted it well over the crossbar. Kim Nam-il attempted to loop the ball over Brad Friedel from range moments later, but the stopper got his 6ft 3in frame back on the goal line quick enough to save himself from any embarrassment.

Seol soon saw his shot saved by Friedel's feet with the Koreans controlling the ball and creating chances. The momentum they were building up was soon halted though, as Hwang required treatment for a nasty cut above his eye after a clash of heads with Hejduk.

Having got the ball back to restart proceedings following the incident, the USA passed it around well. The move suddenly became dangerous when John O'Brien was able to get away from Kim Nam-il. The Ajax midfielder strode away from his opposite number before clipping the ball over South Korea's defence towards Mathis. The mohican-haired USA striker vindicated Arena's decision to pick him by coolly bringing the ball down, letting it bounce and firing past Lee Woon-jae. Most of the Daegu World Cup Stadium fell silent, but the Americans' jubilance was clear to see as Mathis held his arms aloft with his fingers pointing outwards.

South Korea had pretty much dominated the game, but with a bandaged-up Hwang back on the pitch they now found themselves behind after 24 minutes. The buoyed Americans could have easily made it a quick double as both DaMarcus Beasley and Landon Donovan came close to creating clear chances by running in behind. South Korea offered a reminder that they could cause problems when Park forced Hejduk into a wild challenge that earned the full-back a booking. Yoo Sang-chul's effort from the ensuing free kick was just as wild.

Likely due to the kick he had taken earlier on, Park was taken off after just 38 minutes and was replaced by Ulsan Hyundai Horang-i's Lee Chun-soo. And, just moments later, the Koreans had a penalty after Jeff Agoos bundled Hwang over while contesting Kim Nam-il's dinked ball into the box, getting himself a yellow card in the process.

Lee Eul-yong stepped up with the home nation's hopes on his shoulders. The winger side-footed his effort to Friedel's right, but it was at a good height for the goalkeeper who launched himself across the line to stop it. Kim Nam-il came steaming in as he tried to get the rebound but some superb defending from Eddie Pope denied him, turning the ball behind and earning a free kick. Lee Eul-yong looked around in complete disbelief as USA's number 23 received treatment.

This didn't dampen the supporters's spirits; the Korean crowd was largely in full voice as the remainder of the first half was played out without major incident despite both teams continuing to go for it.

The second period began as much of the first had gone, with the Koreans pushing forward, and Seol would have had them back on level terms just a minute after the restart if it wasn't for another impressive stop from Friedel. As Hiddink aimed to get his side back into the game, a battered-looking Hwang was brought off for Ahn Jung-hwan shortly before the hour. Ahn got involved immediately as he won a free kick in a dangerous area, even if it eventually came to nothing.

There was another break in play in the 64th minute. This time it was Reyna who picked up an injury after a coming together with Kim Nam-il and team-mate Pope. While this was a rare moment of respite for the USA's defence, it could be argued that the men in white were actually having the better chances as Brian McBride and Donovan both had opportunities that they couldn't make the most of. Perhaps with this in mind Hiddink stepped up the pressure again in the 69th minute, using his last substitution to bring midfielder Yoo off for forward Choi Yong-soo. The number 11 had his first chance within seconds of entering the fray but scuffed his shot, allowing Friedel to turn it behind.

The pressure continued and South Korea were given a slightly contentious free kick by Urs Meier in the 78th minute when Donovan appeared to win the ball. Lee Chun-soo's delivery was brilliant and his fellow substitute Ahn rose above Agoos to glance the ball into the bottom corner, leaving Friedel rooted to the floor and sending the crowd into elated cheers.

It was Ahn's celebration that eventually caught the eye. The South Korean went to the corner and came to a stop before leaning forward and making striding motions with his arms and legs. It turned out that this was a jibe at United States short track speed skater Apolo Ohno. During the 2002 Salt Lake City Winter Olympics, he had won the 1500m final despite Kim Dong-sung crossing the line first. While carrying the South Korea flag in celebration, Kim discovered he had been disqualified for cross-tracking and slammed the flag into the ice out of frustration.

That image had clearly stuck in the mind, as after the game Ahn told reporters, 'We knew that our people still have some grudge against the United States for the skating incident, so we wanted to allay that with the goal ceremony'. Donovan wasn't too impressed. 'Is that what he was doing? It's kind of a joke. Why do you have to do that? It has no relevance to this game,' he said upon hearing the reasoning.

Back to the game in question, and while Donovan was oblivious to the celebration's meaning at the time, he still wasn't best pleased moments after the goal as he was taken out by Hong Myung-bo while running through for a chance of his own. The Korean captain was given a booking as a result. Shortly afterwards, the goalscorer Mathis was taken off for Josh Wolff as Arena looked to get his side back into the lead with eight minutes left.

It was the men in red who came closest to scoring, though, as Lee Eul-yong ran down the left side before playing a smart one-two with Seol and skipping past Anthony Sanneh to get into the box. The winger stepped over the ball then offloaded it to Choi who was waiting just outside the six-yard box. However, the substitute sent his effort spinning well over the crossbar.

In the end, both teams had to settle for a point – a result that was far from disastrous for either side. They now entered their final group matches in the knowledge a draw would be enough to book their place in the knockout rounds.

*Tunisia 1 Belgium 1 (Group H, 10 June, Ōita)*
After Japan had beaten Russia, both of these teams were looking at this game as an opportunity to increase their

chances of progressing to the knockout stage. Tunisia made two changes, with Kaies Ghodhbane and Mourad Melki replacing Mohamed Mkacher and Adel Sellimi. Meanwhile, Robert Waseige brought Éric Deflandre, Glen De Boeck and Branko Strupar in for Jacky Peeters, Eric Van Meir and Johan Walem.

The opening couple of minutes brought a flurry of free kicks, and Marc Wilmots hit an ambitious effort with the first of those which went straight at Ali Boumnijel. Tunisia's Melki was clearly looking to make his mark as he hit an even more ambitious strike that swerved well wide.

In the 12th minute, Boumnijel – who had a defender taking goal kicks for him – was given a fright as his attempted pass was blocked and he grappled with the opposition attacker to punch the ball away. Despite escaping that moment, the ball was in his net within a minute. Two consecutive deliveries into Tunisia's box were inadequately dealt with before Strupar cushioned the ball down for his Schalke 04 team-mate Wilmots, who was on hand to knock it past the flailing goalkeeper from inside the six-yard box.

Hasen Gabsi couldn't get a convincing contact on his overhead kick as Tunisia looked to respond, but the Red Devils's lead lasted for just four minutes. Tunisia had initially been left frustrated when a free kick was given after Selim Ben Achour was fouled near the edge of the box, just as the ball was smashed into the top corner. Any annoyance towards referee Mark Shield dissipated quickly, though, as Raouf Bouzaiene swept a wonderful shot out of Geert De Vlieger's reach and into the net. As the left-back sprinted off with an unmissable smile drawn across his face, Tunisia were right back in the game.

Buoyed by their first goal in nine matches, Tunisia immediately went for a second and Deflandre blocked

Melki's volley well. However, the Lyon defender was lucky not to concede a penalty in the aftermath as he lunged into a tackle on Tunisia's number 21 and clearly took his legs away, reigniting frustrations towards the referee. Shield must have thought Deflandre had won the ball as he awarded a corner, even though he had got nowhere near it. Still, the Africans were in the ascendancy and Ziad Jaziri latched on to a wonderful through ball but couldn't find the target with his final effort.

In the 22nd minute Shield made himself even less popular among the Tunisians by booking Gabsi for diving – especially as that meant he would miss the next game. Things almost got worse within seconds as a move down the left eventually saw Timmy Simons with the ball in the box, but his shot was deflected over the crossbar.

As the half-hour mark came and went, the game became disjointed, being dominated by the referee's whistle with both teams committing plenty of niggly fouls. There was also a slight break in play as Wilmots went off to get treatment for a cut by his eye. In the 36th minute, Hatem Trabelsi showed the brightness that had also been evident against Russia by getting behind Belgium's defence and trying to pick out Jaziri in the six-yard box, but De Vlieger stretched just enough to divert the ball away from the striker.

There were more fouls to come before half-time as Daniel Van Buyten got booked for sliding through the back of Jaziri, while Ghodhbane saw yellow three minutes later for taking out Peter Van Der Heyden. The half ended with a slight mix-up between De Vlieger and De Bloeck as the goalkeeper went flying into his centre-back, but De Bloeck was decisive enough to clear the ball away before the contact and avoid the pair's blushes. There was also a naughty moment from Goor, who seemed to step on Khaled Badra when getting up after the pair had gone to ground having battled in the air.

Wilmots didn't look overly impressed with how things were going when the whistle was blown for half-time. Waseige clearly wasn't pleased either, making a double change at the break as Verheyen and Strupar made way for Wesley Sonck and Sven Vermant.

Despite the intent from Belgium's bench, an awkward cross was the only challenge Boumnijel faced before Ghodbhane flashed a wonderfully struck volley agonisingly wide of De Vlieger's post in the 51st minute. Van Buyten soon took a moment after Jaziri hit him in the mouth with a stray elbow. Adding to Waseige's frustrations, two Belgian attackers got in each other's way when a superb ball came into the box, leaving Sonck to look around bewildered.

Belgium eventually went up a gear and, in the 64th minute, Boumnijel was forced to impressively rush out to deny Goor as the winger got behind Tunisia's defence and looked to poke the ball goalward. Radhi Jaïdi and Riadh Bouazizi were also called into action to deny clear chances in their box.

Trying to turn the tide, Ammar Souayah brought Gabsi off for Adel Sellimi. However, within two minutes of that change, both Trabelsi and Melki received bookings as the Red Devils continued to push forward in search of a winner. Just after some tireless work from Jaziri put the Belgian defence under pressure, both teams made another substitution. For Belgium, Mbo Mpenza – the brother of Émile, who missed the tournament due to injury – replaced Simons in an attacking change, while Tunisia's Jaziri was replaced by Ali Zitouni a couple of minutes later.

After a spurt of energy in the game, it was slowed down again as Boumnijel took his time getting the ball for a goal kick before Melki received treatment after getting an arm to the head while jumping with Van Buyten. Tunisia were now looking the better side as the final ten minutes arrived, and they got a free kick just outside Belgium's box after Van Buyten fouled Ben Achour. Bouzaiene, who had continued to impress after his equaliser, merely acted as the decoy this time as Ghodhbane's effort was deflected wide by the seven-man wall.

With two minutes left and the lure of a late winner, Souayah made his final change, bringing Zoubeir Baya on for Melki. However Ghodhbane was the only man in white to get shots off in the final minutes, with one being punched away by De Vlieger and the other going over the crossbar. Between those, Sonck had one last try for the Red Devils but his effort on the stretch, also from the edge of the box, went wide before the striker gestured to the referee that his shirt had been pulled.

So, despite both teams' best efforts, they had to settle for a point apiece. This was far from ideal for either side as they trailed Japan and Russia, but it did keep them both in with a chance of reaching the knockout stage. Souayah would have been far happier than Waseige after this result, with Tunisia having come into this as clear underdogs. However Tunisia and Belgium were in the same position in terms of progression: it was now all or nothing for both of them in the final round of group matches.

*Portugal 4 Poland 0 (Group D, 10 June, Jeonju)*
Due to the teams having lost their respective openers, both camps would have known the importance of getting

something from the game if they hoped to progress. For Portugal in particular the match was a chance to earn redemption after a disappointing result.

Manager António Oliveira made two changes from the side that had lost to the United States of America, with Nuno Frechaut and Paulo Bento replacing Beto and Rui Costa. The latter of those alterations was a massive surprise to many, seeing as Costa was AC Milan's most expensive signing at the time. Poland's Jerzy Engel moved things around with Paweł Kryszałowicz coming in for Jacek Bąk, meaning Marek Koźminski moved from the wing to right-back while Tomasz Hajto moved to the heart of defence.

There wasn't an awful lot of quality in the opening exchanges but Pauleta looked in the mood as the first ten minutes played out. He let two shots off from range – one of which flashed agonisingly past the post – and won a corner after some direct running, and in the 14th minute Portugal's number nine really burst into life. By the time Frechaut offloaded the ball to João Pinto in a deep position, he was already peeling away to isolate Hajto. After the ball was floated towards him, Pauleta cut inside the centre-back and fired past Dudek at the near post, with the goalkeeper managing nothing more than the slightest of touches.

Adding to Poland's frustrations, Kałużny was forced off through injury just two minutes after the goal to be replaced by Arkadiusz Bąk. Piotr Świerczewski was booked for throwing an opponent to the floor and while Pauleta continued to look dangerous, the game descended into minor chaos around him in the pouring rain. Within ten minutes of Świerczewski becoming the first name in Hugh Dallas's book, Frechaut joined him for a reckless sliding tackle on Jacek Krzynówek, Jorge Costa was carded for taking out

Emmanuel Olisadebe and Rui Jorge saw yellow after going in late on Bąk – leaving Fernando Couto as the only Portuguese defender without a caution.

For good measure, Bąk got a card of his own in the 39th minute when he brought Pinto down on the edge of the box. Luís Figo took the ensuing free kick but it was a simple effort for Dudek to stop. Portugal's talisman was one of Real Madrid's Galácticos, having joined them from Barcelona in 2000 – getting a pig's head thrown at him for his decision. He had not been at his imperious best in this tournament, though. The 29-year-old had missed a period of Los Blancos's La Liga season through injury and it showed, with a nutmeg being his only major moment of quality in the first half.

Hajto found himself lucky not to be cautioned having kicked out at Pinto after the free kick had already been given, something the Portuguese players made sure to point out to Dallas. It was a scrappy and combative end to the first half but when Olisadebe was almost played through, goalkeeper Vítor Baía showed composure to come out and clear the danger. In one last involvement for the referee in the half, he ended up accidentally getting a touch as he failed to evade a pass, blowing the whistle soon after.

Neither the weather nor the quality initially improved after the restart as small puddles of water splashed up underfoot in several areas of the pitch. Pauleta still remained as alive as ever, steaming in after a poor touch from Dudek invited pressure only for the Polish stopper to reach the ball marginally ahead of him.

Krzynówek had Poland's best opportunity after running in behind, eventually making a complete mess of the finish, while Kryszałowicz's attempted chip was far from the best. The latter actually got the ball in the net in the 59th minute but it was ruled out as he had barged Baía over before doing so.

Oliveira had clearly seen enough of the game's trajectory and decided to bring Costa into the frame following the incident, as the number ten replaced Pinto. Frechaut was brought off for Beto soon after – a decision that was probably aided by the Boavista man's earlier yellow card.

Costa was getting on the ball from the moment he'd come on and when Olisadebe lost possession, the AC Milan star strode forward with it before offloading to Petit, who had run on the overlap down the right wing. The midfielder then saw Figo running forward and slipped in the talisman, who played a first-time pass into the box where Pauleta was waiting to provide a true poacher's finish. It was a devastatingly efficient move and exactly what the game had needed following the scrappy exchanges earlier on. Pauleta looked understandably delighted with himself as he ran to the fans with his arms out wide.

The two-goal man then made his way behind Poland's defence once again almost immediately. This time, with two defenders for company, he played Figo in but the winger could only find the post as he opened up and unleashed a curling effort. Portugal's number nine was involved in pretty much every attack at this point and a difficult header was directed just above the crossbar as he searched for a hat-trick. There was to be no respite for Poland as Nuno Capucho was brought on in the last of Oliveira's substitutions, replacing Sérgio Conceição.

Perhaps seeing the increased threat Portugal were posing, Engel looked to sure things up at the back and replaced Michał Żewłakow with Tomasz Rząsa in the 71st minute. This didn't work and Pauleta secured his hat-trick just six minutes after the change. Costa was certainly making his impact after coming off the bench and released Pauleta, getting him one on one with Tomasz Wałdoch. Pauleta twisted the centre-back inside out and hit his shot past Dudek's outstretched foot, before bringing out the same celebration that would surely dominate Polish nightmares that evening.

Poland came out and attempted to get back into the game. When they finally got a clear opening, Kryszałowicz blazed his effort over the crossbar from just outside the six-yard box with the goal at his mercy after Baía had been drawn out. At the other end Pauleta proved that he was human after all when he hit the side netting after touching the ball past Dudek.

In the 88th minute Costa added an extra layer of gloss to the scoreline for Portugal as he received the ball in Poland's half, offloaded it to Capucho and broke into the box, where he slid in to convert the return pass. There was a defiance in the celebration as Costa hugged his fellow substitute. He could have even had another before the final whistle, but after he rounded Dudek his weak effort was prevented from crossing the line by the recovering Świerczewski.

As the final whistle blew and the players swapped their rain-soaked shirts, it was the Portuguese who did so with joy. Pauleta was the man grabbing all the headlines but there were plenty more positives for Oliveira: Rui Costa showed his quality off the bench, the defence looked far more solid and kept a clean sheet, and there were plenty of encouraging individual performances to build on against South Korea; of course, the 4-0 scoreline was also something to savour.

## 4

# Group Stage – Matchday Three

*Denmark 2 France 0; Senegal 3 Uruguay 3 (Group A, 11 June, Incheon; Suwon)*

All attention going into these fixtures would have been on France, as the defending world champions had to beat Denmark by two clear goals or they would be out. Roger Lemerre's biggest inclusion was Zinedine Zidane, who was finally making his first appearance of the World Cup after returning from injury. He was joined by Vincent Candela, Claude Makélélé and Christophe Dugarry, with Frank Leboeuf out due to the injury sustained against Uruguay, Emmanuel Petit and Thierry Henry suspended, while Johan Micoud naturally gave way for Zizou. While the French were happy to see their talisman back, Real Madrid weren't as they feared that any possible problems could lead to him missing the start of the season. Morten Olsen made three alterations, bringing Niclas Jensen, Christian Poulsen and Martin Jørgensen in for Jan Heintze, Jesper Grønkjær and Ebbe Sand.

In Suwon, Bruno Metsu was forced into a change with Salif Diao having been sent off against Denmark. Moussa

N'Diaye and Papa Sarr also made way to be replaced by Aliou Cissé, Alassane N'Dour and Henri Camara. Uruguay were the only unchanged team going into Group A's final matchday. Like France, they had to win by two goals to be guaranteed a place in the next round.

It was a quick start to the game in Suwon, especially from referee Jan Wegereef. Within eight minutes Camara had been booked for fouling Darío Silva, Omar Daf received a yellow for sliding in on Gustavo Romero – leaving the right-back visibly frustrated as he pumped the ball into the ground – then Romero was cautioned for tripping Khalilou Fadiga, which meant he would miss the next game if Uruguay progressed.

It was a comparatively slow start in Incheon, where Denmark's five-man midfield did a good job of limiting France's attacking talents but couldn't initially find the quality to release Jon Dahl Tomasson. Dugarry came close to reaching the ball after he initially flicked it up with his shoulder, but Thomas Sørensen got there ahead of him. The French forward then got the game's first booking in the eighth minute for taking the ball out of Stig Tøfting's hands as the Dane attempted to take a quick throw-in.

Zidane was getting on the ball and moving it well, but there was very little conviction in France's play whenever they got near the final third. Arguably the greater concern was that Fabien Barthez looked as though he was carrying an injury – he even received treatment while the game was being played. Still, they had a great chance in the 18th minute after Tomasson conceded possession and René Henriksen slipped while trying to stop the break. Sørensen bailed out his team-mates, doing well to close the angle and eventually hold on to David Trezeguet's effort after the striker had been forced wide.

Uruguay had the better of the early exchanges as they adopted a more attacking style than usual in pursuit of the goals they required, but Senegal really came into things around the quarter-hour mark, hitting the South Americans with some blistering attacks. While Sebastián Abreu's flick almost found Silva inside the Senegalese box, Tony Sylva was looking indomitable and rushed out of his goal to collect it.

It was Senegal's quickness of thought and sloppy defending from Uruguay that delivered the first big chance in Suwon. Captain Paolo Montero was far too casual when knocking the ball back to Fabián Carini and undercooked the pass, giving El Hadji Diouf the opportunity to nip in and go down under pressure from Carini, who got a yellow card. Upon closer inspection it seemed there had been very little contact made. Uruguay tried every delaying tactic in the book and even ran into the box before the whistle was blown, but Fadiga kept his head and coolly sent Carini the wrong way to open the scoring with 20 minutes on the clock. As everyone had come to expect, he celebrated by dancing with his team-mates in the corner.

Elsewhere, in perhaps a sign that Zidane wasn't quite 100 per cent the midfielder received a clipped pass from Patrick Vieira, and while his touch was good he couldn't maintain his balance and the ball rolled out of play. After all of France's intricate build-up and possession, it was the Danes who opened the scoring. Tøfting's long throw wasn't cleared convincingly and the ball fell back to him on the wing. The Bolton Wanderers midfielder then delivered an inch-perfect cross for Dennis Rommedahl, who made no mistake in poking it past Barthez.

As Denmark were putting themselves ahead, Uruguay came close to getting back into their game. Silva was denied by some superb defending from Cissé, who tracked the run and made two blocks near the goal line. Uruguayan frustrations only intensified and it wasn't long until the Africans put themselves further ahead with another special goal to add to their growing collection. The men in green retrieved possession and Daf played a first-time pass to Camara, who skipped past his man with ease before breaking up the field and into Uruguay's box. The Sedan star had the composure to slow down so that his team-mates could catch up and laid the ball off to Papa Bouba Diop, who sent it flying into the top corner with the inside of his right boot. As more dancing ensued among the Senegalese, Uruguay were surely wondering how on earth they could stay in the World Cup from here.

Christian Poulsen was booked for a foul on Bixente Lizarazu in the 27th minute, meaning he would miss the next game should Denmark get through. De rød-hvide were looking the better side after going ahead and Zidane was already beginning to cut a frustrated figure. In fact, Les Bleus seemed deflated in the knowledge that they had to score three times without response. In an embodiment of how the entire team probably felt, Lilian Thuram was running around in a ripped shirt, though it didn't seem clear how it had come to be – he eventually switched tops but it wasn't as easy for the team to patch things up.

They gave Sørensen his biggest test so far after half an hour when Trezeguet headed Dugarry's floating cross towards the bottom corner. Even so, the Sunderland man was able to catch it. The game was soon seemingly revolving around Zidane as he saw more of the ball and brought out some eye-catching trickery, including a flick that the crowd audibly enthused over. He even hit a curling chip from outside the box that left Sørensen flapping at thin air but sailed marginally wide of the top corner.

Uruguay's Victor Púa had clearly seen enough from his side and took action in the 32nd minute, putting the forward Mario Regueiro on for centre-back Gonzalo Sorondo. It was an all-or-nothing game and that was already evident from their approach. The extra attacker didn't help the fact that Uruguay had been second best in so many departments, which showed when Pablo García was booked for taking out Papa Bouba Diop after the Lens midfielder was quicker to a loose ball – meaning García would miss the first knockout game in the increasingly unlikely event that Uruguay got that far.

In the 38th minute, the South Americans' defending wasn't the only reason for confusion. Nobody seemed to know whether or not it was a goal when Papa Bouba Diop got on the end of Camara's cross. First of all, the ball hit the crossbar and went over the line before bouncing back across it for Carini to grab and try to convince the referee that it shouldn't be a goal. Then there was uncertainty around whether Diop had been offside. After consultation with the linesman, both of these decisions went in Senegal's favour and Wegereef awarded the goal.

Ferdinand Coly was booked a minute later for bringing down Regueiro, while Darío Rodriguez was booked seconds later for a dive in Senegal's box that was the epitome of Uruguay's desperation. A display of their frustration soon followed as Recoba tried squaring up to Papa Bouba Diop shortly before Abreu failed to hit the target from a half chance. Then there was a summary of Senegal's far greater authority throughout the whole half when Fadiga tracked back and outmuscled Silva before putting the ball through his legs and clearing. Diouf's showboating when the whistle went was the last straw as Uruguay lost their heads and everyone came together before going down the tunnel.

Denmark hardly had a touch of the ball as half-time approached but defended superbly as individuals and a collective unit, meaning France were unable to carve out any notable opportunities. Perhaps that dynamic was why Barthez wasn't brought off during the break despite clearly struggling with injury, while Olsen changed Jørgensen for Grønkjær.

With nothing to lose apart from dignity, Púa went all out again at half-time, using his final two substitutions to bring Richard Morales and Diego Forlán on for Romero and Abreu. Remarkably, this tactic worked within 15 seconds of the restart as Senegal couldn't clear when the ball was pumped upfield. Forlán smashed his shot against Silva, who then had an effort of his own that Sylva couldn't hold on to and Morales swiftly arrived to convert the rebound. It would take a near-miracle for Uruguay to progress after their shocker of a first half, but as Romero showed his undershirt dedicated to Fabián O'Neill – who went to the World Cup but didn't play – Uruguay now had a glimmer of hope. It wasn't long until Romero's header deflected marginally wide.

There wasn't to be any encouragement for France as Zidane, who still had a strapped up left thigh, could be seen limping within three minutes of the restart. While little could be done to help the midfielder, Marcel Desailly came agonisingly close to getting France back on level terms but his header crashed off the crossbar and back out.

Lemerre's first change in pursuit of a comeback came in the 54th minute with Djibril Cissé replacing Dugarry. France's reigning Young Player of the Year was close to making an immediate impact, getting down the wing well before seeing his cross cut out and then having a venomous strike blocked.

Meanwhile, Senegal momentarily regained a degree of control and began asking questions of Uruguay again, with Diouf's header coming close to finding the top corner. That didn't last long, though, as the South Americans started to apply pressure again with Recoba at the forefront. It took a block with a hint of handball to deny his strike, while Silva couldn't hit the target after a peach of a pass from the talismanic number 20, who was also providing some wonderful pieces of skill.

The game in Incheon opened up as the hour passed with France going all out to get back into the game and revive their fading hopes of staying in the World Cup, while Denmark looked to exploit the spaces left as a consequence. The Danes were the ones to benefit from this pattern of play in the 67th minute. After Rommedahl had won a free kick near the halfway line, the ball was swept across the pitch to Thomas Gravesen, who threaded a wonderful pass through for Grønkjær to run on to. The Chelsea winger didn't have to break stride before delivering the ball across the face of goal, and Tomasson left Desailly on the floor after tugging his shirt and calmly placed his shot into the back of the net for his fourth goal of the tournament. If it needed confirming, this goal made it pretty clear that France were going home.

Even so, Denmark were doing everything in their power to ensure Les Bleus didn't get a sniff of a chance as Olsen's side went for top spot in Group A. That was shown when Jensen was booked for bringing down Cissé. There was nothing more for Lemerre to lose at this point, so he used the break in play to bring the more attack-minded Micoud on for Vieira.

Metsu made two changes in four minutes in an attempt to get Senegal back on top, with Habib Beye and N'Diaye replacing Coly and Camara. It was Púa's substitutions that were paying off, though, and Forlán produced a piece of true magic to get Uruguay right back into the game. Senegal's clearance from Recoba's corner only got as far as the Manchester United striker, who chested it down and sent a sensational volley flying into the top corner, giving Sylva absolutely no chance.

With 21 minutes left, the feeling in Suwon was that anything could happen. There would have also been many wondering why Forlán, the forward with the headband, hadn't played a single minute before this final half of the group stage, while Papa Bouba Diop was booked in the aftermath of the goal. This goal coming after Tomasson's also meant that Denmark were top of the group.

Cissé continued to be France's main threat, and the striker seemingly caught Sørensen by surprise when taking a shot early, with the goalkeeper eventually managing to fumble the ball wide. The look of disbelief on Cissé's face encapsulated how pretty much everyone from France felt. That was only compounded by Trezeguet smashing an effort against the crossbar from inside the box moments later and Wiltord completely missing the ball when attempting a cross before watching it roll out of play.

Olsen was even able to give Kasper Bøgelund and then Brian Steen Nielsen their first minutes of the tournament, as they replaced Poulsen and Tøfting. Nielsen was greeted by Micoud's studs flying towards him within 30 seconds of his introduction.

Denmark were momentarily reduced to ten men when Grønkjær received treatment for an injury, while Youri Djorkaeff replaced Wiltord. The best chance of the latter stages fell to Bøgelund as the PSV Eindhoven man waltzed through the middle of the pitch and played a one-two to find himself in acres of space in the box. His shot was eventually blazed wide.

Metsu made his final change in the 76th minute, attempting to alter the game's flow by bringing Amdy Faye on for N'Dour in the middle of the park. Senegal's best chance to get some comfort came seconds later as Sylva's long kick up the pitch released Diouf behind La Celeste's defence. The only criticism of Senegal's number 11 to this point was that he hadn't scored at the World Cup, and that continued as Carini closed the winger down well.

Having scored to make things interesting, Forlán then had a chance to restore parity seconds after Diouf's wastefulness but dragged his own effort wide. It was clear to see that the 23-year-old knew he should have done better as he kicked out at the advertising boards and just about anything that was on the ground in frustration.

Uruguay kept coming, and Daf made a brilliant tackle to deny Recoba. Montero was seemingly losing his head at the back, though, and the Uruguay captain pulled Diouf to get himself booked seconds after having a go at the linesman – the 21-year-old Diouf also saw yellow for his reaction. Fadiga was booked soon after as he held on to the ball for a bit too long, with Senegal desperately trying to see out the game despite being on the back foot. This had bigger ramifications as it meant Senegal's creative star would miss their round of 16 match.

It was also proven worthless within seconds when Uruguay were awarded a penalty after Morales went down under pressure from Beye, who was booked for either the tackle or his protestations. Despite this, his annoyance proved warranted as the substitute had gone down without being touched at all. Recoba stepped up and despite Sylva delaying the penalty, the Internazionale midfielder kept his head long enough to slot the ball away and equalise in the 89th minute. Recoba raced to the ball and tried to kick it back towards the centre circle as Uruguay chased victory, but Sylva got in the way.

Strangely, instead of looking to keep hold of the ball from the kick-off, Senegal smashed it straight out of play and invited more pressure. They were simply booting and heading the ball as far away from their goal as possible at this point but conceded a free kick in the 91st minute. The frantic end was encapsulated by Recoba and Garcia arguing over who would take it, with the latter using his greater physical stature to stand in the way. He soon incurred Recoba's wrath after hitting the wall with his shot.

There was an even better chance to come. Sylva had come flying off his line but got nowhere near the ball as it was cleared, so Gustavo Varela smashed it from range and Lamine Diatta got down for a header which ballooned into the air as the goalkeeper scrambled to get back. With Sylva having also dived for the initial shot, Morales had the goal at his mercy as the ball fell back down to earth, but the man who had started Uruguay's comeback somehow headed wide.

As the final whistle blew moments later, Senegal looked both delighted and drained in equal measure after hanging on to earn a point from a sensational match. The most important thing for the Africans was that they had managed to reach the knockout rounds in what was their first World Cup – a remarkable achievement given the history of the sides going out of Group A. Meanwhile, Uruguay were left to look around regrettably after their terrible first-half performance left them with too much to do in the second period.

Things had slowed down considerably in Incheon. Makélélé kept working and sent an effort just wide, but many of the French looked resigned to their fate as the full-time whistle approached. When it was finally blown, Denmark could celebrate a thoroughly deserved three points won through a performance that showed superb organisation and determination. Meanwhile, the French were left to commiserate themselves for what was deemed a national embarrassment, especially as Les Bleus failed to score a single goal across their three games. For added context, Brazil's team of 1966 were the last reigning world champions to falter at the first round of the next tournament.

Lemerre resisted calls to resign and was eventually sacked less than a month later, with it being reported that he had been negotiating a €2m redundancy payment. The French Federation's president Claude Simonet said, 'Roger Lemerre has been discharged of his mission as the national coach. He will continue to sit on the national coaching management body'. Though he did add, 'I can't say that Roger Lemerre was at fault'.

*Cameroon 0 Germany 2; Saudi Arabia 0 Republic of Ireland 3 (Group E, 11 June, Shizuoka; Yokohama)*
The results from the first two rounds of Group E games meant the final set of fixtures was wonderfully poised to be entertaining and intriguing. Cameroon and Germany went in occupying the top two spots, both with four points to their name. However they both knew that they would likely need

to get a result to progress as the Republic of Ireland were the favourites against Saudi Arabia.

Ireland and Germany kept the same sides that had played out their 1-1 draw. Cameroon manager Winfried Schäfer, who was coming up against his home nation, brought Daniel Kome back in for Salomon Olembé while Saudi Arabia replaced Abdullah Al-Waked and the injured Obeid Al-Dosari with Khamis Al-Dosari and Al Hasan Al-Yami.

In Yokohama, Mick McCarthy had asked for a bright start from his side and that was exactly what he got. Just seven minutes into proceedings, Steve Staunton swept a brilliant ball from the halfway line to just wide of the box, finding Gary Kelly. After the ball bounced, Kelly scooped it high into the air towards Robbie Keane who, having already looked dangerous, watched it on to his foot and controlled his volley magnificently, striking an effort that found its way into the net despite Mohamed Al-Deayea getting a hand to it. As he went off to bring out the usual celebration, Keane was mobbed by his team-mates in a fashion that showed how important that early goal was.

Cameroon were coming under most of the early pressure in Shizuoka but the greatest scare actually came from their own captain, Rigobert Song, whose attempt at clearing Christian Ziege's cross fizzed up off his foot and over the crossbar. There were also signs that things would be combative when Lauren reacted angrily to an especially strong challenge from Torsten Frings that completely missed the ball.

By the ninth minute Marc-Viven Foé had been booked for a high sliding tackle on Frings, while Carsten Jancker got the same punishment for kicking Song in the arm as the centre-back went up for a header. It was going to be a busy day for referee Antonio López Nieto. It was clear that it would be for Song too, as he got his head on to a free kick and ended up converting it on to the roof of his own net.

Cameroon offered a reminder that they could pose a threat of their own a quarter of an hour in: Olembé completely fooled the German defence when he played a one-two with Samuel Eto'o and burst behind them. However, the winger's weak effort wasn't enough to get past Oliver Kahn. While his follow-up was almost deflected in off the goalkeeper's hand, Kahn eventually grabbed hold of the ball.

There was yet another coming together as Eto'o confronted Bernd Schneider after the German attempted to score from the halfway line despite Song being on the floor with a bloody nose, which had been inflicted by Miroslav Klose accidentally stepping on it.

The Irish didn't let up after their goal, especially as they needed another to go through if things stayed level elsewhere. Damien Duff was looking especially dangerous at stages, pulling off a nice piece of skill to beat Abdullah Zubromawi before putting in a cross that Al-Deayea was just about able to collect. The men in white struggled to create much, though, as Abdulaziz Al-Khathran hit an effort from range in the 22nd minute that Shay Given held with ease.

Kahn wasn't quite as comfortable when he dealt with Pierre Womé's free kick. The wing-back fizzed the ball towards goal, causing Kahn to attempt a punch rather than catching it. Having come off his gloves, the ball then bounced off Christoph Metzelder and just wide of the goal – to Kahn and Germany's relief. They were fortunate again moments later as Song was completely unmarked in the middle of their box but still put his header wide.

The cards were soon flowing again when Dietmar Hamann was booked for a sliding tackle on Foé in the 29th minute – meaning he would miss the next game if Germany got through – while Michael Ballack joined him in the book just two minutes later for a challenge on Lauren. Womé could consider himself lucky not to have at least got a booking having caught Klose with his arm during an aerial challenge, the wing-back then jumped over the striker's body and landed on his head. The German feeling was reflected when they returned the ball to Cameroon by putting it out for a throw-in near the corner after the African side had kicked it out.

It wasn't long until there was yet another coming together between the two sets of players, with Foé, Ballack and Jancker central figures this time. Ziege showed some calm with a free kick that was destined for the top corner but Alioum Boukar scrambled back to tip it over the bar.

Despite that momentary showing of composure, it felt as though it was only a matter of time until somebody took things too far and Carsten Ramelow was the man to do so. His first yellow came for a poor challenge through the back of Eto'o in the 37th minute. Then the centre-back was booked for another challenge on the Real Mallorca star just three minutes later, this time bringing the striker down as the ball was shifted out of his reach.

Moments later, Song and Kahn were both booked after they squared up to each other – there weren't too many who chose to go head-to-head with the Bayern Munich stopper down the years. The first half had descended into chaos with various players losing their heads. It seemed the referee was also losing his, harshly booking Bill Tchato shortly before the break.

There was a very different game in Yokohama, but McCarthy wouldn't have been happy with what he was seeing as Saudi Arabia were given hope of getting back into things.

Al-Yami came close to dancing through the Irish defence while inside the box in the 38th minute, but the 29-year-old was eventually crowded out and Staunton did well to recover and steal the ball after initially being beaten. This was a sign that the Saudis were lifting their levels ahead of half-time and Mohammed Al-Jahani then got behind Ireland's defence but couldn't beat Given from a tight angle. Al-Khathran came close to creating another chance for himself with an intelligent flick in the box seconds before the break until Given came out to help his defence.

Ireland may have still been winning, but in *Ireland's World Cup 2002*, McCarthy states that he was 'livid' and that there was 'some very straight talking' in the changing room. With things still level in Shizuoka they needed another goal, and the manager took matters into his own hands with a substitution. Ian Harte had received a knock that agitated an existing injury so was brought off, Kevin Kilbane dropped from the left wing to left-back, Duff went out wide and Niall Quinn went up top next to Keane.

Rudi Völler also recognised that he needed to make a change after a first half that had been characterised by fouls and hot-headedness rather than real quality. He opted to take off Jancker, who had come to represent the game's nature, replacing him with Marco Bode.

Saudi Arabia had a fairly scrappy start to the second half, as was displayed by Redha Tukar slicing his clearance back to his goalkeeper, who then made a mess of his own clearance up the pitch. Duff was the man looking to capitalise on that frailty the most and could have had an assist when Keane's effort on the spin came agonisingly close. The striker would go on to have two more chances in quick succession that he was unable to finish.

It was the Cameroonians who were left to rue their missed opportunities, though, as Völler's substitution paid off. The Africans were playing the ball around nicely until Klose nipped in to capitalise on a loose pass, brought it down and lured the defenders towards him before playing in Bode. The striker had only been on for five minutes but made no mistake, placing his shot past Boukar with a first-time finish. The belly slide that celebrated the game's opener spoke of relief that Germany were ahead despite not being at their best in the first period. Schäfer responded almost immediately, taking centre-back Tchato off for the more attacking option of Patrick Suffo.

Foé gave the ball away in a dangerous area soon afterwards, but Germany were unable to make the most of the error this time around as they were crowded out. Much to his disbelief, Geremi then picked up the game's tenth yellow card for taking a free kick too early. It was only a couple of minutes until Olembé made it a full 11 for stopping Schneider breaking up the pitch by bringing him down.

Elsewhere, despite Saudi Arabia having periods of possession, they were struggling to trouble the Irish. Nawaf Al-Temyat showed this when he was chasing Kilbane and brought the winger-turned-full-back down with a nudge, earning himself the game's first yellow just after the hour mark. The caution wasn't to be his only punishment as Gary Breen lost his marker to get on the end of Staunton's fizzed-in cross and gracefully turned it into the bottom corner.

The goal had the finish of a man who regularly scored but the celebration of somebody who didn't, Breen looking around in disbelief with his hands in the air. Regardless of who scored or how the ball went in, the important thing for Ireland was that even a Cameroon equaliser against Germany wouldn't stop them going through as long as they didn't concede.

The Boys in Green weren't about to rest on their laurels. Some brilliant work from Kelly down the right created a chance for Quinn on the volley moments after the celebrations had stopped, but the striker couldn't find the target. There was still a potential scare for McCarthy when Given ran out to punch the ball and it came to Al-Jahani, but the wing-back's tame attempt was collected by the goalkeeper.

There may not have been another goal in Shizuoka but there were soon to be more cards. Just seven minutes after coming on to the pitch, Suffo went into the book for bringing Bode down. Then, as had been the case throughout the tournament, Schäfer switched Olembé and N'Gom Kome once again.

In an attempt to get his side back into their game, Naser Al-Johar made two substitutions of his own within a minute of each other, swapping Mohammad Al-Shalhoub (who was referred to as 'Baby Maradona' by some in the Gulf region) and Abdullah Jumaan Al-Dosari for Al-Khathran and Zubromawi.

Staunton was the first Irishman to get booked, doing so in the 70th minute for not taking a free kick quickly enough for referee Falla N'Doye's liking. Al-Dosari, who wore his middle name, Gaman, on his back, showed flair when he turned away from Steve Finnan and put the ball through Mark Kinsella's legs but eventually sent his shot sailing over the bar. Al-Yami tried a looping header moments later but it was no trouble for Given.

The Saudis were looking more comfortable again, even if any true cutting edge was still evading them, but this perhaps suited the Irish just as much as it did the men in white. The Saudis gave the ball away in a cheap area and Duff's cross that came as a result of his burst forward was inches away from finding a green head, eventually being met by Al-Deayea's gloves.

There was still far more aggression than quality being shown between Germany and Cameroon – this time with a north London tint – as Tottenham Hotspur's Ziege was booked for holding on to Arsenal right-back Lauren's shirt. The pair squared up and said some venomous words before eventually being separated. Cameroon came the closest they had been all game from the ensuing free kick as Lauren rose highest to meet Geremi's cross and directed it on to the post. Patrick M'Boma came in with a follow-up but Kahn was able to pounce on the ball.

Yet another yellow card soon arrived, this time for Frings after he tripped N'Gom Kome when the winger skipped past him. Another came in the 77th minute and led to Suffo receiving his marching orders less than half an hour after coming on, for sliding in on Ballack without reaching the ball – the chaos continuing while legendary referee Pierluigi Collina acted as the fourth official.

Cameroon hadn't done enough to take advantage of having an extra man, but it took Germany just moments to capitalise on the numbers being equalled. After knocking the ball about, Hamann burst forward and offloaded it to Ballack on the right. He used the space afforded to him to cross for Klose and the striker was never going to miss with his header. Klose didn't bring out his front flip this time, instead throwing a fist into the air.

Jens Jeremies was brought on immediately after the goal, replacing Schneider. Likely taking out the frustrations of

Cameroon's exit now seeming inevitable, Lauren made it eight cards each when he got a yellow for a seriously poor challenge on Hamann. Cameroon made their final change by replacing M'Boma with Joseph Désiré Job – who hadn't played a single World Cup minute up until this point. Oliver Neuville was eventually brought on to replace Klose for Germany.

Saudi Arabia also made their final change with just over ten minutes left, taking Al-Jahani off for Ahmed Doki. McCarthy then replaced Kelly with Jason McAteer – when the officials allowed him, which they puzzlingly didn't at first.

In the 87th minute Ireland added an extra layer of gloss to their result and compounded Saudi Arabia's misery. After some neat play, Matt Holland slipped the ball behind the Saudi defence for Duff to run on to and strike. In truth it wasn't his greatest attempt of the tournament, but there was enough on it for the ball to squeeze through Al-Deayea's hands and over the line for his first goal. Duff didn't care how it went in, putting his hands together and bowing before jubilantly putting his arms in the air and being congratulated by his team-mates.

Ballack almost equalled Ireland's scoreline with a great header, but Boukar pulled off an equally brilliant save to deny the midfielder and keep hold of the ball. Job had the ball in the net soon afterwards with a flicked header but was blatantly offside.

There was a nice touch from McCarthy, who gave Lee Carsley his first World Cup minutes towards the end, bringing the midfielder on for Kinsella after he had 'kept his head down and worked hard all trip without as much as a single moan'.

The Irish fans were in full voice as the game drew to a close, and there was a massive roar when the final whistle set Ireland's round of 16 place in stone. There was also a big charge on to the pitch from the bench as everyone associated with the Republic of Ireland celebrated. McCarthy had opened the group stages with questions surrounding his tenure after everything that had happened with Roy Keane; he ended them by turning down somebody from Saudi Arabia who asked if he would be willing to manage their team after they had finished without any points or goals, as written in *Ireland's World Cup 2002*.

Over in Shizuoka, Jeremies came close with a strong strike from range but Boukar was able to tip it over the crossbar. It then wasn't long until Nieto eventually blew the full-time whistle, putting an end to a game that would be remembered more for his over-enthusiastic refereeing and players losing their heads rather than showings of quality. For Germany, all that mattered as their players applauded the fans was that they topped Group E and progressed to the knockout stage. Meanwhile, Cameroon missed out and would be going home despite their early promise.

### Sweden 1 Argentina 1; Nigeria 0 England 0 (Group F, 12 June, Miyagi; Osaka)

The 'Group of Death' was coming to an end and everybody other than Nigeria had a chance of progressing. That the Africans had still made a memorable contribution with their flair and quality in the first two games, despite not earning a point, spoke volumes about the strength of the group.

In Miyagi, Lars Lagerbäck and Tommy Söderberg only made one change for group leaders Sweden, replacing the unavailable Freddie Ljungberg with Magnus Svensson. With

Marcelo Bielsa knowing that his Argentina side needed to win to progress, El Loco made four changes, taking out Diego Placente, Diego Simeone, Juan Sebastián Verón and Kily González for José Chamot, Matias Almeyda, Pablo Aimar and Claudio López.

With nothing but pride on the line, Super Eagles boss Festus Onigbinde made five changes, including 19-year-old goalkeeper Vincent Enyeama coming in for Ike Shorunmu. Meanwhile, in the knowledge that only a draw was required to be guaranteed a place in the knockout rounds, Sven-Göran Eriksson started Trevor Sinclair, who had come on for Owen Hargreaves following the Bayern Munich man's injury against Argentina.

After the English national anthem was played twice – not for the first time this tournament – Jay-Jay Okocha immediately showed his quality on the ball with some great trickery before switching the play, while Paul Scholes sent the game's first shot wide. Both teams played probing balls into the box that couldn't quite reach their attackers. When Nigeria eventually found Julius Aghahowa inside the penalty area, he was crowded out well by Sol Campbell and Ashley Cole.

Meanwhile, Argentina showed good early intent as a strong defensive header from Andreas Jakobsson was required to deny Juan Pablo Sorín's dangerous cross after mere seconds. While the South Americans were going for it the application wasn't quite there, as shown when Gabriel Batistuta blasted a free kick well over the crossbar.

Still, they were showing more than Sweden in the early stages, their first shot coming from Anders Svensson ten minutes in but trickling harmlessly wide. Sorín was proving particularly threatening for the Argentines, and the Cruzeiro man forced a good save from Magnus Hedman with a strong header from Ariel Ortega's cross. Once again it was Sorín getting his head on the ball a few minutes later, this time sending his effort over the crossbar.

England's best chance of the first quarter of an hour fell to Rio Ferdinand after Enyeama failed to convincingly deal with David Beckham's corner, but the centre-back saw his effort blocked. The first notable save in Osaka came from Enyeama after Danny Mills had got to the byline and delivered a cross to Emile Heskey, and while the striker did well to reach it the eventual effort failed to trouble the 19-year-old.

Argentina were often opting to find space in wide areas and deliver crosses into the box, but the Swedes were doing a brilliant job of nullifying any potential danger. Even so, there were times that Argentina got there first, and another flicked Sorín header whistled past the post with Batistuta coming agonisingly close to latching on to it.

Sweden were offering very little in attack, as was summarised by Anders Svensson attempting a switch but coming nowhere near finding a team-mate. Argentina were doing pretty much all of the probing with Javier Zanetti proving instrumental in various progressions up the pitch. Just before the half-hour, Claudio López had some of the Argentine fans momentarily celebrating before realising the winger had only sent his volley into the side netting.

After a period in which Nigeria had more of the ball than England but were unable to create, there was a slight break in play when Aghahowa went down under pressure from Campbell. They then gave England a scare as Nicky Butt caught Ifeanyi Udeze on the edge of the box, though the Nigerian had already started going down after treading on the ball. David Seaman couldn't keep hold of Okocha's initial free kick, and Aghahowa rushed in as the Arsenal man patted the ball down but could only steer his shot wide.

Michael Owen had been very quiet before the 35th minute but went on a brilliant mazy run that was similar to his one against Argentina. His effort didn't hit the post this time and Joseph Yobo raced across to put in an impressive block. The defender had got so close to Owen to make the intervention that referee Brian Hall somehow didn't see it and awarded a goal kick. Things were beginning to get fairly end-to-end now and Benedict Akwuegbu drove forward into the box impressively but shot straight at Seaman from a tight angle.

In Miyagi, Zanetti was soon back causing problems. The Internazionale star reached the byline before trying a cut-back that Johan Mjällby prevented at the expense of a corner, which was dealt with easily. Five minutes before the break, Sweden had their best opportunity of the half as Walter Samuel fouled Marcus Allbäck from behind. In an encapsulation of an anticlimactic first half, Henrik Larsson hit the wall with his ensuing strike. López had a chance just moments later but went for power from an awkward angle and blazed his shot just off target.

England had the better of the chances in the first half's latter stages and Nigeria survived a scramble in their box before Butt fired his effort over, Mills smashed his strike well over after a nice lay-off from Sinclair and Paul Scholes's venomous shot was superbly tipped on to the post by Enyeama. The final chance fell to Heskey who couldn't find the target with his header.

In one of the biggest moments of first-half entertainment in either of the two games, Argentina's Claudio Caniggia was sent off despite sitting on the bench and not having played a single minute all tournament. The Argentines were aggrieved that Ortega hadn't been awarded a free kick after going down, then a similar incident had gone the way of Anders Svensson seconds later. After saying something to the officials, referee Ali Bujsaim brought out his red card, leaving Rangers forward Caniggia to walk off with an embarrassed look resembling a naughty student being sent out of class.

The whistle was then blown again to mark half-time. Sweden had offered very little in an attacking sense, but with the scores level in both games the two European sides were set to progress. Lagerbäck and Söderberg opted to make a change before the restart, with Andreas Andersson replacing Allbäck – as had been the case in both of their previous matches.

Argentina continued to have the better of the ball in the second half's early stages but Pablo Cavallero gave Larsson momentary encouragement, as a poor touch from the goalkeeper made the Celtic striker pounce towards him. In the end, the Celta Vigo man was able to get off a panicked clearance.

There was also an early second-half mistake in Osaka as Campbell undercooked his pass to Ferdinand, allowing Aghahowa to nip in and drive towards goal. Things were soon made right when the centre-backs crowded him out with the help of Mills before getting a block in and Seaman was even able to get across and stop the ball going out for a corner. Not too long after that, Isaac Okoronkwo almost released Owen while stretching to make a header but his centre-back partner Yobo recovered well to prevent the danger. Owen was then inches from converting a Heskey cross.

In the 55th minute in Miyagi, Chamot got himself booked for using his hand to block the ball as Anders

Svensson attempted to flick it past him to start a rare Swedish attack. Svensson took it himself, and the free kick being far out didn't stop him going for the shot. In the end it fizzed past the left post after sending Cavallero scrambling across his goal.

Within a couple of minutes Svensson was driving his team forward again, with Almeyda taking the booking this time after catching the back of his heel. This free kick was a little bit closer, and there was a delay as Batistuta was taken off for Hernán Crespo after the Argentine protestations against the foul had come to an end. This time, Larsson dummied and Svensson went for the left, directing his effort just inside the post for a wonderful goal despite Cavallero getting a touch on the ball. The Southampton man ran off to celebrate before dropping to the floor and disappearing under a bundle.

Argentina had been on top for almost all of the match but now required two goals in half an hour to go through. Bielsa went for it almost immediately, bringing Verón and González on for Almeyda and Sorín with the latter having faded after his encouraging start.

For a short while the game actually felt more open than it had at any other point, with Sweden freed of the mental shackles that came with one goal being enough to knock them out. There was still care being taken to ensure they weren't hit quickly, and Magnus Svensson was booked for time-wasting as he kicked the ball away in the 65th minute. That was soon followed by Sweden's second change of the game, Anders Svensson making way for Mattias Jonson.

There was a substitute at a similar time in Osaka, where the game had tamely ticked along with very little goalmouth action. Whether it was an effort to change that fact or to simply get some more minutes into Teddy Sheringham's legs, the veteran replaced Heskey. Scholes went on a surging run through the middle but ran in a straight line the entire time and was eventually thwarted by Okoronkwo on the edge of Nigeria's box.

While Argentina were back on the ball regularly as their game approached its final 20 minutes, the men in yellow and blue were putting in a superb defensive display. This meant that the majority of Argentina's moves included delivering balls from wide or deep areas, which had rarely worked all game because of Sweden's dominance in the air.

Substitute Jonson released some of the pressure with a spirited run up the wing before delivering a low cross into the box. Mauricio Pochettino wildly tried to hack it clear only to send it flying towards his own goal. Luckily for him, it went flying off Cavallero's chest and away to safety. This wouldn't have done much for the nerves of Batistuta and his fellow Argentines in the dugout, as they were visibly anxious while watching on.

There was very little happening in the game between England and Nigeria although, with a quarter of an hour remaining, the men in green almost released Aghahowa, forcing Seaman to rush out and unorthodoxly tip the ball on to his own head and out of danger – eventually passing to Beckham having ended up outside his box.

Sheringham had a glorious chance seconds later after Owen's poor touch from Ashley Cole's cross saw the ball fall to him in the box, but the substitute made a complete mess of it. This was Owen's last contribution and he was brought off for Darius Vassell with 13 minutes on the clock.

La Albiceleste were now looking desperate in both attack and defence, with a last-ditch tackle needed to deny Niklas

Alexandersson before González was booked for taking out Larsson. The Celtic striker was back on the floor soon afterwards, having single-handedly led a break by racing up the pitch and being barged over by González. The Argentine substitute would have feared a second yellow card but it was somehow Larsson who ended up in the referee's book and conceding a free kick.

Sweden had another chance to remove any doubt that they would win as Jonson was played behind again, but his ensuing ball into the box was too close to Cavallero. Within seconds Aimar was firing a ball across the box that Jakobsson once again did brilliantly to get a foot on.

It said a lot about Nigeria's game against England that the closest anyone came to a goal was a cross. In the 79th minute Cole had torn down the line and smashed the ball into the box with a first-time effort from the byline. Enyeama took a step out in anticipation but the ball swung back towards the goal and eventually skipped across the entire crossbar before going behind. There were two more substitutions as the game crawled to a close, with Wayne Bridge replacing Cole and Pius Ikedia coming on for Femi Opabunmi.

Zanetti had Argentina's best effort of the game so far in the 83rd minute, latching on to a loose ball and smashing a half-volley that forced a good save from Hedman. Sweden came close to a second moments later when Andersson forced his way into the box well but saw his shot tipped on to the woodwork by Cavallero, while Larsson wasn't able to get the follow-up.

To step things up another level in what had already been a frantic ending, Argentina were awarded a penalty in the 88th minute after Ortega went over Jonson's outstretched leg in the box. Ortega took it himself, although he was made to wait as

Larsson came off for 20-year-old Zlatan Ibrahimović. His initial effort was saved but Crespo converted the rebound, having run into the box well before the ball was kicked and being pretty much in line with Ortega by the time the penalty was taken.

Argentina didn't have much time but they now had hope, especially with four minutes being added on. They launched attack after attack in an effort to secure the win they needed, and López brought another scream from supporters by hitting the side netting with a venomous strike again. The South Americans were displaying pure desperation as the belief seeped out of them with the final whistle approaching.

When it finally came the Argentines could be seen sinking to the floor while Swedes jubilantly jumped on each other. The cruel nature of football was there for all to see as Batistuta bent over in tears, the last image the world would see of the great striker in an Argentina shirt. Ultimately, Sweden had defended well enough to earn their place in the knockout rounds, and despite being among the favourites to win the whole tournament Argentina were going home.

Meanwhile, Nigeria had their first point of the World Cup and England went through, so everyone was left relatively happy, if not completely. There was criticism of the Three Lions as it was felt that they could have gone for it more with top spot up for grabs.

As Scott Murray put it on *The Guardian*'s live blog of the game, 'That's it, England are through, and they're playing Denmark. Is there anything to say about this game? Nope. Oh hold on, there's one thing: if England had won, they wouldn't have been able to face Brazil until the semis. Now they're lined up to meet in the quarters'.

*South Africa 2 Spain 3; Slovenia 1 Paraguay 3 (Group B, 12 June, Daejeon; Seogwipo)*

The impetus was on South Africa going into the final round of Group B games as any result against Spain would see them through. Jomo Sono kept the exact same team that had overcome Slovenia, while Spain had made eight changes. It would be harsh to suggest that José Antonio Camacho was fielding a weak side, as Fernando Morientes had already shown that he could score on this stage and was joined by Real Madrid's Iván Helguera and Barcelona's Xavi, while they still had Raúl up front.

Over in Seogwipo, Slovenia had no hope of getting through and there were plenty of changes. There was so much unrest within the squad that there were reports that with the game being on the Wednesday, some players were willing to downgrade their flights to leave South Korea earlier than their planned Saturday departure. Alexander Knavs missed out through injury but there were three more changes in personnel. There was even a change in the dugout as Danilo Popivoda took charge after Srečko Katanec's dismissal against Spain. Meanwhile, Paraguay would have been keeping an eye on the result in Daejeon but primarily had to sort out their own business, and Cesare Maldini only made one alteration to his team: Diego Gavilán replacing Guido Alvarenga.

Goals were exactly what Paraguay needed and it took just seconds to highlight that they would have chances to get them as a long ball forward found Roque Santa Cruz in space in the box. He couldn't quite get his head around the ball to guide it towards goal, however. It was clear that their aim was to dominate from the beginning but Carlos Paredes took that a step too far when he was booked for a foul on Miran Pavlin four minutes in.

In the same minute, Bafana Bafana – more specifically their goalkeeper, Andre Arendse – got off to a truly horrible start. When Arendse dived on to a misplaced through pass from Morientes, what should have been a simple collection somehow saw the ball slip through his fingers. Hardly believing his luck, Raúl got the loose ball, took a couple of strides forward and passed it into the empty net.

South Africa responded strongly and it wasn't long until MacBeth Sibaya was letting off one of his thunderous strikes. Unluckily for the midfielder, this one was straight at Iker Casillas who punched it away. South Africa were up against an incredibly talented Spain side and Joaquín carved their defence apart with a small slice of luck before setting up Gaizka Mendieta who eventually saw his shot cleared off the line by Aaron Mokoena.

Another sign that South Africa were struggling to deal with Spain's attack came in the 16th minute, when Cyril Nzama picked up a caution for sliding in on Mendieta as the winger spun away from him, getting nowhere near the ball. If the Spaniard's shot a few minutes later was anything to go by, he needn't have bothered as the defence had parted ways before Mendieta struck an awful effort that went well wide.

Paraguay had their chances to take the lead, with José Cardozo glancing a header wide and José Luis Chilavert's balls from deep making life awkward for Slovenia defenders – one of which came from a free kick after Pavlin was cautioned for sliding in on Roberto Acuña from behind. Things became far more difficult for the South Americans in the 22nd minute as Paredes received a second yellow for recklessly fouling Milenko Ačimovič. The lack of protestations and a guilty look on the midfielder's face spoke volumes about the incident. Some things never changed, though, and when

Paraguay got a free kick on the edge of the box Chilavert was the man taking it – this time it came off the top of the wall before being cleared.

In the other game, Arendse went some way to redeeming himself by leaping across the goal line to superbly save Morientes's header, which had seemed destined for the back of the net. That save looked even better moments later as South Africa shocked their opponents and most of the world by grabbing an equaliser just after the half-hour mark. Siyabonga Nomvethe did brilliantly to reach Quinton Fortune's cross and head it down for Benni McCarthy. Nomvethe's strike partner showed his predatory instinct and got to the ball ahead of Casillas as it slowly dropped, volleying it past the goalkeeper and into the back of the net.

Despite being a man down, Paraguay continued to create opportunities: long-range efforts from Francisco Arce and Alvarenga forced awkward saves from Mladen Dabanovič, Cardozo peeled away before getting a good header off, while Santa Cruz's header was deflected over the bar. In addition, there were problems for Slovenia – who had offered little so far – as Pavlin was forced off through injury and replaced by Mladen Rudonja.

The equaliser gave South Africa a very obvious boost of confidence, with McCarthy pulling off a nice flick and Bradley Carnell providing a good piece of skill to get out of a tricky situation. The game was now far more even than it had been beforehand but Mendieta ensured that the teams wouldn't go into the break on level terms in the first minute of added time. Having won a free kick on the edge of the box after being fouled by Nzama, the Lazio man took it himself. The wall was edging forward but this tactic was futile as Mendieta sent his effort beyond the goalkeeper, leaving him completely wrong-footed and stuck watching the ball glide past him. Scored in the first minute of injury time, this proved to be one of the last kicks of the first period in Daejeon.

Despite their enforced change, Slovenia finally looked like they were enjoying themselves as the half-time whistle approached. Rudonja made a good run up the left before getting a shot off, Sebastjan Cimirotič danced through the defence before being impressively denied by Chilavert, while it took a last-ditch tackle to prevent Milan Osterc getting through.

All of this spelt disaster for Paraguay in the very same minute Mendieta's goal had given them hope. Ačimovič danced through the red and white defence before driving the ball across goal but in trying to cut it out Chilavert could only deflect the pass into his own net, leaving the Tottenham Hotspur man to celebrate by revealing an undershirt with his baby on. After the game, Ačimovič admitted, 'I'm happy to score against the great Chilavert, it was a great feeling'.

There was another scare before half-time when Chilavert had to come out and smother Osterc to prevent the striker getting a clear chance. Paraguay were given the opportunity to regroup seconds later, though, as the whistle went. There was plenty of chat about South Africa's result in the build-up but going behind meant Paraguay now had to get into the lead before even considering what was happening in Daejeon.

The last thing they wanted to do was gift Slovenia another goal, but that's what Julio César Cáceres almost did after allowing himself to be dispossessed by Rudonja. Even after being saved by Chilavert the centre-back didn't learn his lesson, dawdling on the ball before handing possession back to Slovenia high up the pitch – Paraguay and Cáceres eventually got away with it. Chilavert had a near miss of his own seconds later, when a terrible first touch allowed Osterc to steal the ball but the striker slipped as he lifted his leg to swipe it into the empty net.

Mendieta's goal didn't seem to dent South African confidence too much and Bafana Bafana came out strongly in the second half. Perhaps in response to this, Camacho opted to bring on Sergio for David Albelda just eight minutes after the break. The first challenge after the substitution was a corner, and an unconvincing Spanish header flicked the initial delivery towards Lucas Radebe. The Leeds United man made no mistake, sending a header of his own just inside the post and past Casillas's flailing arms – sparking wild celebrations that included the centre-back being bundled by his team-mates.

However, parity only lasted for three minutes. After Spain had sprung up the left they switched the ball to Joaquín, who sent a cross in from deep towards Raúl. The striker masterfully peeled off Radebe's shoulder and powered his header past Arendse's outstretched hand.

Meanwhile, Slovenia's confidence was clear to see as Ačimovič curled an effort on to the crossbar – leaving Chilavert sweating as he stood and watched it fly through the air – while Cimirotič produced a nice piece of skill before having his shot saved. In an effort to change the game's flow, Alvarenga was brought off for the more attacking Jorge Campos in the 54th minute.

As news started to roll in from Seogwipo, Nelson Cuevas – who hadn't played a single minute of the World Cup up until now – replaced Cardozo; it seemed urgency was making way for desperation. Nastja Čeh was brought on for Ačimovič, who had a rare moment to take in Slovenian applause after scoring their only goal of the tournament so far.

After being in the shadows for so much of this tournament, it took Cuevas just five minutes to put himself firmly in the spotlight. The River Plate striker received the ball under pressure by the corner flag but immediately drove inwards to beat a defender, jinked his way past another and completely wrong-footed Dabanovič – leaving the goalkeeper on the floor while the ball went over the line. Suddenly, Paraguay had hope.

Having been the first man to get South Africa back on level terms, McCarthy came close to doing it again but his powerful effort from just outside the box went narrowly wide. At the other end, Joaquín had Carnell firmly on the ropes now and beat the left-back at pretty much every attempt. It got to the stage where Carnell was bringing Spain's number 22 down just to stop him running through. After one particularly blatant hack in the 67th minute, the Stuttgart defender finally received a yellow card. The men in yellow and green now appeared desperate and Nomvethe was booked for a lunge on Helguera a couple of minutes later – it wasn't long until he was brought off for George Koumantarakis.

There had been a clear shift in momentum in Seogwipo with Paraguay continuing to come forward and Cuevas troubled Dabanovič once again. Amir Karić resorted to kicking chunks out of the substitute and getting a yellow card; Rudonja's tactic was to pull Cuevas's shirt and trip him, but the outcome was the same. Cuevas was causing complete havoc, and plenty of onlookers would have been wondering why he wasn't used earlier.

The game was now wide open with Slovenia risking it all in an attempt to claim their first World Cup win, while

Spain being in the lead gave Paraguay a glimmer of hope that they could still progress. Osterc was the main European threat and his deflected cross went off the top of the crossbar before staying in play.

It was Paraguay – thanks to another substitute – who took the lead in the 74th minute via a Campos strike from range. It wasn't the most powerful of shots but the direction allowed it to roll past Dabanovič's fingertips and into the bottom corner. As Campos took off his shirt and dropped to his knees before looking to the sky, it was apparent that he didn't care in the slightest how the goal had been scored. It meant that either one more from Spain or Paraguay would see the South Americans through.

There was a break in play in Daejeon as Radebe was treated for a head injury that eventually forced him off to be replaced by Thabang Molefe. Camacho used that break to make a change of his own, with Albert Luque replacing Morientes.

The Spanish substitute was involved immediately as he was released behind a South Africa defence that was still adjusting to losing their captain, but Luque's effort was impressively saved by Arendse. South Africa were struggling to get any real foothold on the game, and Mokoena was booked for flying through Mendieta while attempting to win the ball back.

There was also another booking for Slovenia when Željko Milinovič took his turn to foul Cuevas. It may have been far out but Chilavert came up to take the free kick and only had eyes for goal, backing his technique with good reason. The 36-year-old sent a powerful strike curling towards the target but Dabanovič was able to get the slightest of touches on the ball to tip it on to the bar and over. The disbelief was clear for Chilavert as he jogged back to his goal, which was worsened by the fact this effort would have made him the first goalkeeper to score at a World Cup finals. The stopper didn't lose his head, though, denying Cimirotič at the other end moments later.

Paraguay were given a boost in the 81st minute when the numbers were levelled as just 19 minutes after coming on, Nastja Čeh got himself a straight red card for an ugly challenge on Arce, for which he lunged in late and left his leg knee-high for good measure.

Things were heating up in both games, so to protect his main attacker Camacho opted to bring Raúl off in the 82nd minute, bringing on Luis Enrique. While the Barcelona man's arrival was not as bad as Nastja Čeh's impact, Enrique somehow failed to score the goal that would have knocked South Africa out when he got on the end of a pinpoint cross into the box.

Perhaps seeing this and hoping Slovenia would keep Paraguay out in the final minutes, Sono brought Fortune off for Jacob Lekgotho who went in at left-back, with Carnell moving up to the left wing. That plan was scuppered moments later, however, as just after Santa Cruz failed to convert a cross, Cuevas took matters into his own hands. Having received the ball on the edge of Slovenia's box, the attacker faked to go out wide before turning back inside and taking two defenders out of the game immediately. He carried the ball past one more defender and smashed it as hard as he could, sending his shot off the bar, back on to the ground and into the roof of the net before sprinting off to celebrate with his team-mates and coaching staff. Paraguay were now set to pip South Africa to second spot thanks to Cuevas's miraculous impact.

Sono's visible nerves indicate that South Africa knew they were going out if nothing changed, but there was no real difference in the game's tempo. McCarthy came close to reaching a ball in behind but it was Spain who continued to dominate possession.

Paraguay immediately sat back and protected their lead as soon as they got it. Cuevas was one of their only players who roamed forward enough to get a shot off but injured himself doing so. This meant he was replaced by Juan Carlos Franco, who filled in to play a much deeper role.

As the respective final whistles were blown, South Africa's players were left standing in discussion, likely focusing on how close they had come to the round of 16. They had the same points and goal difference as Paraguay, eventually missing out because the South Americans had scored once more than them. Maldini's side didn't care how they had got through; it was abundantly clear that they were just overwhelmed that it had happened as the substitutes spilled on to the pitch to join in with the celebrations.

## Costa Rica 2 Brazil 5; Turkey 3 China 0 (Group C, 13 June, Suwon; Seoul)

All of the focus ahead of these fixtures was on Costa Rica and Turkey, as Brazil were already guaranteed a place in the round of 16 while China were definitely out. It was imperative that Turkey beat their Asian opponents if they were to progress, while a draw would be enough for Costa Rica to get through.

In Suwon, Costa Rica kept the same team that drew with Turkey, unable to worry about six of their players being one booking away from suspension. Meanwhile Luiz Felipe Scolari made three changes, bringing out Roque Júnior,

Ronaldinho and Roberto Carlos with the first two having already been booked, while the latter had complained of pain in his calf and was withdrawn as a precaution. They were replaced by Edmílson, Júnior and Edílson.

In Seoul, Şenol Güneş left out Ümit Özat and Ergün Penbe for Bülent Korkmaz and Hakan Ünsal – who was coming straight back in after his suspension. Bora Milutinović replaced Qu Bo and Ma Mingyu with Yang Pu and Yang Chen.

As was to be expected, both Brazil and Turkey started their respective games on top. Within two minutes China's Du Wei had to make a desperate attempt to stop Hasan Şaş breaking through the middle, eventually getting away with pulling the Galatasaray winger's shirt. It was Şaş who put Turkey ahead after just six minutes, capitalising on the ball falling to him following a mix-up between Wei and Li Weifeng to fire past Jiang Jin.

It took just three minutes for the men in red to double their lead with Şaş playing a one-two with Emre Belözoğlu from a corner before whipping a ball into the box. Bülent Korkmaz rose above Li Xiaopeng and looped a header over the scrambling Jiang. Hakan Şükür, who hadn't scored yet in the World Cup, nodded the ball home as Li Weifeng tried to reach it, but the ball had already crossed the line by the time the striker touched it. Hao Haidong came close to an immediate response after stealing the ball away from Fatih Akyel in a dangerous area, eventually seeing his shot easily collected by Rüştü Reçber. The goalkeeper did well to hold on to two of Wu Chengying's corner deliveries moments later.

In the other fixture, Costa Rica's Walter Centeno hit a low free kick that had to be awkwardly cleared in the eighth minute, not long before Mauricio Wright sent a header over the crossbar. Even though it took Brazil longer to open the scoring than Turkey, they also did so swiftly. Ronaldo latched on to Edílson's low cross to let off a shot that deflected in off Luis Marín, giving Erick Lonnis no chance.

After Gilberto Martínez was unable to prevent the ball going out of play, Rivaldo's corner went into Ronaldo's chest within minutes of the opener. A mixture of the striker's ingenuity and Costa Rica's poor defending allowed Ronaldo to turn in the box and get a shot off that went through Carlos Castro's legs and Lonnis's hands before nestling in the bottom corner. The records initially said that this was O Fenômeno's third goal of the World Cup with it being questioned whether the game's opener was an own goal, but it was eventually recognised as his fourth. Costa Rica had gone into this game in second place, but with Turkey 2-0 up they found themselves in a precarious position less than a quarter of an hour into the match.

China were doing their best to change that scoreline as they continued to respond well after the second, with Li Weifeng sending an effort wide after some good link-up play down the right. It wasn't one-way traffic, though, as Ünsal's cross flashed through the box and was inches from finding Şükür. Undeterred, China almost released Yang Chen behind the Turkish defence, but Emre Aşık pulled him down and earned himself a booking 20 minutes in – meaning he would miss Turkey's first knockout game in the likely event that they got there.

In an incredibly open game in Seoul, Centeno had a chance to give Costa Rica a glimmer of hope moments after Brazil's second, eventually hitting a horrible effort well wide after chesting the ball down nicely. There was a slight break in play after as Marcos stopped the game so that he could get treatment for a shoulder injury. The CONCACAF nation kept coming and while Brazil's defence was holding up well, Ronald Gómez's cross towards Paulo Wanchope forced a stretched header from Ânderson Polga to turn the ball behind.

Brazil almost caught them out again when Juninho Paulista's free kick slipped through Lonnis's hands in the 25th minute. As the goalkeeper looked back in a panic, he realised the ball had fortuitously floated wide. Costa Rica kept responding and Wright sent another header over the crossbar before shaking the net in frustration, realising that these chances needed to be taken if they were to get close to progressing.

While this was going on, there was evidence that Rüştü clearly wasn't 100 per cent after previously picking up a hamstring injury. Having gone up to ensure a Chinese free kick didn't sail into the net, after it eventually went wide the goalkeeper was left on the floor in agony and required treatment for the same hamstring he had injured before. The most worrying part was that he hadn't been near anybody or jumped that high, but the stopper continued after receiving treatment.

China were still looking for their first goal of the World Cup and Yang Chen came closer than any other had so far in the 27th minute, bursting on to Hao's cross and eventually smashing his effort against the post. While the attempt didn't open China's account, it was close enough to leave the St. Pauli man looking around in disbelief while Güneş stepped forward to get his team going again. Soon after, Emre was given the game's second yellow card for pulling back Li Xiaopeng.

Rüştü was eventually taken off in the 35th minute, having battled on for over ten minutes and made defenders take his goal kicks. He was replaced by Ömer Çatkıç, who played his club football for the now dissolved Gaziantepspor.

Having performed brilliantly throughout the tournament so far, Cafu showed that everyone is human when his attempted flick rolled out for a Costa Rica corner. That was dealt with well before Mauricio Solís's shot from range forced Gilberto Silva to deflect it wide for another corner. That wasn't defended quite so well, but Brazil were let off as Gómez completely wasted the chance with an unconvincing header that pinged wide.

For all of Costa Rica's attacking, Brazil always looked like they could get through again and they did just that in the 38th minute through the unlikely source of Edmílson, who had only just come back into the team after missing out against China. After playing a one-two with Rivaldo, the Lyon defender passed the ball out to Júnior and floated into the box. There, he produced one of the goals of the tournament with a phenomenally hit bicycle kick after the wing-back's cross looped up into the air off a Costa Rican boot.

The men in red responded immediately, winning a corner within a minute of the goal. After the initial delivery was cleared, a scuffed shot from range made its way to Wanchope on the edge of the box. The Manchester City striker then played a one-two with Wright and placed the ball past Marcos via a slight deflection off Lúcio. Soon after that, Marín would have feared an immediate own goal as he stuck out a leg to stop Ronaldo's cross reaching Edílson, feeling grateful as it went off his thigh and behind for a corner.

In a scintillating end to the first half in Suwon, Brazil could have had another goal after Gilberto won the ball on the edge of the opposition box but Ronaldo tried to selflessly set up Edílson and conceded possession. Rivaldo had an even better chance after Brazil's number nine successfully slipped his team-mate through, but he couldn't find the target on the stretch. Rivaldo then beat a seven-man wall with a free kick but not the post, before Júnior sent the follow-up wide and referee Gamal Al-Ghandour blew the half-time whistle to give Costa Rica's defence some respite.

Meanwhile, things had become a bit scrappy in Seoul, with Yıldıray Baştürk smashing a wild effort high and wide from inside the box. In a sign of how sloppy things were getting, the game even had to be stopped after Du cleared his lines due to Akyel's poor attempt at a pass coming inches from hitting a stray ball that was just outside China's box.

Çatkıç wasn't forced into a single save between his introduction and the half-time whistle. He did see Yang Pu get booked after blatantly initiating contact with Akyel in Turkey's box in an attempt to win a penalty. As Óscar Ruiz blew up for the break, this felt like a continuation of China's World Cup so far: they had given a good account of themselves but lacked any true cutting edge and paid for momentary lapses at the back. Milutinović brought Wu off for Shao Jiayi during half-time.

Alexandre Guimarães's only interval change saw Harold Wallace come off for Steven Bryce – a substitution that had now been made in all three of Costa Rica's games. His side continued trying to come forward and within two minutes of the restart, Gómez hit a strike from just outside the box that Marcos was able to gather. Brazil also threatened with Ronaldo being a superb last-ditch Martínez tackle away from securing his hat-trick. He uncharacteristically smashed a horrible effort high and wide moments later.

Wanchope rounded Marcos within seconds of that miss but saw his eventual shot brilliantly cleared off the line by

Ânderson Polga. Then the goalkeeper saved two separate efforts from Castro, while Wright's mazy run and cross only resulted in the ball going out off Gómez's midriff.

China were showing more signs of sloppiness in the early stages of the second half. The worst was Du back-heeling the ball out for a corner while trying to be smart, but they were getting away with these lapses. The first real test for either goalkeeper came in the 50th minute as Şaş shifted the ball well to create space for himself before hitting a shot that was collected by Jiang at the second attempt. Çatkıç was finally called into action soon after, with Yang Pu delivering a dinked cross that threatened to loop into the far corner before being caught.

Just moments later, after already having received one yellow card, Yang Pu likely had Ruiz tempted to give him another when hitting Emre with a big challenge. Within seconds of that free kick being taken, Shao got himself sent off just 14 minutes after his introduction for a shocker of a tackle on Emre, sending his studs flying into the Internazionale midfielder's calf.

Meanwhile, in a scintillating game that seemed devoid of even the slightest of lulls, Costa Rica clawed themselves within a goal of an equaliser. Centeno slipped a smart ball through to Bryce who immediately clipped a cross towards the back post for Gómez to dive and head into the net. There was a clear sense of defiance as their number 11 didn't bother to celebrate, instead picking the ball up and taking it back to the halfway line.

Atlético Paranaense's Kléberson had already been prepared to come on before the goal and replaced Edílson. It was Costa Rica who had the first chance after the substitution, though, as Centeno came close to finding the top corner after a short-corner routine. Scolari was soon making another change with Ricardinho replacing Juninho for his fifth cap and first game under the current manager.

He was able to celebrate with his team-mates just moments after coming on when Júnior ran down the left flank and put in a delicious cross for Rivaldo to convert before taking his shirt off and swinging it around in the air. This saw the Barcelona man join Ronaldo in having scored in all three of Brazil's group matches.

Just a couple of minutes later, Júnior made a superb run up the left wing to get on the end of Edmílson's through pass. This time the Parma man scored himself by slotting the ball inside the near post to beat Lonnis. As Júnior celebrated, it almost felt a shame that Roberto Carlos's presence meant there wouldn't be much seen of him again in the tournament.

In Seoul, China were struggling to keep up with Turkey and Li Weifeng was booked for cynically bringing down Akyel. They did manage to get forward and create the occasional chance of their own, with a brilliant intervention from Aşık required to deny Yang Chen an easy header at the back post. Looking to assert Turkey's dominance, Güneş brought Baştürk off for İlhan Mansız in the 70th minute. Şükür almost did that for him, getting a strong head on to Ümit Davala's cross but being denied by an equally strong hand from Jiang. Milutinović made his final two changes soon after, with Qu and Yu Genwei replacing Hao and Yang Chen.

In Suwon, Costa Rica's record scorer, Rolando Fonseca, was brought on for Solís immediately after the second of Brazil's quickfire goals, but it felt impossible for Guimarães's side to turn things around. While the game calmed down after a scintillating couple of minutes, there was still plenty of action and Ronaldo had a penalty call turned down after going over following a tackle attempt from Martínez.

Costa Rica were soon formulating their own attack, which resulted in Marcos needing a moment after bravely saving Castro's shot with his face. From the resulting corner Kléberson made a complete mess of his clearance, sending it spinning off the post and then Marcos's leg, with that touch being enough to make Wright divert it wide.

In the 72nd minute Rivaldo was withdrawn and replaced by 20-year-old São Paulo midfielder Kaká. Moments later, Guimarães made the final substitution in Suwon as Winston Parks replaced Martínez – a sign that Costa Rica were going for it. Parks had the ball within seconds of his introduction but couldn't find the space to shoot and his intelligent back-heel wasn't controlled by Wanchope, allowing Brazil to clear.

As was typical of the game in Suwon, Brazil had a chance of their own within moments, though with men in yellow queueing up to shoot Kaká let off a strike that was blocked. A minute later, Fonseca had the chance he would have been desperate for after a one-two with López got him into the box, but the Alajuelense forward sent his shot whistling past the far post.

Turkey really should have had a third goal in the 78th minute after Emre's corner delivery flashed across the goal to find Emre Aşık at the back post, eventually defying all logic and somehow lifting his shot over the crossbar.

With ten minutes remaining in Suwon, Kaká showed a glimpse of the supreme technical quality the world would get used to down the years, dribbling through the crowd as if he had the ball stuck to his foot before slipping a pass through to Cafu. The wing-back was halted by the offside flag, while Kaká was guilty of being a tad greedy in his youthful exuberance moments later.

There was another break in play with eight minutes remaining when Júnior was left in pain after his ankle bent under the pressure of a poor López tackle. While Brazil were down to ten men, a rapid break up the pitch resulted in Ronaldo hitting the post from a tight angle as he pursued a hat-trick. Júnior was then back among the action after receiving lengthy treatment on the side.

At this point Şaş stupidly got himself booked for flying into a high challenge on Xu Yunlong. Soon after that, the final Turkish substitution was made with Beşiktaş midfielder Tayfut Havutçu replacing Tugay Kerimoğlu. Within seconds of the change – and 76 minutes after their second goal – Turkey went 3-0 up as Emre picked out Şaş. He burst up the left wing and delivered a cross for Davala to volley past Jiang and in off the far post.

İlhan Mansız came close to compounding Chinese misery moments later after some lovely Turkish linkup play, but Jiang got down to tip his effort around the post well. The Beşiktaş forward produced a shocking miss at the back post from the ensuing corner.

By the standards of Brazil's meeting with Costa Rica, there had been a bit of a lull before Bryce made a darting run past Edmílson and through the middle of the pitch in the 87th minute. He was eventually stopped by Marcos, but the goalkeeper couldn't hold the ball and while he was on the floor, Wanchope latched on to it and got a shot off, being left in disbelief after hitting the crossbar.

If there was one Turk who would leave this game frustrated, it was undoubtedly Şükür. Şaş's ball in the final moments was just behind the striker, meaning that while he got on to it with the goal gaping he couldn't wrap his foot around it enough to capitalise. Still, as the final whistle blew moments later, Turkey's substitutes and staff were dancing around on the touchline before coming on to congratulate those on the pitch for reaching the last 16 – a brilliant achievement for a nation competing in just their second World Cup. Meanwhile, China were leaving their first without a goal or point to their name.

Suwon's match saw its first yellow card in the 93rd minute when Cafu caught Castro with a stray arm as the winger tried to burst forward. Wanchope was on the attack within seconds, though his mazy run took him to a tight angle that made the eventual save simple for Marcos. Soon after that Ronaldo was denied yet again, this time by a block.

Seconds after that effort, the referee blew the final whistle to end a true feast of wonderful football that was a pure delight for anybody watching. While Turkey's win brought jubilation to their country, any neutrals watching that game rather than Brazil's meeting with Costa Rica would surely have felt as though they missed out.

## *Mexico 1 Italy 1; Ecuador 1 Croatia 0 (Group G, 13 June, Ōita; Yokohama)*

All eyes will have been on Italy going into their game as their defeat against Croatia meant Gli Azzurri needed a two-goal victory against Mexico to guarantee a place in the knockout stages, whereas a draw would do for El Tri. With Alessandro Nesta back from his injury sustained during that disappointing result, Giovanni Trapattoni's only change in personnel saw Cristiano Doni replace Filippo Inzaghi. Meanwhile, Javier Aguirre understandably stuck with the team that had beaten Ecuador.

As Ecuador themselves continued to pursue their first World Cup point, Edwin Tenorio and Iván Kaviedes made way for Marlon Ayoví and Carlos Tenorio in Hernán Gómez's line-up. Meanwhile, knowing that a win would likely get Croatia through, Mirko Jozić brought Dario Šimić and Ivica Olić in for Zvonimir Soldo and Davor Vugrinec.

In Ōita, Mexico clearly weren't taking their position for granted. Jesús Arellano was booked within 90 seconds having mistimed a sliding tackle on Christian Panucci, before Nesta produced the game's first shot after the ensuing free kick was cleared, blasting it comfortably over the crossbar.

It didn't take long for Yokohama to see its first opening either, after a long ball over the top found Alen Bokšić, who was unable to control it convincingly and allowed Ecuador to clear.

The indication was that it would be a real battle between Italy and Mexico with Fabio Cannavaro booked for scything down Cuauhtémoc Blanco in the fifth minute, which meant that he would miss the first knockout game if Italy got there. Panucci had a yellow card of his own in the tenth minute, for diving. Having raced past Arellano and into the box the Roma man spotted Manuel Vidrio's outstretched boot and went down without delivering anywhere near it.

Despite Croatia's early opportunity, Ecuador were having the better of the play in Yokohama. They looked particularly effective down the right with Ulises de la Cruz getting inviting crosses into the box. They were still struggling to test Stipe Pletikosa in the Croatian goal as Marlon Ayoví sent their first effort wide.

Meanwhile, Italy were looking stronger than Mexico. Inzaghi even had the ball in the back of the net inside the first 15 minutes after Francesco Totti found him on the edge of the box. However Trapattoni's men were left frustrated by the offside flag once again in this tournament, with the linesman making a call that looked incredibly tight.

Croatia got their first effort away five minutes after Ecuador. This was just as far off target, as Milan Rapaić did well to bring down an awkward lofted pass before sending off a wild strike. De la Cruz finally hit the game's first shot on target in the 17th minute but it rolled into Pletikosa's arms from his weaker left foot.

Mexico were having plenty of the ball and nearly moments of their own, but Christian Vieri was able to get his first sight of goal shortly after, striking a first-time effort from outside the box that fizzed marginally over the crossbar. Gerardo Torrado then hit an ambitious effort that also sailed too high.

The best chance of the game so far came in the 19th minute when Damiano Tommasi found Inzaghi, who drove towards the box and drew in the Mexican defence before offloading the ball to Totti. With Óscar Pérez racing towards him, Italy's number ten placed his shot wide – much to his and the whole team's disbelief. Vieri showed better technique with a volley from outside the box but that was also straight at Pérez, while Totti smashed a free kick agonisingly past the post.

Croatia's Olić had a chance to make the breakthrough when Bokšić intelligently played the ball into his strike partner's path as he sprinted into the box. He couldn't control the ball though, and it rolled harmlessly towards José Cevallos. Édison Méndez soon responded with a strike from range that bounced dangerously enough for Pletikosa to awkwardly drop it, but the Hajduk Split stopper was able to collect it at the second attempt.

Bokšić was looking the most likely player on the pitch to carve out a goal. Soon after attempting to set up Olić, he hit the outside of the post having received the ball in the box, turned away from Iván Hurtado and wedged the ball from underneath his left boot.

Throughout all of the earlier play, Italy had looked incredibly comfortable defensively with Gianluigi Buffon barely being worked at all. Despite this, Mexico took the lead in the 34th minute as they won the ball in their own box and worked it forward well. Instead of going direct, El Tri showed great patience and knocked the ball about until Blanco found his opportunity to loft it into the box, where Jared Borgetti was on hand to provide a simply outstanding header. While running away from goal to reach the ball ahead of Paolo Maldini, he flicked it into the far corner and left Buffon rooted to the spot. It was a goal that deserved every bit of the striker's emphatic celebrations.

With Croatia and Ecuador drawing, Italy were currently on their way out of the competition and Cannavaro showed frustration, desperation or a mixture of the two with a speculative effort from outside the box moments later. While Trapattoni looked on anxiously and Mexican fans jubilantly chanted, there was a break in play when Rafael Márquez went down injured.

As the captain received treatment, Italy came close to an equaliser when Vieri superbly brought down Panucci's ball from deep under pressure and laid it off to Gianluca Zambrotta, who sent a wild effort wide on the stretch. Márquez was soon back on the pitch and battling with Vieri again, while his centre-back partner Salvador Carmona went up the other end and flashed an effort agonisingly wide of the post.

Bokšić, again, was looking to change the result in Yokohama, threatening to get behind Ecuador's back line. This time Hurtado was equal to his run and blocked the shot, though he was left on the floor after a tangling of legs in the aftermath. While he wasn't in pain, the Croatian striker was visibly frustrated that he hadn't managed to hit the back of the net yet. Despite it being the 40th minute, Gómez used the break in play to make a substitution and took Alfonso Obregon off for Álex Aguinaga.

Borgetti could have had a second after being played in by Torrado, but Cannavaro raced across to make a brilliant block and deny him. Within seconds Totti was racing up the pitch but having jumped over Márquez's leg without being touched, the referee Carlos Simon gave him a yellow card for diving. Mexico were able to see the half out with relative comfort despite Italy continuing to push forward.

Seconds before the break in Yokohama, Bokšić must have thought that he had finally got his goal. Rapaić had launched a ball from inside his own half that went over Augusto Poroso's head and towards the striker, who reached it ahead of Cevallos and looped the ball over the goalkeeper's head. The ball looked destined to nestle in the back of the gaping net until Poroso recovered brilliantly, sprinting back to head the ball behind for a corner. After the corner was played short, William Mattus blew the half-time whistle before Croatia could get their shot off as a tame first half ended shortly after its greatest moment.

Italy came out aggressively in Ōita, winning a corner within 20 seconds of the restart which was eventually flicked behind by Braulio Runa after hanging precariously in the air. While Gli Azzurri couldn't hit the back of the net themselves, there was a goal that helped them as Ecuador went ahead in the 48th minute. The half had started with Daniel Šarić taking a kick to the face from Cléver Chalá but there was soon a pain that ran throughout Croatia as Ecuador patiently played the ball around until Aguinaga's pass sent De la Cruz running up the line. With Robert Jarni standing him up, the Hibernian captain delivered a cross that Agustín Delgado jumped up to head down for Méndez. Coming on to the ball perfectly, Ecuador's number 19 hit it into the floor and past Pletikosa despite the goalkeeper getting both hands to it. As Méndez ran off with a massive grin drawn across his face and arms out wide to celebrate with those in the dugout, Ecuador were on course for their first World Cup win, Italy were on their way to the knockout stages and Croatia were going home.

Inzaghi had a glorious chance to further improve Italy's chances of progression in the 50th minute after being found by Totti. The striker took an unconvincing touch and Pérez authoritatively came rushing out to swipe both the ball and man to stop the danger.

Back to Yokohama; Jozić made his first change four minutes after the goal, with forward Vugrinec replacing centre-back Šimić. That was quickly followed by a Rapaić free kick which deflected off Tenorio's head and over as the Balkans tried to keep their World Cup dream alive. However, they were facing an Ecuadorian team that looked full of confidence and determination, with Aguinaga bringing out an eye-catching flick and various men in yellow chasing the ball down.

Mexico were also showing those qualities, and there was an unorthodox piece of skill from Blanco as he put the ball between his legs and hurdled a challenge, but the move eventually came to nothing. The striker was soon involved again when Arellano broke into Italy's box before playing a one-two with him and getting an improvised shot off that Cannavaro made another last-ditch intervention to clear.

Another sign that Italy were being stretched was that Zambrotta was booked for a late lunge on Ramón Morales moments later. That was immediately followed by Trapattoni bringing Inzaghi off for Vincenzo Montella after a frustrating game for the AC Milan frontman. Montella didn't have the initial impact he would have hoped for, seeing yellow for catching Carmona in the face while being dispossessed mere seconds after his introduction. It was Morales who had a chance soon after, though his swerving strike flashed over Buffon's crossbar.

In the 58th minute Croatia boss Jozić made another alteration as he brought off Niko Kovač for Bayer Leverkusen's Jurica Vranješ. Ecuador goalscorer Méndez remained the most likely to hit the back of the net again, playing a quick one-two before smashing a first-time effort that he couldn't quite keep down. Still, it didn't take Vranješ long to get involved as the midfielder hit a weak shot that was saved before kicking Cevallos as he pushed the ball away. The offside flag went up anyway.

Around the same time, it seemed as though Italy had run out of ideas – a sense that was only worsened by a passage of Mexican play that had Cristiano Zanetti chasing shadows. Moments later, the Italian midfielder swiped Borgetti's legs to halt a potential counter after Maldini cheaply conceded possession. The ensuing free kick was played short and eventually led to a sweet strike from Johan Rodríguez that whistled past the post.

In an attempt to improve the situation, Trapattoni brought Panucci off for Francesco Coco in the 63rd minute. The defender was immediately involved, winning the ball back to start a move that resulted in fellow substitute Montella bravely getting on the end of Totti's through ball ahead of Pérez. He lifted the ball over Pérez and into the net before being taken out. Montella didn't care as he got up and started celebrating, but frustration soon took over when he was rightly called offside. The fury almost grew further as Mexico quickly carved out a move of their own but Blanco's effort eventually ballooned over the crossbar.

After Vranješ had also taken out Méndez before executing a nutmeg, Croatia made their final change with Mario Stanić replacing Šarić. They were still struggling to get a hold of the game and Stjepen Tomas got the game's first booking for pulling Aguinaga back as he looked to drive forward in the 72nd minute.

Mexico had looked in complete control for a short period, but they were reminded of Italy's quality when a pass from Totti carved them open and released Vieri in behind. However, as the ball bounced up, it hit the Internazionale striker on the shins, allowing Pérez to tip it wide. The ensuing corner was awful, sailing well over everybody and out for a throw.

Ecuador also got themselves into a good position as a flick-on found Delgado one on one with Josip Šimunić, but the centre-back did brilliantly to stand up and steal the ball away from him before the move broke down. Gómez sought to further strengthen their position in the 76th minute, bringing Kaviedes on for Tenorio. Croatia had a chance to break after a poor Ecuadorian corner seconds later, but having raced up the pitch Rapaić sent a shocking cross from deep straight into Cevallos's grateful arms.

Meanwhile, Aguirre made two changes with Rodríguez and Morales making way for Rafael García and Gabriel Caballero. That was soon followed by Trapattoni's last throw of the dice, bringing Alessandro Del Piero on for Totti. Moments after that change, Mexico also made their final substitution when Francisco Palencia replaced the goalscorer Borgetti.

In the 83rd minute, Italy had a free kick in a dangerous position when García bundled Del Piero over on the edge of Mexico's box. There was a big debate among the Italians to decide who would take it, but having won that, Montella sent a poor effort into the wall. Seconds later, a long ball into the box saw an opportunity wonderfully present itself to the Roma man who proceeded to blaze his shot miles over the crossbar before understandably burying his face in the turf.

Pérez was booked for time-wasting while taking the ensuing goal kick, but the ball was in his net within a minute of his clearance. Montella made up for those missed opportunities with a masterful cross into the box that Del Piero latched on to with his head and glanced into the corner, leaving Pérez helpless. It had been an underwhelming World Cup for the Juventus talisman so far, but he had just scored the goal that meant Italy didn't have to rely on the result in Yokohama so much in their quest to progress. Italy's number seven sprinted off pointing to the sky in jubilation while Trapattoni barked instructions to the players who would listen. With five minutes remaining, Mexico were more than happy to see out the game and keep hold of the draw that saw them secure top spot in the group.

Even before it became known that they needed two goals to get through, Croatia's main tactic had been to get hopeful crosses into the box from pretty much anywhere. Ecuador were looking indomitable at the back and even came close to countering when Pletikosa raced out of his box to reach a through ball ahead of De la Cruz. When Bokšić finally found Vugrinec unmarked in the box, the substitute sent a volley spinning horribly off his boot.

Chalá picked up a yellow for cynically fouling Rapaić as he looked to sprint through in the 86th minute. While this stopped the initial danger, the subsequent free kick inadvertently saw Croatia come as close as they had done all game. The initial ball from deep was headed out wide, forcing Chalá to concede a corner. Rapaić sent his delivery towards the front post where Olić ran back to glance his header into the corner. Aguinaga – who had been among the game's best players since his introduction in the first half – did his job on the back post and cleared with his thigh. There was a scramble of bodies as players attempted to reach the rebound, but a yellow shirt was able to clear.

Croatia continued to flood the box, and while Stanić climbed well to win a header the Chelsea man could only direct his effort straight at Cevallos. Olić thought he had got behind in injury time, but having made the header to deny Bokšić at the end of the first half Poroso recovered once again – even if Olić asked for a handball after the ball hit the defender's arm as he fell. With less than a minute left, Šimunić was booked for catching Kaviedes as the ball went over their heads.

Ecuador understandably took as long as they could to take the free kick and by the time their effort was cleared, Mattus had blown the final whistle. As he did so, Aguinaga threw his arms into the air and Ecuador rejoiced after securing what would go down as a historic result for the nation. While they hadn't got through, they had secured Ecuador's first win at their first World Cup and given a good account of themselves.

Meanwhile, four years after finishing third at the 1998 World Cup, Croatia had now finished third in their group. Pre-tournament questions surrounding Jozić's ageing squad now appeared to be warranted as the Balkans took an early flight home. They wouldn't win another World Cup finals match until 2014 – with Olić on the scoresheet in a 4-0 victory over Cameroon – having missed the 2010 edition completely, while their 2018 progression to the final was their next time out of the group stages.

As the news came through that Ecuador had beaten Croatia and both teams playing in Ōita were going through, nobody bothered going for a winner. Mexico spent almost all of injury time passing the ball around the back under minimal pressure. Referee Simon put a stop to the understandably boring finish by blowing for full time 40 seconds before expected. The teams had drawn 1-1, as had been the case during the 1994 finals, and just like that tournament it was enough for both of them to progress to the knockout stages.

## Tunisia 0 Japan 2; Belgium 3 Russia 2 (Group H, 14 June, Osaka; Shizuoka)

After their draw saw them go into the final round of group games behind Japan and Russia, the onus was on Belgium and Tunisia to win. In Osaka, Tunisia's only change was that the naturalised Brazilian-born Espérance Sportive de Tunis winger José Clayton came in for the banned Hassen Gabsi. Meanwhile, table-toppers Japan went unchanged as they looked to create history by getting out of the World Cup group stage for the first time.

Over in Shizuoka, Belgium's Robert Waseige took action after their disappointing draw against Tunisia, bringing in Jacky Peeters, Nico Van Kerckhoven, Johan Walem and Mbo Mpenza for Éric Deflandre, Peter Van Der Heyden, Timmy Simons and Branko Strupar. Russia's Oleg Romantsev also rotated his team with Dmitri Khokhlov, Dmitri Alenichev and Vladimir Beschastnykh replacing Marat Izmailov, Igor Semshov and Ruslan Pimenov. Aside from the pursuit of a place in the knockout stage, this was an especially important occasion for centre-back Viktor Onopko who became the first player to earn 100 caps for Russia after the fall of the Soviet Union.

There was a real sense of excitement among the Japanese supporters in Osaka as the game got going, which only grew as the ball fell fortuitously to Shinji Ono on the edge of the box just seconds into proceedings. The atmosphere cooled a little as Hatem Trabelsi got a block in but there was still plenty of chanting. Japan continued on the front foot and Radhi Jaïdi hacked Takayuki Suzuki down from behind. The men in blue couldn't quite turn that early dominance into a test for Ali Boumnijel, though.

In Shizuoka, it had been an even start when Belgium were awarded a free kick on the edge of Russia's box after Andrei Solomatin was adjudged to have fouled Marc Wilmots – despite the defender coming away from the off-the-ball incident holding his face. It seemed inevitable that the captain would take it, but Walem stepped up instead and sent a wonderful curling effort into the top corner, leaving Ruslan Nigmatullin rooted. After just seven minutes the Red Devils were now in place to reach the knockout stage and it was the perfect time for the Standard Liège midfielder to get his second international goal.

Belgium weren't about to sit back now and Mpenza continued a bright start to the game by getting behind the Russian defence then testing Nigmatullin with a confident strike. Solomatin's tough time with referee Kim Milton Nielsen continued in the 12th minute as he was booked for pulling Wilmots's shirt while defending a corner – meaning the CSKA Moscow defender would miss Russia's round of 16 game if they got there. As the incident played out before the corner was taken, there was no penalty and Glen De Boeck couldn't hit the target despite getting a free header. Alexey Smertin joined Solomatin in the book two minutes later for sweeping De Boeck's legs away with a sliding tackle.

Tunisia's Ziad Jaziri was looking busy up top, as he had been all tournament, but his isolation made it difficult for him to pose any real threat to a well-organised Japanese defence. As the first 20 minutes went by, neither team was particularly troubled after the Asian side's initial flurry of activity. Then Atsushi Yanagisawa made a burst through the middle of the pitch without seeming to have the ball under control at all but Riadh Bouazizi still brought him down and needlessly received the game's first yellow card.

At that same point, Russia provided their biggest threat so far. Alenichev jinked his way past Belgian bodies and down the left wing before Geert De Vlieger got a vital hand to his cross. The pressure didn't end there as Valery Karpin touched the ball back to Solomatin, whose first-time shot was deflected wide. After a slight lull, Belgium came close to doubling their lead in the 27th minute when Gert Verheyen chested the ball down for Wilmots, but Yuri Kovtun blocked the captain's strike before then making a last-ditch intervention to deflect Mpenza's follow-up wide.

Hidetoshi Nakata had played some nice passes without really hurting Tunisia, but just before the half-hour his corner delivery came inches away from finding Junichi Inamoto in the six-yard box before eventually being headed away by Khaled Badra.

It took 34 minutes for Osaka to witness its first real effort on goal as Yanagisawa received a pass on the turn around 25 yards out, but the striker's shot from range was saved with relative comfort by Boumnijel. A greater test came for the Tunisian goalkeeper soon after as Ono's inswinging corner soared towards goal, but the Bastia stopper was able to punch it away.

Russia boss Romantsev had already made half-time changes in the opening two games, but he moved even earlier this time around and after just 34 minutes he brought Smertin off for teenage attacker Dmitri Sytchev. There was a slight scare for Belgium when Wilmots went down with an ankle problem before eventually being able to continue, while Yves Vanderhaeghe was forced to trip Khokhlov as the Russian midfielder tried to start a break forward.

Soon after Sytchev's speculative shot was easily saved, Verheyen came inches away from a Belgian second. He latched on to Wilmots' flicked header behind Russia's defence with a first-time lob that had just too much on it to find the top corner. That was followed by an effort from Vanderhaeghe as Belgium worked the chance well following a mistake from Yuri Nikiforov.

The PSV Eindhoven centre-back picked up an injury in the process and Romantsev was forced into his second change in the 43rd minute, with Lokomotiv Moscow's Dmitri Sennikov coming on for his fifth cap. A chance came

Verheyen's way as the Russian defence tried to settle, but he smashed the ball marginally wide.

As the half came to a close in Osaka, Tunisia had their biggest opportunity so far thanks to more impressive work from Jaziri winning a corner. After Selim Ben Achour's first effort was put behind for another corner by the first man, the teenager's second attempt was far better. This one found the head of Khaled Badra, whose attempt flashed across goal and Jaïdi couldn't quite sort his feet out at the back post as he tried to turn it in.

Seconds after that scare, Trabelsi jinked his way into the penalty box before Kazuyuki Toda slid in through the back of the Ajax defender. The Japanese midfielder had got nowhere near the ball but Gilles Veissière didn't think to give a penalty. As Trabelsi looked around with an expression of disbelief, Toda got in his face, clearly thinking the Tunisian had gone down too easily.

Japan had controlled most of the first half but had the two biggest moments of concern towards the end. While they were still in the better position in terms of the group, Philippe Troussier wasn't completely happy with what he had seen, bringing Inamoto and Yanagisawa off for Hiroaki Morishima and Daisuke Ichikawa. Ammar Souayah also made a switch, with Zoubeir Baya replacing Mourad Melki.

Morishima had clearly come on full of energy and keen to make an impact; the Cerezo Osaka midfielder did just that within three minutes of his introduction. It was poor defending that saw possession come his way as Raouf Bouzaiene's challenge on Suzuki poked the ball straight into the danger zone. However, nothing could be taken away from the 30-year-old's finish and his first-time effort sent the ball curling away from Boumnijel and inside the far post. Nobody in Osaka or the rest of Japan cared how the goal came to be while the Osaka Nagai Stadium instinctively erupted.

Japan's substitutes had really helped step up their game, and the pair linked up to almost double their lead just four minutes after the opener. Ichikawa had done well down the left before whipping in an inviting ball for Morishima. Despite his 5ft 6in frame, the midfielder stooped down to get his header off, though it eventually spun off the post before Boumnijel gratefully pounced on it.

At the same time, there was nothing De Vlieger could do to stop the reversal of roles between Belgium and Russia from the first half. Seven minutes after the break Khokhlov led a Russian counter and slipped through Sytchev, whose attempt at a dinked finish bounced off the onrushing goalkeeper to Beschastnykh. The striker successfully applied the finishing touch despite Daniel Van Buyten getting a toe to the ball on its way over the line. As things stood, Russia would join Japan in the knockout stages despite not having looked their best.

Belgium really should have been back in front within moments of parity being restored after some dazzling dribbling and a pinpoint pass from Mpenza. However, Wilmots completely scuffed his shot towards Walem, who controlled the ball and then sent it into the side netting. Russia had a brilliant chance of their own after Karpin's pass released Yegor Titov, who found Beschastnykh with a pinpoint cross. The goalscorer couldn't add to his tally, though, producing a mistimed header that was so wide it could have been nodded in by Sytchev if it wasn't so high.

With half an hour remaining Japan had another great chance to go two ahead when Boumnijel came out of his box to make a pass to Badra, who was dispossessed. As the ball fell to Ichikawa, the Shimizu S-Pulse man couldn't capitalise, jinking his way into the box before hitting what was either a poor shot or confused cross that Hidetoshi Nakata was unable to reach. Whatever it was, the ball trickled harmlessly wide and Tunisia used the break in play to make a change with Imed Mhedhebi replacing Clayton.

It made no difference to the game's flow, and Bouazizi had to make a brilliant last-ditch header to prevent Köji Nakata's cross from finding Suzuki at the back post. There were soon more problems when a free kick routine saw Ono get a free header in the Tunisian box, but Boumnijel pulled out an impressive save to deny him.

While Tunisia were largely on the back foot, some good work from Ben Achour and Mhedhebi almost released Jaziri behind Japan's defence, but captain Tsuneyasu Miyamoto – still wearing his protective mask – came steaming over to block the shot.

In the 64th minute in Shizuoka, Alenichev stupidly got himself booked for kicking the ball away out of frustration when he couldn't reach a pass that went out of play. While it didn't have any massive ramifications during the match, it did mean the winger would be unavailable if Russia made it to the round of 16. The men in white had been on top for most of the second half but were now beginning to sit back.

Perhaps looking to capitalise on that fact, Waseige brought Mpenza off and replaced him with Wesley Sonck. However it was Russia who came agonisingly close to going ahead in the 74th minute, when a clinical counter saw Titov receive the ball from Alenichev in the penalty area and provide a pass that glided invitingly across the six-yard box. Neither Beschastnykh nor Karpin could reach the ball as it trickled out of play despite the latter's desperate slide.

Following a brief period in which it felt as though Japan had gone into their shells, Hidetoshi Nakata got their all-important second goal with a quarter of an hour left on the clock. Ichikawa received a pass from Toda and immediately attacked Bouzaiene before getting a yard and sending a pinpoint cross towards the Parma man who headed into the ground. Boumnijel got his feet to the ball but his efforts were futile as it rolled into the back of the net. It would now take the greatest of capitulations for Japan to be knocked out and the celebratory atmosphere indicated that. Their talisman grabbing his first goal of the tournament only helped.

Tunisia refused to throw in the towel with Ben Achour delivering a brilliant cross that sailed agonisingly over Jaïdi's head moments after Japan's second. With nothing to lose, Souayah brought forward Ali Zitouni on for left-back Bouzaiene in the 78th minute, and there was a coming together while that was happening after Jaziri pushed Toda. When the free kick came in, a game of head tennis in Japan's box resulted in Zitouni attempting an overhead kick that went harmlessly wide despite a fairly clean connection.

As this was going on, over in Shizuoka Verheyen was brought off for Simons in Belgium's second substitution. He didn't play a part in what happened next but the midfielder was celebrating with his team-mates immediately. Walem's corner delivery sailed over his head and fellow substitute Sonck outfought Khokhlov to glance his header past Nigmatullin before bringing out some acrobatics. There were also jubilant scenes on the bench, with the goal setting Belgium up for a place in the knockout stages.

With Tunisia now playing for pride against Japan, they were struggling to reach balls first and Badra was booked in the 81st minute for catching Suzuki while trying to get ahead of him. They were still going, though, and Zitouni came even closer with a half volley, hitting the crossbar on this occasion.

Belgium had absolutely everything to play for and Wilmots gave them a vital cushion with eight minutes left, taking an intelligent touch from Bart Goor's pass to get a yard of space from Kovtun. The Belgian captain then unleashed a strike that nicked off his Russian counterpart Onopko's outstretched leg and left Nigmatullin stranded. In the space of four minutes Russia had gone from booking their place in the knockout stages to seemingly having no chance of progressing. Still, it was all about the Belgians in the moment as Wilmots ran to the dugouts with even Waseige going wild. Romantsev took action immediately as Aleksandr Kerzhakov replaced Karpin.

In the 84th minute Hidetoshi Nakata was brought off for Mitsuo Ogasawara, who wore a big smile on his face while coming on for his first minutes of the tournament. Japan were still looking for more joy as Ono's ambitious volley went wide with the Feyenoord man still in search of his first goal of the World Cup. Tunisia's Baya also came close to finding the top corner with a free kick from an acute angle.

In the other fixture, Russia had turned to desperation and Sennikov was yellow-carded as he rushed in to try to steal the ball. It felt as if they had run out of ideas as long balls started being pumped forward, but Titov and Kerzhakov showed the cunning needed to slip Sytchev through for an opportunity that he took with astounding composure given the circumstances. There were no celebrations, though, as the teenager picked up the ball and ran back towards the halfway line.

The game in Osaka maintained its intensity until the end, though Ogasawara audaciously tried to score from near the halfway line with an effort that Boumnijel was able to deal with relatively easily. Ben Achour had his own effort from range that hit the side netting. Seconds later, Veissière blew his whistle to confirm that Japan had made it out of the group stage at a World Cup for the first time in their history, doing so on their own turf. Tunisia may have left the tournament bottom of the group with one point to their name but they did so with their heads held high in the knowledge they were far from the pushovers expected by many.

In Shizuoka, Pierluigi Collina showed the board that indicated there were three minutes of added time to play. Having helped to carve out the goal, Kerzhakov was unable to find the target with a header. This was followed by De Boeck being replaced by Eric Van Meir having picked up a knock a few minutes earlier – though Waseige likely would have appreciated the time eaten up by the substitution. A foul on Sonck used up enough time for the referee to blow his whistle before Russia, who had given everything, could muster another attack.

Belgium were through. This would have felt even sweeter considering their neighbours the Netherlands had failed to qualify for the tournament, while France had already been knocked out in the group stage. However, as assistant Mikhail Gershkovich had outlined before the tournament, failing to get through the first round spelt the end of Romantsev's tenure. He handed in a resignation letter to the Russian Football Union along with his fellow coaches the same day.

'It was not an immediate or emotional decision,' insisted the team's press officer, Alexander Lvov. 'The coaches discussed their move for almost 40 minutes before they decided to resign.'

## *Portugal 0 South Korea 1; Poland 3 USA 1 (Group D, 14 June, Incheon; Daejeon)*

Going into the final round of fixtures, Poland were the only Group D team with no hope of reaching the knockout rounds. Most eyes would have been on Portugal's match against South Korea in Incheon. António Oliveira's only change was to put Beto back into the starting line-up instead of Nuno Frechaut, while Guus Hiddink made two alterations as Lee Young-pyo and Ahn Jung-hwan – the goalscorer against the USA – came in for Lee Eul-yong and Hwang Sun-hong.

Over in Daejeon, Poland brought Radosław Majdan in for Jerzy Dudek while Jerzy Engel changed the entire back four and both of their central midfielders. Bruce Arena's only alteration was to replace DaMarcus Beasley with Earnie Stewart.

The USA had gone into the final round of group matches in a strong position, with South Korea leading them on goal difference, but a terrible start put them at the mercy of the result in Incheon. In the third minute Jacek Krzynówek delivered a corner ball that Emmanuel Olisadebe reacted quickest to, getting a header off that was deflected off Anthony Sanneh and back towards him. As the loose ball bounced and Brad Friedel ran out in an attempt to close the angle it was once again Poland's number 11 who was fastest, smashing his strike off the underside of the crossbar, on to the ground and into the roof of the net.

Landon Donovan thought he had equalised seconds after the restart, but was adjudged to have fouled Arkadiusz Głowacki before nodding the ball into the empty net – much to his fury, as was shown to the referee, Lu Jun. In a blistering turn of events, Poland went and scored from the free kick. Majdan – who kissed the ball before kicking it – sent it up the field and Tomasz Kłos got above Donovan to win the flick-on, then Maciej Żurawski played a one-two with Cezary Kucharski and suddenly Poland were in. The ball was swiftly moved out to Krzynówek, who put a pinpoint low delivery into the box that Paweł Kryszałowicz gratefully slotted into the back of the net.

There were jubilant celebrations from the Polish, but it was Portugal who benefited most from the two goals. They had come into their game needing to beat South Korea, but the goalposts had already been moved in their favour as their superior goal difference meant Oliveira's men only needed a draw to go through in second place. There was visible frustration from the Americans and Olisadebe felt that, as he took a blow to the face after colliding with Eddie Pope.

If the news of the USA's debacle filtered through to Incheon, it certainly didn't lessen the intensity there. Within the first ten minutes Fernando Couto took a blow to the head, while Beto was lucky to escape without a booking after taking out Seol Ki-hyeon. There was a real lack of conviction from the Portuguese, whose attacking play was devoid of the quality expected from players who represented clubs such as Real Madrid, Internazionale, Sporting Lisbon and Bordeaux – Kyoto Purple Sanga's Park Ji-sung looked far more dangerous than any of them.

There was to be a flurry of cards, though, as Beto was booked in the 22nd minute after bringing Seol down again, while Kim Tae-young saw yellow for fouling João Pinto just two minutes later. The game was then completely changed before even 30 minutes had passed. Pinto got himself sent off after jumping through the air and hitting Park with a terrible two-footed challenge at knee height. There was outrage from

Portugal's number eight and his team-mates when Ángel Sánchez brandished the red, but the referee couldn't have done anything else.

Pinto lost his head and punched the official in the stomach in retaliation, a stupid act that earned him a six-month ban and ensured the 30-year-old would never play for his country again. Oliveira looked on in disbelief from the dugout as the ruckus unfolded.

Seol thought he had scored moments later, but the goal was ruled out as Choi Jin-cheul had barged Vítor Baía in mid-air to make the goalkeeper drop the ball.

There was almost another goal elsewhere but Brad Friedel made an incredible double save with his legs to deny Krzynówek and Żurawski. He closed down the former before rushing to his feet and diving to get enough contact on the latter's shot to somehow tip it on to the post. Things did get worse for Arena, though, as Jeff Agoos went off injured in the 36th minute, having tried to play on for ten minutes after a collision with Kucharski. He was replaced by Beasley, who filled in at left-back with Frankie Hejduk going to the centre of the USA's defence.

Still, the Americans had definitely made improvements, with Claudio Reyna beginning to dictate play and John O'Brien getting shots off from range. Majdan earned himself a yellow card in the 44th minute for time-wasting when retrieving one of those efforts, aiming to ensure Poland made it to half-time with their two-goal lead intact.

Portugal hadn't fared any better than the USA when it came to creating chances late in the half. They only really got Pauleta through on goal once, but having been so clinical against Poland their number nine failed to hit the target this time around. So, despite Arena's men struggling, the

Portuguese were still one South Korea goal away from being knocked out.

When the co-hosts re-emerged, it was clear they weren't going to let Portugal walk through to the next round as the players gathered their focus in a huddle. They soon went inches away from taking the lead when Seol lost Couto and Beto to get his head on Kim Nam-il's cross but sent his effort narrowly past the post. Yoo Sang-chul out-jumped Rui Jorge moments later only to see his header deflect off Jorge Costa and wide.

Once again it was Poland who carried the attacking threat at the beginning of the half in Daejeon, but all Marek Koźmiński earned himself was a yellow card for diving as he reached the American box, having run all the way up from his left-back position. Koźmiński wore a smile as he jogged back but it was difficult to tell if it was one of amusement or embarrassment.

In the 58th minute Joe-Max Moore was brought off the bench to replace Brian McBride, who had struggled to make his presence felt. Meanwhile, South Korea attacker Seol got a booking for a sliding challenge on Petit. There was also a scare for the Koreans and Americans as Pauleta stooped low to get his head on Luís Figo's corner ahead of the front post. The Bordeaux striker flicked it goalward but Lee Woon-jae palmed it away before Yoo headed the ball behind.

The Americans had already picked up some momentum and it was beginning to show when Kucharski saw yellow in the 63rd minute after committing one foul too many – he was soon replaced by Marcin Żewłakow.

That change turned out to be an absolute masterstroke from Engel. Within seconds of the forward being introduced, a short corner was played to Koźmiński who delivered a delightful cross that Żewłakow steamed in to head past the motionless Friedel. With that goal the USA's destiny was placed firmly out of their own hands and into those of South Korea – as the Asian outfit beating Portugal or having a complete capitulation was the only way they could progress. It was a sense of helplessness that wouldn't have been aided by Clint Mathis's dinked effort going just over the bar and on to the roof of the net. Nevertheless, Arena made his last substitution when bringing Cobi Jones on for Stewart.

Oliveira would have been wishing that he had made a substitution of his own when Beto clumsily fouled Lee Young-pyo in the 66th minute. Pauleta led the protests while Figo also tried to convince Sánchez not to give their teammate a second yellow, but all they did was test the referee's patience. Pauleta was eventually sacrificed so that Jorge Andrade could join the defence.

This was a decision Oliveira would regret almost immediately. Having been the man fouled by Beto, Lee Young-pyo won a corner which was headed back out to him by Couto. The winger was fronted up by Figo but took a touch out of his feet and sent in a deep cross towards Park. What happened next was pure magic, as Park controlled the ball with his chest, flicked it out of Sérgio Conceição's reach with his right foot, and, as it bounced, smashed his shot through Baía's legs with his left. The stadium absolutely erupted as the midfielder ran to hug Hiddink with the entire team in celebratory pursuit.

South Korea were in dreamland. On the flip side, having just gone down to nine men and taken off the player who had accumulated half of their goals at the tournament, Portugal now needed to score if they were to avoid elimination.

Oliveira's initial response was to replace Rui Jorge with Abel Xavier, and an attacking change was finally made in the 77th minute with Nuno Gomes coming on for Petit – who got Kim Nam-il booked for a foul on the edge of the box before his departure.

There was relief for anybody associated with the USA, but it looked as though the scoreline was heading for embarrassing territory when Sanneh lunged in and caught Kryszałowicz in the box. Żurawski got the ball from Olisadebe but his weak penalty effort was held by Friedel, who had already started stepping to his left before the shot was even struck.

Donovan scored a consolation goal for the USA in the 83rd minute with a well-controlled volley on the stretch after Jones's pass was flicked towards him. Olisadebe was brought off for midfielder Paweł Sibik as Engel attempted to take any potential heat out of the situation, and the striker was booked for how long it took him to depart.

While there was the slightest glimmer of hope for the Americans in this game, many would have been keeping a closer eye on Incheon in the hope that South Korea could maintain their lead. This was reflected by the Stars and Stripes fans as Kłos slowly came off the pitch with Tomasz Wałdoch replacing him while they jubilantly chanted 'USA, USA, USA' despite the match that had unfolded in front of them.

There were scares for the States and South Korea as desperation set in and Portugal got closer to scoring. Costa epitomised his side's tiredness when he got himself booked for fouling Park after the South Korean was quicker to the ball. With Choi down injured, substitute Gomes had a glorious chance in the box but allowed the ball to get underneath his feet and he tamely rolled it towards Lee Woon-jae.

Song Chong-gug then came close to making it 2-0 in the 88th minute but Baía sprinted towards him and slid in to block the effort with his legs. Just moments after that strong save, with the Portuguese dugout screaming at their team to get up the pitch, Conceição hit a strike that connected with the inside of the post and stayed out. Following such a close call, it felt as though the belief was seeping out of A Seleção. Ahn had a great chance of his own but a poor touch allowed Baía to smother him and win the ball back.

Portugal were going direct and while one blocked clearance from Baía gave them a scare and Figo made a futile attempt at winning a foul, they were simply trying to get the ball in South Korea's box as quickly as possible. The men in white stood strong at the back, heading everything away, and the only surprise was that their attackers didn't exploit the gaping holes in Portugal's defence.

Having danced his way into the box, Conceição hit a venomous strike that was parried wide by Lee Woon-jae – the winger looked incredulous in response to the save. Baía even came up for the ensuing corner but neither he nor anybody in red could get near it. A momentous roar echoed throughout the stadium moments later as the final whistle was blown.

Portugal were out of the World Cup. Of the seven groups that contained two European teams, this was the only one to see both of them fail to reach the knockout stage. Pauleta had put in one of the best individual performances of the tournament against Poland, but Oliveira's men simply weren't good enough against the USA and South Korea. The defence looked criminally shaky in the opener while the attack was nowhere near potent enough in their curtain-closer.

Arena let out a smile after hearing the news coming from Incheon, but American celebrations were fairly muted considering they had just qualified for the next stage. Still, this set up a fascinating tie between the States and their neighbourly rivals Mexico in the round of 16.

Among all of this, the real story was South Korea's triumph in the group. The co-hosts had never even won a World Cup game before this tournament despite having made the previous four editions – let alone winning the entire group and going undefeated. This was a monumental achievement for the entire nation, but while the celebrations were jubilant the focus of staff and players would soon turn to their upcoming match against Italy.

# Round of 16

*Germany 1 Paraguay 0 (15 June, Seogwipo)*

Germany's battle against Cameroon had secured their safe passage through to the knockout stages, but it was costly in terms of suspensions. Carsten Ramelow missed out after his first-half sending off while Dietmaar Hamann and Christian Ziege were also unavailable due to an accumulation of bookings. Carsten Jancker was the only man Rudi Völler voluntarily took out, with Marko Rehmer, Jens Jeremies, Oliver Neuville and Marco Bode the quartet to be introduced.

Paraguay boss Cesare Maldini was also forced into a change due to Carlos Paredes being sent off during the dramatic victory over Slovenia, while Guido Alvarenga dropped back out of the team. Estanislao Struway and Carlos Bonet were the two who went into the midfield in their place. Despite their heroics to reach this stage, Jorge Campos and Nelson Cuevas both had to settle for a place on the bench.

Centre-back Thomas Linke had the game's first effort when the ball fell back to him after his initial attempt from a corner was blocked, but he couldn't direct his shot on target.

The stop-start first half was devoid of pretty much any creativity, as the main tactic for both sides was seemingly to smash the ball up the pitch and see what happened – Oliver Kahn and José Luis Chilavert were usually the men to do the honours.

However there were slight flashes of quality, with Michael Ballack's effort from outside the box going marginally over the crossbar, while Francisco Arce hit a firecracker of a free kick at goal that Kahn had to punch away. Even Miroslav Klose wasn't looking as sharp as he had done during the group stage, failing to capitalise on a poor pass and eventually being crowded out.

There had been plenty of fouls from the Paraguayans, but Roberto Acuña took things a step too far in the 26th minute and was booked after leaping into a challenge on Jeremies, completely missing the ball and taking out Germany's number 16.

Paraguay's chances weren't helped by an injury to star striker Roque Santa Cruz. Coming up against the nation in which the 20-year-old played his club football, he would have likely been especially keen to impress. However, over ten minutes after initially getting treatment for a groin injury and trying to play through the evident pain, he was eventually replaced by Campos just before the half-hour.

It appeared that José Cardozo would receive a gift from a short back pass just moments after that setback but Kahn rushed out to clear. As was fairly fitting for a game that had been so bitty, Bernd Schneider was booked in the 35th minute for a stray elbow which caught Caniza. Even more characteristic of this match was that when Kahn punched away Chilavert's overhit effort from the ensuing free kick, the ball was worked to centre-back Celso Ayala, who made a complete mess of his volley and wasted by far the best chance Paraguay had up to this point.

In a reminder that this match was played in the tournament accepted to be football's pinnacle, Campos turned and let off a venomous strike from outside the box which Kahn leapt across his line to palm away from the top corner. Just before the break, Arce was lucky not to add to the list of players booked when getting away with a petulant kick out at Jeremies after the midfielder had brought him down.

There was one change at half-time, Rehmer being replaced by Sebastian Kehl. Considering Germany had been the joint highest scorers in the group matches, while Paraguay showed against Slovenia that they can produce magic when it matters, the hope was that the second half would be more thrilling than the first.

Die Mannschaft seemed to have much more urgency and carved out a couple of chances within minutes of the restart; Schneider had the best of them, but sent his first-time effort straight at Chilavert. With Paraguay largely being pinned back, their main outlet was to hit long balls and attempt to turn them into counter attacks. While that resulted in Campos getting off a shot that stung Kahn's palms, Cardozo also ended up getting booked for over-enthusiastically trying to get in behind Christoph Metzelder.

Perhaps it was out of hope more than anything, but there were cheers in Seogwipo when Schneider's 53rd-minute free kick had the net rippling. However it had just comedically come back off the advertising boards and into the back of the netting. Having struggled since Cardozo's tackle, Metzelder was eventually substituted on the hour and replaced by Frank Baumann.

Paraguay felt they deserved a penalty 65 minutes in when Ballack and Bode both had their arms wrapped around the men they were marking and bundled them over while defending a free kick. Referee Carlos Alberto Batres simply waved play on. While Kahn wasn't being tested, Paraguay were certainly asking questions and German substitute Baumann was booked for crunching through Bonet on the edge of his own box. Chilavert made his way up the pitch and stamped down his authority while Germany tried to get an advantage by moving both ball and wall. Such was the perceived threat that Linke retreated to the line and covered the post behind the wall. Despite the build-up, Chilavert's effort eventually flew harmlessly over the crossbar.

Germany responded with an effort from the Klose-Ballack partnership that had worked so brilliantly for them throughout the tournament. While Klose jumped highest to get his head on the ball, he couldn't control his effort enough to keep it under the crossbar. Still, it was a warning for Paraguay as the stalemate continued into the game's final ten minutes. Perhaps heeding that warning, Maldini made a change in midfield as he brought Bonet off for Diego Gavilán.

It was all Germany, and Paraguay struggled to get any substantial hold on the ball. It seemed as though they would do enough to hang on for extra time until Torsten Frings's headed flick-on from Kahn's long ball had Schneider racing into space up the right flank. He got his head up and picked out Neuville who had run across his defender. Upon reaching the ball, the Bayer Leverkusen man hit a half volley that flew past Chilavert before the goalkeeper could even react. It had all happened in a flash, but it would have a lasting impact as Paraguay only had one minute plus added time to restore parity.

Cuevas – the man who had got Paraguay past Slovenia and was presumably being saved for extra time – was called upon almost immediately with Struway making way. The substitute was a livewire and tried to make things happen. Alas, all his introduction did was give him a front-row seat to watch Batres brandish a red card for Acuña following an off-the-ball incident involving Ballack, for which the German was also booked. Neuville was substituted before the end and received an understandably warm ovation, while Gerald Asamoah got his first taste of tournament football.

The final whistle was blown moments later, confirming Germany's place in the quarter-finals. This had been far from a classic following the blistering nature of the group stage but the cold efficiency that has so often characterised Die Mannschaft down the years paid dividends. Paraguay went home after giving a good account of themselves and providing some wonderful memories – even if Chilavert didn't manage to become the first goalkeeper to score at a World Cup.

## Denmark 0 England 3 (15 June, Niigata)

Consistency was key as Sven-Göran Eriksson kept the same team that had faced Nigeria and played most of the game against Argentina, while Martin Jørgensen was the only man to come out of Morten Olsen's starting line-up to be replaced by Ebbe Sand, despite injury concerns for Jon Dahl Tomasson and Stig Tøfting.

Tøfting was given the first opportunity to pose England a problem after the ball was surrendered easily, but the Bolton Wanderers midfielder overhit his cross into the box, allowing David Seaman to comfortably collect it.

The Three Lions' first opportunity also came from a mistake as Martin Laursen misjudged his header back to Thomas Sørensen, conceding a corner from a harmless situation. Unlike England, Denmark were made to pay and David Beckham delivered the ball to the back post where Rio Ferdinand rushed in and beat Thomas Helveg to the header, diverting it towards goal. Sørensen could only fumble the ball over the line before scraping it away. Emile Heskey made sure with a follow-up, but there was no need as Ferdinand was already running off to celebrate putting England a goal up just five minutes in.

Not only had Helveg been unable to prevent Ferdinand scoring, but the AC Milan defender also picked up an injury that forced him to be replaced while receiving treatment by the advertising boards. Kasper Bøgelund was the man to come on.

Both teams came close to creating chances in the following minutes, but Michael Owen couldn't do much with an awkward pass and the Danish crosses were unable to find their men in the box. Heskey bullied Laursen – who was really struggling – to get behind after 15 minutes, although Sørensen did well to smother the Liverpool man and save his team-mate further blushes.

Just as it looked like Denmark were beginning to settle into things, they were cut open by a superb England move in the 22nd minute. It started with a free kick deep in their own half from which the ball was switched to Ashley Cole and moved around nicely until Paul Scholes launched a crossfield pass to Beckham, who retreated under pressure and passed back. Trevor Sinclair was in space on the left three pinpoint first-time passes later, took a couple of touches and sent a low cross to Nicky Butt, who intelligently poked the ball forward for Owen to masterfully take a touch and score his first goal of the tournament. It was a wonderful team effort in every sense.

England had really turned up and Denmark simply couldn't deal with them. Tøfting showed his frustration by hitting the ball away after a foul was given to England moments after the goal. Sand had Denmark's best chance of the game so far a couple of minutes later, but having done well to work space for himself his final effort went agonisingly wide to compound Danish disbelief.

England were soon in with a chance again but Heskey was unable to convert Beckham's cross. As the heavens opened in Niigata and the rain started pouring to reflect Denmark's mood, their misery was further encapsulated with a shot that almost went out for a throw.

The Danes showed good resilience to carry on chasing the goal that would get them back into the game but they were hit with a sucker punch just before half-time. Danny Mills's quick throw reached Beckham with a slice of luck, allowing the England captain to lay the ball off for Heskey to smash past Sørensen with his first-time effort from the edge of the box.

Thomas Gravesen soon hit a speculative strike from range that Seaman was able to tip over, maintaining England's three-goal lead going into the break and leaving Denmark with virtually no hope of getting back into the game.

England were the only ones to make a half-time substitution, with Robbie Fowler replacing Owen. Denmark created a chance within a couple of minutes of the restart as Scholes gave the ball away to Dennis Rommedahl, who did well to pick out Jesper Grønkjær with an inviting ball to the edge of England's box. The winger skied his effort and showed the frustration that many Danes would have been feeling.

It was a matter of seconds until the Three Lions had a chance of their own with Heskey doing brilliantly to get down the right and put a precise ball into the box for Fowler. Bøgelund produced a superb piece of defending to get in ahead of the Leeds United striker, though. Eriksson then opted to make another change, taking Scholes off for Kieron Dyer.

Considering the scoreline, it was a surprisingly action-packed start to the second period. That continued when there was a big coming together as Mills hit René Henriksen in the face after being tripped while bursting forward with the ball. Beckham made sure to hold the right-back immediately so he didn't respond to the Danish retaliations, and Mills was eventually given a yellow card.

Things calmed down considerably after a blistering first five minutes of the second half, with England getting their foot on the ball in an effort to see it out – though Mills almost put Campbell in trouble with a short pass. Beckham also came close to bagging a fourth goal, hitting one of his trademark curling efforts with that eye-catching technique and forcing Sørensen to punch the ball over the crossbar.

Tøfting was taken off to be replaced by Charlton Athletic's Claus Jensen after a foul was given against Campbell from the ensuing corner. The substitute's namesake Niclas Jensen gave Seaman a test moments later, as the goalkeeper couldn't hold on to his venomous shot from range, but Campbell came rushing in to help his team-mate out.

There was a lull until Gravesen burst forward and hit a strike that deflected out for a corner and Sand's attempt after the set-piece delivery required a good block from Campbell.

The next corner was overhit but retrieved and laid off to Bøgelund, who smashed a piledriver that seemed destined for the top corner. However, in trying to make sure it went in, Tomasson got his head on to the ball, sending it up into the air and well over.

Eriksson made his final change with just over 20 minutes left on the clock, trusty substitute Teddy Sheringham replacing Heskey. With their place in the quarter-finals all but confirmed, some England fans weren't paying too much attention to the actual football and were showing their celebratory mood with a conga down the aisles while chanting 'Let's all have a disco'.

Perhaps that was also down to the men in white not causing Denmark too many problems for a while. Sinclair eventually flew in to get his head on a floating Fowler cross, though the West Ham United winger couldn't quite find the top corner.

While Denmark weren't giving up, the game had dulled down as it progressed towards the final ten minutes and Gravesen attempting to score from all of 40 yards indicated how hopeless their attempts were becoming. Beckham had a chance from inside the Danish box but eventually sent his strike straight at Sørensen.

Denmark admirably kept pushing for a consolation goal and Gravesen was denied by a superb block from Cole, while Claus Jensen jinked away from Beckham and dinked the ball goalward, forcing Seaman to awkwardly tip over the crossbar. As if things weren't frustrating enough, the Danes' route to the ball was even blocked by German referee Markus Merk at one point.

After Rommedahl had a couple of late attempts that didn't hit the target, Denmark were eventually put out of their misery and denied the chance to get a consolation when the full-time whistle cut through the sound of the English band and chanting. England had done all the damage needed in the first half and now waited to see whether they would be meeting Brazil in the next round or if Belgium could pull off a shock. Meanwhile, the Danes were going home and could reflect on a positive group stage performance that had seen them overcome the French – even if they didn't get the desired result in the round of 16.

## Sweden 1 Senegal 2; after sudden-death extra time (16 June, Ōita)

Senegal – the only African side left in the competition – were making even more history by reaching the knockout stages. Having already drawn against one Scandinavian opponent the Lions of Teranga were now hoping to win against another.

Bruno Metsu was forced into a change after Khalilou Fadiga's late yellow card against Uruguay made him unavailable. Alassane N'Dour was the only other player to come out, with the pair replaced by Amdy Faye and Pape Thiaw. Salif Diao was still suspended after his red card, but captain Aliou Cissé and Ferdinand Coly were able to play despite being injury doubts. Meanwhile, with Freddie Ljungberg limited to supporting from the stands, Lars Lagerbäck and Tommy Söderberg opted to field the same Sweden team that had drawn against Argentina.

It was all about Tony Sylva in the early stages with the goalkeeper making a decisive start and rushing out of his box to clear a ball through. Tobias Linderoth then hit a powerful strike from range straight at him with the game's first shot. Soon after that, Sylva was forced to save Olof Mellberg's effort with an outstretched leg before Magnus Svensson failed to get his follow-up on target. Sylva looked furious with his defence as all of this had come within the space of four minutes with Senegal having hardly got a touch of the ball. The stopper wasn't quite as convincing when collecting a cross, fumbling it but eventually clearing his lines with a long ball up the pitch.

Senegal had their first foray forward in the ninth minute. Thiaw tried to lift the ball over Magnus Hedman after getting on the end of Omar Daf's intelligent through pass but couldn't keep his attempt under the crossbar.

It was mere moments later that Sweden turned their early dominance into a goal advantage. Anders Svensson's first corner had been cut out by Coly at the front post, but his second was met by Henrik Larsson, who got in ahead of Sylva and headed the ball into the gaping net. Cissé would have been able to intervene if he had stayed on the post.

It was a goal indicative of Senegal's poor start and they now had plenty of work to do. El Hadji Diouf made his first notable burst forward with a quarter of an hour played, eventually being clumsily barged off the ball by Andreas Jakobsson. While there was a big penalty call, referee Ubaldo Aquino showed no interest. Still, Senegal were already having a far greater impact on the game as they started getting on the ball and hitting shots from range. Pape Malick Diop almost got them into trouble as he was dispossessed by Magnus Svensson on the edge of his own box, but the Swede was unable to make the most of it.

There was a slight break in play in the 24th minute when Niklas Alexandersson sustained a cut to the head after Daf caught him with a stray elbow while going up for a header. The game had been in a lull anyway, but play continued without the Everton midfielder and Senegal used the man advantage to get the ball in the back of the net. Diouf had done well to work space for himself, before hitting a shot that looked destined to go wide before being touched in by Papa Bouba Diop. However, Diouf was left throwing his arms around in dismay as Diop was adjudged to be offside in what was an incredibly tight call. Around four minutes after going off, Alexandersson finally returned to the action with a big bandage around his head.

Even with equal numbers on the pitch, Senegal continued to apply pressure while being backed by drummers in the stands. Marcus Allbäck was hoping for a penalty after breaking forward and going down under pressure from Daf only to be ignored, seconds before Diouf failed to convince the referee with a dive at the other end.

Henri Camara ensured Senegal didn't need any help from the referee to get back into the game by scoring a wonderful equaliser in the 39th minute. The striker chested the ball down after a long free kick was headed in his direction, then faked to shoot before opening up a yard for himself. He then sent his actual shot into the bottom corner from outside the box with pinpoint precision. Of course, he went to the corner and started a celebratory dance with Papa Bouba Diop.

Diouf was still looking dangerous but having retained the ball despite the company of three men in yellow, the number 11 couldn't get his shot on target. Camara could have had another goal just a couple of minutes after his first following some superb play down the left from Faye, but the Sedan man didn't get a clean connection on his header at all. Sweden were largely on the back foot but Anders Svensson forced a good save from Sylva with a free kick.

Papa Bouba Diop had the half's last attempt, firing off a shot from range that Hedman was able to collect at the second attempt. Senegal stayed on top for the two minutes of injury time that followed and Sweden would have likely been thankful for the half-time whistle.

Sweden looked rejuvenated after the break, and Anders Svensson nipped in to steal the ball before getting a shot off within seconds of the restart. Cissé was soon struggling more than his other team-mates in the early stages after Magnus Svensson ended up clipping the ball in to the Montpellier man's private parts. Allbäck then tested Sylva with a volley that sprung up awkwardly off the turf, but the Monaco stopper was equal to it.

Despite these moments, it was far from a breathtaking start to the half with the extreme heat potentially playing a part in that – some fans were even sitting with makeshift head dresses on to protect them from the sun's glare.

There was a moment of excitement in the 56th minute as indecisiveness from Hedman and Teddy Lučić allowed Camara to nip in and steal the ball. However his touch was just too heavy and the ball went out of play, meaning the Swedish pair's embarrassment was mild and inconsequential. Anders Svensson had another chance of his own seconds later after a nice knockdown from Allbäck, eventually making a mess of his strike. Thiaw had a similar problem after Daf had got forward well to provide him with an opportunity.

Diouf was risking a yellow card again on the hour by trying to punch Coly's cross, which had floated too high for him to reach with his head. The Swedes protested while the winger gave the referee an apologetic explanation, which somehow got him off the hook.

There was a break in play as Pape Malick Diop received treatment for an injury and was carried off on a stretcher, eventually being replaced by Habib Beye. Sweden then made their customary change of Allbäck making way for Andreas Andersson. Diouf won a free kick soon afterwards and softly lifted the ball over the wall for Hedman to tip over the bar fairly routinely.

The second half had seen some miserable efforts, and Andersson added another with a first-time strike that sailed high and wide after Larsson had set the ball nicely for him. The game had its first yellow card in the 73rd minute, given to Coly for going through the back of Larsson. Camara was still looking one of the most threatening players on the pitch – even if that wasn't a particularly tough competition in this game – and saw a cross-shot float on to the roof of the net.

Diouf was also still making a nuisance of himself and after winning a free kick, the winger delivered a ball that Sweden failed to deal with convincingly. The ball eventually fell to Thiaw at the back post, but the Strasbourg striker didn't get a clean connection on his shot and it went behind off Mellberg.

Alexandersson was brought off before the corner to be replaced by Zlatan Ibrahimović. The Ajax youngster got involved with some defensive work almost immediately, and then the 20-year-old was soon doing what he was actually brought on for. After a speculative ball forward he out-muscled Coly before jinking his way past Cissé. Instead of laying the ball off to Larsson, he went for goal himself and was denied by Sylva at the near post.

After the last 15 minutes of a tame second half had crawled along, it suddenly came to life right at the end with both sides seemingly hoping to wrap the tie up inside 90 minutes. Despite this, Thiaw's header going wide of the post was the closest either team came to taking a late lead.

Extra time arrived for the first time in the tournament and fans continued beating their drums and chanting, hoping that the players could conjure something special. Sweden were made to wait for the game to restart as Senegal gathered in a huddle.

When the game did get going, the lure of a golden goal meant both teams were going for it far more than they had done in the second half of normal time, with both creating goalscoring opportunities within the first two minutes. That period was quickly followed by a powerful strike from range by Faye that teasingly moved around in the air before eventually whistling over the crossbar. In the 94th minute, Thiaw went down with what was a poorly disguised dive with Johan Mjällby for company and was booked.

Within a minute of that, Anders Svensson came a post's width away from ending the contest; Mellberg's delivery into the box had been masterfully met by Larsson and Coly couldn't clear convincingly under pressure from Ibrahimović, meaning the ball landed at Svensson's feet on the edge of the box. The Southampton man pirouetted around Lamine Diatta with ease as the Senegalese midfielder came flying in, but smashed his effort off the upright and out for a throw-in. Larsson did brilliantly to dance out of the corner moments later despite the company of two men in green, but was then hit with a perfectly timed challenge from Cissé in the box.

It was Senegal's turn to feel disbelief a matter of seconds later as Diouf danced through the Swedes like they weren't there – even nutmegging Mellberg – but went for power with his strike and drilled the ball wide. It would be a near miracle if this game went to penalties at this rate.

There was a slight break in play when Thiaw received treatment and was stretchered off, but unlike Pape Malick

*The infamous image of Roy Keane walking his dog after leaving the Republic of Ireland squad.*

*Papa Bouba Diop bundles the ball over the line to secure Senegal's historic win against France.*

*Miroslav Klose celebrates one of his three goals as Germany inflict an 8-0 humiliation on Saudi Arabia.*

*Rivaldo holds his face to get Hakan Ünsal sent off in an incident that would be watched over and over again.*

*Japan rejoices after Junichi Inamoto scored in their 2-2 draw against Belgium.*

*The Republic of Ireland celebrate Robbie Keane's dramatic equaliser against Germany.*

*David Beckham celebrates laying his demons to rest after scoring England's winner against Argentina.*

*Pauleta celebrates one of his three goals against Poland in what would prove to be a rare moment of joy for Portugal.*

*Christian Ziege and Lauren square up in a game that saw Germany and Cameroon pick up a record 16 cards.*

*Park Ji-sung gleefully runs to Guus Hiddink after masterfully striking South Korea's winner against Portugal.*

*Henri Camara celebrates with his team-mates after scoring the golden goal to take Senegal past Sweden.*

*Landon Donovan heads home to ensure USA beat bitter rivals Mexico in what has contributed to the 'Quinto Partido' curse.*

*Ümit Davala heads home to leave Seigo Narazaki and Japan in despair while Turkey progress.*

*Ahn Jung-hwan celebrates his winner against Italy, unaware of the ramifications that would come.*

Iván Helguera is restrained having confronted the officials after Spain controversially bowed out against South Korea.

Turkey's İlhan Mansız ends Senegal's incredible World Cup run with a dramatic golden goal.

Moments after being ruled out of the final, Michael Ballack celebrates scoring the goal that ensured Germany got there.

Hakan Şükür celebrates with Emre Belözoğlu after scoring the quickest goal in World Cup finals history.

*The smile, the finger wag, the haircut. Ronaldo brings out his iconic celebration after scoring in the final.*

*A dejected Oliver Kahn ponders what went wrong as his impressive World Cup ended in disappointment.*

*Brazil were all smiles as Cafu lifted his nation's fifth World Cup trophy.*

Diop the striker was able to continue despite Souleymane Camara having got stripped off. Instead Sweden made their final change in the 99th minute, taking Magnus Svensson off for Mattias Jonson. There was a moment where Daf almost lost his cool after Ibrahimović had excessively grabbed hold of him, but the referee calmed the situation down quickly so the intense affair on the pitch could continue.

With half-time of extra time approaching, Metsu prepared Makhtar N'Diaye to come off the bench. All the Stade Rennais midfielder eventually got on to the pitch for was to join the emphatic celebrations for Senegal's 114th-minute winner. Cissé collected the ball inside his own half and offloaded it to Faye in the centre circle. He passed forward and Thiaw ran sideways, seemingly harmlessly, before finding Camara with an intelligent back-heel. It was all up to Senegal's number seven from there as he jinked his way into the box and sent his effort rolling over the line off the inside of the post.

The striker took off his shirt before being mobbed by his team-mates, who all eventually went to dance in the corner, while the coaches embraced in the dugout. As Swedish players lay disconsolate on the floor, Camara was lifted up on to Amara Traoré's shoulders and swung his shirt around in the air. He hadn't got the cleanest connection on the strike but nobody associated with Senegal would have cared in the slightest.

The game was over and Senegal were only the second African nation to reach the quarter-finals after Cameroon had done so in 1990. Meanwhile, Sweden were going home just one game after making it through the 'Group of Death'.

*Spain 1 Republic of Ireland 1; after extra time, Spain
won 3-2 on penalties (16 June, Suwon)*

There were plenty of changes made by Spain after a plethora
of José Antonio Camacho's men were rested against South
Africa. Iván Helguera and Fernando Morientes were the
only ones to hold on to their place without previously playing
regularly, while Iker Casillas and Raúl also remained in the
starting line-up. The decision to replace Miguel Ángel Nadal
with Helguera was widely seen as a way of combating the
Republic of Ireland's speed up top.

Whether or not it was down to a foot injury he carried
into the tournament, Ian Harte had been on the receiving end
of plenty of criticism for his performances so far. However,
the backing that mattered came from his manager and the
Leeds United left-back had it as Mick McCarthy started
with the full XI that had overcome Saudi Arabia. McCarthy
remained confident that his side could beat Spain despite
being the underdogs, with Robbie Keane and Damien Duff
instructed to stay high at all times.

The Irish showed this intent from the very start, pressing
Spain hard in attempts to win the ball back as soon as they
lost it – with Mark Kinsella getting an especially nice tackle
in early. The Boys in Green's approach almost paid dividends
just a few minutes in as Keane sent the game's first shot
curling agonisingly wide of the far post after nutmegging
Carles Puyol.

They had started superbly, with Duff looking particularly
dangerous, but it was Spain who took the lead after eight
minutes. For all the talent La Roja had at their disposal, it
was such a simple goal: Puyol threw the ball to Luis Enrique
before getting it back and whipping the ball in first-time for
Morientes to clinically glance out of Shay Given's reach. The

Irish had been expecting Puyol to go with a long throw but the Barcelona man's quick thinking caught them out.

Still, Ireland refused to stray from the game plan as they continued going at the Spaniards. Javier de Pedro angrily shoving his shoulder into Steve Finnan – getting both players a telling off from referee Anders Frisk – indicated that the approach was at least frustrating their opposition.

That was added to when Spain had a goal ruled out for offside, with a slick move seeing Raúl flick the ball to Morientes who then played it through for Enrique to run on to and touch into the net. However, the midfielder had gone a fraction too soon. Steve Staunton required treatment in the aftermath but was able to continue.

Given's goal was soon at Spain's mercy again, but this time Fernando Hierro was denied his chance at a volley by an outstanding diving header from Matt Holland after a pinpoint cross to the back post.

Ireland were dominating the ball at times and had moments where they stretched the Spain defence well, but the offside flag was turning out to be the true nemesis of the men in red. Having already had one goal ruled out, there were numerous times where the flag went up to nullify an attack. One of those, which came 40 minutes in, denied Morientes after he had been slipped in behind as Gary Breen stepped up before the striker flicked the ball over Given's head and knocked it into the empty net. Replays showed that the goal should have stood.

Things almost got worse for Spain when Ireland had their best chance of the game so far just moments later. Holland looped a pass that completely split the Spanish defence and released Keane behind them. With his back to goal, Keane managed to get a boot on to the rising ball ahead of Casillas after it bounced but couldn't quite control it, sending his acrobatic effort over the crossbar.

Another Spain move was stopped by the offside flag – rightly so this time – and a speculative long-range effort from Harte followed, but there was no genuine threat before half-time. So, even if the Republic were playing catch-up, they still had a chance.

The second half's first chance came to Morientes after some incredibly tight control and brilliant ingenuity from Raúl allowed him to keep possession despite being swarmed by men in white. His strike partner couldn't make the most of the opportunity though, firing his effort straight at Given.

McCarthy was forced into his first change just five minutes after the break with Staunton still struggling because of the injury he picked up before half-time. The captain was replaced by Kenny Cunningham and Breen was handed the armband. With questions having been asked about whether or not Staunton would retire from international football after the tournament's culmination, it was felt this would be the centurion's final action for his nation.

Ireland's biggest chance of the game to that point came seconds after the change, when Kevin Kilbane nudged Puyol while trying to get on the end of Steve Finnan's long ball into the box. Puyol went flying into Casillas as he jumped to catch the ball, leading to the goalkeeper dropping it. With both Spaniards on the floor and the ball bouncing up nicely, Kilbane hit a first-time effort but Hierro and Helguera had got back on the cover and the former sent the ball behind for a corner. While Puyol was furious with the referee, he would have been thankful to his defensive partners.

With 35 minutes left to either score a goal or face elimination, McCarthy made the change that had secured the equaliser against Germany: Niall Quinn replaced Gary Kelly and Duff went out to the right. The Blackburn Rovers man had caused carnage at times when drifting wide, so it seemed a natural move to make.

It worked a treat. Harte picked Quinn out with a long ball from deep and the striker chested it out to Duff, who shaped like he was about to cut inside before blazing past Juanfran down the wing. Just as Duff broke into the box the Spain left-back slid in and took him out, getting a yellow card for himself and giving Ireland the chance to get back on level terms from the penalty spot.

Harte stepped up to take it and sent the ball to the goalkeeper's right. Unfortunately for him and Ireland, it was nowhere near the corner and at a good height for Casillas, who even came close to jumping past the ball. Kilbane came in for the follow-up but the ball spun horribly off his foot and wide. Spain had been let off the hook and their celebrations indicated that they knew it. The Irish were left with their heads in their hands.

It wasn't long until Spain made their first change, bringing Gaizka Mendieta on for De Pedro. His first involvement was taking out Duff, who remained undeterred by his earlier efforts coming to nothing. Mendieta's second showed that he could cause problems of his own as he stretched to put a dangerous ball into the box that eventually evaded Morientes's head by a matter of inches. Spain were close to a goal again just seconds later but Raúl had strayed offside before slotting the ball into the net. There may not have been any more goals but the second half had certainly been lively so far.

Morientes was brought off for defensive midfielder David Albelda. Spain still proved that they weren't about to sit back as Raúl got the ball after Cunningham had failed to convincingly clear a cross into the box under pressure, but Given rushed out to smother him. Ireland's main man, Keane, had a half chance of his own with just over ten minutes remaining when Harte fizzed in a cross-shot from a free kick, but the man wearing number ten got too much on it and sent his header well over the bar. That was followed up by Duff's strike from range that whistled agonisingly past the post after he had masterfully created space for himself.

Raúl had seemingly been struggling with injury after a collision with Breen, and Spanish fears were realised as he trudged off in the 80th minute to be replaced by Albert Luque. It wasn't long until McCarthy made another necessarily bold move and brought striker David Connolly on for Harte in an effort to draw level. As written in *Ireland's World Cup 2002*, the manager thought, 'We might as well throw caution to the wind now and go for it'.

The Irish were throwing absolutely everything they had at La Roja, and Casillas bravely jumped at Keane to prevent the striker's shot from beating him in the 86th minute. They may not have been earlier but Spain were now hanging on for dear life. In a rare attack, Luque tried to lob Given from just inside the Ireland half but his effort was hopeless. Rubén Baraja was then booked for time-wasting with three minutes left on the clock.

It was now a case of Ireland getting the ball into Spain's box as quickly as they could and Spain doing everything in their power to get it back out again. Hierro went a step too far as he almost took the shirt off Quinn's back when defending a free kick from deep, leading Frisk to award Ireland's second penalty of the game.

Having missed once, it was now or never with this spot-kick coming in the 90th minute. Keane took the responsibility and stepped up with pure focus in his eyes. The striker's straight run-up completely wrong-footed Casillas and Keane stuck the ball to the same side Harte had done, this time finding the bottom corner before pulling out that trademark celebration with the Irish supporters. There were four minutes of added time and it was Ireland who looked the likeliest to score, with Duff having a strike blocked and Keane putting an effort over the bar. They couldn't breach Casillas's defences again, however, so extra time awaited.

Not only were they the side looking wearier and playing without their star striker, but Spain were also a man down as Albelda went off through injury with all three substitutes already used. Luque often looked isolated and with no Morientes or Raúl, Mendieta was Spain's largest threat – the winger created one chance for himself but curled it wide of the post.

The Irish side full of hungry attackers looked the most likely to grab a golden goal, with Duff continuing to dance past defenders, Keane producing pieces of trickery in and around the box, Quinn getting up to win headers and hold the ball up while Connolly linked play well. Even Breen got a shot off when the ball made its way towards the back post but he couldn't get enough on his strike to trouble Casillas, while Kilbane's effort from range went over.

The expression on Spain's bench was one of collective concern as time went on, with Ireland still the more likely to score as extra time entered its second period. La Roja seemed as though they were merely holding on for penalties and Keane flashed a volley wide.

The Spanish finally found some extra energy to get forward with ten minutes left and Baraja's strike was palmed away well by Given. Connolly responded and came millimetres from writing his name into Irish folklore with a strike from outside the box that went just the wrong side of the post. Both sides went in search of a final goal in the latter stages but neither could find it, meaning the game would be decided by this World Cup's first penalty shoot-out.

Spain won the coin toss and Ireland were up first. Keane had shown so much confidence at the end of normal time and did so again here, sending Casillas the wrong way and emphatically striking the ball into the top corner. Hierro had scored two penalties during the group stages and Spain's captain was just as assured with his effort as he knocked it into the bottom corner.

Holland stepped up next and went for power but ended up smashing the ball off the crossbar and over. 'I've gone from probably the highest moment in my career [against Cameroon] to the lowest moment in the space of how many days,' he says looking back. 'I'd already decided that I was going to try and put my laces through it. I guess the adrenaline maybe took over and got too much of it and obviously the rest is history. There's flashbacks now seeing the ball just rising and thinking, "Oh no, it's going over the bar." I took eight penalties in my career and I scored seven and missed one and that's the only one I ever missed – and it's the only one I ever blasted.'

Baraja confidently took the opportunity to put Spain ahead, sending Given the wrong way and shaking a jubilant fist towards the Spanish bench. Connolly went pretty much straight down the middle but Casillas outfoxed him, taking one step to his right and batting it away. Juanfran could have had the game almost wrapped up if he had scored, but after stuttering in his run-up to send Given the wrong way the full-back sent his shot wide.

Kilbane stepped up to get Ireland back on level terms but Casillas went the right way again and was able to palm the ball wide with relative ease. That save gave Juan Carlos Valerón the opportunity to win the game, but the midfielder couldn't take it as his shot kissed the post on its way wide.

Finnan absolutely had to score if Ireland were to have any chance. Despite that immense pressure, he confidently stroked the ball into the top corner and gave Casillas no chance of repeating his previous heroics. Now it was all on Mendieta: score and Spain go through, miss and it's sudden death. To add to the tension, he had to re-place the ball after initially putting it too far ahead of the spot. Unfettered, the substitute passed his shot down the middle as Given dived away from it and couldn't get his trailing leg to connect with the ball.

Ireland had looked the better team but they were the ones consoling each other while the Spaniards celebrated reaching the quarter-finals. The Boys in Green had given a great account of themselves, not just on the day but throughout the entire tournament despite everything that had gone before it. As McCarthy said in *Ireland's World Cup 2002*, 'This World Cup, all five weeks and four games of it, should not be remembered for three penalty misses'.

When Holland reflects on the reception the squad received on their return to Ireland, he says, 'When we were out there [in Asia], you're hearing the odd story about what's going on, but you don't really have a sense of it because you're so far away. To come back and see the numbers that greeted us was phenomenal. I was in total shock – it was amazing. We knew they'd get behind us but to sense that feeling of everyone and the pride that they had in us – we felt the same with them. It was amazing'.

Nevertheless, the World Cup would continue without them while Spain marched on, waiting to see if they would face Italy or co-hosts South Korea.

## Mexico 0 USA 2 (17 June, Jeonju)

Both Mexico and the USA had exceeded expectations, throwing up an intriguing match-up that not too many would have expected pre-tournament. It also promised to be an even game with the two rivals having won their respective home matches against each other in qualification. It was also a continuation of CONCACAF's greatest rivalry.

With Mexico coming in off the back of an unbeaten group, while the USA had been beaten by Poland in their final match, perhaps it was no surprise that Bruce Arena was the only manager making changes. The suspended Frankie Hejduk and injured Jeff Agoos were joined by Clint Mathis and Ernie Stewart in making way for Gregg Berhalter, Pablo Mastroeni, Eddie Lewis and Josh Wolff – with the first two getting their very first minutes of the tournament.

Mexico controlled the ball in the opening couple of minutes and had the first free kick after Ramón Morales was blocked off by Claudio Reyna. Cuauhtémoc Blanco took the dead ball from deep, delivering an effort that fizzed through the packed box and popped up off the turf. While it took two attempts, Brad Friedel was able to hold on to it.

The USA were struggling as Mexico continued to assert their early dominance. Eddie Pope almost made things increasingly awkward by getting in the way of Friedel's clearance – which eventually went out for a throw as the goalkeeper had words with his defender.

Despite all of this, it was the Stars and Stripes who made the breakthrough after just eight minutes. When the men in white won a free kick in Mexico's half, the ball was quickly rolled out wide to Reyna who raced up the right flank until he reached the byline and produced a cut-back into the box. Under pressure, Wolff expertly touched the ball back to Brian McBride who emphatically took his first chance of the game with an immediate finish. That goal made the Columbus Crew frontman the USA's joint-highest goalscorer in World Cup history, as well as giving his nation the lead against the run of play.

Mexico continued to dominate possession as they pursued a quick equaliser. They had their first real chance after a quarter of an hour after Rafael Márquez had pushed up the pitch before offloading the ball as he was fouled. Vítor Melo Pereira gave the advantage as the ball went out to Morales on the left, but while the Guadalajara winger cut into a good position he couldn't find the target.

Landon Donovan showed that his side weren't about to sit back all game, racing forward on his own and winning a foul off Márquez, although Reyna's strike only hit the wall. It has often been said that possession is nine-tenths of the law. This game is one of many to disprove that theory as Mexico had plenty of the ball but were struggling to cause any danger against a USA side that had visibly grown since their goal.

It took until the 26th minute for Friedel to be tested again, Blanco hitting an effort from range that the Blackburn Rovers goalkeeper was able to palm away to safety. In the same minute, Pope received the game's first yellow card for catching Mexico's number ten as he flicked the ball around the defender. Gerardo Torrado also tried his luck from range – as the midfielder had done various times throughout this World Cup – but the ball floated tamely into Friedel's arms.

Javier Aguirre was clearly dissatisfied with what he was seeing and made his first change in the 28th minute. There was no sign of injury as Morales jogged off the pitch to be replaced by Luis Hernández, the country's all-time top goalscorer at the time. The striker was looking to make things happen and managed to flash a ball across the six-yard box, but it was convincingly cleared.

Then a pair of USA mistakes in the 35th minute gave Mexico their greatest sight of goal so far. First of all Pope hit a weak pass straight to Blanco, who set up Jared Borgetti for a first-time shot that was blocked by Tony Sanneh and looped into the air. Friedel watched the ball as it came back down but his attempt at punching it away was a poor one that created a chance for Blanco to shoot. The striker's effort eventually went directly above Friedel for the goalkeeper to parry it away before Hernández acrobatically hit the side netting.

Mexico's fans were in full voice but there was only more frustration for the men on the pitch, as Manuel Vidrio was booked for catching Lewis with a high leg. Seconds later, Óscar Pérez did brilliantly to prevent Mexico going two goals down when saving with his legs after Wolff had found space in the box.

The men in green continued to struggle in the final third and Borgetti headed wide having beaten Friedel's diving fist to meet Blanco's cross. He was called offside anyway, while Pope soon did well to cut out Torrado's cross with seconds remaining before half-time.

Aguirre was the only manager to make a change at the break, throwing on midfielder Sigifredo Mercado to replace booked centre-back Vidrio. His side came out strong with the USA immediately on the ropes. Within two minutes

Mastroeni didn't release the ball quickly enough and committed a foul. After McBride conceded a free kick on the edge of his own box, Blanco had two attempts blocked by a seven-man wall. Wolff was then booked for time-wasting with a throw deep in Mexico's half.

Moments later, Braulio Luna's wicked free kick saw Friedel tip the ball on to his crossbar and behind having misjudged its flight. The ensuing corner caused a scramble in the box before being poked behind for another. Berhalter was booked for holding on to Mercado before it was taken and while Mexico were pointing to the penalty spot, they only got another corner that was awkwardly cleared. All of this had come within nine minutes of the restart.

The biggest act of desperation came shortly afterwards as John O'Brien clearly punched the ball when Blanco jumped up to meet Luna's corner delivery. Aguirre and plenty of the Mexicans vociferously appealed for the penalty they should have been awarded, but Pereira hadn't seen it.

Reyna had the chance to intensify Mexican frustrations when a move that included a complete miskick saw the ball roll to him invitingly, but his shot was directed straight at Pérez. It was soon becoming a heated affair as there were two comings together in quick succession, while Mercado smashed a cross from deep that came tantalisingly close to the head of Hernández and then Borgetti. Just before the hour, with the relentless Mexican pressure continuing, Wolff was brought off for Stewart.

Soon afterwards, McBride unleashed a header from the edge of the box that was calmly dealt with by Pérez. There was nothing the goalkeeper or his defence could do five minutes later, though, as Lewis raced down the left wing and delivered a pinpoint cross that found Donovan at the back post. The USA's number 21 kept his composure and clinically headed into the net before ripping off his shirt, falling to his knees and being mobbed by his team-mates. Mexico had been so dominant throughout the second period but the USA had stood firm and the 20-year-old ensured they now had breathing space.

Within seconds of the restart, Hernández took a blatant dive in the USA's box as Pope's outstretched leg went nowhere near him. Rather than the penalty the striker had hoped for, Hernández received a yellow card. Another American move out wide resulted in the ball popping out to the edge of the box for O'Brien to hit first-time, but the Ajax midfielder's strike fizzed over the crossbar.

In the 70th minute Mastroeni should have considered himself fairly lucky as he got away with seemingly kicking out at Blanco after conceding a free kick, while the Mexican saw yellow for his retaliation. Blanco followed that up by whipping a ball into the box that was too high for Márquez to control after getting his head on to it.

There was soon a heart-in-mouth moment for Pérez when the goalkeeper failed to control a back-pass, though he was lucky enough to see it roll harmlessly into the side netting. He was still extremely composed from the following corner, leaving Stewart's shot as it hit the outside of the post and went behind. At the other end there was a headed chance for Borgetti but he was on the stretch and opted to find Hernández, and while he managed it his strike partner was at too tight an angle to capitalise.

It wasn't long until Friedel was called into action again, this time tipping Carmona's curling effort from outside the box over. The USA had another effort from range after Sanneh made a burst up the pitch and played a pass inside to

Stewart, but the NAC Breda man wasted it as the ball spun comfortably wide.

In the 78th minute Aguirre made his final change as Mexico looked to get back into the game, with Torrado making way for Alberto García Aspe. That was swiftly followed by McBride being substituted for Cobi Jones. It was the day after Jones's 32nd birthday but García Aspe was in no mood for niceties as the Mexican was booked for a poor sliding tackle on the man who had been introduced seconds after him.

With seven minutes remaining, Friedel became the ninth player booked – much to his disbelief – after side-footing away a ball that had been smashed towards him after the whistle was blown. The tenth arrived swiftly when Carmona brought down Donovan on the edge of his own box with the game descending into a bitty affair.

Things went up a notch in the 88th minute and Márquez saw red. Shortly after showing his frustrations by taking out O'Brien after the whistle had gone, the Mexico captain blatantly kicked Jones in the back as the pair went up for a header – with Márquez clearly more interested in the man than the ball. Mercado was lucky not to get the same marching orders after stamping on the back of O'Brien's leg.

In the second of the five minutes added on, Arena made his final change when taking Mastroeni off for Carlos Llamosa at the heart of their defence. The USA could have even got a third goal when Jones made a run down the left and picked out Donovan in an almost identical position to that from which he had scored. Going for the volley this time, Donovan's effort went comfortably over the crossbar.

Despite that miss, the USA were never going to be troubled in the final moments. The whistle was eventually blown and brought joyous scenes after one of the most significant results in their history. It was the reward for a resolute display.

On the other hand it was misery for Mexico, with this result playing into what would be known as the 'quinto partido' or 'fifth game' curse. El Tri had only ever made it to a World Cup quarter-final on home soil in 1970 and 1986. After being banned for Italia '90 due to an age manipulation scandal for the Under-20 tournament, they went into the 1994 World Cup looking to restore honour. Instead, it became the start of an unwanted trend as, ahead of the 2022 finals in Qatar, the defeat against USA was the third of seven consecutive tournaments in which they would make it to the round of 16 without playing in that elusive fifth game.

## Brazil 2 Belgium 0 (17 June, Kobe)

Having made numerous changes against Costa Rica, Brazil reverted back to the line-up they had used for a lot of the tournament with Roque Júnior, Roberto Carlos and Ronaldinho replacing Ânderson Polga, Júnior and Edílson. For Belgium, Timmy Simons was the only person coming into the team as he replaced the injured Glen De Boeck.

Brazil were the joint highest scorers in qualifying and clear favourites to go through, but it was Belgium's Mbo Mpenza who had the game's first effort. He forced Marcos to scramble across his goal line within the first minute to claw the Belgian's audacious chip from outside the box over the crossbar. The Red Devils had the better of the game's early encounters and when Juninho Paulista hit Brazil's first effort from range, in the sixth minute, he was unable to work Geert De Vlieger.

The men in yellow shirts built up some pressure after that moment, and Gilberto Silva came agonisingly close to getting on the end of Rivaldo's whipped corner delivery. Roberto Carlos then had a free kick effort from range that went over but was close enough to make De Vlieger nervous.

With a quarter of an hour gone, Ronaldo had by far the best chance of the game so far. Some dazzling footwork and a pass from Ronaldinho found the striker in space, but his curling effort was set marginally too far wide of the post. Another chance soon came without seeing Brazil hit the back of the net as Ronaldo jinked his way to the byline and sat up a cross for Rivaldo to hit, but the number ten sent his acrobatic effort flying into the stratosphere. With Belgium fighting to stay in the game, Yves Vanderhaeghe was booked for bringing Ronaldinho down moments later.

Marc Wilmots had been largely limited and when the ball floated above his head outside the box, the Schalke 04 man tried his own overhead kick. It was further out than Rivaldo's attempt and didn't go quite as high, but he still couldn't work Marcos. Roberto Carlos was then booked for a lunging tackle that Gert Verheyen appeared to run straight into – something the left-back made sure to take up with the Club Brugge forward. The Brazilian's frustrations continued when he mishit a volley to send it trickling wide after lung-bursting work from Juninho down the right flank.

Having scored in all of Belgium's group games, Wilmots had the ball in Brazil's net 35 minutes in after climbing above Roque Júnior to head in Jacky Peeters's cross. However, what seemed like a perfectly good goal was harshly ruled out with referee Peter Prendergast indicating that it was for a push. Whatever it was, the look of dismay on Wilmots's face told a story of its own.

Ronaldo almost capitalised immediately as he burst into the box, but De Vlieger bravely dived at his feet to stop the ball and took a hit to the face. The stopper kicked the ball out so he could receive treatment.

When the game resumed, it seemingly had a greater competitive edge than ever before due to Belgian frustrations and Brazil being shocked into action. Rivaldo was soon bursting down the left before drilling in a cross for Ronaldo, and while the Internazionale frontman did well to get ahead of Simons and reach it he couldn't steer his strike on target.

As half-time approached, Ronaldinho danced his way into the box again surrounded by men in red. He was eventually stopped when Daniel Van Buyten got over quickly enough to block the shot and send it spinning mercifully into De Vlieger's arms. Seconds later, another intervention from the Marseille defender was followed by Roberto Carlos smashing a ball across the face of goal that nobody was able to get on the end of. Prendergast blowing up for half-time soon followed.

Robert Waseige's Belgium side had been described as 'workmanlike' various times throughout the tournament, but they were displaying attacking promise against the best while also keeping them out. They will have even felt hard done by as they went in goalless after seeing the ball in Marcos's net.

The Brazilian was the first goalkeeper to be called into serious action after half-time. Predictably, Wilmots was the man behind the shot; he finished off a nice passage of play with a neat turn and strike that seemed destined for the bottom corner, only for the Palmeiras stalwart to tip it past the post. It wasn't long until Marcos had to sprint out of his goal to smother Mpenza, blocking the Royal Excelsior Mouscron attacker's shot. With Belgium on top, Scolari made the decision to bring Denílson on for Juninho just before the hour.

While the Real Betis man looked bright, the change didn't initially alter the game's flow as Belgium continued to push. Mpenza did well to create a chance for Wilmots who cut across Lúcio and let off a curling effort that looked destined for the top corner. However, once again, Marcos was able to parry it away before the rebound went off target.

In the 67th minute, just as many people around the world would have started believing that Belgium could get through, Brazil showed the magic that made them formidable. Denílson sprinted down the left before keeping his cool to retain possession as the ball was moved methodically to the right. It was when Ronaldinho got it that things really came to life, as the Paris Saint-Germain attacker got a yard from Nico Van Kerckhoven and sent the ball flying towards Rivaldo with a flick of his right boot. Rivaldo then chested the ball down, took a touch and smashed it past De Vlieger via a deflection that left the goalkeeper helpless. As Brazil's number ten ran off swinging his shirt around in celebration, the Belgians looked on in disbelief once more.

The goal undoubtedly shifted the game's momentum, which Waseige attempted to swing back to his team's favour by bringing Peeters off for Wesley Sonck five minutes after the opener – hoping the Genk forward could replicate his heroics off the bench against Russia. It was Bart Goor who came agonisingly close to restoring parity, coming mere inches from getting his head on to a sweeping ball forward.

That was soon followed by another overhead kick attempt, this time seeing Ronaldinho's effort go wide. It was then Sonck's turn to try to make his mark and he came very close, turning near the edge of the box and unleashing a strike that whistled past the post. The Europeans weren't giving up as the final ten minutes approached and Verheyen unleashed a shot, though he couldn't control it and sent the ball up into the air. Soon after that, Scolari opted to bring Kléberson on for Ronaldinho.

Brazil had started to sit back and attempt to soak up Belgium's pressure. That almost proved costly as Roque Júnior's unconvincing block on a shot saw the ball dribble into the six-yard box. Marcos eventually cleared, but Vanderhaeghe was inches away from reaching the ball ahead of the goalkeeper and took him out.

Denílson soon offered a reminder that Brazil could pose problems of their own going forward, even if he ran the ball too far and went into De Vlieger when yellow shirts were queueing up for a pass.

There was to be no such wastefulness in the 87th minute. After Vanderhaeghe conceded possession cheaply, Kleberson immediately raced up the right flank before delivering a pinpoint low cross to Ronaldo. Barely breaking stride, O Fenômeno side-footed the ball off De Vlieger's legs and into the net. Ronaldo now had five goals from four matches and Brazil had their place in the quarter-finals wrapped up, much to the visible delight of the bench.

Goor soon missed a clear-cut opportunity to give Belgium a glimmer of hope, but his blushes were somewhat spared as the offside flag was raised. That was followed by Rivaldo getting a warm ovation as he was brought off in the 90th minute to be replaced by Ricardinho. Moments later, the final whistle confirmed that Brazil were through to the next round while Belgium were heading home.

'On that day, we were better than Brazil,' Wilmots told FIFATV in 2014. 'Six months later, Scolari gave me a memento for the 100th anniversary of Real Madrid and in his book, he wrote, "The hardest was against Belgium. We were close to being out." Sometimes a tournament goes like this with a decision that hurts you, but life goes on.

'It leaves a bitter taste but you have to see the overall performance. You're out, but you go out with honour. We were welcomed in Brussels like we won this match.'

### *Japan 0 Turkey 1 (18 June, Miyagi)*

This was an incredibly big game for both teams involved, as neither had ever reached the knockout stage of a World Cup before now. Philippe Troussier made two attacking changes for Japan, replacing Atsushi Yanagisawa and Takayuki Suzuki with Alessandro Santos (otherwise known as Alex) and Akinori Nishisawa. Meanwhile, Alpay Özalan and Ergün Penbe replaced Emre Aşşık and Emre Belözoğlu – who were both suspended after picking up bookings against Costa Rica and China. However, Şenol Güneş would have been encouraged by Rüştü Reçber being available.

There were goosebump-inspiring levels of noise in the Miyagi Stadium when the two teams emerged, before it died down for the national anthems that both nations sung wholeheartedly. The chanting soon resumed once Pierluigi Collina got the game under way.

Yıldıray Baştürk was looking a real threat within the first minute and after already being fouled, the Bayer Leverkusen man danced his way into the Japanese box before being abruptly halted by the onrushing goalkeeper Seigo Narazaki.

The ensuing exchanges were fierce. Tackles flew in from both teams as Japan started formulating attacks of their own and the two sides tried to assert their dominance on the game. The opening ten minutes were played at a blistering pace but both defences were competing brilliantly, meaning there were no meaningful shots on goal.

Eventually a mistake from Kōji Nakata allowed Turkey in after he gave the ball away and then put it out for a corner with his recovery challenge. That proved costly as Ümit Davala rose through the air unchallenged and reached Penbe's delivery. Once up, he executed a header that left Narazaki rooted after initially coming out and retreating back to his goal line, putting Turkey ahead with 12 minutes on the clock. The winger's joy was unmistakable as he ran to do a knee slide before being congratulated by his team-mates.

Japan came close to responding within minutes as Nishizawa turned behind and attempted to get a shot off, but Hakan Ünsal did well to get a block in after initially being beaten. What seemed to be a mishit cross from Alex troubled Rüştü moments later but it eventually looped on to the roof of Turkey's net.

With the pace back up and both teams competing well, Alpay got the game's first yellow card in the 21st minute for lunging in and taking out Alex's legs. There was no further punishment, though, as Japan made a complete mess of their short free-kick routine.

Hakan Şükür was still yet to score in the tournament but wasn't looking low on confidence at all and attempted to chip Narazaki from a tight angle. While the goalkeeper looked worried, he was able to get back quickly enough to catch the ball. Şükür was soon heading it down for fellow forward Hasan Şaş's first effort of the game but the strike sailed comfortably over the crossbar.

As the half hour came and went, the game was turning into a bit of a scrappy affair, with a break in play while Şaş was seemingly caught in the eye by Hidetoshi Nakata's outstretched hand as the midfielder turned. Even with the Galatasaray forward back on the pitch, there wasn't much improvement in terms of attacking quality and Japan struggled to find the pass to break Turkey's resolute back line when it really mattered, while Yıldıray Baştürk hit a tame shot.

Some Japanese fans will have been forgiven for thinking they had been awarded a penalty in the 41st minute when Alpay committed a foul by going through the back of Hidetoshi Nakata on the very edge of his own box. However it was just a free kick and it seemed inevitable that the man fouled would take it as he stepped up. Instead, Alex struck the ball and was desperately unlucky to see it cannon back off the point where the post and crossbar meet – Rüştü had barely bothered to move.

Just moments later, Penbe was booked for bringing down Alex, who was showing signs that he could make an impact in his first start of the tournament. The Shimizu S-Pulse man was involved once again when Shinji Ono smashed the free kick delivery into the box, but couldn't quite control his header to find the target.

Kazuyuki Toda, who showed a fiery side at various points throughout the World Cup, saw yellow for a cynical foul on Baştürk to stop a break on the stroke of half-time. Troussier made two interval changes as he brought off Junichi Inamoto and Alex for Daisuke Ichikawa and Suzuki – despite Alex's late flurry of activity before the break.

Ichikawa got a warm welcome from Ünsal, who mercilessly smashed into him during a 50-50 challenge just a couple of minutes after his introduction. It was soon Bülent Korkmaz's turn to writhe in pain on the floor after a late tackle from Nishizawa.

There was what seemed to be another foul within moments as Alpay tripped Suzuki in the box, though Collina waved play on despite the outrage raining down from the stands. In the aftermath, Hidetoshi Nakata hit an effort from outside the box that flicked up to cause Rüştü problems, but the stopper was able to pat the ball down and reach it before Nishizawa could get there.

Alpay wasn't looking completely comfortable despite Turkey's clean sheet remaining intact, panicking and stealing the ball from Rüştü's gloves when Toda's cross came in – eventually getting away with it due to the follow-up delivery going behind. That didn't mean the Aston Villa centre-back escaped a questioning from his goalkeeper, though.

Şaş brought some extra life to Turkey's play on the hour as he slalomed his way through the middle of the pitch, but the number 11's eventual strike was saved with relative ease. Japan responded immediately, surging up the other end and delivering a cross for Nishizawa to attack, but his header was also straight at the goalkeeper.

Suzuki was then incredibly close to being played through but the substitute was let down by a touch that allowed Korkmaz to recover and clear. With the game's levels rising, Baştürk saw the half's most eye-catching effort sail marginally wide of Narazaki's post. Hidetoshi Nakata brought another satisfying moment, pulling off a nutmeg before being fouled by Ümit Davala. Ono was unable to beat the first man in the box with his free kick, though.

Köji Nakata put his team in trouble after it was cleared, seeing his overly relaxed pass intercepted by Şaş near the halfway line. Unlike what happened with the opener, the centre-back got away with it. The Galatasaray man ran into the box and went down after being nudged by Tsuneyasu Miyamoto but was completely ignored by Collina.

In the 74th minute Güneş made his first change of the game, taking Davala off for Real Sociedad's Nihat Kehveci. It wasn't long until there was another stoppage, this time coming so that Tugay Kerimoğlu could get treatment.

As the game entered its final ten minutes it was apparent Japan weren't going to get too many chances to equalise because Turkey were managing the game well. There was a big sigh from the crowd when Nishizawa's shot from the edge of the box sailed over the crossbar but that didn't stop them trying and plenty of crosses were attempted without finding a Japanese head.

There was a flurry of late changes as Turkey aimed to maintain their lead and Japan looked to force extra time. Şaş was replaced by Tayfur Havutçu, which was followed by the substitute Ichikawa being replaced by Hiroaki Morishima, who had handed Japan the lead against Tunisia.

However, for all of the nice football being played, Japan simply couldn't muster enough to get through. Naoki Matsuda's speculative shot from range looped up and into Rüştü's arms after being blocked. There was a half chance for Nishizawa as the 90th minute approached, but the striker was left holding his leg after hitting his shot high and wide. That was followed by Turkey's final change with Baştürk making way for İlhan Mansız.

It looked as though Morishima was about to finally make the burst forward Japan needed as he went through the gears, but Turkey captain Şükür took one for the team, being carded for cynically pulling down the substitute. Ono delivered a dangerous whipped free kick but Penbe hurled himself at the ball to head it behind, before a Japanese foul was committed while trying to make the most of the ensuing corner.

In the end the Turkish wall was just too much for the co-hosts to surmount and the red flags came out as Turkey celebrated with history continuing to be made. On the other hand, there were plenty of Japanese tears shed by players and supporters alike as they realised their tournament was over as a team, even if there were more games to be played in their home.

## South Korea 2 Italy 1; after sudden death extra time (18 June, Daejeon)

Hours after seeing their co-hosts knocked out, South Korea looked to continue their own journey on home soil. Guus Hiddink understandably stuck with the same starting line-up that beat Portugal to secure top spot in Group D.

Giovanni Trapattoni was forced into two of his changes with Alessandro Nesta's foot injury keeping him out, while Fabio Cannavaro was suspended. Filippo Inzaghi was replaced by Alessandro Del Piero after the Juventus talisman's equaliser against Mexico, with Francesco Coco and Mark Iuliano also coming in.

There was a real buzz among South Korea's fans in the Daejeon World Cup Stadium as Byron Moreno blew his whistle to get the game off to what proved to be a blistering start. Even the shortest period of Italy possession was met by boos, while chants and cheers rang out whenever South Korea had the ball.

The noise cranked up considerably in the fourth minute when Coco got the game's first yellow card for taking out Park Ji-Sung as the winger sprinted past him and threatened to burst into the box.

Then they were awarded a penalty after two Korean men hit the floor when Song Chong-gug whipped in the ensuing free kick delivery. Italy were furious, but Moreno pointed to the spot with Ahn Jung-hwan standing over the ball. The Perugia forward confidently stepped up and sent an effort towards the bottom corner but Gianluigi Buffon had read his intentions and got down to his right, parrying it behind for a corner. As the Italians jubilantly jumped around, Christian Panucci showed his frustrations towards the referee for the initial decision.

There was soon a break in play as Kim Tae-young sustained a head injury after an aerial duel with Christian Vieri – Hong Myung-bo indicated to the referee that he thought the striker had thrown an elbow.

Both teams maintained their intensity as play resumed, with Vieri marginally clearing the crossbar from Italy's first shot and Buffon sprinting out of his box to deal with a threatening through ball. Francesco Totti soon had his first opportunity of the game from a free kick but smashed it against Damiano Tommasi.

In the 17th minute, a bloodied Kim Tae-Young was the first Korean to go into the book, perhaps harshly being cautioned for a challenge on Vieri. Lee Woon-jae did well to punch Del Piero's delivery away ahead of Totti, but there was nothing he could do when it was the number ten taking a corner. Totti whipped the ball in towards the front post where Vieri out-jumped Choi Jin-cheul and powered his header into the back of the net before putting a finger to his lips while facing the stands.

South Koreans soon surrounded Moreno demanding a yellow for Totti after Kim Nam-il went down holding his face when the Roma talisman caught him while using his arm for momentum. Moreno obliged, leaving Totti looking perplexed.

At this time, South Korea were doing a lot of attacking but rarely called Buffon into action. A great move found Lee Young-pyo in a threatening area, and while the 25-year-old pulled off some nice step-overs to create space his cross was comfortably headed away. The Asians continued to show patience as they moved the ball around well, with their big opening coming in the 36th minute when Song's attempted pass deflected off Coco and into Ahn's path. The forward turned brilliantly to create space but couldn't show the same composure with his shot and failed to find the target.

Tommasi had a chance to double Italy's lead moments later after Totti received his pass and masterfully returned it to the shaggy-haired midfielder. Lee Woon-jae rushed out to deny him, the ball hit Kim Nam-il and Choi cleared as Del Piero speculatively dived in an optimistic attempt to block it into the net.

Nothing came from the ensuing corner, but there was a stoppage in play as Coco was caught in the face by Tommasi while heading it behind. As the centre-back walked off with blood staining his hair, South Korea took another corner that was easily cleared. Ahn had a shot from range moments later, but it was comfortably saved by Buffon.

Down to ten men until a bandaged-up Coco returned to the pitch, Italy were initially content to hold on to possession. By the time the defender returned the whistle was being blown for half-time.

South Korea flew out of the traps for the second half with Seol Ki-hyeon's cross being unconvincingly cleared before a shot went so wide it returned to the Anderlecht forward.

While the final application wasn't there, the intensity certainly was.

In a game that would be known for its controversy for years to come, Kim Tae-young was incredibly lucky not to be given a red card in the 50th minute when he looked at Del Piero as the Italian pulled his shirt and elbowed him in the face with force. Somehow the defender only got a talking to from Moreno.

Italy's frustrations around that incident will have only increased when Tommasi was booked five minutes later for pulling down Lee Young-pyo. That was swiftly followed by Totti feeling he was fouled by Kim Tae-young before South Korea got another free kick. Song thought quickly as he attempted to release Ahn, but Buffon rushed out to meet the ball. Seconds later, Gianluca Zambrotta's pinpoint cross was met by a thunderbolt volley from Del Piero that Choi got across brilliantly to block.

In the 59th minute Cristiano Zanetti became the fourth Italian to enter Moreno's book for nudging the referee while protesting after Coco had fouled Park. He looked on in disbelief as the Italians crowded the official. When the free kick was finally taken, Park laid it off and Ahn smashed it over the crossbar as Italian bodies flew towards him.

It wasn't long until Trapattoni made his first change and Gennaro Gattuso replaced Del Piero. Hiddink responded quickly with forward Hwang Sun-hong replacing centre-back Kim Tae-young. While his namesake Kim Nam-il was on the floor, Italy were soon on the attack as they cut the depleted South Korea open but Zambrotta couldn't quite find the final pass and the ball was cleared. The Koreans played with ten men until Lee Chun-soo was able to come on.

Lee was involved immediately, bursting forward with the ball at his feet before shifting it out wide to Seol, who delivered a cross for Ahn. After initially bringing the ball down well the Perugia man tried and failed to dribble it past Coco then nutmegged him before being dispossessed. With a wall of noise coming from the stands, the intensity that had been evident throughout the game was in no danger of fading. Angelo Di Livio was soon introduced to proceedings, replacing Zambrotta in the 72nd minute.

Italy had a marvellous opportunity to double their lead almost immediately as Zanetti hit a 40-yard pass over the Korean defence and into Vieri's path. As Vieri approached the goal with just Lee Woon-jae to beat, he uncharacteristically missed the target altogether with a poor shot. Vieri soon had another go after brilliantly winning possession and driving into the box but his shot was blocked by Lee Young-pyo and – after a concerned look from the goalkeeper – eventually nestled on the roof of the net.

Totti soon had an attempt of his own, embarking on a mazy run from inside his own half that eventually reached the edge of South Korea's box. He was then blocked off, being left a frustrated and bewildered figure on the floor. As the final ten minutes approached, there was more outrage from Italy as Lee Chun-soo tried to get a shot off but ended up kicking Maldini in the head as he nipped it away. Then no yellow card was given when their breakaway was illegitimately brought to an end.

With South Korea still far from out of this contest, Hiddink made his final alteration in the 83rd minute as another defender, Hong, made way for another attacker, Cha Du-ri. The hosts were well on top but Italy still had a chance to extend their lead, with Totti's free kick delivery coming inches from finding Vieri's head before being cleared.

When another Totti cross went into Lee Woon-jae's arms, the goalkeeper sprung an attack that carried on despite Gattuso and Maldini both managing to get tackles in. Following the latter attempt, the ball was worked to Hwang who clipped a cross towards the back post that evaded every man in a white shirt and landed on Panucci's thigh. It bounced up off the Italian and on to his arm as he fell back, providing Seol with the opportunity to shoot. He took it gratefully, firing a first-time effort into the bottom corner and giving Buffon absolutely no chance. While Hiddink remained focused on the sideline, South Korea's number nine and the rest of the nation jubilantly celebrated.

Vieri had a glorious chance to immediately restore Italy's lead after Di Livio whipped a brilliant low cross into the box but sent his effort over the crossbar with the goal at his mercy. There was hardly any time left, so much so that Inzaghi mistakenly walked on to the pitch for a second when Buffon kicked the ball out of play following the ensuing attack.

The striker's return to the bench was swiftly followed by an attack led by Cha down the right. A roar arose as he won a corner with the game entering injury time. While it wasn't the greatest delivery, the ball made its way to Cha who hit a clean bicycle kick straight at Buffon. A long ball towards the back post then found Seol who was able to chest it down, only to send his final strike into the side netting. Twenty seconds and a very slowly taken goal kick from Buffon later and the whistle was blown. Extra time awaited.

Within a minute of the restart, both sides were a last-ditch defensive intervention away from getting a clear chance on goal. The game was being played at a blistering pace –

especially considering 90 minutes of football had already passed – with the players vying for the golden goal that would secure their passage to the quarter-finals, but the defences were standing strong and refusing to be breached.

In fact, when Lee Chun-soo was booked in the 100th minute for going into a challenge with his studs up, neither team had registered a shot on target since the restart. It wasn't too long after that incident that Park came to life, showing great footwork to find space near the edge of Italy's box before being taken out by Maldini and winning a free kick. Hwang intelligently hit his effort under the jumping Italian wall but Buffon patted it away impressively.

In the 103rd minute a period of extra time that had been a magnificent spectacle descended into controversy when Totti was given a second yellow card. As Totti danced his way through the box trying to find enough space to shoot, he had been clipped by Song and went tumbling to the ground, which Moreno interpreted as him diving. Upon seeing the replay people across Italy would have been incredulous, feeling they were owed a penalty. However, they were now down to ten men despite the Italian protests on the pitch led by Di Livio. There was still a game to be decided, and a speculative effort from Hwang was all that could be managed before the whistle ended the first period of extra time.

After the restart, Panucci came agonisingly close to finding Vieri with his cross from a free kick that was cleared brilliantly. While the intensity remained as high as ever, the game wasn't being played at quite the same pace. There was a renewal of Italian frustrations towards the referee when Tommasi was adjudged to be offside when a pass from Vieri released the midfielder into a position where the goal was at his mercy. Hwang had South Korea's best chance of extra time so far within seconds, but his header was comfortable for Buffon to deal with.

At the other end, Gattuso really should have scored after a ridiculous defensive back-heel attempt saw the ball bounce off the midfielder and put him through on goal. However, Lee Woon-jae pulled off a brilliant stop to keep the game going. Choi was then booked for a late challenge on Vieri.

The match's sustained pace was potentially beginning to get to the players but Ahn ensured they wouldn't have to go on any longer by scoring the golden goal in the 117th minute. The ball had been swept out wide to the left flank, where Lee Chun-soo collected it and passed back to Lee Young-pyo. Lee delivered a pinpoint cross into the packed box and with Maldini on the back foot, Ahn was able to jump highest to head past Buffon and spark the wildest of celebrations in the Daejeon World Cup Stadium.

As Ahn, the only South Korean who played his domestic football in Italy, ran off with his arms out wide in celebration before succumbing to tears of joy, Hiddink threw his fists into the air and the whole of South Korea rejoiced. It was confirmed that they would be going through and Italy were on their way home.

Gli Azzurri hadn't been at their best for large periods of the tournament, but there was outrage towards Moreno across Italy. This was captured by the headline emblazoned on the following day's *La Gazzetta dello Sport* front page. Translated, it read 'The scandalous Ecuadorian referee, Italy out of the World Cup' with 'Vergogna!', which translates to 'Shame!' written in large font underneath, accompanied by an image of Di Livio angrily pointing at Moreno while Vieri looked on in disgust.

The fury didn't stop there and speaking to the same outlet about Ahn, Perugia chairman Luciano Gaucci said, 'That gentleman will never set foot in Perugia again,' before adding, 'He was a phenomenon only when he played against Italy. I am a nationalist and I regard such behaviour not only as an affront to Italian pride but also an offence to a country which two years ago opened its doors to him. I have no intention of paying a salary to someone who has ruined Italian soccer'.

Ahn later told BBC Sport, 'I don't understand why they did this to me,' unable to comprehend the Italian feeling towards him. He added, 'Even now, I cannot find any reason to convince myself, I still cannot accept it. When I scored that goal, the feeling was unbelievable. It was the best moment of my career'.

Issues surrounding Moreno would be even more long-lasting. With his reputation in tatters internationally, it was soon equally ruined back in Ecuador. During a match between Liga de Quito and Barcelona of Guayaquil, he signalled for six minutes of injury time before proceeding to play 13, in which Quito came from behind to win 4-3 while two contentious penalties and as many red cards were given. This came at a time in which Moreno was running for election in the local council of Quito. The Ecuadorian Football Federation banned him for 20 matches.

Soon after returning, he was banned for one game after sending off three Deportivo Quito players in a match against Deportivo Cuenca. Realising his reputation was now broken beyond repair, Moreno retired and made television appearances; he provided analysis in Ecuador and went on comedy shows in Italy to be mocked for his ineptitude as a referee. Having become accustomed to the finer things in life, he ran up huge debts and eventually resorted to drug-smuggling, being caught in September 2010 by United States Customs at JFK Airport in New York. After two years in jail, he was released and extradited back to Ecuador.

# 6

# Quarter-Finals

*England 1 Brazil 2 (21 June, Shizuoka)*

In this World Cup's first quarter-final, England lined up with the same team that had comfortably beaten Denmark. Meanwhile, Luiz Felipe Scolari's only alteration from the side that overcame Belgium saw Juninho Paulista replace Kléberson. The England team had been in attendance for that match but would have expected a better performance than the South Americans had provided in their last outing.

After what had seemingly become a customary two verses of the English national anthem and the more traditional one-run through of Brazil's, England had a corner within seconds thanks to a brilliant burst forward from Ashley Cole. Nothing came of it and Marcos authoritatively punched away David Beckham's deep delivery. The Three Lions also had the game's first effort on goal, but it was routine for Marcos after Emile Heskey headed Beckham's free kick from deep straight at him.

Rivaldo wasted no time in getting a shot off from range – as had been the case so often throughout the tournament – but his latest attempt flew harmlessly wide. After this, Brazil began to control the ball and pinned back England's resolute defence with Danny Mills and Beckham doing a particularly good job of doubling up on Roberto Carlos.

Sol Campbell also got in on the act, doing brilliantly to head a dangerous corner clear after a quarter of an hour before coming across intelligently to end a Ronaldo burst forward. Brazil were firmly on top at this point with quick link-up play between Rivaldo and Ronaldo seeing the latter get a decent shot off that went straight at David Seaman.

Despite all of this, England got their noses in front in the 23rd minute. After Campbell had blocked an overly ambitious shot attempt from Rivaldo, Paul Scholes switched the ball out wide to Mills, who played it forward to Heskey in space. The Liverpool man turned and was immediately looking for Michael Owen. He hit a lofted pass behind that was awkward for Lúcio to deal with but the centre-back still insisted on taking a touch, which allowed Owen to nip in and steal the ball away. Breaking into the box, England's number ten sat Marcos down before making sure of the goal by lifting the ball into the net.

There was unbridled joy among the English in the stands, but those on the pitch had to concentrate immediately as Edmílson played a one-two that saw him break into the box before being halted. There was another scare soon afterwards as Beckham went down with a knock after making a challenge on Ronaldo, but the England captain was able to continue after receiving treatment – his return to the pitch inspired a massive roar from the stands. It wasn't long until English nerves returned, however, as Ronaldo beat Cole in the box before his toe-poke came back off Seaman.

Beckham was soon in the thick of the action again, smashing a loose ball on the edge of the box but being unable to keep it down. Another England chance soon followed, this time seeing Heskey reach Mills's cross to loop a threatening header on to the roof of Marcos's net. Roberto Carlos replied with a venomous strike that only found the side netting – still managing to cause gasps from the crowd.

As Brazil continued to hold plenty of possession, Cafu had two shots blocked with the first seemingly destined to play Ronaldo through before Mills raced over to deny him. There was another injury scare for England as Heskey went down following a collision with Roque Júnior, but once again the Europeans were soon restored to their full contingent. It was soon Seaman's turn to go down after he came out to gather a deflected shot, going over bodies in the box and hitting the floor.

With the first half approaching injury time when Seaman got up, it seemed as though England would be able to see out their lead. Their spirited defence had taken the sting out of the game, the midfield was showing real discipline and Heskey was fighting to give those behind him respite whenever possible as he fought for balls and ran the channels. They couldn't make it, though. In the second minute of injury time, Ronaldinho burst through the middle of the pitch and attracted England men towards him before releasing Rivaldo as he got into the box. The Barcelona man made no mistake, opening up his body to place the ball across Seaman and into the bottom corner.

In a familiar sight during this tournament, Rivaldo took off his shirt and swung it around in the air to celebrate. He was still working out how to get it back on by the time the game restarted, but England were unable to do anything as the half-time whistle was blown just seconds later. Post-match, defender Gareth Southgate admitted his disappointment at Sven-Göran Eriksson's half-time team talk, 'We were expecting Winston Churchill and instead got Iain Duncan Smith'.

England seemed to have recovered from the blow, coming out strong after the restart. However they were hit with another in the 50th minute after Scholes fouled Kléberson in a seemingly harmless area. Brazil had originally tried to take a quick free kick before referee Felipe Ramos made them re-take it. When the whistle blew again, Ronaldinho sent the ball flying over Seaman and into the top corner. The goalkeeper had taken up an aggressive position, seemingly presuming that the Paris Saint-Germain star would cross, and was simply unable to claw the ball away despite staggering back in his efforts to do so.

Many questions followed, looking at whether Ronaldinho meant it and how Seaman let that happen. Speaking to *FourFourTwo* years later the goalscorer insisted, 'I saw he was off his line. About five metres off. I really aimed at the goal'. Intent didn't really matter; what did was that as Ronaldinho ran off to celebrate, Brazil were ahead five minutes into the second half having been down with moments left of the first.

With Brazil refusing to sit back, both teams were on the search for goals. Within a few minutes of the South Americans going ahead, Owen came close to getting behind their defence before losing his balance, Roberto Carlos hit the side netting and Edmílson did well to cut out Heskey's dangerous ball across the box.

In an effort to get back into the game, Eriksson made his first substitution in the 56th minute when taking Trevor Sinclair off for Kieron Dyer. An even bigger change came a minute later as Ronaldinho was sent off for a challenge on

Mills, much to his disbelief. He went over the ball while attempting to get it and came down on the right-back's ankle, sending Mills towards the floor in pain. Ronaldinho had been the thorn in England's side all game but he was now going to miss the final half an hour.

He certainly took his time coming off and looked devastated, but the match continued without him as both teams struggled to release the attacking talents that remained. Beckham soon had a half-hearted penalty shout turned down, which led to Brazilians claiming that he should be booked for diving. Both defences were standing strong at this point and Roberto Carlos smashed his free kick against the sturdy England wall.

In the 70th minute Edílson was brought on for Ronaldo, ending the latter's run of scoring in every match at the finals. The game was being played at a pedestrian pace now, as Brazil did everything they could to slow it down while the Three Lions were struggling to find a way to create meaningful opportunities. That continued when Rivaldo went down holding his face after the slightest of contacts from Campbell as the pair jumped for a header.

Mills almost made a breakthrough, brilliantly turning his marker in the box and getting a left-footed shot off, but it was deflected over the crossbar by Roque Júnior's outstretched leg. There seemed to be growing frustrations among the men in white when Campbell was penalised for his efforts to reach the ensuing corner, which was swiftly followed up by Scholes going into the referee's book for a foul on Rivaldo.

As the game approached the final ten minutes, Brazil seemed largely content to keep possession and run down the clock while England looked as though they were waning. In an effort to change that, Eriksson brought Darius Vassell on for Owen up top, which was soon followed by Teddy Sheringham replacing Cole.

The next few minutes mostly consisted of balls flying into the Brazilian box but not even Beckham could find an English head. One of his passes almost played through a man in blue after being mis-controlled by Mills, but the right-back managed to retrieve the ball just before it reached Edílson.

The game threatened to become end to end at one point but after some back and forth, Roberto Carlos slowed it down having initially burst up the pitch to win a free kick from Nicky Butt. It spoke volumes about the South Americans' approach to the final few minutes that rather than whipping the ball into the box, they opted to play short and knock it about. Even when Cafu dispossessed Scholes, what initially looked like a counter culminated in the right-back going to the corner and winning a throw off Campbell.

Dyer was showing moments of trickery and trying to make things happen but England's final delivery was letting them down. There was a hopeful roar from the stands when Gilberto Silva headed behind for a corner with 30 seconds of normal time remaining. That quickly subsided, though, as Campbell and Butt rose in the air but the ball went off Rivaldo, on to Butt and out for a goal kick.

There were four minutes added on but England could do nothing. Campbell and Seaman narrowly escaped with the ball after a mix-up, while nobody in white could muster the quality to test Marcos at all with aimlessly hopeful crosses floated into the box. As Seaman smashed a ball forward the referee's whistle was blown, confirming that Brazil were going through to the semi-final while the Three Lions were left forlorn and Seaman could be seen in tears in the knowledge that his and England's World Cup was over. They could hold on to that victory over Argentina, but the overriding emotion looking back would be disappointment.

## Germany 1 USA 0 (21 June, Ulsan)

As USA entered their first World Cup quarter-final, Bruce Arena's only change saw Josh Wolff come out for Frankie Hejduk, who was returning from suspension. Rudi Völler also benefited from returning players as Christian Ziege and Dietmar Hamann were available again, while Sebastien Kehl joined them in the starting line-up with Marko Rehmer, Jens Jeremies and Marco Bode all missing out.

Within the opening minute Landon Donovan thought he had got behind the German defence, but a free kick was given as he had accidentally tripped Christoph Metzelder on the way through. Just seconds later Donovan was seemingly through again, but was this time called offside – though it looked a tighter call than it first seemed.

While the Americans had enjoyed the better of the opening five minutes, a swift Germany move showed what they were up against and their defence scrambled back to deal with Oliver Neuville's dangerous cross. The Bayer Leverkusen frontman also hit an ambitious volley when the ball came out to the edge of the box, but his effort skewed wide. In the tenth minute Eddie Lewis hit the USA's first real shot but was unable to find the target with his free kick.

Lewis was soon getting down the left flank and delivering a wicked ball, but Oliver Kahn did brilliantly to dive and palm it away with two men in blue waiting for the simplest of finishes. Tony Sanneh also got towards the byline before cutting back well and this time it was Metzelder who nullified the threat.

Donovan was looking really bright, and seconds after being denied by the offside flag he embarked on a run that included nutmegging Hamann before hitting a sweet strike that was miraculously tipped wide by Kahn. Neuville missed what would have been Germany's best chance so far when he didn't get enough on his glancing header from Bernd Schneider's cross. He was offside anyway as Pablo Mastroeni had done well to step up in line with his team-mates.

After Hejduk – who had been getting up and down well all game – was fouled by Ziege, Lewis delivered a cross that was attacked brilliantly by Gregg Berhalter but eventually sailed over. There was then a brief stoppage in the 27th minute when Michael Ballack required treatment for a bloodied nose after being caught by John O'Brien's elbow while the pair jumped for a header.

The USA had been the dominant force in the opening half an hour and Donovan almost provided the opener as he finally sprung the offside trap but was forced wide by the recovering Thomas Linke. With the angle narrowed, Kahn was able to come out and stop the strike at the expense of a corner. Brian McBride came flying across in an attempt to reach Claudio Reyna's delivery but the ball eventually went out for a goal kick.

Germany were just beginning to pose a threat of their own: one free kick almost found Miroslav Klose in the box, Neuville hit a bicycle kick that smashed Lewis in the face from point-blank range and Ballack wasted a headed opportunity.

The USA also conjured a good effort as McBride broke down the left and found Donovan, who controlled well before laying the ball back for Lewis to strike, but Kahn was there once again with a strong reaction save. After all of the good work done by Arena's side it was Germany who took the lead in the 39th minute. A relatively soft foul had been given against Lewis, which allowed Ziege to deliver a pinpoint cross that Ballack rose to head into the net. Brad Friedel had actually got a hand to it, but his efforts were futile and the USA now had a massive challenge on their hands against a side that had conceded just one in four games across the tournament so far.

Any frustrations felt by Lewis would have only grown when he was booked for persistent fouling seconds after the restart. With the USA on the back foot, Eddie Pope was given a yellow card just one minute later, with the free kick seemingly destined for another Ballack header before Berhalter superbly flicked it away. Klose came even closer to doubling Germany's lead with his header bouncing off the post and back out. McBride almost got through in the first half's final seconds but couldn't quite keep hold of the ball and Hugh Dallas's whistle saw the Euopeans go into the break 1-0 up.

Both teams went for it as soon as the second half got under way, with Sanneh coming close. The Nürnberg defender made an incredible run that saw him beat Ballack, pass the ball wide and sprint into the box. Throwing himself at Lewis's cross, Sanneh came agonisingly close to heading it in, but he couldn't reach far enough and Metzelder put the ball behind. Donovan was soon getting in on the action as he broke into the Germany box but Hamann was able to get across and block his shot when it seemed there had been an opening.

The ensuing corner saw the USA get about as close as they possibly could without finding their equaliser. Reyna's delivery was initially flicked on by Sanneh with Berhalter flying through the air to get on to it. The defender's shot bounced off Kahn as he dived and would have gone over the line had it not been handled by Torsten Frings. Having got away with a handball against Mexico, it was the USA who felt wronged as referee Dallas didn't spot this from the German. It was impossible to miss Berhalter repeatedly trying to kick the ball as Kahn held on to it and Germany were awarded a free kick. O'Brien's strike from outside the box moments later was far easier for the goalkeeper to deal with, while McBride would have had a great chance if he had been able to control Berhalter's ball over the top.

As had been the case for large periods of the first half the USA were mostly in control of the play, although there was a scare when Reyna conceded possession near the halfway line, resorting to pulling Ballack's shirt to ensure Neuville couldn't play him in and the move broke down, while the USA's number ten escaped a booking.

The first substitution came after 58 minutes as Clint Mathis replaced McBride up top, which was swiftly followed by Germany's Jeremies coming on for Schneider. But it was Germany who came close to the game's second goal soon after the changes when Neuville made a wide run and squared the ball to Klose who looked sure to convert with a first-time finish until Sanneh came flying across to block it. The USA could have had an equaliser seconds later, as Kahn raced out of his box to make a header that only went as far as Reyna, but the first-time volley that sent Kahn helplessly sprinting back to his goal line also went wide of the mark.

There was another change in the 65th minute, this time seeing Hejduk make way for Cobi Jones. This was a sign that USA were far from giving up on their World Cup place, and so was a Mathis run that ended in Kehl getting a yellow card for fouling him. There was a delay to the free kick being taken due to a coming together that resulted in yellow cards for Neuville and Reyna.

As it was cleared and Neuville led a break up the pitch, Mastroeni joined them in the book after blatantly blocking off the German with no intention of going for the ball. This meant the Colorado Rapids man would be ineligible if the USA made it through to the semi-final. With it looking as though things may get slightly too heated, Berhalter got the game's fifth booking in as many minutes for his late lunge on Klose, making him unavailable too.

Having created regular problems, Neuville did so again with the game entering its final quarter of an hour as he hurdled a challenge and cut in on the edge of the USA's box. However the striker was left frustrated with himself after curling his strike over the crossbar.

Both teams made changes ahead of the final ten minutes with Bode replacing Neuville and Mastroeni making way for Earnie Stewart. While the Americans were seeing plenty of the ball in their quest to restore parity, Germany looked in control and Bode almost played a part in a breakaway goal after nodding down the long ball that came his way. However, with Klose, Friedel and Pope all hurtling towards the loose ball, it was the latter who reached it first to clear.

Sanneh had a half-chance to get the USA back on level terms when Reyna crossed the ball into the box from a free kick. It was a difficult one to take with his back to goal, and the defender got too much on his flicked header to send the ball wide. Undeterred, Sanneh stayed up top for the final five minutes in the hope another opportunity would come.

Likely with the aim of running down the clock and disrupting proceedings, Völler made his final change in the

88th minute with Klose coming off for Oliver Bierhoff. It looked like Sanneh was going to have his moment of glory when Mathis planted a cross on to his head at the back post but the defender-turned-frontman could only find the side netting. With the USA throwing everything they had forward, Bode had another chance of his own having got behind the defence. The German also hit the side netting, having forced himself wide. Hamann then had a chance when he dispossessed Reyna on the edge of the USA's box, but the captain redeemed himself by winning the ball back.

Just preventing another German goal wasn't enough, and Mathis saw his strike bounce back off Jeremies. While Germany wasted two chances to wrap things up, Dallas's whistle eventually did that for them and Kahn laid on his back breathless having made a series of brilliant saves to ensure his nation went through. It had been an incredibly valiant display from the USA, who could feel hard done by that they were out of the tournament but proudly look back at a time in which they exceeded expectations.

### Spain 0 South Korea 0; after extra time, South Korea won 5-3 on penalties (22 June, Gwangju)

Both teams had required extra time in the round of 16, with Spain going to penalties, but the two managers took slightly different approaches in setting up their teams. Guus Hiddink kept the exact same XI that started against Italy, while José Antonio Camacho made three changes as Enrique Romero, Miguel Ángel Nadal and Joaquín replaced Juanfran, Luis Enrique and Raúl – though the latter came out through injury.

As proceedings started, the atmosphere in the stands was about all there was to admire. Both sides took their time to settle into the game and struggled to maintain meaningful possession. Fernando Hierro almost released Fernando Morientes with a ball over the top but Kim Tae-young used his body well to see the ball through to Lee Woon-jae – having already got into a couple of tangles.

South Korea responded with a long ball of their own to Ahn Jung-hwan, but Hierro stretched to get his head on it and force the Perugia man wide, with his cross eventually being easily headed away. As the Asians began to get on top but struggled to provide much cutting edge, Park Ji-sung could have had the game's first real chance in the 12th minute if he had been able to judge Kim Nam-il's ball into the box, though it eventually trickled behind. There was no shortage of dedication, though, with a slight break in play required after Choi Jin-cheul and Hong Myung-bo collided while going for the same ball.

In the 18th minute Rubén Baraja had the game's first real effort after Carles Puyol's long throw bounced towards the midfielder, but his acrobatic attempt went wide. There was another Spain chance after Joaquín drove inside and won a free kick on the edge of the box. In keeping with much of what had gone before, Hierro sent a weak effort into the wall.

Another throw-in saw Morientes attempt a bicycle kick, but that simply popped up into the air and the men in white were able to break up the pitch until Ahn was fouled. The Spanish striker got far closer with a header moments later but Lee Woon-jae was able to pluck the ball out of the air and hold on to it despite colliding with the post and requiring treatment. It was another header that saw Spain come close just after the half-hour, with Hierro's effort nestling on the roof of the net.

There was a blow for South Korea in the 32nd minute as Kim Nam-il was forced off with a knock to be replaced by

Lee Eul-yong. The Bucheon midfielder immediately showed his worth by nipping in to break up a passage of Spanish play. In a game that was struggling to get going, there was yet another break in play five minutes later while Hierro got some attention for a head injury.

Spain came as close to making a breakthrough as either team had so far in the 42nd minute when Joaquín turned and delivered a delicious cross that sailed inches away from both Lee Woon-jae and Morientes – with the goal gaping if the latter had got even the slightest touch. Spain did have the ball in the net soon after, but Romero was adjudged to have been offside before crossing into the box.

Joaquín was looking by far the brightest player on the pitch and drove straight towards the heart of South Korea's defence before seeing his shot blocked by Lee Eul-yong. With Spain finishing the half strongly, Javier de Pedro sent a strike spinning marginally wide, while the final touch before the break saw another Hierro header hit the roof of the net.

Spain had the ball in the net again in the 49th minute when a free kick was headed in by Baraja after a slight deflection. The celebrations were cut short by the referee's whistle after Baraja had tugged Kim Tae-young's shirt. There was a great chance for Morientes soon afterwards as Joaquín produced more sterling work down the right before crossing, but the striker's shot lacked conviction and went well wide.

With South Korea seemingly struggling, Yoo Sang-chul got the game's first booking after preventing Baraja from starting a break. De Pedro swiftly joined him in the book for doing the same thing to Song Chong-gug with an even larger dose of cynicism.

The Asian side had shown very little threat throughout but Park offered a reminder of his quality by showing quick feet and nutmegging Romero in the Spanish box before Hierro smashed the ball away for a corner. From that, the ball went to the edge of the area for Lee Eul-yong to strike but he scuffed it comfortably wide.

Moments after another exciting Joaquín run was finished with a weak shot, Yoo made way for Lee Chun-soo. Lee came close to creating a chance for Ahn with a ball flashed into the box but it was too far ahead of him and Hierro knocked it behind. The ensuing corner caused Spain their first real problems of the game as Lee's blocked shot went to Park, who chested it down and smashed the ball goalward. Considering how little action Iker Casillas had seen, he was impressively alert to get a strong hand to the ball.

It wasn't too long until Camacho made his first change of the game, with De Pedro making way for Gaizka Mendieta. One thing that wasn't changing was Joaquín's status as the most dangerous man on the pitch, and the Real Betis winger played a one-two with Juan Carlos Valerón to get into the box. There was also more frustration for the 20-year-old, whose shot hit the side netting. Park thought he was in seconds later after a poor touch from Hierro gifted him the ball but the veteran defender held his nerve and retrieved it.

There was a chuckle between Hiddink and referee Gamal Al-Ghandour as the former offered his water bottle while getting a talking to for being too animated. However, with a quarter of an hour remaining, there was no mistaking how important a period this was. Five minutes later Valerón made way for Enrique as Camacho went in search of that elusive opening goal.

Iván Helguera provided an opportunity by winning a free kick in a dangerous position. While the ensuing delivery was unconvincingly headed into the air by Choi Jin-cheul, Lee

Woon-jae showed authority to rise above the jumping bodies and punch the ball away. With four minutes remaining, Enrique was played through but didn't have the legs to beat Kim Tae-young, who recovered brilliantly but got a knock. The Jeonnam Dragons man ended up going off for Hwang Sun-hong – even if he stayed on the first time Hiddink went to make the substitution.

Moments after that change, Lee Chun-soo hit a shot from outside the box that Casillas was equal to. That proved to be the last shot before the whistle was blown despite three minutes of injury time being added, with neither side coming close to breaking the opposition down. So, following 90 minutes that were fairly forgettable, there was now the opportunity for players to score a golden goal and provide a moment that would be remembered for a lifetime.

South Korea had the first attacks of extra time, only to see Spain valiantly clear everything that came their way. South Korea couldn't return the favour when Joaquín drove towards the byline and dinked a cross to the back post for Morientes to head in what should have been the winner. It would have seen the game finish just two minutes after it had restarted, but the linesman said Joaquín had carried the ball out of play even though that clearly wasn't the case.

The celebrations were cut short and Joaquín trudged back with a look of disgust on his face as play continued. It was shortly afterwards that Helguera limped off to be replaced by Xavi. A break in play came when Lee Chun-soo was ordered to take off a necklace – if it was a lucky charm, he was certainly missing it upon seeing his free kick sail tantalisingly close to the crossbar moments later.

In the 100th minute Morientes came close to hitting the back of the net again. Having forced Choi to kick the ball into touch with his running in behind, Joaquín quickly threw the ball to the striker who swept his effort against the post, while Mendieta's follow-up took a nick and went over.

There was a bit of sparring at the end of the first half of extra time but no goal was threatened – a trend that continued into the beginning of the second period as things became scrappy. There was soon plenty of action, however.

Hwang got a shot off from outside the box in the 109th minute but Casillas was able to catch the ball, although it was going wide anyway. The same man had a chance to finish things off seconds later when Lee Chun-soo dinked a cross to him, although an unconvincing finish was easily dealt with. Spain immediately went up the other end and Morientes was played through before being left so furious that he was booked for dissent after being called offside.

It looked like Romero was going to seal the game for Spain when Choi's header from Hierro's free kick pinballed around the box and into the Deportivo La Coruña man's path, but it was blocked and went out for a corner.

With five minutes left, signs of fatigue were showing as Joaquín tried to stretch off an injury. Both teams were still going for that all-important winner, though, and Ahn launched a superb crossfield pass over to Seol Ki-hyeon who whipped in an inviting cross that whistled past Lee Chun-soo and into Casillas's gloves.

Enrique had a late shot from the edge of the box but it was a tame one and that turned out to be the game's final shot as the ball rolled out for a corner when the clock struck 120 minutes. It was deemed that there was no time to take it – something the Spanish players mentioned to the referee after his whistle was blown. There was to be no golden goal for South Korea this time and Spain would have to win on penalties again.

South Korea's Hwang was first up, calmly making the walk from the halfway line to the penalty spot. The number 18's celebrations weren't quite as relaxed as he had got enough power on the strike to send it bouncing off the underside of Casillas's body and over the line, with the goalkeeper just unable to get his hands on it. Hierro's penalty was straightforward as he confidently converted just like he had previously throughout the tournament.

Next up was Park, who left Casillas rooted and the ball flying into the right side of the net while making the whole thing look simple. Baraja was equally as clinical, sending Lee Woon-jae the wrong way and slotting into the bottom corner.

Seol also sent Casillas the wrong way, sticking the ball just right of the goal's centre. Xavi responded by producing the best penalty of the lot so far, placing it wonderfully into the top corner.

Having been the hero against Italy, Ahn avoided becoming the villain here by smashing the ball down the middle while Casillas dived to his right – left obviously frustrated by the South Korean's choice. Joaquín had been brilliant all game but there was a lack of confidence in his eyes as he approached the ball. His penalty was a predictable one and Lee Woon-jae was already on his way left before Joaquín had even struck the ball and eventually palmed it away with ease.

As the goalkeeper put his arms out while looking at the crowd in celebration and the winger walked back full of despair, Hong knew that he could win the game for South Korea with his kick. The captain put the ball down with composure, took his time after the whistle was blown and sent the ball into the top-right corner while Casillas dived low the other way. The hosts had won, a realisation that hit as Hong joyously wheeled away and the supporters went into rapture. Having never even made it out of the group stages before, South Korea were now the first Asian team to reach a World Cup semi-final.

'I've never seen anything like it,' Ahn told BBC Sport years later. 'There were so many people and cars on the street and all the bars were open after midnight, some of them serving drinks free of charge. It was like the whole nation was having a big party.'

On the flip side, Spain were left furious with the referee and his assistants to the point that Helguera had to be pulled away while leading the inquisition aimed at them. After the game, he seethed, 'Everyone saw two perfectly good goals. If Spain didn't win it's because they didn't let us win'. Hiddink's thoughts on this matter were simple. 'The losing team must look in the mirror,' he said, as quoted by *The Guardian*. 'If an experienced team doesn't take advantage of the mistakes we made they should not look at external circumstances.'

Before the period of success that would come for the Spaniards in later years, their reputation as perennial underachievers continued while South Korea went on to try and create more history.

### Senegal 0 Turkey 1; after sudden death extra time (22 June, Osaka)

The last quarter-final saw two teams who had already outdone anything they had previously achieved in the World Cup – a win for Senegal would even see them become Africa's first semi-finalists. Bruno Metsu made two changes from the side that overcame Sweden, as Khalilou Fadiga and Salif Diao returned from their respective suspensions to replace Amdy Faye and Pape Thiaw. Meanwhile, Turkey benefited from Emre Belözoğlu's return and the midfielder went straight into Şenol Güneş's team in Hakan Ünsal's place.

Senegal immediately went on the attack, winning a throw deep in Turkey's half that Ferdinand Coly launched into the box. While Papa Bouba Diop did well to reach it, the midfielder could only loop his header on to the roof of the net. Turkey soon responded with Yıldıray Baştürk making a run down the left before driving the ball into the box, though it was cleared convincingly. Papa Bouba Diop came close to releasing El Hadji Diouf through on goal moments later before the winger frustratingly got the ball stuck under his feet.

A long Tony Sylva ball up the pitch caused chaos for Turkey as Diouf ran behind the Turkey defence again, with Rüştü Reçber tempted to come out and claim it. The Lens man's cross was behind Fadiga, who did well to pluck it out of the air, but his touch was heavy enough to lure Rüştü into coming out only for Henri Camara to nip in and get there first. As the goalkeeper retreated, Fatih Akyel was able to come across and win the ball back.

With a backdrop of drums, the first ten minutes had been played at a blistering pace that was unaffected by Hasan Şaş going off for treatment. In the 12th minute Omar Daf received the first yellow card having dived into a challenge on Baştürk.

Senegal thought they had gone ahead in the 19th minute with another long throw from Coly causing problems. Again, Diop won the initial header, this time playing it across the box where Diouf was tempted to go for a bicycle kick before leaving the ball for Fadiga. His sweet strike was actually blocked by team-mate Camara, but the number seven didn't stop, firing in an effort that hit two men in red on the line before being converted by Diouf. The potentially jubilant scenes were disrupted by Óscar Ruiz running in with his arms waving in the air, signifying that the goal was being ruled out because Camara had been offside.

Having just returned from a suspension due to an accumulation of yellow cards, Emre got another for a late challenge on Diao as Senegal continued to apply pressure. A Senegalese attack soon after resulted in Fadiga hitting the side netting, surely wondering how he hadn't scored at least once yet. He almost turned provider thanks to a wonderful free kick from deep but Lamine Diatta couldn't connect as he tried to guide the ball goalward.

Turkey had been firmly on the back foot but Hakan Şükür had a glorious opportunity to put them ahead when he was played in behind in the 27th minute. After initially taking a superb touch to get through on goal, with Diatta putting the striker under pressure, he cut back with a heavy touch that allowed Pape Malick Diop to make a tackle and hold him up. That only saw the ball get as far as Hasan Şaş, who passed it back to his strike partner for what should have been the simplest of finishes, but Şükür clumsily let the ball creep under his foot and Sylva collected it. Another good cross was then directed towards Şükür but he made no effort to strike it at all.

Şaş was down again just before the half-hour following a clash of heads with Coly. The Galatasaray attacker's frustrations started to show shortly after as he was then fouled by Aliou Cissé. It was soon Emre's turn to go down holding his thigh, while Şükür completely missed the ball for what would have been another sitter – this time failing to latch on to Penbe's low cross.

With Turkey now in the ascendancy, Şaş almost had a great opening but Diatta stood him up authoritatively and poked the ball away. There was soon another Turkey injury, this time for Tugay Kerimoğlu. Şaş still caused further problems just before the break, looping a pass through for Baştürk, who got his head to the ball ahead of Sylva as it bounced up. He and Turkey would have thought they were finally getting the game's opener but Daf dived to make a miraculous clearance off the line. The ensuing corner agonisingly rolled across the six-yard box without anyone getting a touch on it.

Camara did brilliantly to play Diouf through but as the winger cut back and shot, Alpay Özalan did even better to make the block mere seconds before the half ended. It was unbelievable that the scoreline was still 0-0 at the break.

The second half started where the first had left off as both teams showed attacking intent but found the defensive solidity facing them too much to overcome. Diouf was the first to cause concern for a goalkeeper, doing so with a free kick in the 53rd minute. Even then, the ball eventually floated on to the roof of Rüştü's net.

Baştürk created an opening brilliantly within moments of that effort but Diatta did equally well to make up the ground required to get a block on his eventual shot. A cross from Akyel that Şükür was unable to reach soon followed.

As the hour came and went, Diouf was left frustrated by the officials after being fouled numerous times in quick succession, feeling at least one man in red should have seen yellow. That only worsened when the referee didn't even give a foul moments later. It was soon followed up by a moment of expressiveness from Diao in his own box as he did an overhead kick under little pressure – though that did see him unnecessarily concede a throw. Then Cissé picked up a yellow card when Şaş had gone down despite there being little if any contact.

Şükür's game had been a frustrating one and it was finally brought to an end in the 67th minute when he was brought off for İlhan Mansız. The substitute's first contribution seemed to be a misplaced pass, but it came agonisingly close to going under the crossbar – eventually finding the roof of the net after forcing Sylva to scramble back on to his goal line.

Despite the intensity remaining, creative ideas were seemingly drying up. A sign of this came in the 77th minute when Baştürk managed to get in behind the Senegalese defence but overhit his cross with two Turkish players waiting in the box. Perhaps out of desperation, Mansız went down in the box under pressure from Daf soon afterwards but the referee showed no interest in awarding a penalty and the full-back was left wondering why a card wasn't given for diving.

With just under ten minutes remaining there was a break in play while Alpay received treatment after sustaining a knock while tackling Papa Bouba Diop – ending a seemingly unstoppable burst forward that had seen the midfielder glide past many a man in red. He was able to continue, as was the game with Hasan Şaş getting behind Senegal's defence, only to see his cross headed behind by Pape Malick Diop.

In the 87th minute Mansız got himself booked for repeatedly fouling, with one challenge on Pape Malick Diop near the corner flag tipping him over the edge. The pace of the game was dropping and Senegal's attacking threat was regressing as extra time began to feel inevitable.

There was a late flurry from the Africans as Fadiga passed to Diao, who nutmegged Tugay before lunging to take the ball away from Akyel and pass to Diouf. The winger laid the ball off to Fadiga with a first-time pass after he had ghosted into an attacking area, with the number ten offloading to Camara. The first-time strike didn't have quite enough on it to beat Rüştü. Diouf almost got through with the final touches of normal time but the red defence managed to crowd him out, so extra time and a possible golden goal awaited.

Senegal restarted the game and immediately switched the ball out to Camara on the right. He sprinted his way to the byline and through the red shirts before being stopped by Rüştü. It looked as though it should have been a corner, but the goal kick was given.

Turkey eventually got two corners of their own but Senegal defended them both convincingly, with the second clearance falling to Tugay outside the box. While the midfielder attempted the spectacular, he ended up scuffing a shot comfortably wide.

Then the big moment happened. After 90 minutes without a goal in normal time, it took just three minutes and five seconds of extra time for Turkey to make Sylva's net ripple. Daf had done well to make a tackle as Turkey broke forward, but all that did was move the ball to Ümit Davala. He sent the ball into the box towards Mansız, who clinically flicked a boot at the ball to give Sylva absolutely no chance.

As Turkey's bench jubilantly ran on to the pitch to celebrate their passage to the semi-finals, Senegalese bodies sunk to the floor. They had provided such a show throughout the tournament and offered unforgettable memories. However, having experienced the joy of a golden goal against Sweden, they now felt despair as their dream ended.

Metsu would go on to leave his post after the finals due to differences with the country's football officials. Having come in after an Africa Cup of Nations quarter-final defeat to Nigeria, making the same stage in international football's biggest competition secured the legacy behind a man nicknamed 'The White Sorcerer'.

Cissé has the greatest legacy of all. Having captained Senegal during this historic campaign, he was the man in charge in 2018, when they next appeared at a World Cup finals. He then lifted the 2021 Africa Cup of Nations trophy (the tournament was played in 2022 due to the Covid-19 pandemic), the first time Senegal had ever won the competition.

# 7

# Semi-Finals

*Germany 1 South Korea 0 (25 June, Seoul)*

In a situation like this, most of the world would usually have wanted plucky underdogs South Korea to win on their own turf. However many people were still discussing their route past Italy and Spain and the questionable refereeing decisions that helped them reach this point – were they honest mistakes from referees out of their depth or signs of corruption?

Whatever public opinion was, the bottom line was that South Korea were playing in their first World Cup semi-final and coming up against Germany, a nation of serial winners. Rudi Völler made two changes with Sebastien Kehl and Christian Ziege making way for Carsten Ramelow and Marco Bode. Meanwhile, Guus Hiddink made three as Ahn Jung-hwan, Seol Ki-hyeon and the injured Kim Nam-il came out for Lee Chun-soo, Cha Du-ri and Hwang Sun-hong.

Surprisingly, it was Germany centre-back Ramelow who had the game's first shot after bursting up the pitch before being tackled and winning a throw. Instead of retreating, the Bayer Leverkusen man kept going to receive the ball before cutting in and letting off a strike that was comfortably dealt with by Lee Woon-jae.

The pace had largely slowed down, but South Korea quickened it again to release Cha down the right. The man who was still playing his football for Korea University found Lee Chun-soo in the box and he let off a curling shot that forced Oliver Kahn into his first impressive save of the match – having made so many already throughout the World Cup.

This was a sign of things to come as the Asians were getting most of their joy down the right, while they were also winning plenty of their individual battles in midfield. Germany's main point of attack was attempting to get Miroslav Klose on the end of crosses, but South Korea were looking dominant in the air.

When Christoph Metzelder's run forward allowed Bode to pick out Oliver Neuville, the cross was just too high for the striker to turn goalward. Moments later, Thomas Linke got a toe to Cha's attempted cross, sending the ball to Park Ji-sung who couldn't get enough on his shot to trouble Kahn. Neuville then tried to catch Lee Woon-jae out with a shot from distance but the goalkeeper was aware enough to deal with it.

Lee Young-pyo went down injured in the 20th minute and while there was confusion about whether the ball would be put out, South Korea tried to continue their attack before being tackled. They ended up kicking it out when tackling Ramelow so that Anyang LG Cheetahs defender Lee could get treatment.

For all the talk of refereeing decisions, it was South Korea who were left hard done by in the 23rd minute. Hwang spun behind Ramelow and would have had only Kahn to beat had Urs Meier not blown for a free kick that seemed soft.

In a game of few chances, Neuville thought he was in with a sniff after Klose headed a free kick across to him but Kim

Tae-young did brilliantly to force him wide, meaning the German's volley couldn't find the target. Neuville suffered the same fate when being played through moments later, this time due to Kim Tae-young and Choi Jin-cheul teaming up on him.

As the half-hour came and went, the main battle of note was between Hwang and Ramelow. The former was growingly increasingly frustrated with the referee, as he felt the defender was often going down easily and getting the call each time. Hwang almost got enough space to let a clear shot off but Linke was able to intervene and deflect it wide.

At the other end, a German corner routine almost worked as the ball was played short to Frings, who found Bode with a lofted cross. However the knockdown meant for Klose was hacked behind for another corner. Neuville went with a more direct delivery that was headed away before Hamann saw his shot blocked and South Korea scrambled it to safety.

Germany were beginning to really apply pressure as the half entered its final five minutes, but South Korea defended valiantly and with plenty of discipline as Choi dived in front of Klose's shot. Bode attempted a bicycle kick but didn't connect, while the Koreans headed plenty of crosses into the box clear. When they finally missed one, as Neuville's corner skipped off the turf and into the six-yard box, Bode was caught off guard and couldn't react in time to turn the ball goalward – handling it instead.

It wasn't long until the whistle was blown for half-time, meaning everything was in the balance ahead of the second period. This was reflected in the opening stages after the restart with both teams looking to make something happen, and Song was required to make a brilliant recovering header to prevent Klose's cross from finding Bode at the back post within four minutes. The Werder Bremen forward couldn't find the target despite managing to get his head on the ensuing corner.

There was a scare for Germany in the 50th minute when Ballack went down holding his calf after stretching for a loose ball. Moments later, Kim Tae-young was down holding his head, though both players were able to carry on. South Korea came agonisingly close to releasing Cha, who was played through and seemingly had the goal at his mercy, but Frings did superbly to race back and slide in to stop the winger running through – also knocking the ball back to Kahn. The Werder Bremen man's attempt at the other end wasn't quite as good as he dragged his shot from range wide.

Hiddink was the first manager to look to his bench for further inspiration and Ahn replaced Hwang in the 54th minute, which was swiftly followed by Lee Min-sung coming on for Choi. Despite the stoppages, Germany remained on top and Ramelow's ball from deep forced Song to awkwardly head behind for a corner.

South Korea were struggling to make an attacking impact as the game passed the hour, signified by a free kick being sent into Germany's one-man wall. They were still defending resolutely, though. When Ballack's lofted cross was met by Klose, Lee Min-sung put enough pressure on the tournament's joint top scorer at the time to ensure he couldn't generate the power required to beat Lee Woon-jae.

Ahn finally got his first sight of goal 12 minutes after his introduction, but the hero of South Korea's World Cup let off a wild strike that came nowhere near hitting the target. When Ramelow made another burst up the pitch, Klose's effort was equally wayward.

In the 70th minute there was German concern as Klose hobbled off to be replaced by Oliver Bierhoff. That would only grow a minute later when Ballack got himself booked. Lee Chun-soo slalomed up the pitch then showed quick feet to get around his team-mates on the edge of the box. Ballack took action and dived in to stop the Ulsan Hyundai Horangi winger, who could have carried on himself or passed to Ahn, who was in acres of space, had Germany's number 13 not done so. This was the ultimate definition of taking one for the team as it meant he would miss the final if Germany got there.

This was another moment of frustration for the UEFA Midfielder of the Year with Ballack's Bayer Leverkusen having just finished as runners-up in the Champions League, Bundesliga and DFB-Pokal. Having had so many near misses for moments of incredible glory, he was doomed to watch on from the sidelines during world football's biggest match no matter which team got there. The devastation that came with that knowledge was written across his face when Meier lifted the card aloft. In this game the decision paid off as the ensuing free kick was deflected over the crossbar, while the corner was cleared before Song's shot from range was comfortably saved.

Just four minutes after being ruled out of the final, Ballack bounced back in the most emphatic way possible as he put Germany ahead. Neuville did well to get to the byline and pull the ball back into a dangerous area, Ballack gave Bierhoff a call to leave it as he was coming on to the ball and let off a first-time shot that was saved well. However, Lee Woon-jae had no chance of catching it and Ballack touched in the rebound. There was joy and relief for the European outfit in equal measure.

With just under 15 minutes to find an equaliser, South Korea came forward immediately. It looked as though Lee Chun-soo's cross would find Ahn at the back post until Kahn stretched to knock the ball behind for a corner that he comfortably punched clear. Germany posed a far greater threat from their set piece soon afterwards and the ball was shifted from a free kick before Bode smashed it towards goal, with Lee Woon-jae palming it away well.

As the game approached its final ten minutes Hiddink went for it, bringing centre-back and captain Hong off for Seol. It was Neuville who came close to scoring, though, as his intelligently flicked header forced another good save from Lee Woon-jae. Even so, Germany seemed content with their one-goal lead, and Metzelder took his opportunity to waste a few seconds after being fouled while dispossessing Cha.

With five minutes remaining, Völler opted to bring Jens Jeremies on for Schneider. Seconds after that, Neuville thought he had won a penalty when touching the ball past Lee Woon-jae and taking a tumble as it went out of play. Instead he received fury from Yoo Sang-chul and a yellow card. A few minutes later, the booked striker made way for Gerald Asamoah.

Time was running out for South Korea and their desperation was beginning to grow – as was reflected by Lee Young-pyo's shot from range that went harmlessly wide. It looked as though they might just get that vital equaliser when Seol worked space in the box and laid the ball back to the edge, but with Linke flying at him Park couldn't get a clean connection on his shot and sent it spinning wide.

There was yet another stoppage as Frings went down with a facial injury, while Lee Min-sung was booked for grabbing Bierhoff as the striker tried to get the ball. Ahn then came painfully close to slipping Yoo through in the final seconds but the midfielder was offside anyway. There wasn't enough time for them to try again as Kahn's kick was the final one before Meier blew for full time.

Germany may not have been the most exciting team to watch, but they had shown great efficiency and booked their place in the World Cup Final and were understandably delighted. While Ballack would not be on the pitch in Yokohama, his goal meant that his team-mates would and he deservedly looked ecstatic. Meanwhile, South Korea's players dropped to their knees as their hopes of a fairytale final came to an end. Still, they had another game to play against whoever lost in the match between Brazil and Turkey the following day.

## Brazil 1 Turkey 0 (26 June, Saitama)

As had been the case in the first semi-final, Brazil versus Turkey saw one of world football's most historically successful teams face a nation that had never even made it out of the group stage before 2002. On a side note, a thought could be spared for Costa Rica and China who had come up against both semi-finalists in Group C.

Luiz Felipe Scolari's only change was a forced one as Edílson replaced the suspended Ronaldinho. Meanwhile, Şenol Güneş stuck with the starting line-up that secured victory against Senegal, which would have felt harsh on İlhan Mansız considering that he had scored the winner, while under-fire captain Hakan Şükür kept his place.

There was a lighter topic of discussion going into the game, though: Ronaldo's new haircut, which saw him shave all of his head apart from a little bit at the front. 'I had an injury in my leg and everybody was talking about that. I

323

decided to cut my hair and leave the small thing there,' he later told *ESPN*. 'I came to training and everybody saw me with bad hair. Everybody was talking about the hair and forgot about the injury. I could stay more calm and relaxed and focused on my training. I'm not proud about the hair itself because it was pretty strange. But it was a good way to change the subject.'

As Şükür and Hasan Şaş kicked off, there was no time for thoughts about hair or past form. The only focus was on reaching the World Cup Final. Lúcio made a brilliant burst forward in the opening minutes, and it looked as though things would open up for the centre-back until Alpay Özalan intervened at the expense of a corner. Eventually that was cleared with ease and Turkey responded with an attack of their own as Fatih Akyel crossed into the box, but Şükür was edged away from its flight by Cafu.

In the sixth minute Emre Belözoğlu's effort from outside the box was another sign that Turkey weren't going to hold back, even if its path was always destined to end in Marcos's arms. The Turks had actually enjoyed the better of the opening ten minutes but Brazil showed moments of quality, especially when Rivaldo used his trickery to win a free kick when seemingly in trouble.

Then Ronaldo was almost slipped through but was eventually denied by another impressive intervention from Alpay. Emre's challenge on Edmílson down the other end wasn't quite as great as he swiped the defender's legs while trying to keep the ball in play, leading to a couple of questioning gestures from the Lyon man.

As Brazil got a greater foothold on the game, Roberto Carlos posed a threat with his crosses and long throws. One of his launched balls almost created an opportunity for

Rivaldo, whose touch behind was just too heavy and allowed Rüştü Reçber to collect the ball.

Turkey were still going, though, and a 20th-minute free kick was worked wide to Fatih Akyel, whose cross was headed goalward by Alpay. The Aston Villa defender had executed the game's best effort so far but was left visibly frustrated as Marcos tipped it wide. Within seconds of the ensuing corner being dealt with, Brazil had worked the ball to Cafu in the box and the right-back unleashed a strike that hit the underside of Rüştü's hand, bounced off the turf and over the crossbar. A game that had been entertaining from the start was also beginning to bring its fair share of opportunities and Roberto Carlos cut in but could only find the side netting with his right foot.

Rivaldo gave Rüştü a scare just moments later, working space away from two men in red before smashing an effort from outside the box that skipped off the turf and was impossible for the goalkeeper to hold on to. Rüştü did well to get his body behind it before scrambling to stop Ronaldo's follow-up and grabbed it at the second attempt. As much as the haircut had distracted from Ronaldo's injury concerns, they were clear to see when he attempted to replicate Rivaldo's effort, hobbling away from a strike that was easily saved.

Turkey were still very much in this game, which was benefitting from great intent from both sides. Şükür almost found a breakthrough when a defence-splitting pass came his way but Cafu did well to steal the ball. There was more frustration for the Turkey captain soon after, as having just received treatment, Şaş burst down the wing to receive the ball and tried to pick him out, only to pass agonisingly behind him.

As evidence of this game's end-to-end nature, it wasn't long until Rivaldo forced Rüstü into a fingertip save with an innovative effort from outside the box. Moments later he then left the goalkeeper diving helplessly after another blistering attack, but this time saw the ball whistle agonisingly past the post. Having come tantalisingly close to a searching cross into the box, Rivaldo took another shot from range with this one being blocked by Alpay. There was concern as the attacker held his foot after a tackle that took Ergün Penbe's boot off, though he was able to continue.

Yıldıray Baştürk had shown real ingenuity with his dribbling at points throughout the first half and drove straight at the heart of Brazil's defence in the 41st minute. In the end Gilberto Silva was forced to grab his shirt, surrendering a free kick on the edge of his box and receiving a yellow card as a result. After an argument between the two sides as they tried to shift the ball a yard towards or further away from the goal, Emre stepped up to take the kick with yellow shirts in the wall trying to edge forward and those in red looking to put them off. After all of that, the midfielder sent it over the crossbar.

The resultant goal kick saw Roberto Carlos fly into the Turkish box, but there was to be no delight as his right-footed shot was comfortably saved. In the seconds before the clock reached 45 minutes, Rüştü had his biggest challenge so far. Roberto Carlos had delivered a wonderful pass that sailed inches from Ronaldo's outstretched toe and the goalkeeper was unable to hold. He then did superbly to get back up and knock the ball away as Edílson raced in to tap home. There was a break in play as Rüştü was treated for a head injury, while things got heated among both sets of players as almost everyone seemed to be pushing everyone else – Ronaldo and Bülent Korkmaz were at the centre of it all.

Not long after the game restarted, Kim Milton Nielsen blew the whistle for half-time. It had taken an 87th-minute winner for Brazil to win this fixture in the group stages and this was looking like being a tight affair too.

Ergün almost played himself into trouble when overcomplicating things as Kléberson drove him back, but the Galatasaray man eventually did enough to win a goal kick. Turkey's number 18 was involved again moments later, this time finding Şaş who burst forward before dinking a cross that was agonisingly too high for Şükür and calmly chested back by Roberto Carlos.

Brazil went straight up the other end with Gilberto Silva eventually finding Ronaldo. Despite having four men in red around him, O Fenômeno dribbled his way into the Turkish box before nonchalantly poking the ball goalward. Rüştü got a hand to the shot, but his efforts were futile as it clipped off the inside of the post and nestled in the back of the net while Brazil's number nine ran off wearing a big smile and wagging his finger. After all of the battling in the first half, it had taken just four minutes in the second period for the South Americans to edge ahead.

The goal was followed by a period of quiet compared to the rest of the game. There was a scare for Marcos in the 56th minute, though, as Baştürk's cross took a heavy deflection that saw the ball loop awkwardly down under the crossbar, forcing the Palmeiras goalkeeper to tip it behind.

Moments later, Cafu robbed Turkey of possession and offloaded the ball to Ronaldo for him to lead the counter. Instead of returning the ball to his captain as he sped up the wing, Ronaldo played it to Edílson who should have doubled Brazil's lead but took too long, allowing Fatih to recover and stab the ball wide. There was soon another clear opportunity for Brazil, once again set up by a Ronaldo pass, but Kléberson hit his effort straight at Rüştü.

As the game entered its final half an hour, Güneş made his first substitution and brought on Turkey's goalscorer against Senegal, Mansız, in place of Emre. Rivaldo hit plenty of audacious attempts throughout the World Cup but his effort to lob Rüştü from over 30 yards out was among the most speculative, eventually sailing comfortably over the crossbar.

While Mansız and Şaş were lively, Turkey were unable to breach Brazil's defence and didn't look like scoring. Perhaps with his injuries in mind, Scolari took Ronaldo off for Luizão in the 68th minute. After some brilliant work from Rivaldo, the substitute had a great opportunity to play Edílson through at the back post but overhit his pass and brought a collective groan from the stands. It then looked like Roberto Carlos had expertly released Luizão until Rüştü surged out of his goal and slid in to clear. In what was proving to be an action-packed introduction, Luizão's improvised attempt at an acrobatic volley bounced off the floor and agonisingly over the crossbar on to the roof of the net.

In the 74th minute Turkey made another change as Ümit Davala made way for Leicester City's Muzzy Izzet, which was swiftly followed by Denílson replacing Edílson. In a stop-start couple of minutes there was then a break in play after Edmílson got a knock as he protected the ball from Mansız so Marcos could collect it.

Since his introduction, Mansız had seemed to be a central figure whenever Turkey posed any kind of threat, and that was the case again when his wayward cross forced Marcos to hurriedly touch the ball behind for a corner. He then received the ball in the middle of Brazil's box but was denied as Roque Júnior rushed in to block his shot.

Turkey were now applying more pressure than they had at any other point in the game, but with ten minutes remaining a long thump forward and flick-on gave Denílson the opportunity to make things more comfortable for Brazil. However, with Rüştü off his line, the Real Betis man got far too much on his attempted lob. Seconds later, Turkey had a free kick that saw Şaş find Şükür, who spun Roque Júnior to get off a brilliant volley that was palmed wide by Marcos.

In the 85th minute, having gone down injured, Kléberson was brought off for Juliano Belletti. With Brazil controlling the game, Denílson had the chance to strike from the edge of Turkey's box following a nice move but his weak effort rolled tamely into Rüştü's arms. Baştürk continued trying to make things happen and when he drove forward, a tackle from Lúcio left the ball loose in the Brazilian box. Cafu went flying in on Ergün as he met it, timing his challenge perfectly and striding away from the potentially precarious situation with the ball at his feet.

Just moments later, Baştürk was taken off for Arif Erdem, giving the Galatasaray forward two minutes plus injury time to get his country back on level terms. He certainly had ambition – if not the application – immediately smashing a first-time effort well over the crossbar.

At the other end, Rivaldo could have slipped in either of his attacking partners but instead went for a chip that gifted the ball to Rüştü. Denílson was next up to have a chance, though he was chased wide by five men in red before eventually winning a free kick near the corner – not bad considering the clock was almost at 90 minutes. As Turkish frustrations grew, Şaş was booked for flying into a tackle and getting nowhere near the ball when Brazil played the free kick short. Four minutes were added on but the first two of those saw Denílson toy with the Turkish defence before winning a free kick that Rivaldo struck wide.

Turkey's big chance – even though it was a difficult one – came to Mansız as Şaş found him with a cross. Leaning back, the attacker was unable to control his header enough to get it on target.

After Brazil had taken the ball up the other end, the referee was blowing his whistle for full time by the time Turkey had won possession back and smashed it up the pitch. Cafu and his team-mates immediately jumped for joy as they could begin to look forward to a World Cup Final. Turkey, meanwhile, looked on in dismay as a tournament that had seen them exceed expectations wasn't ending in the match they would have allowed themselves to begin dreaming of.

# 8

# Third Place Play-Off

*South Korea 2 Turkey 3 (29 June, Daegu)*
This wasn't the game that either side would have been
dreaming of before their respective semi-finals, but
nonetheless they would have wanted to end a magical
tournament with a medal. Guus Hiddink made four changes,
with Lee Min-sung, Lee Eul-young, Ahn Jung-hwan and
Seol Ki-hyeon replacing Choi Jin-cheul, Kim Tae-young,
Cha Du-ri and Hwang Sun-hong. Şenol Güneş's only
alteration saw İlhan Mansız come in for Hasan Şaş.

Before the match started, there was a moment of silence
after at least four South Korean servicemen were killed after
an exchange of gunfire between North and South Korean
frigates earlier that day.

After one false start that required South Korea to retake
the kick off, they then had another that saw them concede
after a mere 11 seconds, which was – and remains at the
time of publication – the fastest goal in World Cup history.
The ball had been routinely passed back and then across to
Hong Myung-bo until the captain got it stuck under his feet
and Mansız seized his opportunity to win it. Then, having

previously failed to score in the entire tournament, Hakan Şükür calmly slotted past Lee Woon-jae. The Turkey captain certainly made the most of his moment as Emre Belözoğlu joined him for a choreographed celebration.

South Korea's first attack saw Lee Chun-soo released down the left wing, but his cross was comfortably collected by Rüştü Reçber. With the men in red coming again, Hwang's cross found Lee Eul-yong whose eventual shot was a wild one. At the other end, Lee Woon-jae's attempted clearance went straight to Şükür but there were enough defenders back to deal with it at the expense of a free kick that Emre fired wide.

In the ninth minute, South Korea were awarded a free kick near the edge of Turkey's box when Yıldıray Baştürk went through the back of Song Chong-gug. Despite others staking a claim to take it, Lee Eul-yong was the man to step up. That decision was vindicated as he beautifully curled the ball over the wall and into the top corner to restore parity.

The co-hosts kept coming, and Lee Chun-soo smashed an effort from the edge of the box that was straight at Rüştü but so venomously hit that he could only palm it away, but Turkey regained the lead just three minutes after the equaliser. South Korea stopped, thinking they had won a free kick, and instead Turkey kept going and burst forward with the ball finding Mansız, who passed to Şükür. Instead of going himself, Şükür returned the ball to his strike partner who converted despite Lee Min-sung diving in to try to stop him.

After the flurry of early action both sides would have been forgiven for trying to catch their breath, but they continued playing some brilliant football with moments of flair on display. Ahn was one of those as he turned brightly but shot wildly over the crossbar, inspiring an unimpressed shake of the head from the man himself in frustration at his effort. The forward soon had another opportunity after turning Bülent Korkmaz inside out, this time getting off a shot that was destined for the top corner until Rüştü sprung through the air to keep it out.

South Korea kept the pressure on with three corners ensuing, but a Turkey break forward forced Lee Eul-yong to pull back Baştürk for a yellow card. Soon after that, Ahn came agonisingly close to latching on to a through ball but was eventually disrupted enough to allow Rüştü to rush out and collect it. In the space of a couple of minutes the attacker almost got hold of the ball again, this time fouling Alpay on the edge of the box while Bülent Korkmaz made a last-ditch intervention to stop the ball reaching him.

Despite that period of dominance, Mansız managed to double Turkey's lead in the 32nd minute. The goal stemmed from a simple ball up the pitch from Rüştü that Şükür knocked down for his strike partner. The pair then played an intricate one-two to create space for Mansız, who masterfully dinked the ball over Lee Woon-jae as the goalkeeper rushed out towards him.

Lee Chun-soo had the opportunity to quickly respond after Seol set him up having embarked on a mazy run, but the Bucheon FK man couldn't find the target. It wasn't long until Song came close to creating an opening but was denied by an emphatic sliding tackle from Ümit Davala. At the other end, Şükür's powerful header demanded a big save from Lee Woon-jae to parry it wide.

The game remained incredibly open and South Korea had the ball in the net again in the 42nd minute after a sweeping move resulted in Park finding Ahn, who stroked his shot home calmly. However he was adjudged to be offside, despite replays showing that he had been played on. As play was stopped, Emre went off injured to be replaced by Hakan Ünsal.

Just before half-time, another pump forward from Rüştü released Şükür, but this time he was put under enough pressure by South Korea's defence to force him into a weak shot that was smothered by Lee Woon-jae. Rüştü then ran the clock down and the whistle was blown seconds after Seol's ambitious effort went wide. In an attempt to get his side back into the game, Hiddink used the break to bring Kim Tae-young on for Hong.

There was no chance of a goal coming as quickly in the second half as it had in the first, as a long Turkish ball forward was miscontrolled and went out of play. Seol almost found a route to goal in the 48th minute after patient build-up play saw him receive the ball out wide. While his big touch took him past the defender, it also meant he had to slide to get a shot off that was routinely stopped by Rüştü. After Turkey cheaply surrendered possession, Lee Chun-soo's looped ball into the box found Ahn but he chested it on to his own arm and a free kick was given.

With South Korea enjoying a strong start to the second period, Tugay Kerimoğlu picked up a yellow for a sliding tackle from behind as South Korea played out from the back. Lee Chun-soo soon had another chance but sent it wide, with Bülent Korkmaz having to take the ensuing goal kick as Rüştü continued to struggle with the injury that had been evident for large parts of this tournament.

Moments later, Song showed quick feet to work space for himself on the edge of the box. He couldn't find the target with his final effort and while Lee Eul-yong could from a similar position, Rüştü was equal to it. Despite his leg problem, with South Korea's early pressure in the second period proving relentless, the goalkeeper was forced to rush out of his goal to clear the danger after a probing ball was played behind the Turkish defence.

Turkey were finally able to apply pressure of their own again in the 57th minute as Ergün Penbe latched on to Fatih Akyel's long pass before turning Song inside out and dinking an inviting cross towards the back post, but Şükür was unable to reach the ball and it was put behind for a corner that Alpay headed wide.

As the game passed 60 minutes it became a stop-start affair as both teams were caught offside multiple times. Even when they were onside, there was a mix-up for Turkey as a cross into the box was perfectly set for Ergün to hit on the volley, but Mansız flew through the air to control it before he could do so – much to Ergün's frustration.

It was soon South Korea's turn to be left frustrated as Rüştü showed great authority to catch Song's threatening ball into the box. Having then dropped the ball after going over Alpay, the goalkeeper miraculously got up to deny and gather the follow-up effort. Hiddink responded by bringing Cha on for the goalscorer Lee Eul-yong.

Turkey came close to cutting South Korea open in the 70th minute but Kim Tae-young did brilliantly to race back and get a block on Hakan Şükür's nonchalant pass across the box before clearing. Moments later, Mansız did a rainbow flick over the defender's head but merely ended up putting the ball out of play. Cha then had a chance of his own when a cross came into the box, eventually mistiming his attempt at a flicked header. Another opportunity was wasted as Seol cut in on the edge of the area but sent a wild effort high and wide, while a cross from the Anderlecht attacker gave Rüştü a scare before eventually hitting the side netting.

With 15 minutes remaining, Okan Buruk replaced Ümit Davala for his first minutes of the tournament. The Internazionale man got involved immediately by making a recovery tackle, and Hiddink soon gave Choi Tae-uk his first appearance of the World Cup as Seol made way. Choi Tae-uk also made his presence known with a cross that wreaked havoc in the Turkish box, only for Lee Chun-soo to let off a weak shot.

There were more Korean bursts forward but Cha made a mess of his strike, sending it horribly high and wide. Ahn then hit an effort that flashed agonisingly past the post after getting a touch on its way to goal. As Turkey protested, South Korea took a quick corner but Lee Young-pyo's shot was saved, Ahn couldn't quite catch the ball with his attempted overhead kick and the ball was touched back to Rüştü from the ensuing cross.

Remarkably, Turkey's two-goal lead was still intact as Cha let off a venomous strike that the goalkeeper gathered at the second attempt. The shots kept raining down on Rüştü, with Lee Chun-soo the latest to be stopped.

Tayfur Havutçu was given the last five minutes as Baştürk made way. It was South Korea who created another chance after a wayward pass was intercepted, although it ended disappointingly as Cha raced up the line before delivering a cross that Ahn was unable to control. Then Song was the latest to see a shot from range denied, while a Lee Chun-soo header went agonisingly over the crossbar.

The ferocity with which South Korea were flying forward meant there was always going to be another chance for Turkey, which came in the 92nd minute, but Şükür couldn't take it and set a weak effort wide with the outside of his boot when he would have been better served slipping Mansız through. Within seconds the ball was in the back of Turkey's net as Song's speculative strike from range hit Cha's back and span out of Rüştü's reach.

There was no time for a magical comeback as the kick-off was almost immediately followed by the final whistle. South Korea initially slumped to their knees after being unable to crown a historic World Cup with a bronze medal, but soon rose to link arms with third-placed Turkey's players and thank the supporters while both teams waved their country's respective flags. This was a fitting ending for two nations that had captured the imagination of world football throughout the tournament – even if there were questions surrounding South Korea – and represented the underdog in the biggest of competitions.

# 9

# Final

*Germany 0 Brazil 2 (30 June, Yokohama)*
After 63 other games had been played in the 2002 World Cup, the biggest one of them all had finally arrived as Germany and Brazil faced off in the final. While the South Americans had dazzled on their way to Yokohama, the Europeans had often shown a cold efficiency without too many frills or goals – aside from that 8-0 win against Saudi Arabia.

As was expected, there weren't many changes and the only ones made were forced by one star man being suspended and another returning. Rudi Völler opted to replace Michael Ballack with Jens Jeremies, while Luiz Felipe Scolari predictably brought Ronaldinho back in for Edílson.

There was a roar of anticipation as Pierluigi Collina got the game started. While Roque Júnior raced forward in an attempt to reach a ball that was smashed up the pitch, he couldn't quite get there and it trickled out for a goal kick. With Brazil starting on the front foot, Ronaldinho had won a corner off Torsten Frings within a minute but his delivery was slightly too high for those in the box.

Rivaldo looked in the mood to entertain with some eye-catching flicks in the early stages. Meanwhile, Roque

Júnior was more concerned about disrupting Germany and was booked for pulling Oliver Neuville as the attacker tried to race away from him.

In the seventh minute, Germany had their first attempts as two shots rained in from range in quick succession, but both were repelled by a Brazilian block. That was soon followed by a scare when Frings's sloppy pass surrendered possession to Kléberson on the edge of Germany's box. The midfielder couldn't capitalise, only producing a weak strike that Oliver Kahn saved with ease.

Klose joined Roque Júnior in Collina's book in the ninth minute after catching Edmílson in the face with a stray elbow. Bernd Schneider then delivered a low cross that gave Brazil their first real moment of concern. Marcos and Edmílson teamed up to deal with it at the expense of a corner – German efforts to head in the ensuing cross only leading to a free kick for Brazil.

After nutmegging Kléberson, Schneider put in another low cross, this time for Klose, with that being put behind for a corner too.

While Germany had got themselves on top as the clock passed 15 minutes, Brazil carved open the best opportunity yet as Ronaldinho split Die Mannschaft's defence with a pass that Ronaldo latched on to. However, the man still sporting his unorthodox haircut prodded the ball wide.

Despite that moment and Marco Bode almost playing himself into trouble, Germany continued to look authoritative as they enjoyed more of the ball but they were struggling to translate that into chances. Brazil almost made a breakthrough when Lúcio burst up the pitch and attempted to play a one-two with Ronaldo, but Carsten Ramelow ensured the return pass didn't reach its desired destination.

As had been the case at various points throughout the World Cup, Germany's main method of attack was getting crosses into the box. Brazil were dealing with them valiantly, though there was a slight physical cost as Edmílson limped away from one aerial duel. There would have also been concern for Ronaldo when he winced after being caught by a tackle from Thomas Linke, but he was able to continue. Ronaldo then had a chance within seconds after a mazy run saw the ball end up with Ronaldinho, who lofted it back into his path, but he couldn't quite get it under control and Kahn came out to gather.

If there was a question regarding Ronaldo's confidence after that moment it was quickly answered by the frontman doing kick-ups in Germany's box, although there was soon a reminder of what was at stake in this game as Linke hit him with a hard but fair challenge. Rivaldo was also on the receiving end of a hard one to take when Schneider landed on his face after tackling him.

As the half entered its final five minutes, Jeremies let off a strike that rose well above the crossbar and into the stand. Moments later, Cafu slipped Kléberson through but while the Atlético Paranaense midfielder's shot under pressure had Kahn rooted, it also fizzed past the far post.

Kléberson then came closer than anybody in this final had so far by opening up his body to unleash a curling effort that crashed off the crossbar and away to safety. In the final seconds before Collina blew for half-time, Roberto Carlos smashed in a cross from deep that was masterfully controlled by Ronaldo, but his shot was met by Kahn's outstretched leg to keep the scores level going into the break.

Germany had a corner within a minute of the restart and Jeremies's header seemed destined for the back of the net until Edmílson blocked it. The Europeans were flying and a couple of minutes later, despite having no right to shoot from 35 yards out, Neuville smashed a free kick that Marcos managed to get his fingertips to and tip on to the post despite it swerving away from him. The striker was understandably in visible disbelief.

When they finally got some respite, Brazil showed their own attacking qualities as Ronaldo won a corner that was played short and swung into the box for Gilberto Silva to attack. Having risen well for the header, the midfielder was denied by both Kahn's save and Collina's whistle. Ronaldo was soon back on the ball after being found by Rivaldo but saw Ramelow block his shot.

In what had become an end-to-end match, both Frings and Dietmar Hamann let off strikes from outside the box that were unable to find the target. Shortly before the hour, Brazil won a free kick in a dangerous position when Rivaldo's flick was handled by Hamann but Ronaldo's effort hit the wall and Germany fought to repel attempted passes through until Ramelow was fouled. Moments later, Cafu was released down the right but was unable to find any of his onrushing team-mates having smashed the ball across the box.

This was followed by a break in play as Edmílson took what seemed like an age to sort out his top and put it on. While the fans laughed, there was no time for jokes among the players and Neuville soon came agonisingly close to getting a foot on Schneider's innovative ball through with a goal almost inevitable had he connected. There was then another break in play as Jeremies went down injured after a 50-50 challenge from Cafu that Ramelow took issue with, even if Collina didn't.

While Brazil's captain had certainly left his mark on Jeremies's leg the midfielder was able to continue, but Germany went a goal down shortly after his reintroduction. In the 68th minute Ronaldo caught Hamann on the ball and laid it off to Rivaldo, who took it upon himself to strike from range. It should have been a routine stop for Kahn – who had only been beaten once in the entire tournament – but he couldn't keep hold of the ball and Ronaldo was on hand to convert the rebound.

While Ronaldo and his entire nation celebrated, the look on Kahn's face encapsulated how cruel football can be. The goalkeeper was one of the main reasons Germany had reached the final in the first place, making a plethora of outstanding saves at key times. He would even go on to win the tournament's Golden Ball for those displays but his mishap, and that of Hamann, had allowed Brazil to steal a lead.

But Germany weren't about to lie down and accept their fate, instead pushing forward immediately with Frings hitting an ambitious strike that went over. Jeremies then saw a shot deflected wide, though the initial corner was authoritatively punched behind by Marcos while the second was wasted.

Lúcio responded by making a lung-bursting run out from the back right up to the far byline, but his cross to Ronaldo was eventually cut out. There was soon more frustration for the Brazilian striker, who had words with Linke after being left wincing when hit by another tough tackle.

With 16 minutes to play Völler made his first move from the bench as Oliver Bierhoff replaced Klose. Germany were still being limited to speculative shots from range and crosses that were largely being won by Brazil's resolute defence, and that first change was swiftly followed by the introduction of Gerald Asamoah in the place of Jeremies.

However there was nothing any German could do just moments later as Ronaldo doubled his and Brazil's tally. Kléberson picked up the ball and burst up the right flank before delivering a pass that had seemingly been intended for Rivaldo until he intelligently stepped over the ball. There, O Fenômeno was waiting to calmly take a touch before clinically slotting his shot into the bottom corner – the ball even kissed the inside of the post on its way in – and running off while wagging his finger with an unmissable smile on his face.

Ronaldo's brace was the perfect response to what had happened four years previously in France. He had scored four goals going into the 1998 final against the hosts, including the opener in the Seleção's semi-final against the Netherlands. But there was to be no joy in the curtain-closer as after having a convulsion and initially being pulled from the starting line-up, Brazil's talisman was reinstated before playing the full 90 minutes. Understandably given what had occurred, Ronaldo hadn't delivered his most electrifying performance with Brazil eventually losing 3-0. There had been so many discussion points around his physical condition ahead of the 2002 final that he even felt the need to sport a silly haircut to distract from it. Still, unlike 1998, this World Cup and its final brought eternal glory for O Fenômeno.

With ten minutes left to get back into the game, it could be seen on German faces that hope was beginning to fade even if they continued to push forward. Brazil were still putting their bodies on the line to ensure their hope didn't grow, with Lúcio going down after blocking a venomous strike from Linke. That was soon followed by Germany's best chance of the entire game when Frings's pass somehow rolled to Bierhoff's feet in the box, but Marcos miraculously leapt across his goal line to parry the shot wide. The ensuing corner reached Hamann on the edge of the area, though his effort bounced off target.

Both managers made changes with just over five minutes remaining as Christian Ziege replaced Bode and Juninho Paulista came on for Ronaldinho – it's safe to say the Brazilian took longer to get off the pitch. A German free kick followed the latter substitution, but Christoph Metzelder couldn't react quickly enough to prod it home as it bounced through the crowd. Juninho was involved almost immediately as he raced through after intercepting a poor pass from Frings, but his attempted pass to Rivaldo was too close to Kahn who came out to collect it.

As the clock approached 90 minutes, Roberto Carlos was happy to simply smash the ball up the pitch, while Metzelder headed wide as German attempts to create chances grew increasingly desperate. Scolari also took his opportunity to help run down the clock as Ronaldo was given an ovation while coming off for Denílson. Straightaway, he darted up the field before being tackled by Ramelow, just as it was announced that there would be three minutes of added time.

Ziege's shot was the best Germany could muster in the game's dying embers, but it was straight at Marcos who was able to bring it in. Kaká was on the sideline waiting to come on, but there was no time as Brazil brought out some tricks and ran the clock down until Collina blew his whistle to confirm their fifth World Cup, sparking wonderful celebrations as men in yellow ran on with flags held aloft.

Kahn and his German team-mates were left standing in bewilderment as they reflected on what had gone wrong in the game. As quoted by *World Soccer*, Kahn said, 'I don't think I can be consoled. I am fully aware that this is the only mistake I made in the seven matches of the World Cup. That one mistake was brutally punished. We have put Germany and German football back where it belongs – among the top four. The memories of the World Cup will be very good and cannot be destroyed by an unlucky goal'.

It was all about Brazilian joy in that moment, though. With a massive smile on his face and '100% Jardim Irene' written on his shirt for the neighbourhood he grew up in, Cafu lifted the World Cup trophy aloft as the rain fell while confetti and smoke rose into the air. There had been plenty of questions surrounding Brazil ahead of this tournament due to bad form and injury, but they left it as champions of the world.

# 10

# Legacy

This should have been a tournament with a wonderful legacy. Ronaldo made up for the 1998 final to take Brazil to a record-breaking tally of World Cup wins; Turkey and South Korea reached the semi-finals; Senegal equalled Africa's best finish; David Beckham scored against Argentina; Japan got out of the group stage; the United States of America exceeded all expectations; the Republic of Ireland created unforgettable memories; it was the last to include golden goals.

The reality is that this has gone down in history as one of the most controversial World Cups of all time – mostly down to refereeing decisions. No matter how much South Korea were able to celebrate their achievements, some from outside will always ask questions about potential corruption.

So many love an upset, but France, Portugal and Argentina falling in the groups had some feeling that something must have been wrong. Adding to that, Brazil's win against England was the only meeting of two historical footballing giants in the knockout stages until the South Americans faced Germany in the final.

Still, there were various transfers that were helped by the tournament, from Park Ji-sung joining Manchester United to Rüştü Reçber making his first transfer out of Turkey and heading to Barcelona – although he only made seven appearances for them. Even if that move didn't turn out the way he wanted, Rüştü will always be a name associated with this World Cup for his unmistakable image and heroic displays, with it often forgotten that he was struggling with injury for the majority.

This tournament was also part of an exciting period for African football. Senegal became the continent's second quarter-finalists, 12 years after Cameroon reached the same stage. Just two years later South Africa was named as the host nation for the 2010 World Cup, in which Ghana also came one game away from the semi-finals. Senegal's achievements would have also helped several of their players move to the Premier League, with El Hadji Diouf and Salif Diao joining Liverpool while Aliou Cissé went to Birmingham City. Henri Camara had followed by 2003.

A big pre-tournament topic had been the co-hosting, which left further debate once everybody had gone home. 'Because of the distance between the two countries, it did feel like two World Cups were going on simultaneously,' Amy Lawrence wrote for *The Guardian*. 'If you were stationed in one country you inevitably felt dislocated from events in the other, and apart from the super-rich or super-dedicated, the majority of visitors experienced either Japan or Korea. That said, both countries put on a hugely welcoming World Cup experience. They may not have been given the chance were it not for co-hosting.'

While the World Cup had a positive impact for the host nations, the stadiums erected in South Korea have not been filled in the years since as would have been hoped – even before the Covid pandemic. Japanese clubs have had far higher attendances, but statistics indicate that they also haven't been able to completely fill their stadia regularly.

In 2018, Nam Kunn attended a match at the Seoul World Cup Stadium. For the website Bled FC, he described, 'An arena with a very low attendance but with a lot of kids, families and a kop of one hundred ultras who tried to do their best to add to the atmosphere. It is truly sad because this stadium which has been created for the 2002 FIFA World Cup in Japan and South Korea is a very beautiful place and pretty well located in the city, where there are many food trucks, a FC Seoul store and a mall around the stadium'.

In addition to the major economic impact the tournament had, those stadiums and the World Cup still hold special memories for those who were able to witness their country's success. When Tottenham Hotspur's official website asked Son Heung-min the first World Cup he remembered, the winger responded, 'The World Cup in 2002 in South Korea, when we hosted it with Japan. South Korea did very well, getting to the semi-finals and I was so inspired by what I was seeing. Just having the World Cup in your country of course makes for a great atmosphere but then when we did very well, the country went crazy! I was very proud of what South Korea achieved and I think everyone was'.

He finished by declaring, 'For South Korean people, this is a memory we will never forget'. Whether it's for special moments or controversies, the 2002 World Cup has also remained in the minds of people around the world ever since.

# Acknowledgements

Thank you to my mum, dad, family and friends for their support while I have been writing this book. I really appreciate the efforts of Matthew Gibbs, Josh Butler, Ollie Sirrell, Oliver Dyer, Matt Dawson, Josh Browne, Haydon Stevenson and Tom Symes-Brown who have all helped with proofreading.

A massive thank you goes to Jane Camillin for deciding to take this book on. In addition, I want to thank Duncan Olner for taking on my ideas and coming up with the brilliant cover.

I also want to thank Matt Holland for speaking so openly about his experiences at the 2002 World Cup and Gareth Maher for helping to put me in touch with him. Further thanks go to Federico Manasse for his advice on how to access *La Gazzetta dello Sport*'s archives.

Finally, I want to thank any reader for giving their time to my book. I sincerely hope you have enjoyed it.

# Bibliography

**Books**

Radnedge, K., *The Official ITV Sport World Cup 2002 Fact File* (London: Carlton Books Ltd, 2002)

McCarthy, M. and Dervan, C., *Ireland's World Cup 2002* (London/Dublin: Simon & Schuster UK Ltd/ Townhouse and Country House Ltd, 2002)

Mustapha, I., *No Longer Naïve: African Football's Growing Impact at the World Cup* (Sussex: Pitch Publishing, 2021)

**Websites**

bledfc.com
btsgoalies.com
collezioni.gazzetta.it
espn.co.uk
fifa.com
footballia.net
goal.com
irishtimes.com
news.bbc.co.uk
news.nike.com
olympics.nbcsports.com
skysports.com
theguardian.com
thesefootballtimes.co

# CRYPTO
## THE DISRUPTOR

# CRYPTO

## THE DISRUPTOR

### THE RISE OF MONEY FROM BARTER TO **BITCOIN**

## MUKESH JINDAL

**PENGUIN**
**BUSINESS**

An imprint of Penguin Random House

PENGUIN BUSINESS

USA | Canada | UK | Ireland | Australia
New Zealand | India | South Africa | China | Singapore

Penguin Business is part of the Penguin Random House group of companies
whose addresses can be found at global.penguinrandomhouse.com

Published by Penguin Random House India Pvt. Ltd
4th Floor, Capital Tower 1, MG Road,
Gurugram 122 002, Haryana, India

First published in Penguin Business by Penguin Random House India 2024

10 9 8 7 6 5 4 3 2 1

ISBN 9780143465850

Typeset in Sabon by Manipal Technologies Limited, Manipal
Printed at Thomson Press India Ltd, New Delhi

www.penguin.co.in

# Contents

# Preface

'For the love of money is the root of all evil', states 1 Timothy 6:10 in the King James Bible. Through generations, this biblical verse has been misinterpreted to mean that money by itself is the root of all evil. Whether the Holy Bible stands against or with money is not the point here. But we should clarify whether money by itself or our love for it is the root of all evil.

Since the days of our hunter–gatherer forefathers, human beings have been social animals. We made a living and survived as a species by exchanging something for another thing. For example, in primitive days, hunting a wild animal was a valuable activity as it brought much-needed food. Therefore, a large piece of wild flesh might have been traded for a spear, or a strip of fur might have been exchanged for a boat.

The exchanges of value took a different form when we started settling down as civilizations. Humans began to perceive the shortfalls of the barter system as societies transitioned from nomadic to more settled lifestyles. For example, consider someone who needs a haircut and has a clay pot to exchange with the barber for the service. The barber wouldn't entertain that exchange if he did not need a clay pot.

Precious metals, stones, even grains and, later, coinage entered human civilization as a common storehouse of value and medium of exchange. When a person can reward the barber for the haircut he provided with a precious stone or a gold coin, the barber, in turn, can buy any product or service of his choice using that gold coin or precious stone. Consequently, a common storehouse of value made the haircut service rewarding for both the barber and the person who availed of the service.

Eventually, the limited portability of heavy, precious metals and grains led to their demise as a medium of exchange. Then, along with the establishment of independent nations and the development of interconnected free-markets worldwide, a promissory note printed by a country's central bank emerged. Today, we call this money cash, paper money and fiat currency, to name just a few terms. But no matter what we call it, it has the power to determine the value and price of every good and service available under the sun. It is also one of the determinants of the holder's social status and purchasing power.

Have you ever wondered how a pen with a 'Made in China' label ended up in your hand? After all, the people who manufactured the pen don't know you personally. So then, how did you come by a pen if you have no personal or professional association with the manufacturers?

No one manufactures a pen to help you write. The company behind your Chinese pen is making and selling pens to make money or profit from their business. Their business will thrive only if they can produce and sell good-quality pens at an affordable price. This is how an economy works.

Let's look at another example—a home nurse who is an elderly man. The nurse accepts a job to care for an older man who lives far from the nurse's hometown. Why would a person in his sunset years take care of an old, sick person whom he doesn't even know personally? The answer is obvious: the nurse needs the money to take care of his family and himself. This is how money works.

Money is an easily portable and transferable reward for all our efforts to create value in an economy. From risky stock market speculation to simple shopkeeping, every human endeavour is undertaken with an eye on the reward it delivers.

When the idea of starting an online retail business struck him, Jeff Bezos, the founder of Amazon, held a high-profile job in the American hedge fund industry. He quit his high-paying job, rented a house and started an online bookstore. It is said that during the initial stages of his business, Bezos himself delivered books to his customers. Why did he give up his lucrative job and take the significant risk of starting his own business? Bezos calculated that if his idea worked out, it would make him millions or even billions.

He was right. He created thousands of jobs and made online shopping a trend on his way to becoming the third-wealthiest person in the world.[1] Amazon has also made products cheaper and easily accessible by eliminating middlemen and warehousing costs. Along with that, books became cheaper and easily portable with the launch of the Kindle e-reader.

Money may never make the world go around. But it can make people, businesses, products, services and ideas go around the world. Money is the lifeblood of a free-market economy. Money can trigger great ideas that can even change the course of human history. Money itself is not the root of all evil, but it is the root of human progress.

Like religious belief, money is also a collective belief. A collective belief that our economy can provide the goods and services worth the money in our purse. The emergence of digital cash has solidified the fact that tangibility doesn't matter in our economic system; only belief matters. You create value in the economy by doing a job or running a business, earning money, physical or digital, and as a reward, buy the things you wish to and lead the life of your choice. Create value and reward yourself, or, in simpler terms, get a job and receive a pay cheque.

World economies run (not very smoothly) on the mutual trust firmly built on the collective monetary belief system. Although this mutual trust has been broken several times throughout history (we will get to that in the following chapters), it has nonetheless stood the test of time as a consistently proven trust. The day when that trust is broken permanently, our beloved money will lose its value.

From the barter system to coinage, paper currency, digital cash and now, to cryptocurrencies, the evolution of money has never followed a smooth trajectory. Whether it is a free-market economy, capitalism, a centralized financial system or even a democracy, not every man-made system is perfect. Everything we create comes with flaws. It would be futile to seek perfection in a world where one species can survive only by eating another.

Money has created wars, motivated corruption, impaired human relationships and triggered stock market crashes and economic downturns. Mutations and flaws are inevitable outcomes of the evolutionary process, and as humans, we should accept the favourable mutations and reject flaws while learning to move on with the process.

The day when digital technology joined hands with the Internet, things started to transform beyond our imagination. The Internet introduced a decentralized communication system, and we, knowingly or unknowingly, became part of a decentralized virtual world. A world that, one way or another, everyone owns. The role of intermediaries began to vanish when people began to share information, products and services over the Internet. As a result, our financial transactions became more transparent, efficient and quicker.

However, the world had to face a deadly pandemic like COVID-19 to realize the immense power and potential of digital technology and the Internet. The pandemic has ushered in a new reality: digital transformation is crucial for our survival in a post-pandemic world. The pandemic displayed the potential of remote working and e-commerce. Most enterprises worldwide accept the new reality and accelerate their digital transformation efforts.

During the pandemic, while most business sectors worldwide were nosediving, information technology (IT) was booming, and crypto markets were hitting new highs. The COVID-19 pandemic, the worldwide digital transformation and the frequent technological disruptions are all signs of a paradigm shift in our day-to-day lives and how we foresee the future. Today, we stand at a juncture where a mammoth disruption lurks around the corner. However, there is nothing to be worried about as technological disruptions are inevitable these days.

Are we losing trust in our centralized financial systems? Is our centralized world of finance about to witness decentralization or public ownership similar to the Internet? Is the decentralized financial (DeFi) system the most transparent way to embrace the technology-driven economy of the future? Are we heading towards a DeFi world altogether? Technologies such as blockchain, artificial intelligence and crypto assets are indeed leading us towards that end. At this juncture, both world history and financial history are about to take an extraordinary turn.

The pandemic has compelled humans to test the waters of uncharted virtual territories. We have realized that along with making our lives easier, faster and safer, the virtual world has immense potential to generate profit for both individuals and enterprises. To a species for which the lust for wars, colonization, exploitation and profit runs through its veins, it would be no surprise if a modern-day Columbus embarked on a virtual voyage aboard the *Santa Maria* in search of a new world.

There is no doubt that we will rely more on the virtual world in the post-pandemic era. And while plucking the fruits of the digital virtual world, our usual way of living, traditional business models and economies will crumble down to ashes. Nevertheless, our never-ending curiosity will ensure that we don't rest until we find new virtual terrains that satiate our lust for profit and growth. As the virtual world is endless, our quest for and conquest of virtual treasure islands and new worlds will never end.

But right now, amid all these technological disruptions, speculations and chaos, we are clueless.

Robert Frost, the nineteenth-century Pulitzer Prize-winning American poet, summed up in three words what he had learnt about life: 'It goes on.' His three wise words can give us solace and hope during these rapidly changing times. Life, without a doubt, goes on. But the future belongs to those who plan and act on the uncertain times ahead.

Ignorance is a matter of decision in today's information age. Learning from the past gives us lessons to apply in the present and insights to anticipate the future. *Crypto the Disruptor* does the same. This book illustrates how various human ideas and technologies have shaped today's world of finance. It simplifies the history of money—how the economic medium of exchange transformed from precious goods to a piece of paper and now to a non-tangible digital token—and speculates on the future course money will take.

*Crypto the Disruptor*, without being didactic, provides valuable information and knowledge that we believe should enable you to embrace the changes the financial world is likely to witness in a fast-paced, digital world. We will consider ourselves successful in our mission if this book empowers you to take a stand in these swiftly changing times and boldly face the challenges ahead.

# 1

# The Rise of Riches

'Money is the most universal and most efficient system of mutual trust ever devised.'

—Yuval Noah Harari

## The Evolution of Money

To know what money is and where it is going, you should first know the story of money.

The ability to communicate and exchange are the two significant attributes that distinguish humans from other animals and allow us to roam planet Earth as the dominant species. Unfortunately, evidence of the means of value exchange employed during the primitive hunter-gatherer days is scarce. Our primitive forefathers lived for today, as the future was always uncertain. They did not save; they hunted and feasted when they wished to or felt hungry. During a shortage of prey, food or other necessities, they raided other tribes and stole their possessions. During those uncivilized, brutish days, it is unlikely that humans would have exchanged one good for another in a civilized manner.

Trading and value exchange became more organized and widespread after the emergence of civilizations around 10,000 years ago during the Neolithic Revolution, or the New Stone Age, but the story of money begins much earlier. The first forms of money were not coins or notes, but commodity money—goods that had value in themselves as well as value in exchange. Some examples of commodity money are cattle, cowrie shells, grain, salt and precious metals.

Humans began to use commodity money as early as the Palaeolithic era, or the Old Stone Age. However, the use of commodity money became more widespread and organized during the Bronze Age, when civilizations, such as the Mesopotamians, Egyptians and Chinese, used items such as cattle, grain, shells and metals as mediums of exchange.

Early evidence shows that the barter system, an ancient method of trading goods and services without using money, existed before, alongside the use of commodity money. 'You give me a knife, I give you an apple' sort of value exchanges were rooted in a 'give and take' policy. It was the Phoenicians, an ancient civilization from the eastern Mediterranean region, who took the barter system across oceans. Numerous civilizations throughout history have used the barter system, including the Egyptians, Mesopotamians, Babylonians, Greeks, Romans and Chinese.

The Babylonians improved the bartering system during the Bronze Age, which lasted from around 3000

BCE to 1200 BCE, by creating common goods that were exchanged for food, tea, spices and weapons. Human skulls and salt were some of the popular items used as the medium of exchange. During the Middle Ages, Europeans travelled around the world to barter furs and other goods, such as food items, weapons and jewellery, in exchange for silk and perfumes. Colonial Americans used deerskins, musket balls and wheat as common goods for bartering.

Even a highly developed civilization like the Inca empire, which was based in present-day Peru, was a moneyless, bartering society until 1524, when Francisco Pizarro González, a Spanish conqueror, set foot on their land.

## The Mountain That Devoured Men

Pizzaro was one of the first Europeans to cross the Pacific in pursuit of his fortune in the early sixteenth century. He was after gold and silver. The Incas believed gold to be the 'sweat of the sun' and silver to be 'the tears of the moon'. They appreciated the aesthetic value of both precious metals, but they couldn't fathom Pizzaro's insatiable lust for gold and silver.

Despite a few failed attempts, Pizzaro carried out a successful plunder of Peru with Spanish royal approval in 1530. He looted around 6000 kilos of pure 22-carat gold and nearly twelve tons of silver. Pizzaro died in Lima in 1541, but his legacy lived on. The Spanish Empire sponsored more expeditions to the Americas or the New World to bring home tons of gold and silver. It is important to note here that North America and South America together are popularly known as the 'New World' since the Europeans discovered these lands much later and these are relatively new civilizations.

But the real treasure was on top of a mountain that stands tall at 15,827 feet above sea level in the Andes Mountains near the Bolivian city of Potosí. The economic history of the world took a dramatic turn when an indigenous Andean named Diego Gualpa discovered traces of silver on Cerro Rico in 1545. Cerro Rico, which means 'rich mountain' in Spanish, is an apt name for this beautiful mountain with vast deposits of silver ore.

Initially, the Spanish conquistadors paid the villagers to work in the silver mines of Cerro Rico. But from the late sixteenth century onwards, they had to introduce forced labour, also known as *mita*, as the environmental conditions in the mines were so harsh that no one was willing to work in them. Under the mita system, men aged between 18 and 50 were forced to work for seventeen weeks a year. Owing to the constant exposure to the mercury fumes generated by the patio process of silver refinement, mortality among the miners soared to new heights. The workers also had to climb up and down through the 700-foot mine shaft, which was filled with toxic air. Hundreds were also killed and wounded by falling rocks.

Potosí became a silver-rush city with a ruthless face. Domingo de Santo Tomâs, a legendary Spanish Dominican missionary, called Potosí 'a mouth of hell, into which a great mass of people enters every year and are sacrificed by the greed of the Spaniards to their "God".'[1] Rodrigo de Loaisa, a Spanish priest, called the silver mines 'infernal pits'. He also noted that 'if twenty healthy Indians enter on Monday, half may emerge crippled on Saturday.'[2] In 1638, an Augustinian monk, Fray Antonio de la Calancha, wrote: 'Every peso coin minted in Potosí has cost the lives of ten Indians who have died in the depths of the mines.'[3]

As the population of the indigenous workers had dropped due to the inhumane working conditions, thousands of African slaves were imported to serve as 'human mules'.[4] Even today, the devilish nature of the mine shafts and tunnels of the Cerro Rico remains.

On the mountain of death of Cerro Rico, Spain found its fortune. The mountain gave 45,000 tons of pure silver to the Spaniards between 1556 and 1783. This silver was turned into bars and coins in mints and then shipped to Spain.

Potosí rapidly turned into one of the major cities of the Spanish Empire, with a population of nearly 2 lakh at its zenith, a larger population than most European cities at that time. *Valer un Potosí*, meaning 'to be worth a Potosí', is still a Spanish expression that means 'to be worth a fortune'.

Pizarro's conquest of the New World had made the Spanish Empire rich beyond its wildest imagination. The Incas, however, could not understand what the Europeans were doing with all the loads of gold and silver they had shipped from their land. It was said that 'even if all the snow in the Andes turned to gold, still Europeans would not be satisfied.'[5] The Incas failed to understand that silver was more than a shiny, beautiful metal for Pizarro and his men. It could easily be turned into money: a unit of account, a store of value and more than anything else, a portable power.

## Coinage

Money is a medium of exchange that can eliminate the inefficiencies of the barter system. It is a unit of account that facilitates valuation and calculation and a store of value that allows longer-term economic transactions, which can cross geographical boundaries. Money must be affordable, available, durable, reliable, fungible (mutually interchangeable) and portable to perform all these functions optimally. Precious metals such as gold, silver and bronze fulfil most of these criteria, and they were for this reason regarded as the ideal monetary raw material for millennia.

Archaeologists unearthed the earliest known coins in the Temple of Artemis at Ephesus (near Izmir in present-day Turkey), which date back to 600 BCE. These oval Lydian coins made of electrum, an alloy of gold and silver, bear the image of a lion's head.

Between 326 BCE and 211 BCE, the Roman Empire began minting coins comprised of the aureus (gold), the denarius (silver) and the sestertius (bronze), ranked according to the relative scarcity of the metals. All the coins bore the image of the reigning emperor's head on one side and the mythological figures of Romulus and Remus on the other, a tradition since the Imperial period, which started in 27 BCE with Emperor Augustus. As per Roman mythology, Romulus and Remus were twin brothers who founded the city of Rome.

Although coinage originated in the ancient Mediterranean, the region can't claim sole possession rights. Qin Shihuangdi, the first emperor and creator of the first unified Chinese empire, introduced to China the standardized bronze coin in 221 BCE. Every coin made of precious metal in various parts of the world was associated with powerful rulers who monopolized the minting of money and exploited it as a revenue source.

But even before these systems of coinage were developed, five thousand years ago, people in ancient Mesopotamia used clay tokens to keep accounts of transactions involving agricultural produce like barley or wool and metals such as silver. Rings, blocks or sheets of silver were used as ready money (like grains), but the clay tablets were more significant. The clay tablets that survived remind us that human beings created written records not to write stories, poetry or philosophy but to trade.

Despite being made of base earth, those clay tablets have lasted much longer than the silver coins and bars made in the Potosí mint. One of the well-preserved Mesopotamian clay tokens is from the town of Sippar (present-day Tell Abu Habbah in Iraq), and it dates back to 1683–1647 BCE, during the reign of King Ammi-Ditana. It states that its bearer should receive a specific quantity of barley at harvest time. Another clay token, made during the reign of King Ammi-Saduqa, the successor of King Ammi-Ditana, states that 'the bearer should be given a specific quantity of silver at the end of a journey'.

Do those inscriptions ring a bell? No? 'I promise to pay the bearer the sum of one hundred rupees'. Does this inscription sound familiar? If not, take out a hundred-rupee note or any Indian banknote from your purse and read the inscription above the signature of the governor of the Reserve Bank of India. You may be filled with awe to learn that the Mesopotamians created something similar to our modern banknotes five thousand years ago.

## Banking

The birth of modern-day banking can be attributed to the Italian Renaissance in the fourteenth century. This historical period is known for a cultural shift that spread across Europe and marked the transition from the Middle Ages to modern times. The word 'renaissance' in French means 'rebirth', and the Renaissance period witnessed the 'rebirth' of culture and a renewal of interest in the Greco-Roman Classical Age after the centuries-long Dark Ages.

The Renaissance arose in Florence in the Tuscany region of central Italy. The Florentine Republic rose to economic and political prominence by providing credit to European monarchs and laying the cornerstone of capitalism and banking.

The story of the birth of modern-day banking and its spread across Europe and the world would be incomplete without a recounting of the significant part played by a man named Giovanni di Bicci de' Medici. Giovanni was an Italian banker who founded the Medici Bank. The primary business of the Medici family was foreign exchange dealing. They were known as 'bankers' (*banchieri* in Italian) because, like the Jews of Venice, the Medicis did their business seated at moneychanger's tables, '*banca*' in Italian, in the open street.

In 1385, after becoming the manager of the bank's branch in Rome, which was run by one of his relatives, a moneylender in Florence, Giovanni built his career as a currency trader. Since it was the age of financial transactions involving multiple coinage systems based on gold, silver and base metal, any long-distance trade or tax payment had to undergo a complicated process of conversion from one currency to another.

In the early stages of his career, Giovanni acted as a broker for the bills of exchange (*cambium per literas* in Italian) that were a means of financing trade developed during the Middle Ages. For instance, if one trader owed money to another and that debt could not be reimbursed until the conclusion of a transaction that may take some months, then the creditor could draw a bill of exchange on the debtor. The creditor could either use the bill as a mode of payment in its own right, or he could use it to acquire cash at a discount from a banker who acted as a broker.

One of Giovanni's most lucrative clients was the Church, as various currencies flowed in and out of the Vatican's coffers. But Giovanni saw even better money-making opportunities in Florence. By the time he passed the business on to his son in 1420, he had established bank branches in Venice and Rome. Later, branches were added in Geneva, Pisa, London and Avignon.

The *Libro Segreto*, Giovanni's 'secret book', sheds fascinating light on the Medici family's rise as influential European bankers. The book also tells the story of meticulous bookkeeping, albeit with imperfections by modern standards. Still, a modern researcher would be impressed by the neatness and orderliness of the financial accounts and balance sheets in the book. Giovanni did not invent these bookkeeping techniques, but he applied and popularized them on a larger scale.

The Medicis achieved massive financial success by learning a vital lesson: playing small in finance is seldom profitable. So, they found a way to spread their risk and made their bank more extensive and more diversified than any other financial institution until their time. By engaging in currency trading and lending, they reduced their vulnerability to defaults.

Eventually, the Italian banking system became the model for notable northern European nations such as Britain, the Dutch Republic and Sweden to attain tremendous commercial success in the coming centuries. The predecessors of modern central banks first appeared in Amsterdam, London and Stockholm, triggering the next wave of financial innovation.

The seventeenth century saw the rise of three novel financial institutions that would serve private and public economic activities in their own unique ways. The Exchange Bank of Amsterdam was set up in 1609 to solve mercantile problems that arose due to the circulation of multiple currencies in the United Provinces of the Netherlands. The United Provinces of the Netherlands was a confederation of seven provinces that existed from 1581 to 1795 and was the precursor of the modern Netherlands. The bank provided a stable and uniform currency for the merchants and traders who used Amsterdam as a hub for international commerce. The bank also issued its own currency, the bank guilder, which was backed by deposits of gold and silver and became the first international reserve currency.

In the United Provinces of the Netherlands, there were nearly fourteen different mints and abundant quantities of foreign coins. The Exchange Bank of Amsterdam allowed merchants to set up accounts denominated in a standardized currency, pioneering modern-day cheques and direct debits or transfers. As a result, more and more commercial transactions took place without actual coins.

A merchant could make a payment to another by simply debiting his bank account and crediting the money to the counterparty's bank account. However, the Exchange Bank maintained a nearly 100 per cent ratio between its deposits and its precious coins and metal reserves. This put a limitation on this system. In 1760, when the bank's deposits stood at just below 19 million florins, its reserve was over 16 million. That meant the bank had enough cash on hand to satisfy most of its customers if they all wanted to withdraw their deposits at once. Without a doubt, this can make the bank secure, but it prevents the bank from performing the defining characteristic of a bank: credit creation.

Nearly half a century later, in 1656, this barrier was broken in Stockholm with the foundation of the Riksbank. Although Wisselbank and the Riksbank operated in similar ways, the latter was designed to engage in lending while facilitating commercial payments. By taking the risk of lending amounts beyond its metallic reserves, the Riksbank pioneered the modern-day practice of fractional reserve banking, the utilization of the money left on deposit for profitable lending to credible borrowers. As there was a slim possibility that customers would liquidate their deposits en masse, only a fraction of their deposits needed to be kept in the bank's reserve at any given time. The bank's liabilities were thus its deposits (on which it paid interest) plus its reserve (on which it couldn't collect interest), while its loans became its assets (on which it could collect interest).

In 1694, the foundation of the Bank of England triggered the third great financial innovation of the seventeenth century. The bank was created mainly to assist the government with war finance. This was done by converting a portion of the government's debt into shares in the bank, and thus, the bank was endowed with distinctive privileges. In 1709 it became the only bank permitted to operate on a joint-stock basis. In 1742, the Bank of England established a partial monopoly on the issue of banknotes, a unique form of a promissory note. These banknotes did not bear interest and were designed to facilitate payments without the need for current bank accounts among both transacting parties.

Though the Italian banking methods successfully improved the banking systems in the financial centres of northern Europe, one country couldn't reap the benefits of it. The cursed country was none other than the mighty Spain. By relying heavily on the merchants and conquistadors of Antwerp for short-term advance cash payments against future silver deliveries, the Spanish Crown failed to develop a sophisticated banking system.

Credit and debt are the two essential building blocks of economic development. They are as crucial to creating the wealth of nations as mining, manufacturing or information technology. Unfortunately, Spain couldn't grasp the idea that money was all about credit, not precious metals. Consequently, the Spanish Empire became debt-ridden, defaulting on most of its debt for more than a century between 1557 and 1696. All the silver from the mountain of Cerro Rico could not rescue Spain from its mountain of debts.

Regarded by many as the 'Father of Economics and Capitalism', Adam Smith explained in his famous book, *An Inquiry into the Nature and Causes of the Wealth of Nations*, that banking is a wise practice that replaces a lot of gold and silver with paper money, which allows the country to turn a lot of idle wealth into useful and profitable wealth that benefits the country. The gold and silver money that is used in any country can be likened to a road, which, while it transports and sells all the crops of the country, does not create any of them. Banking is a clever practice that creates, if I can use such a strong metaphor, a kind of aerial railway, which lets the country change, in a way, a lot of its roads into fertile lands and fields and thus greatly improve the yearly output of its land and work.[6] Many regard him as the 'Father of Economics and Capitalism'.

After he published *The Wealth of Nations* in 1776, there was a great deal of financial innovation in Europe and North America for the next hundred years. This led to several different kinds of banks being opened. Bill-discounting banks had been around the longest. They helped finance both domestic and international trade by discounting bills of exchange that one merchant drew on another. Even in Smith's time, London was home to several very successful businesses, like Barings, which specialized in transatlantic merchant banking (as this line of business came to be known). For legal reasons, almost all English banks at the time were private partnerships. Some focused on the business of the City, a square mile of London that had been the centre of mercantile finance for hundreds of years, while others focused on the business of the landowning elite. The rise and fall of these so-called 'country banks' closely followed the rise and fall of agriculture in Britain.

Financial historians disagree about the extent to which the growth of banking after the seventeenth century can be credited to the rapid economic growth that started in

Britain in the late eighteenth century and spread to Western Europe, North America and Australasia as a result of large-scale European settlement.

Without a doubt, the financial revolution came before the industrial revolution. It is true that the major innovations in iron and textile manufacturing, which served as the industrial revolution's fulcrum, did not heavily rely on bank financing. However, banks were more crucial to the industrialization of continental Europe than they were to that of England. Finding a straightforward causal link—such as whether the development of more sophisticated financial institutions led to industrial growth or whether industrial growth prompted financial development—might be pointless.

It seems very likely that the two processes were connected and helped each other. Both processes also had a clear evolutionary touch to them, with frequent mutations (new technologies), speciation (new types of businesses) and punctuated equilibrium (crises that would determine which businesses would survive and which ones would perish).

A world without money, credit and the exchange of value would be a world much worse than our present money-powered world. The rise and the evolution of the banking system was thus the essential first step in the evolution of money. But, to understand the shortcomings of our current monetary systems and the emergence of financial crises, we need to know the four great pillars of our financial systems: the bond market, the stock market, the insurance market and the real estate market, as well as the remarkable globalization of all these markets that has taken place over the past thirty years.

## The Bond Market

'My name is Bond, Bond Market.' If the bond market were a person, he could have delivered this punchy James Bond line in his hallmark style—seductively and dominantly—to every one of the world's citizens. There are a few reasons for that.

Around 600 years ago, banks created the credit system, triggering a financial revolution worldwide. The second revolution happened in the form of the bond market, another way of borrowing money. Governments and multinational corporations issue bonds to borrow money from a range of people and institutions other than banks.

Since its humble beginnings in the cities of northern Italy around 800 years ago, the bond market has grown to an enormous size. Today, the size of the global bond market stands at about $128 trillion. In India, the value of domestically traded bonds stands at a staggering $30 billion. Consequently, each of us, whether we like it or not (and most of us don't even know it), is affected by the bond market in two significant ways.

First, a large chunk of the money we save for our old age enters the bond market as investments. Second, owing to its enormous size and as big governments are considered the most reliable borrowers, the bond market sets long-term interest rates for the economy. Interest rates and bond prices have an inverse relationship. As a result, a fall in bond prices increases the interest rates, with painful consequences for every borrower.

The bond market is influential and powerful because it is the foundation of all the financial markets. The cost of credit and the bond's interest rate ultimately determine the value of stocks, homes and every asset class. The bond market influences domestic and international politics as it provides a daily barometer of the credibility of a government's fiscal and monetary policies.

Throughout history, from building dams to financing wars to building canals to the Italian Renaissance, bond markets all over the world have helped create wealth and enabled many to taste the sweetness of money and the benefits of credit.

## The Legend of the Rothschilds

The family name of Rothschild is often associated with secrecy and mystery in the financial world. The name 'Rothschild' has a similar impact on finance enthusiasts that the term 'Illuminati' has on conspiracy theory enthusiasts. The Rothschilds have been seen as a family who secretly control the world of finance. As they are of Jewish descent, the Rothschilds have also been the target of anti-Semitic prejudices. They are believed to be the funders of wars, including both the World Wars, the 9/11 attack and the 2003 invasion of Iraq, and to bring chaos to the world. Conspiracy theorists even believe the Rothschilds were behind the sinking of the *Titanic*! Whenever any financial distress or geopolitical conflict happens anywhere in the world, directly or indirectly, the Rothschilds are blamed.

Is there someone who controls the world of finance with vested interests? If so, are they able to manipulate the governments of powerful countries? To understand finance, we should debunk some deep-rooted myths, including the myth of the Rothschilds. Let's take a look at who the Rothschilds really are.

'Money is the god of our time, and Rothschild is his prophet,' declared the German poet Heinrich Heine in 1841.[7] This statement was true during those days. The man Heinrich Heine was referring to was Nathan Mayer Rothschild, the founder of the London branch of the N.M. Rothschild & Sons bank, the biggest bank in the world for most of the nineteenth century. The Rothschild family made their fortune from the bond market and were rich enough to build forty-one stately homes all over Europe.

Nathan Rothschild, the founder of the Rothschild banking empire, was ambitious and a financial genius. His phenomenal drive and innate financial prowess propelled him from the obscurity of a Frankfurt ghetto to mastering the London bond market.

A historic war provided the opportunity to prove his financial mettle and to lay the foundation for the Rothschild family's immense wealth. The war was the Battle of Waterloo in 1815.

On 18 June 1815, thousands of British, Dutch and German troops under the command of the Duke of Wellington faced the troops led by the French Emperor, Napoleon Bonaparte. The Battle of Waterloo was the culmination of more than two decades of sporadic conflicts between Britain and France. But it was also something more than a conflict between two armies. It was a battle between two rival financial systems. The first was the French, under Napoleon, which was based on plundering the conquered; the second was the British, which was based on debt.

Never in human history had so many bonds been issued to fund a war. Between 1793 and 1815, Britain's national debt increased to £745 million, doubling the annual output of the British economy. This abundant supply of bonds took a heavy toll on the London bond market and bond prices.

In 1751, the Bank of England issued a British consol, a type of government bond that has no maturity date and pays a fixed interest rate. The name is an abbreviation for consolidated annuities. The price of British consols, which were considered a safe and reliable investment, sank below £50 from £100 in 1797.

According to popular legend, Nathan earned the first million of the Rothschild family's fortune through successful speculation on British bond prices following the outcome of the Battle of Waterloo. In some versions of the legend, Nathan witnessed the battle of Waterloo himself and took the news of Wellington's victory to London through his private channels ahead of official news channels. He then bought bonds on the London Stock Exchange ahead of the price surge and pocketed between £20 million and £135 million.

The Nazis brilliantly used this version of the story to propagate antisemitism. To this end, Paul Joseph Goebbels, chief propagandist of the Nazi party, promoted the 1940 movie *Die Rothschilds*. This anti-Semitic 'biography' of the Rothschilds showcases Nathan bribing a French general to let Wellington win the war. He then deliberately misreports the outcome in the London stock market and triggers a panic selling of British bonds, allowing him to buy the bonds at bargain prices.

But the reality was entirely different. Rather than making money from Wellington's victory at Waterloo, the Rothschilds were nearly ruined by it. In fact, their fortune was made another way, not because of the Battle of Waterloo.

The British had been fighting Napoleon's French troops since August 1808, and there was a recurrent need for men and money for the battles in the Iberian Peninsula. Britain's government amassed wealth by selling bonds to the public, but paper banknotes were of little use on distant battlefields. Wellington needed a universally acceptable currency to provision his troops and pay Britain's allies against France. The challenge was to convert the money raised on the bond market into gold coins and then get them to where they were needed.

Sending gold coins from London to Lisbon was expensive and hazardous during the war. To make matters worse, the Portuguese merchants declined to accept the bills of exchange that Wellington offered, and he was left with no other option but to ship the gold.

Nathan Rothschild, son of a German antique dealer and bill broker, had arrived in England in 1799. He spent the next ten years in the newly industrializing northern England, purchasing and shipping textiles back to Germany. Nathan didn't venture into the banking business in London until 1811. But he had gained popularity and experience as a proficient gold smuggler on the continent, breaching Napoleon's blockade on trade between Europe and England. Nathan's popularity and gold smuggling skills compelled the British government to turn to him for help during the war.

In truth, the French deliberately closed their eyes to the smuggling of gold from Britain to Europe as they thought that outflows of gold from England would weaken the British war effort.

In January 1814, Nathan took up the biggest and the most challenging gold smuggling operation of his career.

He had to secretly deliver large quantities of gold and silver coins to Wellington, who had already arrived in France with his troops. Nathan's smuggling operation for the British depended on the transcontinental credit network of his five brothers to manage immense bullion transfers.

No doubt, mobilizing such vast amounts of gold during a war was risky. Yet from the Rothschilds' point of view, the hefty commissions they received justified the risks. Moreover, what made the Rothschilds well suited to the task was that the brothers had an established banking network within the family that spanned across Europe—London, Frankfurt, Paris and Amsterdam.

Their strategic banking locations around Europe allowed the five Rothschilds to exploit price and exchange rate differences of gold between markets. This process is also known as arbitrage. Arbitrage and hefty commissions on the gold smuggling operations made the Rothschilds immensely wealthy during the war.

But things took a different turn when Napoleon Bonaparte abdicated in April 1814 and made his comeback in March 1815. Anticipating a war, Nathan Rothschild immediately resumed purchasing all the bullion and gold coins he and his brothers could lay their hands on and making them available for shipment to Wellington.

It has been recorded that the Rothschilds provided gold coins worth more than £2 million and offered a fresh round of donations to Britain's allies, making their total transactions worth nearly £10 million in 1815. With commissions ranging from 2 to 6 per cent, Napoleon's return was a sure-shot path to profits for the Rothschilds. But unfortunately, Nathan underestimated the risk. While buying large quantities of gold in a wild frenzy, he had assumed that, like every other war with Napoleon, this too would be a long one. Yet events proved otherwise.

On Sunday, 18 June 1815, the Battle of Waterloo came to an abrupt end with the defeat of Napoleon Bonaparte. The Rothschild brothers sat on top of a mountain of cash nobody needed, to fund a war that was over.

With peace around the corner, the great armies that had fought Napoleon were disbanded and the coalition of allies dissolved. That meant no more wages for soldiers and no more money for Britain's wartime allies. The price of gold, which had skyrocketed during the war, was about to fall.

Contrary to legend, Nathan was faced with heavy and growing losses. Finally, the light appeared at the end of the tunnel: Nathan was struck by the idea of using the bullion they had bought to make a massive and risky bet on the bond market.

On 20 July 1815, Nathan began to pump his gold reserves into the London bond market. Several evening dailies heralded Nathan's 'great buying spree of bonds'.[8] Nathan's gamble was that the British victory at Waterloo and the subsequent reduction in government borrowing would raise the price of British bonds. So, Nathan bought more bonds, and although their prices duly began to rise, he kept buying. Nathan held his positions for another year despite his brothers' desperate requests to realize profits in the early bull run.

Eventually, Nathan sold his positions when bond prices were up more than 40 per cent in late 1817. His net profits were worth around £600 million in today's money. It was one of the most daring trades in financial history, made in the aftermath of Napoleon's historic military defeat.

Even today, it remains an astonishing fact that, after Waterloo, the Rothschilds dominated the international financial world for half a century. The feat was so extraordinary that contemporaries often explained it in mystical terms. According to one nineteenth-century legend, the Rothschilds built their fortune using a mysterious 'Hebrew talisman', which empowered Nathan Rothschild to become 'the giant of the European money markets'.[9] Similar stories were circulated in the Pale of Settlement, where Russian Jews were confined in the late nineteenth century. As we have seen, the Nazis brilliantly used stories of stock market manipulation and other financial malpractices attributed to the Rothschilds to create anti-Semitic sentiments across Europe.

Such myths remain alive even today. For example, several books have been published that claim the Rothschilds were in charge of the global monetary system through their alleged influence over the Federal Reserve System, the central banking system of the United States.

But the truth is far from these myths. Indeed, the Rothschilds were arguably the wealthiest family in the world throughout the nineteenth and twentieth centuries. They were more affluent than Bill Gates and Jeff Bezos combined in today's dollar terms. But the family, which virtually created the bond market and controlled the international financial system for nearly two centuries, is not as big as today's global financial giants.

The Rothschild's financial empire gradually disintegrated as its wealth was spread among a large number of family members. Some left the field of finance and focused on other interests and careers. Although the Rothschild Bank exists today, theories about them controlling the global financial system are nothing more than childish fantasy.

Markets in the early ages were narrow and shallow with no tight regulations. These conditions made it possible for an individual or a financial institution with deep pockets to easily manipulate them, but only for a short period. On the other hand, today's financial markets and systems are highly sophisticated and too deep in money for a single family or corporation to manipulate. So, you may be thinking: would it be possible to control the global financial systems if two or more financial giants joined hands to do so? Well, no.

The world of finance, as you have seen, is as old as human history. So, it is a fascinating field of study with several exciting myths, legends and conspiracy theories. You will encounter many of these in the coming chapters. All these stories show the ephemeral nature of those greedy monetary treasure hunts.

## Protecting One's Life

In agricultural societies prior to the modern era, life expectancy was low because of poor nutrition, disease and war. People back then couldn't do nearly as much to prevent problems as people today can. They relied on appeasing gods, who, they thought, were most powerful and would protect them from famines, floods, plagues, invasions and other natural and man-made calamities. Men didn't realize that all natural events and phenomena—weather, crop yields, floods, famines and disease—followed regular patterns.

It was only in the eighteenth and nineteenth centuries that our forefathers began keeping track of rainfall, harvests and deaths in a way that made it possible to calculate probabilities. Even before that, though, they knew it was smart to save money for the proverbial (and, in agricultural societies, actual) 'rainy day'. Most people in primitive societies only knew that sometimes things went well, and sometimes they did not. They learned to save money and food for the hard times, like when there was no rain or crops. They also learned to live in groups and cooperate with each other, because that made them stronger and safer. Today, we call it safety in numbers.

Given that our forefathers were always in danger, it made sense for them to ensure their burials. Therefore, the first insurance was probably bought by burial societies, which set money aside to make sure each tribe member had a decent burial. In some of the poorest parts of East Africa, these groups are still the only financial organizations.[10] Saving to provide for an uncertain future is still the main idea behind insurance, whether it is for death, sickness, old age or an accident. The trick is knowing how much to save and what to do with that money to ensure that there is enough in the emergency fund to cover a disaster when it occurs.

In medieval times, life insurance was merely a form of gambling. Canny businessmen bet on the lives of people; for example, Florentine merchant Bernardo Cambi made wagers on the lives of the pope, the doge of Venice and the king of Aragon. Then, in the seventeenth century, came six crucial breakthroughs that provided a theoretical basis for evaluating risks. They were probability, life expectancy, certainty, normal distribution, utility and inference. The following mathematicians exploited these theories and contributed significantly to the development of insurance.

Blaise Pascal was a seventeenth-century French mathematician, physicist, inventor and philosopher. Pascal is well known for his contributions to mathematics and physics, particularly probability theory and hydrodynamics. He invented the mechanical calculator, which served as a forerunner to the modern computer. He is regarded as one of the seventeenth century's most influential thinkers and is often referred to as a 'Renaissance man'. Pascal attributed the insight that fear of harm should be proportional to the probability of the event to a monk in Port Royal, a village in Jamaica.

John Graunt was an English statistician and demographer who is regarded as one of the forefathers of modern statistics. Graunt is best known for his contributions to the development of statistical analysis and his pioneering work in demography, the study of human populations. He is widely regarded as the first person to use quantitative methods to study human populations and analyse mortality rates in a systematic manner. The book *Natural and Political Observations Made Upon the Bills of Mortality*, published in 1662, is Graunt's most famous work. Graunt analysed data from weekly reports of births, deaths and marriages in London, known as 'bills of mortality' in this book. He studied disease and mortality patterns, as well as demographic trends and patterns in the population using this data. However, his data did not include ages at death.

Edmund Halley was an English astronomer, mathematician and physicist best known for predicting the orbit of Halley's comet, which bears his name. Edmund Halley developed the 'Breslau Table' or 'Halley's Table of Mortality', which is an early example of a life table. A life table is a statistical tool used to estimate life expectancy and mortality rates. In 1693, Halley created the table based on observations of the mortality patterns of the population of Breslau, a city in modern-day Poland. His life table, based on 1238 recorded births and 1174 recorded deaths, gave the odds of not dying in a given year.

Jacob Bernoulli was a Swiss mathematician who made significant contributions to calculus, probability theory and differential equations in the seventeenth century. He invented the method of integration by parts, which is used to calculate integrals even today, and he also worked on series theory and the solution of differential equations. The development of the law of large numbers and the concept of expected value were among his significant contributions to probability theory. His law of large numbers states that a sample of two kinds of balls in a jar could be used to make some assumptions about the total number of balls in the jar.

Abraham de Moivre was a French mathematician who contributed significantly to probability theory and trigonometry. He is best known for his work on the complex exponential function, which has since become known as De Moivre's formula. This formula computes the nth power of a complex number in trigonometric form, which is a useful tool in many fields of mathematics and science. He was among the first mathematicians to develop a comprehensive probability theory. He is best known for his contributions to the normal distribution, also known as the Gaussian distribution. De Moivre discovered that the normal distribution occurs naturally in a wide range of situations involving random variables, and his work laid the foundation for modern probability theory and statistics.

De Moivre showed that the outcomes of any iterative process could be distributed along a curve according to their variance around the mean, or standard deviation. This provides the basis for the concept of statistical significance and modern formulations of probabilities at specified confidence intervals. De Moivre and Bernoulli proposed that the value of an item should not be based on its price but rather on the utility it yields.

Thomas Bayes was an English mathematician and theologian who worked in the field of probability theory in the eighteenth century. He was especially intrigued by the problem of induction, which asks how we can draw conclusions about the world based on limited observations. Bayes devised a probabilistic method for solving this problem, which is now known as Bayesian inference. Bayes is best known for his work on conditional probability, which he described in his essay 'An Essay Towards Solving a Problem in Chances'. He introduced the concept of what is now known as Bayes' theorem in this essay, which provides a method for updating probabilities based on new evidence.[11] Bayes' theorem has become an indispensable tool in modern statistics, with applications ranging from machine learning to genetics to finance.

Thomas Bayes proposed that the chance of an event happening in the first instance is not fixed but can be anywhere between two possible chances. The chance of something happening is equal to how much you expect to gain from it if it happens, divided by the chance of that expectation coming true if the event does happen.

In short, mathematicians, not merchants, were the ones who established insurance as we know it today. Still, it was the clergy who put the ideas into action.

Reverend Patrick MacFarlane and Reverend James Grant, both from the Church of Scotland, deserve credit for coming up with the first real insurance fund in 1744. It was named the Scottish Ministers' Widows' Fund. MacFarlane and Grant were concerned about the penury faced by the widows and families of the Church's ministers. They suggested setting up a fund to help them and the General Assembly of the Church of Scotland eventually agreed. The Scottish Ministers' Widows' Fund is one of the oldest pension funds that is still going strong, supporting the widows and families of Church of Scotland ministers.

There were a few insurance companies before that time as well. 'Bottomry', or the insurance of the 'bottoms' (hulls) of merchant ships, was the first form of insurance as a business. Some historians say that the first insurance contracts were made in Italy in the early 1300s when payments for *securitas* (which means 'security' or 'safety' in Latin) started to show up in business records. But these deals were more akin to loans to merchants (as in ancient Babylon) that could be cancelled if something tragic happened, rather than like policies in the modern sense. In Shakespeare's *Merchant of Venice*, Antonio's fleet of ships (argosies) is not insured, which leaves him vulnerable to Shylock's plan to kill him.

True insurance contracts did not start to appear until the 1350s, with premiums ranging between 15 per cent and 20 per cent of the amount insured. These premiums started to fall below 10 per cent by the fifteenth century. After being incorporated into mercantile law, or *lex mercatoria* in Latin, such contracts gradually came to be standardized and this format has stood the test of time for centuries. These insurers, however, were merchants who also conducted business on their own account rather than specialists.

After the Great Fire of 1666, which destroyed more than 13,000 homes, something resembling a specialized insurance market started to emerge in London in the late seventeenth century. Nicholas Barbon founded the first fire insurance company fourteen years later. He was an English economist, physician and stock speculator. Barbon is regarded as one of the first proponents of the free-market by historians of mercantilism.

Around the same time, a niche marine insurance market started to develop in Edward Lloyd's coffee house on London's Tower Street. Edward Lloyd was a Welshman who moved to London in 1680 and opened his coffee house in 1688. He catered to the interests of his customers, who were mostly shipowners, merchants and sailors, by providing them with up-to-date and accurate information about shipping and the marine insurance market. He also held maritime auctions and published a paper called Lloyd's News, which later became Lloyd's List. He facilitated the transactions of his customers, who began to underwrite ships and cargo in his coffee house. His coffee house became the place for obtaining marine insurance and the origin of the Lloyd's of London Market, which is still one of the world's leading insurance markets today.[12]

The Amicable Society for a Perpetual Assurance Office was the first company in modern times to offer life insurance. It was started in London in 1706 by William Talbot and Sir Thomas Allen. Each member paid an annual fee per share for one to three shares. Members were between the ages of twelve and fifty-five. At the end of the year, the wives and children of members who had died got a share of the 'amicable contribution' based on how many shares each heir owned. Initially, there were 2000 people in the Amicable Society.

In the 1760s, life insurance started to be sold in the United States. In 1759, the Presbyterian Synods in Philadelphia and New York City set up the Corporation for Relief of Poor and Distressed Ministers, and of the Poor and Distressed Widows and Children of Presbyterian Ministers. In 1769, Episcopal priests set up a similar fund. More than two dozen life insurance companies were started between 1787 and 1837, but less than half of them survived.

In the 1870s, military officers came together to start the American Armed Forces Mutual Aid Association and the Navy Mutual Aid Association. They did this because they saw how hard it was to survive for widows and orphans left in the West after the Battle of the Little Big Horn and for the families of US sailors who died at sea.

In 1818, the Oriental Life Insurance Company was started in Calcutta to meet the needs of the European community. This was the beginning of insurance in India as we know it today. Before India gained independence, the lives of the English and the Indians were valued differently. For example, Indians had to pay more for their insurance than the English. In 1870, the Bombay Mutual Life Assurance Society was founded as the first Indian insurance company.

At the beginning of the twentieth century, many insurance companies were established in India. In 1912, the Life Insurance Companies Act and the Provident Fund Act were passed to regulate the insurance business. The Life Insurance Companies Act of 1912 stipulated that an actuary had to sign off on the companies' premium rate tables and regular valuations. Nonetheless, Indian and foreign companies were still treated differently.

The National Insurance Company, which was started in 1906 and is still in business, is India's oldest insurance company. On 19 January 1956, the Indian government passed an ordinance that nationalized the life insurance business. That same year, the Life Insurance Corporation (LIC) was created. Later, LIC became India's largest insurance company and the country's largest institutional investor, with nearly $600 billion in assets under management.

The evolution of money, the bond market and the insurance market has been a fascinating and centuries-long journey. From barter systems and coins of precious metal to the rise of paper money and the development of financial instruments like insurance policies and bonds, the history of money shows how it has changed and adapted to different economic conditions.

The bond market has been critical in providing capital to businesses and governments all over the world, while the insurance market has assisted individuals and organizations in managing risk and protecting against unforeseen events.

## The Problem with Money

The real estate market, or the market for land and property, is one of the oldest and most fundamental markets in human history. Since the dawn of civilization, people have been exchanging, buying, selling and renting land and property for various purposes, such as agriculture, commerce, residence and defense. The bond, stock and insurance markets, on the other hand, are relatively modern inventions that emerged along with the advent of capitalism during the early Renaissance. These markets are based on the concepts of debt, equity and risk, which are essential for the development and expansion of trade, commerce and industry.

These three markets have evolved and diversified over time, and they have become interconnected and interdependent with each other and with the real estate market. The bond, stock and insurance markets provide the capital, ownership and security for the realty market, while the realty market provides the collateral, the income and the diversification for the bond, stock and insurance markets. Together, these four markets form the four strong pillars of our modern financial system by facilitating the allocation and management of resources in our economies for centuries.

Throughout history, various factors such as economic, social, political and environmental changes have had an impact on real estate, which refers to the ownership, use and transfer of land and property. The origins of real estate can be traced back to ancient times when people were nomadic and moved from place to place in search of food and shelter. They did not have a concept of private property or land ownership, and they shared the resources of the land with other groups.

As human civilization developed, people began to settle down in permanent locations and cultivate the land for agriculture. This led to the emergence of the first real estate markets, where land and property were exchanged for goods or services. The first recorded real estate transaction in history was in 334 BCE when Alexander the Great bought a large estate in Egypt for 100 talents of silver.

Ancient civilizations like Mesopotamia, Egypt, Greece, Rome, China and India also had sophisticated real estate systems where the state measured, taxed and regulated the value of land and property. The ancient laws and customs of real estate also dealt with issues such as inheritance, ownership rights, leases, mortgages and contracts.

The Middle Ages saw a decline in the real estate market as the feudal system dominated land and property ownership in Europe. The feudal system was a hierarchical system of loyalty and service, where the king granted land and property to the nobles, who in turn granted them to the vassals, who then granted them to the peasants. The peasants, who were the majority of the population, had no rights to the land and property, and they had to pay rent and taxes to their lords. The feudal system also restricted the mobility and trade of the people, and it discouraged the development and innovation of real estate.

The Renaissance and the Age of Exploration revived the real estate market, as the discovery of new lands and the expansion of trade and commerce created new opportunities and challenges for real estate. The European colonists brought their real estate laws and practices to the Americas, Africa and Asia, and they established new settlements, plantations and cities.

The colonists also exploited the land and the resources of the native people, and they often imposed their real estate system on them. The colonization and exploitation of the land and the people also led to conflicts and wars, such as the American Revolution and the French Revolution, which challenged the existing real estate system and demanded more rights and freedoms for the people.

The Industrial Revolution and urbanization transformed the real estate market as the development of new technologies, such as the steam engine, the railroad, the telegraph and electricity, increased the productivity and efficiency of the economy. Industrialization also created a massive demand for labour, and it attracted millions of people from rural areas to urban areas, where they worked in factories, mines and mills. Urbanization also created a huge demand for housing, and it led to the construction of new types of buildings, such as apartments, tenements and skyscrapers. Urbanization also brought new challenges and problems for real estate, such as overcrowding, pollution, sanitation and crime.

The twentieth century and the twenty-first century witnessed the globalization and digitalization of the real estate market, as the advancement of communication, transportation and information technologies connected the world and made the real estate market more accessible and competitive.

Globalization also increased the diversity and complexity of the real estate market, as different countries and regions had different laws, regulations, cultures and preferences for real estate. Digitalization also revolutionized the real estate market, as the Internet, e-commerce, social media and artificial intelligence-enabled new ways of searching, buying, selling and managing real estate. The digitalization also created new types of real estate, such as virtual reality, augmented reality, blockchain and the metaverse.

The history of the real estate market shows how real estate has evolved from a simple exchange of land and property to a sophisticated and dynamic industry that affects every aspect of human life. However, this evolution has not been without conflicts and challenges. Throughout history, land and property have been the sources and targets of wars, as people have competed for control and ownership of these valuable assets.

Money and wealth have been equated with precious metals and land for ages. And that is where all the trouble began. Many wars have been fought, won and lost in the pursuit of land and precious metals. As a result, the four strong pillars of our modern financial system have been shaken several times throughout history. The repercussions of those tremors have been felt even in modern times.

During 800 CE, western Europe faced a severe scarcity of silver, which was the main metal used for coinage. The main reason for this was the trade imbalance with the Islamic Empire, which dominated the markets in the Mediterranean and the Near East. The Islamic Empire had a high demand for silver coins, which they exchanged for luxury goods, such as spices, silks and gems. As a result, more and more silver flowed out of Europe to the East, leaving Europe with less metal money to buy essential goods.

There were two ways by which the Europeans could overcome the shortage of silver. They could either export slaves and goods like timber in exchange for silver in Baghdad or African gold in Cairo and Cordoba. Or they could plunder precious metals by invading the Muslim world. The Europeans chose the second way.

In 1095, the First Crusade was proclaimed and initiated by Pope Urban II at the Council of Clermont. Historically, the Crusades were regarded as a series of religious wars initiated, supported and sometimes directed by the Latin Church during the Middle Ages.

Like subsequent conquests, the Crusades were carried out more to overcome Europe's monetary shortage than to convert heathens to Christianity. The best-known Crusades were carried out between 1095 and 1291 to the Holy Land to recover Jerusalem from Islamic rule. Time has revealed that the Crusades were an expensive affair with modest net returns.

Another big problem lurked around the corner to compound Europe's monetary difficulties. Economists today would have called this big problem a 'small change' problem. Europe struggled to establish stable rates between coins made of different metals. This meant that smaller denomination coins were prone to recurrent shortages, depreciations and debasements. One possible solution to this problem was to increase the supply of silver, the main metal used for coinage. However, this was not easy to achieve, as silver was scarce and expensive in Europe.

Fortunately for some Europeans, especially the Spaniards, a new source of silver was discovered in the New World. Europeans, particularly the Spaniards, had found abundant silver deposits at Potosí and other places in the New World, notably Zacatecas in Mexico. The Spanish conquistadors had broken centuries-old silver mining and shipping restrictions to mitigate their financial troubles. 170 tons of silver were shipped annually from the New World across the Atlantic to the Spanish city of Seville. The convoys of ships could be as large as a hundred at a time. The Castilian monarchy that sponsored the conquests was the initial beneficiary of this wealth. A fifth of all the silver was reserved for the monarchy. At the peak of the silver rush, nearly 50 per cent of the royal expenditure was funded by these silver reserves during the late sixteenth century.

It appeared as if Spain's newfound wealth had provided the entire European continent with a fiscal stimulus. The Spanish silver coins or 'pieces of eight', based on the German thaler (from which the term 'dollar' was derived), became the world's first global currency. It financed not only the recurrent Spanish war efforts in Europe but also the rapidly expanding trade activities in Europe and Asia.

Yet all the New World silver could not help Spain subdue the rebellious Dutch Republic, could not help it conquer England and could not save it from an inexorable economic and imperial decline. So, like the mythological King Midas, the Spanish monarchs of the sixteenth century, Charles V and Philip II, realized that an abundance of precious metal could be a curse rather than a blessing.

The reason?

Spain dug up so much silver to pay for their wars that the metal's value dramatically declined. That meant its purchasing power too declined relative to other goods. This created the Spanish price revolution from the 1540s until the 1640s, the impact of which was felt all over Europe. The cost of food—which hadn't displayed an upward trend for 300 years—rose significantly. In England, the cost of living increased during the same period. The price of bread witnessed a revolutionary increase by medieval standards without a high inflation rate.

The abundance of silver became a 'resource curse' within Spain, much like the surplus oil of the Middle East, Nigeria, Russia and Venezuela in our own time, eliminating the incentives for more productive economic activities.

The Spaniards failed to understand that the value of a precious metal is not absolute, and the value of money depends on what someone else is willing to give you for an exchange. An increase in the money supply will not make a society more prosperous, though it may enrich the government that monopolizes the minting of money. With other economic factors remaining equal, monetary expansion results only in higher prices. The Spanish price revolution was the first recorded instance of inflation in history.

## What Is a Pound?

Sir Robert Peel, the then-prime minister of the United Kingdom, asked one of the most frequently repeated rhetorical questions of the nineteenth century during a parliamentary debate in 1819: 'What is a pound?'

The debate focused on the Bank of England's decision to resume cash payments that was part of a process to restore the British currency to the gold standard, which meant that paper money could be exchanged for gold and silver at a fixed rate. This was seen as a way to ensure the stability and credibility of the currency, as well as to prevent inflation and speculation.

Cash payments were stopped in 1797, during the French Revolutionary Wars, when the Bank of England faced a financial crisis due to the high demand for gold and silver from the government and the public. The Bank Restriction Act of 1797 suspended the convertibility of paper money to gold and silver, allowing the bank to issue more paper money without backing it with metal. This was meant to be a temporary measure, but it lasted for 22 years, until 1819.

The debate over the resumption of cash payments was controversial and divisive, as it had significant economic and social implications for different groups of people. Some argued that returning to the gold standard would restore the soundness and honesty of the currency, while others feared that it would cause deflation and hardship for debtors, farmers and industrialists.

Peel was certain that the question was as perplexing for him as it was for influential philosophers like John Locke and outstanding scientists like Isaac Newton during the Enlightenment era.

Peel later came to the simple conclusion that a pound was a specific amount of gold bullion with an impression indicating its weight and fineness. He believed that forcing the bank to exchange gold for paper money would return Britain to its 'ancient and solid standard of value'.[13]

A few Victorians had questioned whether a pound was a 'definite quantity of gold bullion',[14] and they repeatedly asked the question posed by Peel as they were perplexed as to how gold worked, or didn't work, in British culture because it had different meanings and functions in different contexts. Gold was a symbol of wealth, power and prestige, but it was also a source of conflict, exploitation, greed and corruption. Gold was also a commodity that was traded in the global market, and its supply and demand affected the prices of other goods and services.

Nonetheless, the Victorians strove to determine what their money was and how much it was worth in light of Britain's shifting position in the global economy because Britain faced increasing competition and challenges from other countries, especially the United States and Germany, in the second half of the nineteenth century. Britain's share of the world's GDP declined from 9.1 per cent in 1870 to 7.3 per cent in 1913, while the US and Germany increased their shares from 8.8 per cent to 18.9 per cent and from 6.5 per cent to 14.8 per cent, respectively.[15] Britain also faced political and social unrest at home and abroad, as well as wars and crises in its vast colonial empire. These factors influenced the value and stability of the British currency, and the debate over the gold standard reflected the uncertainty and anxiety of the Victorian era.

From the time of the Sumerians (3000 BCE) until 1873, silver was far more widely used as the global monetary standard than gold. As mentioned earlier, following the discovery of large silver deposits at Cerro Rico in Potosí in the sixteenth century, an international silver standard was established, as was the widespread use of the Spanish 'pieces of eight' and the Spanish dollar.

The Spanish dollar is a silver coin with a diameter of about 38 mm, which contains 0.822 ounces of fine silver. The coin, also known as a real, was produced during the Spanish Empire and was worth eight units of the Spanish currency. The coin's uniformity in standard and milling characteristics allowed it to be widely used as the first global currency. The Spanish dollar was countermarked and used as local money in some nations.

A fixed weight of silver served as the standard economic unit of account in the 'silver standard' system of financial transactions. For nearly 400 years, these silver coins were a significant part of the international trading system.

The switch from the silver standard to the gold standard in international trade began in the eighteenth century when Great Britain adopted gold as its primary currency and increased the value of one gold coin to that of silver relative to other nations. This attracted other countries to trade with Britain and use gold as their primary currency too. This action put Britain on the gold standard, though the term wasn't used at the time.

The gold guinea coin was minted in the United Kingdom between 1663 and 1814. The coin contained roughly a quarter ounce of gold. The term 'guinea' comes from the Guinea region of West Africa, where the majority of the gold used to make these coins was mined. The guinea coin was the first machine-struck gold coin in the United Kingdom.

Following the formalization of the gold standard in 1821, the United Kingdom extended it to its colonies. This historical move triggered a similar trend throughout Europe. In 1873, imperial Germany adopted the gold standard. Except for China, which remained on the silver standard until 1935, the rest of the world followed suit over the next thirty-five years.

In 1935, China abandoned the silver standard, while the rest of the world abandoned the gold standard in favour of government-backed fiat currencies pegged to the British pound or the US dollar.

Now, let's return to the nineteenth-century Victorian era.

Money had a big effect on the way Victorians thought about morality, social class and politics, which are all important areas of thought. Money, according to the Victorian moral compass, sat on a precipice between the sacred and the profane. Victorians determined the value of their money over time by transforming some major contradictions into a celebration of wealth and power. Politicians and bankers defended gold's sacred status as a store of value, while radicals and evangelicals opposed society's worship of Mammon.

Money changed a lot in the 1800s. It was not just something people used to buy things, but also a sign of how powerful a country was. Banks and other businesses helped money grow more and more, but sometimes they also caused big problems for the economy. The Victorians loved to save money. They looked at the stock market, the bank records and the post office books to see how much money they had. At the beginning of the nineteenth century, the French term 'millionaire', which means 'a man of great wealth', entered the English language.

Money told a different story in politics. The ability of the gold standard to stabilize the economy was defended by Britons. At the same time, they conveniently ignored the mixed effects of this standard, which resulted in decades of deflation and the vulnerable position that a strong pound repeatedly imposed on their trading partners.

The main argument in favour of the gold standard was that no other basis would be as effective at providing stable prices—which politicians hoped would be associated with stable social and political relations. In comparison to other nineteenth-century economies—such as those of Austria, Russia and China—and other periods in British history, the Victorian era saw relatively stable prices. They fell from inflated wartime levels in the decade following Waterloo and continued to fall until the Great Depression of 1873-96.

During the Napoleonic Wars, however, the inconvertible paper currency experienced much higher price fluctuations, up to 80 per cent. The gold standard's defenders could also point to this meteoric rise in prices.

The most straightforward cause of price volatility is the amount of actual gold bullion in the bank's vaults at any given time. War and an unexpected demand for imports drained the country's gold reserves, and sometimes there was too much gold coming into the country, which could also affect the value of the paper currency. For example, India was a major source of gold imports for Britain, especially after the discovery of new gold mines in the nineteenth century. This could cause inflation and make the paper currency less stable. Until the end of the Victorian era, people remembered the impact of war on the money supply as rising prices and a thriving economy during the Napoleonic Wars.

Money, or its lack thereof, became increasingly associated with punishment during the Victorian era. In Victorian novels and everyday life, bankruptcy was referred to as 'the hell of the English'. Several laws were enacted between the 1840s and the 1880s to penalize loan defaults. A consensus emerged that debt undermines 'national morality'. On the other hand, while bankruptcies were viewed negatively, rags-to-riches stories gained celebrity status in society.

In this new Victorian moral economy, insurers and bankers managed a person's personal worth. Bank executives boasted that their loans enabled people with good intentions and ideas to obtain elevated social status. Insurers told melodramatic stories of uninsured people on their deathbeds weeping over their inability to provide financial security for their loved ones. Insurance companies went a step further in monetizing life by precisely calculating the payments to be made by the insured person or the breadwinner of the family to provide a financial safety net for their dependents if they died unexpectedly.

The 'detoxification' of money was well underway by the end of the nineteenth century. Victorian moralists focused on money's redemptive capacity, shifting their focus away from money itself and towards its abuse. Money became a status symbol, a legal incentive in the form of reward payments for wanted criminals and a tool of philanthropy—a practice that emerged alongside the Enlightenment as a universal instrument of personal agency. 'Let the world be as corrupt as it is, but why should we blame gold or silver?'[16] emerged as a general Victorian thought pattern. In other words, it is not money that is at fault, but the people who use it.

A closer look at the moral meanings of gold, which was the basis of Victorian currency and a solid sign of wealth, shows that the Victorians had mixed feelings about money. Gold-backed currency supporters called it a 'sacred standard' because it was a fair way to measure how much something was worth that was the same for all goods. During those times, gold also represented an earthly reward. Victorians who excelled in fields ranging from science and sports to the arts received gold medals, cups and plates. The Royal Society of Arts awarded dozens of gold and silver medals each year to encourage invention; endowment reports included the value of each award (typically thirty to fifty guinea coins), and the society always gave the recipients the option of accepting the cash value.

Although gold is corrupted and cankered in the Bible, Victorians found ample biblical evidence that God approved of their choice of gold as a judge of worldly worth. Gold shone as a symbol of purity, truth and value. On one side of the balance, biblical metaphors linked gold to purity, honour and virtue; on the other, to the vices of avarice, miserliness, idolatry and greed.

Avarice is a recurring theme in English literature, including Shakespeare's. Victorians vigorously used these clichés for their favourite moral targets, such as child labour, slavery and financial speculation. The radical evangelists accused factory owners of posing as Christians and employing child labour in factories to amass filthy heaps of gold. They also included a definition of planters as 'slaves of gold'.

As abolitionism and factory reform became solved or forgotten issues, financial speculation became a focus of public ire. The Victorians believed that this more ambiguous symptom of avarice existed somewhere between gambling and investment. The Victorians believed that 'the lust for gold' and the insane desire to amass wealth were symptoms of neural disorders that frequently led to insanity. Misers who saved money in an unhealthy way motivated by avarice had a similar status in the minds of Victorians.

Victorians practised dual worship of God and gold, so their blatant hypocrisy is at the heart of most such depictions. In reality, most Victorians were perfectly content to live with the ambiguity of their chosen value standard. Gold, according to the *Cornhill Magazine*, was the medium of exchange, the enemy of virtue and the exceptional standard of value in all civilized countries. Bank notes, cheques and other credit instruments that were based on gold also had gold status.

The paradoxical nature of Victorian money was linked to Victorian devotion to religiously closing their eyes to unwelcome realities. Because Victorians were able to live with money's contradictory nature, most stopped connecting personal moral failings (money abuse) and institutional culpability. As a result, protests against filthy lucre rarely slowed the nineteenth-century expansion of monetary instruments and institutions throughout British society and the British Empire.

Aside from bank notes, a growing number of other credit instruments found their way into all classes of Victorian society. The most spectacular were the stocks and bonds that fuelled the meteoric rise of railways and other public companies in the 1820s. In comparison to the eighteenth century, when investment was primarily limited to the aristocracy and privileged classes of society and consisted of government bonds and a few chartered company shares, after 1820, a wider variety of stocks became available to more people.

In addition, less spectacular forms of credit became more prevalent in Victorian society. Banks, which had previously rarely paid interest on deposits before 1850, began to compete in this market. Banks expanded their branches across the country, while life insurance companies began to reward policyholders with 'bonuses' similar to interest on their premiums. Savings banks and friendly societies arose as investment vehicles supported by charities, trade unions and the government. To meet local demand, new stock exchanges were established in Manchester and Liverpool in 1836. The major financial journals documented the widespread democratization of financial speculation in the mid-century.

Even those who did not deal with credit in its more esoteric forms could read about it in novels and news accounts that drew readers in with the promise of demystifying the money market. As a result, there was a surge in demand for this type of knowledge, blurring the distinction between fact and fiction. Writers borrowed novelists' storytelling techniques to demonstrate how the new credit economy and commodity culture functioned in a dramatic and natural way.

So, the answer to the question 'What is a pound?' is that money had very different meanings and manifestations for Victorians depending on their social class. However, this did not imply that they were ignorant of money, particularly the coin that jingled in their pockets.

Beginning with shillings and crowns, the Victorians had a distinct advantage over previous generations in terms of the availability of reliable coins. The Coinage Act of 1816 was passed to ensure that the economy had a sufficient supply of shillings. In addition to making gold legal tender, the Coinage Act required the State to mint silver coins that circulated at less than face value and thus could not be melted down and exported as bullion. The mint was able to stamp shillings that were less likely to be counterfeited thanks to new steam technology, and this helped alleviate an endemic shortage that had embarrassed British officials.

Joining the shilling as token coins were crowns (five shillings), half-crowns and sixpence and threepence pieces. These pieces were all in silver. Then came pennies, half-pennies, farthings and half-farthings, which went from copper to bronze in 1860.

In addition to switching from token currency to sterling, the Coinage Act introduced a new gold coin, the sovereign (valued at twenty shillings). The sovereign became more popular and widely used than the guinea, the previous gold coin that was slightly heavier and worth more (twenty-one shillings).

The sovereign was not only lighter and easier to carry, but it also had a fixed value that was unaffected by price fluctuations in the gold market. The guinea, on the other hand, was often overvalued or undervalued depending on the supply and demand of gold. The sovereign achieved success as it was more convenient and stable as a medium of exchange than the guinea.

The term 'sovereign' was not novel: coins with similar names (priced between ten and twenty-two shillings) circulated during the Tudor and Stuart monarchies in the fifteenth and sixteenth centuries.

This plethora of names was accompanied by a consistent set of State-issued coins bearing Queen Victoria's images—a stark contrast to the variety of tokens and foreign coins that had previously circulated in the United Kingdom. Paper money (fixed at a minimum of five pounds in England) increasingly bore the Bank of England's stamp in the nineteenth century. Furthermore, some provincial banks continued to print notes in the 1920s.

The pound sterling became as effective as the British Empire's navy at underpinning colonial trade terms and reinforcing its strength.

By 1914, the aggregate money power of bank deposits, insurance premiums and self-help subscriptions had increased the capital market by more than £2 billion. In addition to becoming creditors for the first time, Victorian workers borrowed in novel ways. Credit became a form of self-help in cooperative societies. Along with this, pawnbrokers proliferated in industrial cities, and shopkeepers established 'guardian societies' to regulate the widespread availability—and frequent abuse—of retail credit.

Foreign and colonial bonds became increasingly prominent on the London Stock Exchange by the end of the nineteenth century. However, Victorian-era money served as a nationalizing agent. It replaced locally minted tokens and regional paper currency with State-minted coins and Bank of England notes, thereby reinforcing national boundaries.

Thus, the national currency became a primary symbol of national unity. The national economy was centred on the national banking system, with everything linked to the national treasury, fuelled by collective effort and dedicated to achieving national goals.

As more Victorians understood what money was, they began to realize it through the instruments of credit, financial institutions and a wide array of cultural activities.

The peculiar quality of money reinforced their understanding of money as both an entity and a sign. It also enabled Victorians to accomplish something that Karl Marx had predicted would fail under capitalism: the capacity to simultaneously pursue the contradictory ideals of Christian morality and the accumulation of wealth.

Robert Peel's definition of a pound as 'a definite quantity of gold bullion', which he had made in 1819 by supporting new legislation that reiterated the gold standard's reach, was not entirely accurate when he first uttered it as he had ignored the historical role of silver as a legal tender in Britain. Before 1797, the British currency system was based on a bimetallic standard, meaning that both gold and silver coins were accepted as legal tender and could be exchanged for banknotes at a fixed ratio. The Coinage Act of 1696, which increased the value of silver coins relative to gold coins and gave people an incentive to hoard gold and export silver, however, distorted this ratio. This led to a shortage of silver coins and a devaluation of the bank notes, which were backed by both metals.

Before 1797, when the Bank of England suspended cash payments, its customers could demand either silver or gold in exchange for their notes. They demanded silver because of its artificially low price relative to gold since 1696. Only after 1816, in anticipation of the resumption of cash payments, did the British Parliament officially declare gold as the nation's only legal tender for all transactions. Once cash payments resumed in 1821, the Bank of England was legally liable to exchange its notes for gold bullion.

Since most other banks held Bank of England notes in reserve against their paper currency, the Bank had to back the nation's supply of paper money with its gold reserves. For most of the nineteenth century, the Bank held ample bullion reserves for this purpose except during the times of 'overtrading', when lenders issued an excess of paper money and other forms of credit or there were sudden drains of gold reserves in exchange for grain during the Great Famine from 1845 to 1852.

Although price fluctuations of the pound never shook Britain's faith in the gold standard, they did invite frequent criticisms. The inflationary repercussions of a weak pound angered creditors, who received interest payments in devalued currency. These creditors included bankers, public debt holders and landlords. A strong pound and a tight money supply favoured financiers throughout the nineteenth century. It also helped export-oriented manufacturers by reducing the cost of wages and imported raw materials.

On the other hand, it punished farmers by increasing rental payments and reducing the price of rival grain imports. Throughout the century, fluctuating prices had mixed effects on workers, which were endlessly debated: a strong pound kept prices low but accompanied higher unemployment; and, while jobs were easier to find during inflation, consumer prices increased faster than wage hikes.

Critics of the gold standard put forth three sources of price instability: gold supplies, the price of gold relative to silver and the role of credit in the economy. Complicating any such diagnosis were the economic activity swings, also known as business cycles, which were both causes and effects of changes in the money supply. Inflation typically accompanied a booming economy, and trade depressions were deflationary. It was seldom possible to disentangle cause and effect.

The only monetary cause of British price instability during the nineteenth century was world gold production, which remained relatively constant until the Californian and Australian gold rush of 1849 and 1852. Gold output averaged forty-two tons per year in the 1840s, but it increased twentyfold during the ensuing decades as immigrants flocked to San Francisco and Melbourne.

British newspapers and magazines forecast that the influx of gold would soon lead to inflation. A minority regarded gold rushes as God's blessing that would give wings to steam engine-driven railways and shipping and boost trade with India and China. Politicians like Robert Peel, who were advocates of tight monetary policies based on the 'natural' scarcity of gold, theorized that inflation would be gradual and unlikely to disrupt the economy.

The inflationary repercussions of the gold rush were relatively mild and remarkably short-lived. One of the reasons was that returns from the gold diggings in California and Australia soon diminished. But the primary reason was that two leading commercial rivals of Britain adopted the gold standard. First, Germany in 1871, and then the United States in 1879.

Germany embraced the gold standard after the reparation payments following the 1871 Franco-Prussian War inflated its coffers. As a result, the United States had to redeem itself from using 'greenbacks'. The United States government first issued greenbacks in the nineteenth century to finance the American Civil War. The currency got its name, the greenback, as the back of the note was green in colour.

Greenbacks that were not convertible into gold or silver caused inflation and the devaluation of the dollar. Meanwhile, Germany, which had emerged as a powerful nation after defeating France in the Franco-Prussian War, adopted the gold standard and used its reparation payments to buy large amounts of gold. This increased the demand and price of gold and reduced the supply of gold to other countries.

The US government, under the influence of the Republican Party, decided to return to the gold standard and redeem the greenbacks for gold at a fixed rate. This was seen as a way to stabilize the value of the dollar and enhance its international reputation and trade. However, this also required the US government to reduce the amount of greenbacks in circulation and to maintain sufficient gold reserves to back up the dollar.

Both countries had sound reasons to adopt the gold standard. German industry relied on British loans, which were cheaper to repay in gold. Americans needed stable prices, as the British needed after Waterloo, and a strong dollar made it easier to attract foreign investments to their growing manufacturing sector.

France and Scandinavia in the 1870s, followed by Russia and Japan by 1900, joined Germany and the United States on the gold standard. So, it turned out to be effortless for the Bank of England to attract enough gold to back its notes. Consequently, British financiers shifted from home to foreign investment and prospered between 1880 and 1914—for the first time, they could depend on repaying most foreign loans in full-value currency.

Not all sectors of the British economy were so lucky, however. Farmers had to pay higher mortgage payments, and manufacturers were fearful as demonetized silver swamped India and China. As a result, imports became expensive in those countries, and foreign investment vanished. It also took its toll on British industry, which now had to contend with cheap and low-quality Asian goods and German and American imports.

A widespread bimetallist movement sprang up in Britain to balance the playing field. A bimetallic standard is a monetary system in which gold and silver coins are considered legal tender. Britain also placed India on a 'gold-exchange' standard, pegging the rupee to the pound. But unfortunately, it achieved little or nothing other than displaying the significance of the banking and service sector.

Credit was a potentially destabilizing force in the Victorian economy. It destabilized the meaning and the supply of money. Bank notes—the most visible form of credit—are the most widely blamed in times of crisis, such as the Panic of 1825. The Bank of England triggered the Panic of 1825, a stock market crash, in part due to speculative investments in Latin America, including the fictional country of Poyais. The crisis was felt most acutely in Britain, where it led to the closure of twelve banks. It was also manifest in the markets of Europe, Latin America and the United States. A number of factors, including the expansion of money and credit following the Napoleonic Wars, the overvaluation of foreign bonds and mining stocks, the fluctuation of gold and silver prices and the absence of effective regulation and supervision of the banking system, contributed to the panic. It has been said that the panic marked the beginning of modern economic cycles, as it was the first crisis of that type not caused by an outside factor, like a war.

Until 1825, the Bank of England shared its right to issue notes with smaller firms, limited to six or fewer. After the Panic of 1825 wiped out most of these financial institutions, the British Parliament legalized joint-stock banks. These banks circulated banknotes as short-term loans by discounting bills of exchange—promissory notes backed by the payments owed to the bill's owner in the future.

These short-term loans were popular during those days. In exchange for bills, the debtor (the bank) accepts the bills drawn by the creditor (the owner of the bills) and agrees to pay the amount stated at maturity. Then, after charging a fee or 'discount', the bank pays the owner the invoice's value. Finally, when the bill of exchange expires, the bank receives payment from the party that accepts the bill. So, discounting a bill of exchange is a self-clearing loan.

By the middle of the century, 'discount houses' emerged to guarantee repayment of these bills, which worked well as long as the bill brokers made good money on these deals. Overend, Gurney & Company in London was the largest discount house, controlling more than half of the discounting of bills of exchange business.

Credit was a seriously debatable issue during those days. Eventually, two schools of economics emerged in the early part of the nineteenth century. The first was the currency school and the second was the banking school. The currency school argued that restoring Britain to the gold standard would be sufficient to prevent financial crises. Two successive stock market speculative bubbles—first, the Panic of 1825 in England and then the Panic of 1837 in the United States—proved them wrong. They accused the Bank of England and the new joint-stock banks of excessive note issues, which had led to this financial mayhem. They opposed rapid economic growth because they saw it as corrupted and deprived of morality.

The banking school was dominated by the Bank of England directors. They reimagined the Bank's role as that of using its prime lending rate to control the overall supply of credit while their definition of money expanded to include bills, checks and bank deposits.

The banking school, representing the new joint-stock banking interests, argued that open competition among all note-issuing banks (instead of relying only on the Bank of England) would ensure steady, crisis-free economic growth.

The currency school won the battle in the early 1840s, convincing Parliament to restrict the Bank's note issues beyond its bullion reserves. But they lost the war to the banking school. In the short term, the main result of the Bank Charter Act of 1844 was to compel creditors to find other means of lending money than Bank of England paper—which they did with a vengeance, feeding a frenzied stock market already flooded with projected railways.

All these legislations and activities led to stock market booms and busts between 1844 and 1847, followed by the Panic of 1857 in the United States ten years later. The Panic was caused by the weakening international economy and over-expansion of the domestic economy. The invention of the telegraph in 1844 turned the Panic of 1857 into the first financial crisis to spread rapidly throughout the United States. The world economy was also more interconnected by the 1850s, making the Panic the first international economic crisis.

The power of human ingenuity and creativity drives the evolution of money, markets and financial instruments. Like every other human-driven system, money and financial systems come with inherent risks that sometimes take them to near death. Banks fail, bubbles burst, markets crash and economies intermittently go for inflation-deflation roller-coaster rides. Credit is a double-edged sword that can cut the hands, even the heads, of those who don't know how to use it wisely and meticulously.

The following chapters take you through historical financial bloodbaths that ruined the lives of millions.

# 2

# The Boom-and-Bust Stories

'October: This is one of the peculiarly dangerous months to speculate in stocks. The others are July, January, September, April, November, May, March, June, December, August and February.'

—Mark Twain

## The First Bubble

Tulip, a Turkish word, means turban. A tulip plant is blessed with a perfectly symmetrical flower bud. The unique shape and texture of the flower made it a prized decorative item during the Dutch Golden Age. Moreover, the petals of this auspicious flower are edible, so they can replace onions in many recipes and be added to wines.

The tulip was introduced in Western Europe in the middle of the sixteenth century. The credit for popularizing the flower goes to Conrad Gessner, a Swiss physician and naturalist. One may wonder what great virtue turned the tulip into a thing of such value in the eyes of the Dutch as it has neither the fragrance of a jasmine nor the beauty of a rose. The tulip became so popular for several reasons. One reason was its novelty and rarity, as it was a new and exotic plant that came from a distant land. Another reason was its variety and beauty, as it had many different colours, shapes and patterns that appealed to the aesthetic taste of the Dutch. A third reason was its symbolism and status, as it represented wealth, power and prestige for the Dutch merchants and nobles who could afford to buy and grow them.

Conrad Gessner first saw the tulip in 1559 in a garden belonging to the learned Counsellor Herwart at Augsburg in Germany. Herwart was famous for his collection of rare exotics. He had procured tulip bulbs from a friend in Constantinople, where it had long been a favourite. Subsequently, there grew a great demand for tulips among the wealthy and powerful in Germany and Holland. In Amsterdam, the rich brought tulip bulbs directly from Constantinople, paying exorbitant prices.

Tulips reached England from Vienna in 1600 and soon became wildly popular. Indeed, it was a shame for a man of wealth to live without an exotic tulip collection. Many wise men and well-known personalities were passionately fond of tulips. The tulip rage eventually spread to the middle class, including merchants and shopkeepers. They began to compete with one another for the possession of the more extravagant varieties of these flowers.

According to a legend, a trader in Haarlem, a city in the Dutch Republic, spent half his fortune on a single tulip bulb, not to sell it at a profit but to keep it for himself out of admiration for it.

Official futures markets appeared in the Dutch Republic during the seventeenth century. Among the most notable was that they centred on the trade of tulip bulbs. The demand for tulips skyrocketed in 1636, and their trading was established on the Stock Exchange of Amsterdam, as well as on the exchanges in Haarlem, Rotterdam, Leyden, Hoorn and Alkmar, among other towns.

For the first time in financial history, speculation emerged. The stock jobbers or the market makers were always alert for new avenues of speculation. Seeing the tulip craze, they dealt mainly in the flower, using every means possible to cause price fluctuations. They made large profits by buying when tulip prices fell and selling when they rose.

At first, as in every speculation mania, confidence was at its height, and everybody made money. Many ordinary people suddenly grew rich. Tulips became the golden bait, and people, one after another, rushed to the tulip dealers and trading floors like flies around a honeypot. Everyone thought that the demand and passion for tulips would last forever. The rich from every part of the world arrived in Holland and paid whatever price was demanded for tulips. Nobles, citizens, farmers, mechanics, seamen, footmen, maidservants and even chimney sweeps dabbled in tulips.

People of all social classes sold their property and invested their money in tulips. Realty and houses were offered for sale at meagre prices or pawned at tulip shops. Foreigners were struck by the same frenzy, and Holland was flooded with money from all over the world. The prices of daily necessities rose, taking with them houses, properties, horses, carriages and luxuries of every sort.

The tulip trade operations became so extensive and intricate that it was necessary to write down a code of laws for dealers. Notaries and clerks were appointed exclusively for the tulip trade. In smaller towns, where there was no stock exchange, the main bar or pub was usually used as the 'showplace', where people traded in tulips over sumptuous entertainment. Sometimes two to three hundred people attended these dinners—large vases of tulips in full bloom were artfully arranged upon the tables and sideboards. The tulips on display were worth more than the diamonds worn by the guests.

At last, however, canny observers began to realize that this folly could not last forever. The rich no longer bought tulips to keep them in their gardens but to sell them at an immense profit. The tulip-buying frenzy could not last unless someone was willing to pay the high prices demanded.

In February 1637, the interest in buying tulip bulbs dried up. Prices plummeted, and the speculative bubble burst.

The tulip speculators sought help from the Netherlands government, which declared that anyone who held tulip futures contracts could nullify the contracts with the payment of a 10 per cent fee. Nonetheless, most of the attempts that were made to resolve the situation proved unsuccessful. Even after the end of the mania, many speculators ended up holding tulip bulbs—no court ruled for the reimbursement of the payment of a contract since judges regarded the contracts as gambling bets.

As consistent price data is unavailable from the 1630s, it is difficult to fathom the depth of the Tulip Mania. However, this 1637 Dutch financial market crash gained global popularity in 1841 with the publication of the book, *Extraordinary Popular Delusions and the Madness of Crowds* by Charles Mackay, a Scottish journalist. In the book, Mackay describes how many tulip traders were ruined by price falls, and Dutch commerce suffered a severe setback. However, while his book is a classic, his account of the Tulip Mania is debatable.

The Tulip Mania is regarded as the first recorded speculative bubble in financial history. In many ways, it was more of a socio-economic phenomenon than a landmark economic crisis. The crisis did not seriously impact the economy of the Dutch Republic, one of the world's leading financial powers in the seventeenth century. The term 'Tulip Mania' is now often used metaphorically to refer to any economic bubble when asset prices diverge from intrinsic values.

After 1637, several tulip manias of lesser impact occurred in various parts of the world. These financial blips were more a display of human behaviour, than serious economic catastrophes, such as the Bandwagon Effect or, in modern terms, the fear of missing out (FOMO).

The financial world is where these human behavioural patterns emerge frequently. It shows the significant role of money in every part of human life.

History reveals that the Dutch Republic experienced a severe economic standstill for several years as a result of the tulip crisis.

By the end of the seventeenth century, a deadlier crisis was raising its head in the United Kingdom.

## The Mississippi Menace

John Law, the son of a successful goldsmith, was born in
Edinburgh in 1671. He was heir to numerous real estate
assets, including Lauriston Castle in Edinburgh. In 1692,
at the age of twenty-one, Law visited London. Being a
spendthrift and a compulsive gambler, he quickly began to
squander away his patrimony in numerous business ventures
and gambling escapades. Two years later, he fought with
his neighbour and killed him. Law was sentenced to death
but escaped from prison and fled to Amsterdam.

Amsterdam was the perfect choice for Law to lead a
low-profile life as the city had become the global capital
of financial innovation by the 1690s. The Dutch modified
the Italian system of public debt to finance their battles for
independence against Spain in the late sixteenth century.
They also introduced, among other things, lottery loans,
which let people gamble while their savings were invested
in government debt. They also reformed their currency
by creating the world's first central bank, the Exchange
Bank of Amsterdam or Wisselbank. This bank solved the
problem of debased coinage by creating a reliable form
of bank money. But perhaps the greatest Dutch financial
invention was the joint-stock company.

The story of the joint-stock company began in the
latter part of the sixteenth century. It had its origins in the
efforts of Dutch merchants to wrest control of the lucrative
Asian spice trade from the Portuguese and Spanish. There
was high demand for spices such as cinnamon, cloves,
nutmeg and pepper, which the Europeans used to flavour
and preserve their food. These commodities had travelled
overland from Asia to Europe along the Spice Road for

centuries. However, the Portuguese discovery of the sea route to the East Indies via the Cape of Good Hope changed the course of history. It opened up new and irresistibly attractive business opportunities.

However, a round trip via this sea route was long and hazardous: only half the ships that set sail would return safely. Thus, merchants had to pool their resources. At the onset of the seventeenth century, around six new East India companies were operating out of the major Dutch ports. However, each company had a limited term specified in advance as per the expected duration of the voyage. After the maturity of the period, the capital was repaid to investors. Unfortunately, this business model couldn't supply enough money to build the permanent bases and fortifications in various locations across Asia and Africa, such as Batavia (now Jakarta), Cape Town, Ceylon (now Sri Lanka), Malacca, Taiwan, Cochin, Surat and Masulipatnam. The Dutch would need these permanent bases and fortifications to replace the Portuguese and Spanish merchants.

Motivated by strategic calculations as well as the hefty profits, the parliaments of the Dutch and the United Provinces of the Netherlands proposed to merge the existing companies into a single entity. The result was the United Dutch Chartered East India Company, or the Vereenigde Nederlandsche Geoctroyeerde Oostindische Compagnie (in short, VOC). The company was formally chartered in 1602 to build a monopoly on all Dutch trade east of the Cape of Good Hope and west of the Straits of Magellan.

The structure of the VOC was innovative in several aspects. The company was supposed to last for a fixed period of twenty-one years but allowed the investors to withdraw their money at the end of just ten years when the first general balance was drawn up. In addition, the scale of the company was unprecedented. The subscription to the company's capital was open to all residents of the United Provinces, and there was no upper limit on how much money might be raised.

People from all walks of life—merchants, artisans and even servants—between 1580 and 1640 rushed to acquire shares. There were 1143 subscribers in Amsterdam alone, raising the capital to 6.45 million guilders and turning the VOC into the largest corporation of the era. The capital of the VOC's English rival, the East India Company, founded in 1600, was around 8,20,000 guilders shared between a mere 219 subscribers.

VOC's ownership was divided into multiple *partijen* or *actien*, which means 'actions' in Portuguese, akin to 'a piece of the action'. The investors could acquire shares—which were more like receipts—in instalments. The VOC stock ledger was the key legal document where all stockholders' names were entered at the time of purchase. The principle of limited liability was applied: shareholders lost only their investment and no other assets if the company failed. On the other hand, there was no guarantee of returns. The charter merely stated that payments would be made to shareholders once a 5 per cent profit from the initial capital had been made.

An innovative venture like VOC was not an immediate commercial success. Trade networks had to be set up, the mode of operation had to be established and bases had to be secured. Over four years (1603 to 1607), twenty-two ships made a voyage to Asia at the cost of nearly four million guilders. The initial business goal was to establish many factories (salt refineries, textile mills and warehouses) in

Asia, mainly in Indonesia, India, Sri Lanka, Malaysia and Taiwan, the products of which would then be exchanged for spices. The trade plan saw early successes at Masulipatnam in the Bay of Bengal and Amboyna (present-day Ambon Islands) in the Moluccas archipelago.

Malacca was a port city on the Malay Peninsula that controlled the Strait of Malacca, a narrow waterway that connected the Indian Ocean and the South China Sea. Malacca was the main hub for the trade of spices, such as cloves, nutmeg and mace, which came from the Moluccas, also known as the Spice Islands, in eastern Indonesia. The Portuguese had conquered Malacca in 1511 and established a monopoly over the spice trade. The VOC wanted to break this monopoly and gain access to the spice markets in Asia and Europe.

Makian was one of the Moluccan islands that produced nutmeg, a highly valued spice in Europe. The Spanish had established a presence in Makian since 1575 and built a fort there in 1603. The VOC wanted to oust the Spanish from Makian and secure a monopoly over the nutmeg trade.

In 1606, a Dutch admiral by the name of Cornelis Matelief de Jonge failed to capture Malacca, and the Spaniards successfully repelled his attack on Makian. The VOC had to resort to other strategies, such as forming alliances with local rulers, building forts and factories in other locations and capturing enemy ships. An attempt to build a fort on Banda Neira, the largest nutmeg-producing Banda island, also failed terribly.

By the time a twelve-year truce was signed with Spain in 1608, the VOC had made a huge profit from its maritime warfare, but it had not yet achieved its goal of monopolizing the spice trade.

Some investors, including the major ones, were so dismayed by the company's warlike conduct that they withdrew from the company in 1605. In addition, a few directors resigned in protest at what they regarded as the mismanagement of the company's affairs. 'We cannot make war without trade, nor trade without war' was the unspoken motto of the company, on which it stood firm. All these events made even the large shareholders realize the little to no power they held over VOC's affairs.

The company's directors petitioned the government to free them from their obligation to publish the company's business accounts in 1612—the date investors could withdraw their capital if they chose to. The government granted permission, and the publication of the accounts and repayment of capital to the investors were postponed. The only benefit to shareholders was that in 1610 VOC's board of directors, also known as Seventeen Lords, agreed to make a dividend payment the following year. VOC was so strapped for cash at this stage that the dividend was paid in spices!

Another surprise welcomed the investors in 1612 as VOC announced that it would not be liquidated as initially planned. That meant that any shareholders who wished to redeem their capital had no alternative but to sell their shares to another investor. This unprecedented event paved the way for the emergence of the stock market. In fact, the stock market and joint-stock company were born just a few years apart.

VOC, or the Dutch East India Company, turned into the first publicly owned corporation, which offered its shares to the public in March 1602. This was the first-ever initial public offering (IPO) of shares. The VOC was also the first company to be listed on a recognized stock exchange, the Amsterdam Stock Exchange, which was established in 1602 along with the creation of the VOC. As soon as the first publicly owned corporation came into existence with the first-ever IPO of shares, a remarkably liquid secondary market emerged to allow these shares to be bought and sold.

One-third of the VOC's shares had been transferred from the original owners by 1607, and the turnover in the shares was high. Moreover, as the account books of the VOC's stock trading were opened relatively infrequently (monthly or quarterly), a lively forward market in VOC shares soon developed, allowing sales for future delivery. In the beginning, such transactions were carried out in informal open-air markets. But, in 1608, the market for VOC stocks turned so lively that it was decided to erect a covered building.

Amsterdam Stock Exchange, the first stock exchange in the world, with its quadrangle, colonnades and clock tower, looked like a medieval Oxford college. But what went on there between 12 p.m. and 2 p.m. each workday was revolutionary. In the words of one contemporary, the trading floor's ambiance was something like this: 'Handshakes are followed by shouting, insults, impudence, pushing and shoving. Bulls did battle with bears. The anxious speculator "chews his nails, pulls his fingers, closes his eyes, takes four paces and four times talks to himself, raises his hand to his cheek as if he has a toothache and all this accompanied by a mysterious coughing."'[1]

It may seem coincidental that this same period witnessed the emergence of the Exchange Bank of Amsterdam, heralding the fact that a stock market cannot readily function without an effective financial system. The day when Dutch bankers began to accept VOC shares as collateral for loans, the nexus between the stock market and the supply of credit had been forged. The next step for banks was to lend money to investors so they could purchase shares with credit.

The companies, stock exchange and banks laid the foundation for the seventeenth-century New Age economy.

The economic and political ascent of the VOC can be traced to its share price. The Amsterdam stock market was volatile as investors reacted to the news of war, peace and shipwrecks. Yet the long-term trend was clearly upward for more than a century after the company's foundation. Between 1602 and 1733, VOC stock rose from 100 guilders to an all-time peak of 786 guilders.

While the VOC stock price ascended gradually for more than a century, its descent was more rapid. It took less than sixty years to fall back to 120 in December 1794. This rise and fall happened closely with the rise and fall of the Dutch Empire. On the other hand, the stock prices of other monopoly trading companies that outwardly resembled VOC behaved very differently, soaring and slumping within just a few months.

To understand why, we must bring John Law back into the story.

John Law was an ambitious Scot, a convicted murderer and a compulsive gambler. Yet, more than anything else, Law was a financial genius. This rare trait made him the protagonist of this story. Not only was he responsible for the first boom and bust of asset prices in financial history, but he also, indirectly, unleashed the French Revolution by comprehensively foiling the best chance for the French monarchy to reform its finances. Law's story is one of the most astonishing yet misunderstood tales of adventure in all financial history. His story continues to be relevant today as well.

Dutch finance was a revelation to John Law as he was fascinated by the mysterious relationships between the Dutch East India Company, the Exchange Bank and the stock exchange. An avid gambler himself, Law found the Amsterdam Stock Exchange more exciting than any casino. He marvelled at the extraordinary skills of short sellers who sold borrowed stocks and profited from the fall in their prices. They also spread negative rumours to drive down VOC share prices, which was termed 'windhandel', literally 'wind trade' or 'wind deal'. That is, trading futures without actual possession of the stocks.

In the Dutch Republic, financial innovation was all around. Yet Law found some shortcomings in the Dutch financial system. For one thing, the stock exchange restricted the number of Dutch East India Company shares even though there was a great demand for them in the market. He was also perplexed by the conservatism of the Exchange Bank. Its 'bank money' was a success, but it largely rested as figures in the bank's ledgers. Apart from receipts issued to merchants who deposited gold or silver coins with the bank, the money had no physical existence.

A grand plan to modify these legendary financial institutions was taking shape in Law's mind. He dreamt of combining the properties of a monopoly trading company with a public bank that issued notes in the same way the Bank of England did. Law couldn't wait to try out the new financial system in France, which he considered a trustworthy nation because he had the support of the

Duke of Orleans, who was the regent for the young King
Louis XV.

John Law first tried his luck in the Italian city of
Genoa, trading foreign currency and stocks. In Venice, he
spent some time trading by day and gambling by night.
Consequently, Law was well-connected in political and
financial circles. He partnered with the Earl of Islay to
build a substantial portfolio on the London stock market.

In 1705 he submitted a proposal for a new bank to the
Scottish parliament. His proposal was later published in
a book he authored titled *Money and Trade Considered:
With a Proposal for Supplying the Nation with Money*.[2]
The book's central idea was that the new bank should
issue interest-bearing notes that would replace coins as
currency. Besides, he proposed a 'land bank' system in
which banknotes would be backed by real estate rather
than gold or silver. In the book, he advocates that the land
bank system would boost the prosperity of Scotland akin
to that of other countries.

The parliament rejected the proposal shortly before
the Act of Union with England in 1707. Disappointed,
Law made a case for a paper currency in Turin with
Victor Amadeus II, Duke of Savoy, in 1711. The duke,
who was concerned that it would jeopardize his position
of power and the stability of his state, also rejected his
plan. Law then moved to France, where he found a more
receptive audience for his ideas under the regent, Philippe
d'Orléans. Law believed that trust alone was the basis
for public credit, and with trust, banknotes would serve
like gold or silver coins. In his heart, he believed he had
discovered the secret of the philosopher's stone: making
gold out of paper.

Despite his failures in Scotland and Italy, Law did not give up on his vision of a paper money system. He saw an opportunity in France, where the monarchy was in dire need of financial reform. The French knew John Law better than anyone. In 1708, the foreign minister of Louis XIV had identified Law as a professional gambler and possible spy. But, above all, France's fiscal problems were particularly desperate. Louis XIV's wars had created a mountain of public debt that brought the government to the brink of its third bankruptcy in less than a century.

A review of the monarch's debts was required, which resulted in the reduction and cancellation of many of them, resulting in a partial default. Nonetheless, 250 million new interest-bearing notes known as *billets d'état* had to be issued to cover the current deficit. The economy was thrown into recession as a result of an attempt to reduce the amount of gold and silver coinage.

John Law claimed to have the solution to all fiscal and political problems in France.

In October 1715, John Law submitted his first proposal for a public note-issuing bank to the royal council of France. But it was rejected because of Law's bold suggestion that the bank act as the monarch's treasurer, receiving all tax payments.

John Law's second proposal for a private bank was more successful. On 2 May 1716, the Banque Générale was established in Paris. The bank, which was under Law's direction, was licensed to issue notes payable in gold or silver for twenty years.

At first glance, the Banque Générale appeared to be a small business. But John Law had a grander plan in mind than just running a small business. He was so confident about his plan that he was determined to sell it to the Duke of Orleans. In 1717, he took another bold step: he persuaded the Duke of Orleans to issue a decree that all tax payments be made using Banque Générale notes. Law succeeded in convincing the Duke of Orleans that paper money was more convenient and efficient than metal coins and that it would help reduce public debt and stimulate the economy. This gave Law's bank a monopoly over the money supply and increased the demand for paper money. This decree was initially opposed in some areas, but the government effectively enforced it.

John Law's ambition was to establish a Dutch-model public bank that could revive economic confidence in France. But this bank would have a significant difference: it would issue paper money. As a result, the government could consolidate its massive debt as money was invested in the bank; simultaneously, the paper money would revive French trade, and with it, France's economic power.

According to Law, the bank was not the only, nor the grandest, of his ideas. He told the Regent that his work would bring more drastic changes in Europe in favour of France. He believed those changes would be more potent than the changes produced by the discovery of the Indies.

Law's finance theory was absolutist in nature. It was based on the idea that only one authority should control the credit in the country, just like the army and the parliament. He wanted to use the king's credit more efficiently than the Regent, who had to borrow money all the time to pay for the wars. Law's plan was to let the king lend his credit to a big trading company. This company would own all the trade goods in the country and become a huge business. In this system, everyone in the country would be a trader who could get money from the royal bank, where all the trade, money and goods were stored.

Law thought that France's colonial empire was as valuable as the Dutch one, but France was not using it well. He wanted to make France's colonies and lands overseas more profitable and productive. So, he devised a plan to take over France's trade with the Louisiana territory in North America, which was a large but underdeveloped strip of land that ran from the Mississippi Delta to the Midwest and was about the same size as a quarter of the United States today. He wanted to make this land better and richer for France.

In 1717 a new 'Company of the West' (Compagnie d'Occident) was granted the trade monopoly of Louisiana and its internal affairs for twenty-five years. The company's capital was fixed at 100 million livres, the French currency unit. This amount was an unprecedented sum in France during that period.

Regardless of social class, Frenchmen and foreigners were encouraged to buy the company's shares, which were priced at 500 livres each (in instalments). They could buy shares using state-issued public securities or billets d'état, which were later converted into government bonds or *rentes* that earned a 4 per cent coupon rate. Law was appointed as the head of the company's directors.

The Regent used his absolute power to support Law's plan, even though many people in France did not like it. Law was happy and grateful for the Regent's help. The government gave the Company of the West some special rights to make its shares more attractive to buyers. In August, the company got the right to get all the money from selling tobacco. In December, the company took over the Senegal Company, which was a French trading company that had the right to trade in Senegal, Africa.

In a further attempt to enhance John Law's position as the head of directors, the Banque Générale was given the royal seal of approval: it became the Banque Royale in December 1718, the first French central bank. Moreover, to enhance the appeal of its notes, the bank allowed them to be exchanged for French units of gold and silver.

The transition in France from coinage to paper money had begun. Meanwhile, the Company of the West steadily expanded. In May 1719, it took over the East India and China companies to create the Company of the Indies (Compagnie des Indes), popularly known as the Mississippi Company.

John Law secured the royal mint's profits for a nine-year term in July. In August, he took over the lease of the indirect tax collection from a rival financier, who had been in control of it a year before. In September, the company agreed to lend 1.2 billion livres to the monarchy to pay off the entire royal debt. A month later, Law took control of the collection of direct taxes.

John Law was proud of his financial system. According to him, what had existed before was nothing more than 'a method of receipts and disbursements'. He claimed that in contrast, his financial system had a chain of ideas that supported one another and clearly displayed their foundation principle.

In modern terms, what Law was trying to explain was reflation. His extension of the money supply with banknotes provided a much-needed stimulus for the French economy, which had been in recession in 1716. At the same time, he was trying to convert a massive yet mismanaged public debt into the equity of a large, privatized, tax-collecting and monopolistic trading company. Had Law succeeded, the French monarchy's financial problems would have ended.

John Law acquired various other companies and tax collecting areas not with the company profits but simply by issuing new shares. In 1719 the Mississippi Company issued 50,000 shares for 550 livres apiece. Law underwrote it by himself to ensure the success of the issue. To avoid the accusation that he alone would profit if the share price rose, he gave the shareholders of the company the exclusive right to acquire these new shares. These new shares became known as 'daughters' since the earlier shares were called 'mothers'. In the same year, Law issued a third tranche of 50,000 shares, the 'granddaughters', priced at 1000 livres each to raise 50 million livres.

Logically, this dilution of the existing shareholders would have caused the share price to decline. But what happened was the opposite.

Apparently, the share price rose on Law's promise of future profits from Louisiana, a colony he painted as a Garden of Eden, inhabited by friendly primitives eager to supply France with exotic goods. For trading, a grand new city was established at the mouth of the Mississippi: New Orleans, named to flatter the Duke of Orléans, who had always suspected Law's business ambitions. A few thousand impoverished Germans were recruited to act as colonists. But in a stroke of bad luck, those immigrants who reached Louisiana encountered a sweltering and insect-infested swamp. In less than a year, most of them had died of starvation or contagious diseases like yellow fever.

A different justification was needed to back the 40 per cent dividends Law paid using paper money. From the summer of 1719, the Banque Royale generously supported investors who wished to buy the 'daughters' and 'granddaughters'. The investors could borrow money using their shares as collateral and invest in more shares with the borrowed money.

Soon, something predictable happened: the share price soared. Within a month, the price of 'mothers' rose from 2750 livres and stood at 5000 on 4 September 1719. John Law was happy to issue 1 lakh more shares at this new market price, and two further issues of the same number of shares followed in September and October. A smaller block of 24,000 shares was also issued to private shareholders. The share price reached 9000 livres in November and touched a new high of 10,025 in December. The unofficial futures market saw them trading at 12,500 livres.

The market mood began to shift rapidly from euphoria to mania.

Some smelt a rat. A few sensible bankers and economists sold their shares and left Paris in 1719. But many aristocratic Parisians were trapped in Law's seductive venture. With the phoney money of his own making, John Law offered to pay pension arrears and advance pension payments—a sure-shot way to build support among the privileged classes.

By September 1719, hundreds of people began to throng the share-issuing office of the company. The crowd that stood there from early morning to late night included princes and princesses, dukes and duchesses as well as some of the prominent people in France. They sold estates and pawned jewels to purchase Mississippi Company shares.

John Law turned invincible when he was duly appointed Controller General of Finances in October 1719. This position made him the head of the collection of France's indirect taxes; the French national debt; the twenty-six French gold and silver coin mints; the colony of Louisiana; and the Mississippi Company. By that time, the Mississippi Company held a monopoly on the import and sale of tobacco, the fur trade with Canada and all the French trade with Africa, Asia and the East Indies. More than that, in his own right, John Law owned the Hotel de Nevers (the present Bibliotheque Nationale), the Mazarin Palace, more than twelve country estates and several plantations in Louisiana and Mississippi Company shares worth 100 million livres.

When Louis XIV, the king of France, would say, 'I am the state,' John Law could confidently say, 'I am the economy.'

But things were taking a different turn by the end of 1719. Even before Law was appointed Controller General of Finances, the first signs of the bubble had begun to manifest themselves. First, the share price of the Mississippi Company began to decline, touching 7930 livres in December 1719. As a cunning response, Law offered the first of many fabricated promotions to prop it up—he opened a branch at the Banque Royale that offered a guaranteed purchase and sale of the shares at a floor price of 9000 livres. Then, in February 1720, the company announced that it was taking over the Banque Royale.

However, inflation was accelerating alarmingly outside the stock markets. It peaked in September 1720, with prices in Paris roughly double what they had been two years before. Furthermore, the majority of the price increases had occurred in the previous eleven months. All this was a reflection of Law's aggressive increase in note circulation. Within a little more than a year, he had more than doubled the volume of paper currency. By May 1720, the total money supply, including banknotes and shares held by the public, was roughly four times larger in terms of livre than the gold and silver coinage circulated previously in France.

Unsurprisingly, some people began to anticipate a value depreciation of the banknotes and turned towards payments in gold and silver. As an absolutist, Law resorted to compulsion. As a consequence, banknotes were made legal tender. He banned the export of gold and silver along with the production and sale of gold and silver jewellery. The decree of 27 February 1720 made it illegal for a citizen to possess more than 500 livres of metal coin. This decree was enforced by giving the authorities the power to search people's houses for illegal possessions.

Voltaire, a French Enlightenment-era writer, called this law enforcement 'the most unjust edict ever rendered' and 'the final limit of a tyrannical absurdity'.[3]

Simultaneously, Law obsessively manipulated the exchange rate of the banknotes in terms of gold and silver—altering the official price of gold and silver twenty-eight times and thirty-five times, respectively, between September 1719 and December 1720. His effort was to make banknotes more attractive than coins to the public.

But these contradictory regulations served only to bewilder French citizens and illustrate the inclination of an absolutist regime to manipulate the economic rules to suit itself. On 5 March 1720, under pressure from the Regent, John Law took another U-turn—he reinstituted the floor price of 9000 livres by reopening the bureau to buy the shares at this price. But by his action, he released the money supply from the previous commitment to a 1.2 million livre limit and negated the decree that asserted that the banknote was immune to the alteration of value.

Between February and May 1720, the public holdings of banknotes increased 94 per cent. Meanwhile, their holdings of shares slumped to less than a third of the total number of shares issued. It seemed inevitable that all the shares would be unloaded on the company within no time, unleashing a further flood of banknotes and a surge in inflation.

On 21 May, in a desperate effort to avert a financial meltdown, Law induced the Regent to issue a deflationary decree to reduce the official price of company shares from 9000 livres to 5000 in monthly steps. Simultaneously, he also halved the number of banknotes in circulation and devalued them, revoking the previous order which guaranteed that a devaluation would not happen. All these measures exposed royal absolutism, the foundation of Law's financial system.

Violent public outcry compelled the government to revoke these measures within a week of their announcement, but by that time, confidence in the system was irrevocably damaged. The share price slid from 9005 livres to 4200 in May 1720. Angry crowds gathered outside the Banque Royale, which failed to meet the demand for notes. Stones were thrown and windows broken.

Law was roundly denounced at a parliament meeting. The Regent retreated and revoked his decree. Law offered his resignation but was dismissed and put under house arrest. Later, Law faced jail for the second time in his life, conceivably even death. An investigation quickly found evidence that Law's issues of banknotes had breached the authorized limit, and he deserved prosecution. The Banque Royale closed its doors.

In May 1720, Law was dismissed from his position as Controller General of Finances after he tried to reduce the price of the Mississippi Company's shares and limit the amount of paper money in circulation. He was accused of fraud and embezzlement and faced arrest and prosecution. He escaped to Belgium, where he stayed for a few weeks.

In June 1720, Law was recalled to power by the Duke of Orleans, who was the regent of the young King Louis XV. The Duke hoped that Law could restore confidence and stability in the financial system, which was in chaos after his departure. Law's return sparked a rally on the stock market, and the Mississippi Company's shares rose back to 6350 livres. However, this was a temporary relief, as the underlying problems of the system remained unsolved.

In October 1720, the government was forced to reintroduce the use of gold and silver in domestic transactions, as paper money had lost most of its value and credibility. This caused a sharp decline in the Mississippi Company's share price, which dropped to 2000 livres in September and 1000 in December. A full-blown market panic was imminent as investors rushed to sell their shares and withdraw their money from the bank.

Law, who had become the most hated man in France, was vilified by the people and ridiculed by the press. He was blamed for the financial disaster and the social unrest that followed. He finally fled the country in December 1720, never to return. He died in poverty and obscurity in Venice in 1791.

However, the losses caused by Law in France were more than just financial. The bust of the Mississippi bubble fatally set back France's economic development, putting the French off paper money and stock markets for generations. The French monarchy's fiscal crisis went unresolved. The crown essentially lived from hand-to-mouth for the remainder of the reigns of Louis XV and Louis XVI, teetering from one failed reform to another until royal bankruptcy triggered the French Revolution.

England soon imitated the Mississippi bubble with her South Sea bubble.

It all began in 1711. A British joint-stock company known as the South Sea Company was founded that year by an Act of Parliament. The company was a public-private partnership designed to consolidate, control and reduce the national debt and help Britain enhance its trade and profits in the Americas.

In 1713, the South Sea Company was granted a trading monopoly in the American region. Part of this was the Asiento de Negros: the contract for trading African slaves in the 'South Sea' islands and Spanish-Portuguese colonies in the Americas. The slave trade had been a profitable venture for over two centuries, and public confidence in the scheme was tremendous.

At the time of the company's inception, Britain was engaged in the War of the Spanish Succession, while Spain and Portugal controlled most of the colonies in South America. Despite these challenges, many Britons believed that the war would soon end and the profits from the slave trade would increase dramatically.

Unfortunately, things didn't quite play out as expected.

The War of the Spanish Succession ended in 1713, but contrary to widespread speculation, the explosion in the slave trade didn't happen. At that time, the South Sea

Company offered shareholders an incredible 6 per cent interest. Spain only allowed Britain to engage in limited slave trade and even took a percentage of the profits. Spain also levied a tax on Asiento de Negros and put strict limits on the number of British ships carrying out the trade: just one ship a year. These steps prevented the company from generating the profits required to sustain it.

However, the company's share prices increased as it expanded its management of the government's various debt instruments. Most of them were created to fund the War of the Spanish Succession. The company offered to take over part of the government's debt in exchange for new shares of the company, which paid a guaranteed interest rate of 6 per cent. The company also agreed to pay an annual sum to the government, which reduced the interest payments on the debt. The company's scheme was attractive to both the government and the investors, as it reduced the cost of the debt and increased the value of the shares. In fact, the company converted government debt to the stocks of a business chartered to monopolize trade with Spanish-Portuguese colonies in South America.

In 1718, King George took over the governorship of the company. This endorsement by the ruling monarch boosted investor confidence and inflated the stock further. Soon after the monarch took over the company, its shares began to give out 100 per cent interest. In reality, the company was not making the promised profits. Instead, it was just trading its stock. The company's promoters encouraged—and in some cases bribed—their friends to purchase stock to further balloon the price and keep demand high.

In 1720, the parliament allowed the South Sea Company to take over the national debt, assuring interest would be kept low. The agreement was that the company would use the profits generated by the ever-increasing stock sales to pay the interest on the debt or swap the stocks for the interest on the debt. The stocks sold well, generating higher interest and boosting their demand and price.

In August 1720, the stock price hit £1000 with no solid fundamentals—the company kept dabbling with its stocks against the national debt. Then in September 1720, the bubble burst. The company's share price plummeted to £124 (lower than its face value) by December of the same year. This notorious stock market bubble, which ruined thousands of investors and the British economy, became known as the South Sea bubble.

In Britain, although the South Sea bubble ruined thousands of investors and damaged the British economy, it did not cause a systemic banking crisis or a major political upheaval. This is because the South Sea Company did not have the same degree of influence and control over the British financial system and government as John Law's Mississippi Company had over the Banque Royale. The Bubble Act of 1720 was promoted by the company itself soon before its collapse. The Act forbade the creation of joint-stock companies without a royal charter.

A parliamentary inquiry was held soon after the bubble burst to find its root causes. It was found that the company's promoters had engaged in insider trading, using their advanced knowledge of national debt consolidations. Huge bribes were paid to politicians to support Acts of Parliament favouring the company. The company's profits were used for trading in its shares, and cash loans on the company shares were given to selected individuals to buy more company shares.

Without a doubt, the South Sea bubble was a financial disaster. It bankrupted even the greatest thinkers of the time, including Isaac Newton. Several politicians were displaced, and the personal assets of people who profited from the South Sea scheme were confiscated. Even after that, most of the culprits remained rich until their death. Ultimately, the company was restructured and operated for more than a century after the bubble.

## Black Friday

In 1775, the Gurney family in the prosperous district of East Anglia in England decided to expand its business to banking. The family were prominent wool traders in the county, and they soon created a company that later became Gurney & Co., a bank that facilitated investing in London. The Gurney family had a reputation for wealth and trustworthiness, which were significant prerequisites for running banks that operated as unlimited liability partnerships at the time. The family successfully attracted the savings of the local aristocracy and tradesmen.

Eventually, Gurney & Co. became the largest bank in East Anglia. In 1807, Samuel Gurney, the heir of the original founder of Gurney & Co., further expanded the family business. He did so by acquiring and restructuring Richardson, Overend & Company, the London bill broker. The amalgamation of these companies became known as Overend, Gurney & Company. It was one of the first companies to offer the matching of buyers and sellers of bills in exchange for a brokerage fee. Bills of exchange were a crucial financial instrument in the nineteenth century.

Overend, Gurney & Company soon became a discount house as it began investing in the market for bills on its own account. Being a bill broker and discount house, Overend Gurney helped lenders sell their bills to commercial banks with excess deposits and receive funds before the due date of their loans. These deals were conducted smoothly because of the strong nexus between bill broking, the London discount market and the Bank of England.

With Samuel Gurney at the helm, Overend Gurney became the largest and most influential discount house of the nineteenth century, standing next to the Bank of England. By the 1850s, it had accumulated deposits that rivalled the total net worth of Smith, Payne & Smiths, Barnett, Hoares & Co. and Glyn, Mills & Co. combined. Moreover, its annual turnover of bills of exchange equalled half of the United Kingdom's national debt.

The first half of the nineteenth century was plagued by recurrent money market panics following enormous credit expansions. To bring the panics under control, the Bank of England typically provided liquidity to the market. The 1844 Bank Charter Act restricted the issue of Bank of England notes relative to the value of its gold reserve. However, the financial situation demanded the suspension of this Act to enable the bank to provide the needed liquidity in the market, unconstrained by its total gold stock. During these financial panics, the ability of the Bank of England to provide liquidity brought solid confidence to the market.

The first worldwide financial crisis in 1857, which began in the United States, caused several financial catastrophes in the United Kingdom. The financial panics in the United Kingdom resulted in a flood of applications for assistance from bill brokers to the Bank of England. Overend Gurney was one of the largest beneficiaries of this assistance. Gurney's size in the market partly helped it acquire the assistance.

In the middle of the nineteenth century, bills of exchange—a tradable financial instrument—were used to record most business transactions. Commercial banks that received bills from their customers and desired to sell those on the market at a discount could obtain a guarantee from a merchant bank. This bank was responsible for settling the debt in case the commercial bank's customer defaulted. The merchant bank could sell their bills through brokers to commercial banks that channelled their deposits into productive investments. They also had the option to sell the bills directly to the Bank of England.

From 1830 onwards, bill brokers became discount houses as they started investing in bills of exchange for their own accounts, using the term deposits they collected from commercial banks. This way, they became competitors of the Bank of England, which had been purchasing bills at a discount since its foundation more than a century ago.

Despite being a privately owned bank, the Bank of England enjoyed privileges, such as controlling Britain's gold reserve and monopoly over the banknote issue in London. The bank also operated an office called the Discount Window. This office provided 'discounts' and 'advances' on the bills of exchange of merchants, brokers and other banks. The discount rate the Bank of England charged on those bills is similar to today's bank rate.

During a crisis, commercial banks got liquidity from the Discount Window as advances or discounts. In addition, commercial banks would get back their deposits with discount houses. In that case, the discount houses had to rediscount the bills on their balance sheet with the Bank of England to meet the cash requirements of the commercial banks.

After the 1857 crisis, the Bank of England was increasingly concerned that the provision of unlimited liquidity to bill brokers had led to moral hazard. The idea was that when the Bank of England gave bill brokers unlimited incentives, they would be inclined to become highly leveraged, hold few reserves of their own and rely on the Discount Window whenever a crisis occurred.

In March 1858, the Bank of England began to restrict bill brokers' access to its Discount Window to compel them to hold more reserves rather than rely on the bank for liquidity. This move proved to be controversial even inside the Bank of England. However, the move was publicly seen as one planned against Overend Gurney.

Two years later, the Bank of England unexpectedly raised its bill discount rate. By this surprising move, the bank broke the principle that it would never raise interest rates during peak dividend season because many dividend payments brought tight liquidity for bill brokers. This was a highly criticized attack on the bill market.

Infuriated by the Bank of England's actions, Overend Gurney's partners joined with other discount houses to withdraw a large chunk of the funds they had deposited at the bank. Overend Gurney argued that it was irrational to leave large deposits with the Bank of England, as they could be used by the bank to compete with them in the bill market. The goal was to bring the bank's reserves as low as possible to prove to the bank that it was dependent on the bill brokers and that it should give bill brokers access to its rediscounting facilities again. Within a few days in April 1860, the Bank of England witnessed a 22 per cent reduction in banknote deposits, and a significant part of the fund withdrawal came from Overend Gurney.

The number of banknotes in circulation had been closely watched since the passage of the 1844 Bank Charter Act. Within a week of the massive withdrawal of banknotes, the number of Bank of England's notes in circulation rose dramatically. Despite the mass withdrawal of funds, the rise in the number of banknotes in circulation and an attempt to cause a run on the bank, the Bank of England immediately hiked its bill discount rate by one percentage point, to 5 per cent.

The matter was raised in the House of Commons, and Chancellor of the Exchequer Gladstone expressed sympathy for the bill brokers over the issue of access to the Bank of England's Discount Window. However, the bank refused to change its position. In response, Overend Gurney redeposited their notes with the bank and apologized. Thereafter, the relationship between the Bank of England and Overend Gurney remained strained.

As the bill brokers were no longer able to access the Discount Window, they were forced to restructure their business model. Unfortunately, this included holding higher reserve levels, which ultimately rendered bill discounting (their core business) less profitable.

In the late 1860s, Overend Gurney, although making profits from the bill-broking business, was facing heavy losses from more risky and speculative lending activities, such as railway construction, mining and land development. The company lost around £500,000 a year from 1860 onwards on these activities. By 1865, the company was on the verge of bankruptcy. The partners tried to save the company by injecting new capital, bringing in new partners and even selling the firm to a competitor, the National Discount Company. However, none of these options worked, as the National Discount Company rejected the offer, and the new shareholders were deceived about the true state of the company.

Given its financial difficulties, the partners decided to incorporate Overend Gurney as a limited liability company in 1865. In 1862, this company structure had been extended to discount houses, insurance companies and banks. The firm raised £5 million in equity and a portion of uncalled capital. This meant that shareholders initially paid a low price for their shares, but the company could call up a larger payment if necessary. Furthermore, the partners guaranteed the losses on any assets transferred to the new company, providing comfort to the new shareholders. A partner, John Gurney, had removed any mention of bad investments from the prospectus. The guarantee was for a limited period of time, which was stated in the special deed of arrangement. However, no one really bothered to examine this deed.

The new directors, like the general public, were victims of a lack of due diligence. They concluded that there was no need for an accountant to look over the books. Overend Gurney's limited liability conversion elicited a mixed reaction from political, economic and social circles. The company was expected to focus on bill broking rather than lending in the future. Furthermore, as a public company, it was required to disclose the nature of its business in order to increase public trust in the company. The shares performed well at first in October 1865, but by January 1866, the price had begun to fall.

By the evening of 10 May 1866, a note was posted on Overend Gurney's door stating that it was suspending all payments. A sudden panic spread across the City of London on 11 May 1866. It was as if the city were shaken by an earthquake. Depositors began queueing in front of all banking institutions to withdraw their money, seizing up the entire money market. On the other side, bankers ran to the Bank of England's Discount Window for funds.

The day has been marked as 'Black Friday' in the annals of financial history.

Chancellor Gladstone suspended the 1844 Bank Charter Act. He did so because, unlike the crises of 1847 and 1857, which were commercial, the 1866 panic was a purely financial catastrophe. The suspension of the Act allowed the Bank of England to extend liquidity by printing more banknotes without the backing of gold. This measure was rolled out in the hope that it would ease the financial markets and ensure confidence in the currency. The bank had taken much of its reserves and extended over £4 million to support market participants. The Chancellor also placed an obligation on the bank: the discount rate should be raised to 10 per cent, and the control to hike it again, if necessary, should be given to the government.

To cover the losses, Overend Gurney was forced to call in uncalled capital. As a result, shareholders filed a lawsuit against the partners, alleging that the prospectus was false. In an unexpected turn of events, the shareholders lost their legal battle and were forced to pay the full value of their shares. This event caused investors to avoid investing in limited liability companies, particularly with uncalled capital.

Several factors contributed to the collapse of Overend, Gurney & Company, the biggest discount house in Britain, which controlled more than half of England's bills of exchange discounting business. The company was already insolvent when it became a limited liability company. This fact was brilliantly hidden from its new investors.

The spread of rumours about the company's financial troubles started to circulate in the London financial market in early 1866 when the company faced difficulties in collecting its debts and paying its obligations. The rumours were fuelled by the political and economic instability of the time, such as the fear of war in Europe, the fall in cotton prices and the high interest rates. The failure of Watson, Overend & Co., a railway contractor with no connection to Overend, Gurney & Company but with a similar name, was one unfortunate coincidence that added to the rumours. The rumours eroded confidence and trust in Overend, Gurney & Company and made it harder for the company to raise funds or sell its assets.

Overend Gurney's downfall was caused by poor lending practices and a lack of good management. As a result of poor management by its new-generation partners, they had expanded into riskier customer lending. Fees were paid to the partners by both the investors who funded the loan and the borrowers. No prudent steps were taken to verify the accuracy of the collateral, such as the borrower's properties.

The fall of Overend Gurney marks a turning point in Britain's financial history. The panic triggered valuable debates on the Bank of England's role as the lender of last resort (LOLR) and moral hazard.

This historical event also inspired Walter Bagehot, the *Economist*'s Editor in Chief, to publish his treatise, *Lombard Street: A Description of The Money Market*, in

1873. In it, he describes many principles, including the role of LOLR and liquidity assistance during a panic. Notably, some of these principles can be seen in the approach of the Bank of England toward liquidity assistance today.

By the time Overend Gurney crashed in 1866, a group of financial journalists, Bank of England directors and joint-stock bank managers had helped to quickly create a new consensus on central banking policy. Subsequently, the Bank of England was able to prevent major financial panics in the United Kingdom for the rest of the century, aided primarily by joint-stock banks. However, they faced a tense period in 1890 when Baring Brothers & Company, a British merchant bank, declared insolvency after making reckless loans to Argentina.

Let's look at this infamous sovereign debt crisis of the nineteenth century.

## The Baring Crisis and the Great Latin American Meltdown

The Baring crisis, also known as the Panic of 1890, began in Argentina. It then spread to London through the Baring Brothers & Company, an investment bank in London that held large amounts of Argentine debt that could not be placed on the London market. The Baring crisis was mostly a regional phenomenon, but it impacted all the Latin American countries.

Argentina and the rest of Latin America had been severely impacted by the recession that preceded the 1873 global debt crisis. The financial crisis lasted six years and impacted many countries. Several factors contributed to it, including the failure of several European banks and the inability of American railroads to repay European bank loans. From 1873 to 1879, many countries and regions suffered as a result of the crisis. But some suffered more than others. Great Britain, Germany, France, Austria-Hungary, Russia and Latin America faced deflation, unemployment and political instability. The period was known as the 'Long Depression'. The crisis had a significant impact on the global economy and caused a significant re-evaluation of the international monetary system.

The Conquest of the Desert, also referred to as the wars with the native people of the Pampas, was a series of military operations carried out by the Argentine government against the indigenous tribes of the southern Pampas and northern Patagonia. The wars lasted from the 1870s to the 1880s and resulted in the annexation of Patagonia by Argentina and the displacement or extermination of most of the native population. The Argentine army, under the command of General Julio Roca, who rose to national prominence and won the presidency in 1880, fought the wars in large part.

After the wars ended, Argentina entered a period of economic recovery and growth, thanks to the increase in trade with Europe and the return of funds from European investors. Argentina exported mainly agricultural products, such as wheat, beef and wool, and imported manufactured goods and capital goods.

The funds were used to build railroads and public works projects, such as ports, bridges and telegraphs, which connected the interior provinces with Buenos Aires and the rest of the world. The largest and capital city of Argentina, Buenos Aires, underwent a similar modernization process that resulted in its emergence as a cosmopolitan metropolis with influences from European immigration, culture and architecture.

The first big loan that Roca got was for a railroad project that connected two major trunk lines. The building of a transportation network across the country gave the central government even more power and boosted the economy by making the market for commercial agriculture more accessible.

Roca also made Buenos Aires the 'Paris of South America' by building wide streets, large parks, a well-planned water supply and drainage system and a modern port. Between 1880 and 1886, the national government and the government of the province of Buenos Aires executed several state-run development projects that had never been done before in Latin America.

Since capital markets were open in the 1800s, Argentina was able to borrow a lot of money from other countries. It was the fifth-largest borrower in the world at the time. Between 1884 and 1890, it purchased about 11 per cent of all new issues on the new London market and between 40 per cent and 50 per cent of all loans made outside the UK in 1889.

North America, on the other hand, had twenty times as many people as Argentina, but only 30 per cent of the new issues in London came from there. The 1880s stand out as the only time in history when so much money went into an emerging market all at once. From 1884 to 1889, the average share of GDP taken up by the current account deficit was 20 per cent.

Even though Argentina's economic policies of the 1880s helped the economy in the short term, they made it hard to pay for things in the long term. Finances for railroads and land development projects were meant to help with domestic growth, exports and economic growth. However, the slow pace of completion of the development projects made it harder for the country to pay its debts, a situation termed a maturity mismatch. The growing national debt could only be paid off if the country had enough tax money to pay off the debt.

Unfortunately, it would take years for the government to profit significantly from increased business activity as a result of infrastructure investments. Argentina also sold sterling or gold bonds on European capital markets while operating on a paper standard. This was due to the failure of several attempts in the early to mid-1880s to switch to a gold or bimetallic standard. Because of the currency mismatch, a decline in the value of the paper peso made it more difficult for the country to pay its gold debts.

When President Roca's brother-in-law, Miguel Celman, took over as president of Argentina in 1886 through a rigged election, the new president sold the Central Norte and Andino railways to British capitalists to pay off the country's growing debt.

Even though the government stopped borrowing money to pay for new railway projects, it did not bring back fiscal discipline. Instead, it started issuing more debt through state banks. Between 1886 and 1890, Argentina passed several 'banking reforms' that made it easier to get credit and paper money.

In 1887, national and provincial banking authorities passed the Free Banking Law. This law stated that any banking association could print notes as long as it bought gold bonds for the same amount as the notes it printed. Even though the law was based on what was used in the US under the National Banking Acts, it had several flaws. The Argentine government let banks with a certain amount of capital issue paper notes that were backed by government gold bonds. The banknotes, on the other hand, could not be redeemed for gold, and since the gold bonds were new issues, they showed up on the government's balance sheet as a new liability.

The banks that took part in the scheme to issue notes gave out loans in Europe to pay for the purchase of domestic gold bonds that backed the notes. This plan worked as long as foreign investors were willing to buy Argentine bonds and as long as new notes were fully backed by specie, or money in the form of coins made of gold or silver. In the past, gold and silver coins were used to buy and sell things and to store value. They were an important part of the global monetary system.

Foreign investors, on the other hand, sponsored a credit boom in Argentina, which was paid for by the printing of new paper money. By 1890, provincial banks in Argentina had borrowed more than 30 million pounds from international capital markets.

Starting in the middle of the 1880s, loose monetary and fiscal policies made Argentina's economy a lot worse. Between 1884 and 1890, the paper peso lost value at an average rate of 19 per cent per year. This was caused by the issuance of paper money, which grew the monetary base by an average of 18 per cent per year.

Argentina had a large budget deficit as well. At the end of the decade, the Argentine economy got worse. As much as 40 per cent of foreign borrowing went towards paying off debt, and 60 per cent of imports went towards buying consumer goods. The net profits of railways were going down, and gold pesos were worth 94 per cent more than paper pesos.

Till the end of 1887, there was still a chance to save the economy, but by 1888, it was too late. By the end of the decade, it was clear to the financial world that paper pesos weren't enough to pay the normal interest on internal and external debt.

In 1889, the government broke its promise and used paper money to pay off some of its gold-based debts. In response, there wasn't much interest in primary issues on the London market, and investors dumped paper pesos in anticipation of their value going down even more. The government used the gold that backed the notes to protect the exchange rate, but by December 1889, the Banco Nacional de la República Argentina had so little gold that it could no longer do this. When prices went up in 1889 and 1890, Argentine workers' real wages went down. This led to strikes, protests and a failed military coup.

The political instability in Argentina discouraged foreign investors from buying Argentine securities. The government's questionable fiscal and monetary policies drained the banking system of specie, which led to runs on several banks starting in 1890. This led to a financial crisis. In the summer of 1890, a series of last-minute tax and budget changes helped slow down the economy's decline, but they did not stop the coming financial crisis.

Even though the Baring crisis started in Argentina, it quickly spread to other places around the world, including London. The problems in Argentina beset Baring Brothers as well, which backed most of that country's foreign debt. The investment bank was stuck with the Buenos Aires Water Supply and Drainage Loan, a new debt issue that the investment house failed to sell on the London market. Early in November 1890, the Baring Brothers & Company notified the Bank of England that it was on the verge of going out of business and couldn't pay its debts.

The Bank of England put together a rescue fund with money from the Bank of France, Russia's central bank and British financial institutions to help a troubled bank that was threatening to bring down the British financial markets. The rescue operation worked, and it stopped the European markets from going bankrupt as a whole.

Even though the Bank of England stopped a major financial collapse in European markets, it didn't do much to help Argentina, which was deep in debt. In 1890, Argentina didn't pay back close to $48 million in debt, which was nearly 60 per cent of the world's defaulted debt at the time.

After the Argentine government and Baring Brothers & Company couldn't reach a deal, Nathan Rothschild put together a group of top financiers to restructure the country's debt. The committee told the Banco Nacional that it needed to send money to pay the country's short-term debts. In exchange, the committee agreed to support a bond issue that could pay Argentina's remaining debt service for three years.

In January 1891, Argentina faced a serious banking crisis, which was partly caused by the fact that Banco Nacional's finances had gotten worse after it gave assets to British creditors and helped the Bank of the Province of Buenos Aires. The financial downturn worsened. The only banks that did not fail during the crisis were the Bank of London and River Plate. In real terms, Argentina's GDP fell by 11 per cent between 1890 and 1891. The country went through a deep recession for several years. It did not fully recover from the crisis until the turn of the century, after a debt restructuring and more than a decade of monetary and fiscal reforms.

The Argentine crisis spread to other countries in the region, such as Brazil, which took longer to get back on its feet than Argentina. A Bank of England bailout was made possible by pledges of £15 million from London banks, and the final cost of the bailout was paid for by Argentine taxpayers. The effects of Argentina's default were felt around the world, all the way from Argentina to Australia.

The Barings crisis showed, among other things, that the cash nexus had become a global nexus by the end of the 1800s. This meant that the Victorians were connected to the rest of the world, whether they liked it or not. People who worked put their money and savings into colonial and foreign bonds through voluntary associations and the post office. Life insurance companies used their customers' monthly premium payments to pay for intensive farming, urban renewal and colonization, while they waited for their customers to die.

In the meantime, the Bank of England, a few sizable joint-stock banks and a few merchant banks dominated London's banking industry. By 1900, the provincial banks Barclays, Midland and Lloyds had moved to the city, where they joined two huge London banks that would later become the National Westminster Bank or NatWest. The boards of these 'Big Five' banks were composed of prominent politicians from across the country, and their branch networks covered thousands of towns and villages. Private investment companies like Grenfells, Rothschilds and Barings invested a significant portion of the money they raised abroad. These firms financed various overseas projects, such as railways, mines, plantations and infrastructure, especially in the colonies and former colonies of the British Empire. These investments not only generated profits for the banks and their shareholders but also facilitated trade, migration and cultural exchange between Britain and the rest of the world.

Conversely, these ties were not always visible or appreciated by the British people, as they were often indirect, mediated by private investment firms and not always transparent to the public or the government. Moreover, these ties were sometimes challenged by political and economic conflicts, such as wars, revolutions and crises, that threatened the stability and security of British interests abroad.

The Barings crisis exposed the fragility of the British empire and its financial system, which relied on the confidence of investors and creditors. One of the symbols of this confidence was the coinage that circulated in the empire, which bore the inscriptions of Queen Victoria's titles and honours.

In 1888, Victoria, who was anxious about her role as the head of the Church of England and eager to assert her imperial authority, wanted to replace the Latin abbreviation 'D.F.' (Defender of the Faith) with 'Imp.' (the Empress) on the new coins. However, George Goschen, the chancellor of the exchequer, opposed this change, arguing that it would violate the Royal Titles Act of 1876, which had granted Victoria the title of Empress of India but not of the whole empire. They eventually compromised by keeping both 'D.F.' and 'Ind. Imp.' (the Empress of India) on the coins.

These inscriptions reflected Victoria's dual role as the spiritual and temporal leader of a vast and diverse empire, which she sought to maintain and expand with God and gold as her allies. The coins, therefore, were not only a medium of exchange but also a tool of propaganda and education, which aimed to instil loyalty and faith among the subjects and to impress and intimidate their rivals. The late nineteenth-century economic and political crises posed a significant threat to the British Empire's institutions, including the monarchy, parliament, the church, the army and the navy, which relied heavily on the money that conveyed these messages.

## How Did the Roaring Twenties Fade Out?

If you are a jazz lover or a fan of French fashion and have read *The Great Gatsby* by F. Scott Fitzgerald or *The Sun Also Rises* by Ernest Hemingway, you probably know about the Roaring Twenties or the Jazz Age. If you don't, here's a brief overview of the 1920s and how those years affected the global financial system and led to the Great Depression, the worst economic crisis in modern history.

The Roaring Twenties were a time of economic growth and widespread prosperity in North America, Europe and a few other developed countries such as Australia. People were getting back on their feet after the First World War and spending the money they had saved through the hard times.

At first, the end of wartime production led to a short but deep recession in 1919 and 1920. This was called the 'post-World War I recession'. However, the economies of the US and Canada quickly rebounded as soldiers returned to work and factories that had made weapons switched to making consumer goods.

The Roaring Twenties witnessed a construction boom and a rapid rise in consumer goods, like cars and electronic products. The United States was able to make a smooth transition from a wartime economy to a peacetime economy. Their economy grew, and they were able to help Europe grow as well by giving them loans. Some areas, like farming and coal mining, stayed the same. Since the late 1800s, the US had been the richest country in the world in terms of per capita income and GDP. Its economy was based on mass production, and its society embraced consumerism. In contrast, it was harder for European economies to get back on their feet after the war, and they didn't start to do well again until about 1924.

During the First World War, industrial and agricultural production in the Western countries outside of Europe grew. When peace returned to Europe and production started up again, there was chronic overcapacity, which had been driving down the prices of basic goods for a long time before 1929, the year the Great Depression began. This made it even harder for countries with big foreign war debts, like Germany, which had to pay reparations, to earn the hard currency they needed to pay the interest on their debts to their foreign creditors. In most of the countries at war, the war had also made unions stronger, making it harder for employers to cut wages when prices fell. As wages went up and profit margins got smaller, companies had to lay off workers or risk going out of business.

Still, the United States, which was the epicentre of the financial crisis, was in many ways in good economic condition when the Great Depression hit. During the time between the two World Wars, companies such as DuPont (nylon), Procter & Gamble (soap powder), Revlon (cosmetics), Radio Corporation of America (RCA—radio) and IBM (computers) developed several new technologies that made workers more productive. America was using science, technology and new ideas in business in ways that no one had ever done before.

Yet, it may have been these strengths that caused the first shift that set off a classic stock market bubble. As more and more American households wanted to buy cars and other durable consumer goods that they could pay for in instalments, it seemed like there was no limit to what they could buy. Between 1925 and 1929, the stock price of RCA, the tech stock of the 1920s, went up by a staggering 939 per cent.

This euphoria triggered a rush of new IPOs. In 1929, stocks worth $6 billion were sold, with $1 billion of that in September alone. There were a lot of new financial institutions called 'investment trusts' that were established to take advantage of the stock market boom. Goldman Sachs announced its own expansion plan in the form of the Goldman Sachs Trading Corporation. If the Goldman Sachs Trading Corporation hadn't been a separate company, its failure during the Great Depression could have brought down Goldman Sachs as a whole.

After the presidency of Herbert Hoover was inaugurated in January 1929, the stock market boomed for the first six months. During the great 'Hoover bull market', stock prices went through the roof, and everyone from bankers and industrialists to cab drivers and cooks rushed to brokers to invest their cash or savings in securities that they could then sell for a profit. Billions of dollars were taken from banks and put on Wall Street in the form of loans to brokers so they could keep their margin accounts going. It was as if the Mississippi and the South Sea bubbles had risen again. People sold their Liberty Bonds and put their homes up as collateral so they could put their money in the stock market. About 300 million shares of stock were bought on credit in the middle of the summer of 1929. This caused the Dow Jones Industrial Average (DJIA) to reach its peak level of 381 points in September. No one paid attention to the warning signs that this financial system was built on shaky ground.

Prices started to go down in September and early October, but speculation kept going. In many cases, this was because people had borrowed money to buy shares, which could only be done profitably as long as stock prices kept going up.

On 18 October, the market went into a free fall, and people rushed to both buy and sell stocks in a frenzy. On 24 October, the first day of real panic, a record 12.9 million shares were traded as investors tried to make up for their losses. This day is known as 'Black Thursday'. Still, the DJIA lost only six points by the end of the day. This was because several big banks and investment firms bought up large blocks of stock to stop the panic. Their efforts, however, did not help the market in the end.

On 28 October (Black Monday), when the market closed with a loss of 12.8 per cent, the panic started up again. More than 16 million shares changed hands on 29 October (Black Tuesday). The DJIA dropped another 12 per cent and ended the day at 198, which was a drop of 183 points in less than two months. The prices of prime securities fell like the shares of fake gold mines.

From 3 September to 29 October, General Electric's stock went from 396 to 210. The stock price of American Telephone and Telegraph (AT&T) fell 100 points. From their summer highs, DuPont fell from 217 to 80, US Steel from 261 to 166, Delaware and Hudson from 224 to 141 and RCA common stock from 505 to 26.

At first, political and financial leaders tried to reassure the public by saying that the problem was just a hiccup in the market. President Hoover and Treasury Secretary Andrew W. Mellon led the way by saying that business was 'fundamentally sound' and that a great return to prosperity was 'just around the corner'. Even though the DJIA almost reached 300 again in 1930, it fell quickly in May of that year. It would take another twenty years for the DJIA to break through the 200-point mark again.

The stock market was doomed for a variety of reasons. First, this was a period of rampant speculation. People who bought stocks on margin not only lost the value of their investment, but they also owed money to the companies that had given them the loans to buy the stocks. Second was the Federal Reserve's tightening of credit. In August 1929, the discount rate went from 5 per cent to 6 per cent. Third was the rise of holding companies and investment trusts, which often led to debt, the number of large loans that couldn't be recovered and a recession in the economy that started earlier in the summer.

Some people say that the Great Depression was partly caused by the way the global economy was thrown off by the crisis of 1914. In July 1914, when it became clear that a war in Europe was almost certain, London, which was the most important international financial centre in the world, went through a serious financial crisis. The stock market crashed, the financial markets froze and depositors couldn't get to their money for days. The London Stock Exchange ceased operations, and it didn't open again for five months. People worried that a run on the banks had begun, which would threaten the country's payment and credit systems. This was happening as Britain teetered on the edge of war and then fell into Armageddon.

Even though the US stock markets crashed, the worst of the crisis didn't happen until after 1929. In December 1930, there was a run on the privately held Bank of the United States, which caused panic. The bank failed because it couldn't pay all its debts. The Bank of the United States had a third of the $550 million in deposits that were lost when 608 American banks closed in November and December 1930. When it closed, the number of bank failures reached a critical level. Even though the market went up between 14 November and 17 April 1930, it went into a long slump after that. From 17 April 1930 to 8 July 1932, the value of the market dropped by 89 per cent.

Four things played key roles with varying levels of significance in the longest and worst economic downturn that the industrialized Western world had ever seen. It led to major changes in economic institutions, macroeconomic policy and economic theory. First, when the stock market crashed in 1929, people lost faith in the American economy. This made people spend and invest less. Second, banking panics in the early 1930s led to the failure of many banks, which made it harder to get loans. Third, under the gold standard, foreign central banks had to raise interest rates to make up for trade imbalances with the US. This made people spend and invest less in those countries, damaging their economies. Finally, the Smoot-Hawley Tariff Act of 1930 imposed heavy taxes on many industrial and agricultural goods. This led to retaliatory measures that cut production and shrank global trade. Most economists agree that protectionist policies such as the Smoot-Hawley Tariff Act made the Great Depression worse or even started it.

We have already talked about stock market crashes and banking panics, so let us now take a look at the gold standard.

The gold standard was the main medium through which the Great Depression spread across the world. Even countries that had never had a bank failure or limited money supply had to adopt a deflationary policy since higher interest rates in deflationary countries caused gold to leave low-interest-rate countries. Under the price-specie flow mechanism of the gold standard, countries that lost gold but still wanted to use the gold standard had to let their money supply and domestic price levels go down, inviting deflation.

On the other hand, the economy was able to recover after the suspension of gold convertibility or the devaluation of the currency in terms of gold.

The Great Depression saw the withdrawal of the gold standard for every significant currency. The first to do so was the UK. In September 1931, the Bank of England stopped exchanging pound notes for gold and allowed the pound to float on foreign exchange markets in response to speculative attacks on the currency and declining gold reserves.

In 1931, the United Kingdom, Japan and the Scandinavian nations abandoned the gold standard. France, Poland, Belgium and Switzerland, which formed the so-called 'gold bloc', continued to use the standard until 1935–36. Italy and the United States also kept the gold standard until 1932 and 1933, respectively, before giving it up.

The speed at which a nation abandoned the gold standard accurately predicted that nation's economic recovery. For instance, Scandinavia and the UK, which departed from the gold standard in 1931, recovered much more quickly than France and Belgium, which relied on gold for a much longer period of time. Countries with a silver standard, like China, almost avoided the depression. For dozens of nations, including developing nations, leaving the gold standard was correlated with the severity of a nation's depression and the time it took for recovery. This helps explain why different nations experienced the depression differently and for shorter or longer periods of time.

John Maynard Keynes, one of the most influential economists of the twentieth century, famously called the gold standard a 'barbaric relic' in 1924. But it took a long time for money created by banks to be untied from a precious metal anchor. There's no doubt that the gold standard had its pros. Stable exchange rates made prices in trade more predictable and cut down on transaction costs, and the long-term stability of prices helped keep inflation expectations in check. Having a currency based on gold may have also made it cheaper to borrow money because it forced governments to use good fiscal and monetary policies.

The problem with tying currencies to a single commodity-based standard or even to each other is that policymakers have to choose between free capital flows and independent national monetary policy. Both are not possible. As the central bank tries to keep the price of its currency stable in terms of the peg, this can make short-term interest rates more volatile. If the supply of the peg is limited, it can cause deflation (just as the supply of gold in the 1870s and 1880s was proportional to the demand for it). It can also make financial crises worse, as happened in several countries, including Britain, France, Germany, Italy, Japan and the United States, when the gold standard was brought back after 1929.

On the other hand, these rules don't apply to a money system that is mostly based on bank deposits and exchange rates that change all the time. The gold standard had been dead for a long time, and there were few people who cared when the last important piece of it was ended on 15 August 1971. That was the day President Richard Nixon closed the so-called 'gold window', through which dollars could still be exchanged for gold under certain limited circumstances. From then on, the link between money and precious metals, which had existed for hundreds of years, was broken.

The end of the gold standard marked a new era of monetary policy and global finance. It also coincided with the emergence of new technologies and innovations that would transform the world economy and society. One of these innovations was the Internet, which gave rise to a new wave of businesses and industries that relied on digital networks and information. However, the Internet also created a frenzy of speculation and overvaluation in the stock market, leading to the first global stock market bubble of the information age: the dot-com bubble.

## The First Bubble of the Information Age

When the Mosaic web browser came out in 1993 and other web browsers came out in the years that followed, they made the World Wide Web accessible to computer users all around the world. The 'digital divide' shrank, making it easier for more people to connect to the Internet and learn how to use it. This led to more people using the Internet. In the US, the number of households with computers went from 15 per cent in 1990 to 35 per cent in 1997, as computers went from being a luxury to a necessity. This was the beginning of the 'Information Age', a time when the economy was based on information technology (IT) and many new-age businesses were started.

At the same time, the availability of capital in the United States went up because interest rates went down. The Taxpayer Relief Act of 1997, which lowered the top marginal capital gains tax rate, also made people more willing to make riskier investments. Alan Greenspan, who was chairman of the Federal Reserve at the time, is said to have encouraged more people to invest in the stock market by making the stock prices look attractive and enticing, as they showed a rapid and steady increase over time. People hoped that the Telecommunications Act of 1996 would lead to a lot of new technologies that they could use to make money.

Because of these factors, many investors were eager to invest in any dot-com company, no matter how much it was worth, especially if it had an Internet-related suffix or '.com' at the end of its name. It was easy to get money for a business idea. Investment banks, which made a lot of money from IPOs, fuelled speculation and pushed people to invest in technology. Many investors were willing to ignore traditional metrics like the price-to-earnings (PE) ratio and instead put their faith in technological advances.

The combination of rapidly rising stock prices in the quaternary sector of the economy and investors' confidence that the companies would make money in the future led to a stock market bubble. This Internet bubble is also known as the 'dot-com bubble'. In terms of history, the dot-com boom can be compared to several other technology-driven booms, such as the railroads in the 1840s, automobiles in the early twentieth century, radio in the 1920s, television in the 1940s, transistor electronics in the 1950s, computer time-sharing in the 1960s and home computers and biotechnology in the 1980s.

The Nasdaq Composite stock market index went up 400 per cent between 1995 and 2000. It reached a PE ratio of 200, which was much higher than the Nikkei 225's peak PE ratio of 80 during the Japanese asset price bubble of 1991. In 1999, the value of Qualcomm shares went up by 2619 per cent. The value of several large-cap Internet company stocks went up by more than 1000 per cent. Even though the Nasdaq Composite went up 85.6 per cent and the S&P 500 went up 19.5 per cent in 1999, more stocks went down in value than up because investors sold stocks in companies with slower growth to buy booming Internet company stocks.

During the boom, people invested more than ever before, and it was common to hear about people quitting their jobs to trade on the stock market. The media used people's desire to invest in the stock market to make money. For example, an article in the *Wall Street Journal* said that investors were starting to 're-think' the 'quaint idea' of profits, and CNBC covered the stock market with the same level of edge-of-the-seat excitement with which sports networks covered sporting events.[4]

During the height of the boom, a promising dot-com company could go public through an IPO and raise a lot of money even if it had never made a profit or, in some cases, any real money. People who had employee stock options became instant millionaires on paper when their companies went public. But most employees couldn't sell their shares right away because they had to keep them for a lock-up period.

Most dot-com companies had net operating losses because they spent a lot of money on advertising and promotions to attract more users and gain market share as quickly as possible. Slogans such as 'get big fast' and 'get big or get lost' became the mantra of these companies. Many provided their services for free or sold them at a discount in the hope of building up enough brand awareness to bring in more money for their services in the future.

Some companies spent a lot of money on fancy offices and expensive vacations for their employees because they believed growth was more important than making money. When a new product or website was launched, a company would throw an expensive party, which came to be known as a 'dot-com party'.

Near the turn of the twenty-first century, companies spent a lot of money on technology as they got ready for the Year 2000 problem, or the Y2K problem. The Y2K problem, also called the 'Millennium Bug', was a problem that could have arisen because many computer systems used a two-digit format (like '97' for the year 1997) instead of a four-digit format to show the year (e.g., '1997'). This meant that when the year 2000 dawned, the two-digit representation of '00' would be read as '1900', which could cause problems with the way computers and software worked.

Many critical systems such as financial, utility and transportation systems relied on computer systems that could be affected by the Y2K problem. Dates could be incorrectly calculated, mistakes could occur when processing data and system failures could happen, which could stop essential services and cause widespread chaos.

But in the years leading up to the year 2000, organizations and governments around the world took steps to deal with the Y2K issue by updating their computer systems and software to make sure they could handle the change in date. Most of the work done to fix the Y2K problem was successful, and when 2000 came, it didn't cause any serious disruptions. 'The first challenge of the twenty-first century was successfully met,' stated Bill Clinton, the US president at the time, after coordinating efforts to mitigate the effects of Y2K.

Meanwhile, Alan Greenspan was contemplating a troublesome idea: the US stock market was overvalued and in danger of a speculative bubble, especially in the technology sector. He coined the phrase 'irrational exuberance' to describe the excessive optimism and high expectations of investors that drove up the share prices of dot-com companies, many of which had no profits or revenues.

Early in 2000, he raised the interest rates slightly (not once, but several times) to cool down the economy and curb inflation. Raising interest rates means it costs more to borrow money, which makes it harder to invest. Expensive borrowing reduced the demand for stocks. This move by the US Federal Reserve panicked the investors in dot-com companies, and they soon started selling off their holdings, triggering a market crash that lasted until 2002.

Between March 2000 and October 2002, the NASDAQ
fell from 5048 to 1139, wiping out almost all its gains
made during the dot-com bubble. By the end of 2001,
most publicly listed dot-com companies had failed. This
happened when investors who had been excited realized
that web businesses that didn't make money were worthless
in the long run.

Companies that were worth billions when they went
public were now worth zero. Even great companies like
Cisco lost 86 per cent of their market value. The price of
Amazon's stock went down from $107 to $7. Within a
year, there was a recession all over the world. Few people
who were there will ever forget it. The bursting of the dot-
com bubble is still one of the most significant events in
modern economics.

Not everyone lost money during this financial
downturn. The dot-com bubble's burst was a boon for
some who had smelled trouble before everything went
down. Successful businessmen such as Mark Cuban, a
billionaire entrepreneur and former owner of the Dallas
Mavericks basketball team, sold their shares in Internet
companies or hedged them to protect their profits.
Sir John Templeton, a legendary fund manager and
philanthropist, sold short a lot of dot-com stocks at the
peak of the bubble, which he called 'temporary insanity'
and a 'once-in-a-lifetime opportunity'.[5] He sold eighty-
four Nasdaq stocks that had gone up three times their
initial public offering (IPO) price and had insider lock-up
periods of six months. He expected that the stock prices
would plummet when the insiders could sell their shares
after the lock-up expired. He was right and made $80
million in six weeks.

These are some examples of how some investors managed to profit from the dot-com bubble while many others lost their fortunes. The dot-com bubble was one of the most significant global financial events of the late twentieth century, and it had ripple effects across the world. How did it affect the Indian economy? Was India immune to the financial shocks that hit other countries? Let us explore the history of financial crises in India and how international events influenced them.

India's first stock market collapse in recorded history occurred even earlier, in 1865. This crisis, triggered by the American Civil War, was popularly linked with the first 'big bull' of the Indian financial market: Premchand Roychand. In nineteenth-century Bombay (present-day Mumbai), Roychand was also known as the Cotton King and the Bullion King. His life is depicted in historian Sharada Dwivedi's book, *Premchand Roychand: His Life and Times.*[6]

Premchand began his stockbroking career following his education at Elphinstone Institution (present-day Elphinstone College). He is believed to have been the first Indian broker to be fluent in English—speaking, reading and writing. Young Premchand's professional success came quickly, as he was lucky enough to start working as an assistant to wealthy and successful broker Ratanchand Lala in 1852. Lala was smart enough to realize how useful the young man would be as an assistant, especially when he went around to European merchants and bank managers as he grew his business as a broker.

According to a legend, Premchand started his prosperous career as a broker under the shade of a grand, spreading banyan tree at the western end of the lovely Horniman

Circle Garden in South Bombay, where travellers, clerks, strangers and cotton and opium brokers came to quench their thirst. The Native Share and Stock Brokers Association was founded with a contribution of one rupee by around twenty-two of these brokers who started trading under the banyan tree. The Bombay Stock Exchange (BSE) is the name of that organization today.

Premchand prospered by dabbling in the trade of cotton and opium, both of which were in demand in China at the time and were legal. Roychand and his son had amassed a modest fortune of about Rs 1 lakh by 1858. But Premchand didn't really make it big until the start of the American Civil War in mid-April 1861.

Cotton plantations in the United States were the primary source of cotton for Lancashire mills in the United Kingdom. However, the supply of American cotton abruptly halted following the outbreak of the American Civil War. Britain then looked to India. This historical occurrence is described by Naresh Fernandes in his book *City Adrift*.[7] He recounts how India filled the void by shipping a sizable portion of its cotton harvest to England through the port of Bombay. As the price of Indian cotton increased from about four pence per pound in the Liverpool market to between twenty and twenty-four pence over the course of the following five years, the value of Indian cotton exports to the UK increased from Rs 16 crore to Rs 40 crore.

A frenzy ensued. People of all economic strata and social standing, from merchants and traders to aristocrats and serfs, worshipped at the shrine of King Cotton. As cotton became scarce and expensive, people began to sell their old cotton-filled mattresses and buy new ones made of coir fibre, which is cheaper and more abundant than cotton but also less comfortable and durable. People began flocking to Bombay to make a quick buck during this prosperous time, and as the city consequently grew, it was felt that land needed to be reclaimed from the sea to cater to the expanding population. Many financial institutions and reclamation companies emerged.

Premchand was undoubtedly at the centre of this boom. After starting the Back Bay Reclamation Company, he became immensely wealthy during the Indian cotton boom. He was the most illustrious of the 'Share Kings', and his exploits would contribute to the development of yet another stereotype: that of a prominent Bombayite who placed profits before morals. The clever merchant had ties to about seventy mushroom businesses and was a promoter and shareholder in the Commercial Bank and Mercantile Bank. The Bank of Bombay was also put under his control. He had a keen eye for regulatory grey areas and loopholes.

Premchand could be considered the Nathan Rothschild of nineteenth-century India. Legend says that Premchand informed his fellow cotton traders of how the Liverpool cotton market was doing long before anyone else by sending boats out to sea. Since there were no telegraph lines between England and India, other means had to be devised to get news as soon as possible. At what was called the 'outer lighthouse', Premchand stationed fast-sailing boats that would set out to meet and gather news from steamers coming into port, then swiftly return and report to Premchand.

The Bank of Bombay doubled its capital to Rs 104 lakh in 1863, at the height of the boom. It also relaxed its lending rules and allowed people to borrow money based on their shares or personal guarantees without any collateral. Every day, huge speculative transactions involving crores of rupees were carried out, frequently at fictitious prices. Future delivery prices for Back Bay shares reached nearly Rs 50,000 during this frenzy. Premchand Roychand was the brains behind these wild speculative ventures. Company promoters often relied on his help to rally their share prices in the market.

The strategy was simple. A bank would help launch a financial company by lending money against its shares. The founders of the financial company would then start a reclamation company, and both the bank and the financial company would lend money against the shares of that company. The shares would then be sold at ridiculously high prices.

All of this changed when the American Civil War ended. Britain resumed cotton imports from the United States on 1 May 1865. The Indian cotton story was over. The price of cotton dropped from twenty pence to ten pence on the Liverpool market, resulting in panic and chaos in Bombay. Everyone who owned shares in the bubble companies tried to sell them. However, no one was interested in purchasing them.

By the middle of May, many of the city's wealthy businessmen had gone bankrupt, led by Behramji Hormusji Cama, Kharshedji Furdunji Parekh, K.J. Readymoney, Rustomjee Jamsetjee Jejeebhoy, K.N. Cama and, of course, Premchand Roychand.

Premchand took the Bank of Bombay along with him on his way down. A share of Bank of Bombay, which had reached a high of Rs 2850 at the peak of the market, fell to just Rs 87. The Back Bay Reclamation Company's stock fell by 96 per cent. As a result of the closure of numerous businesses, the city's population fell by 21 per cent.

The Indian government established a commission in 1868 to investigate and provide a report on the factors that had led to the Bank of Bombay's collapse. Sir Charles Jackson, a judge from Bombay's Supreme Court of Judicature, was chosen to lead the commission.

It was found that Act X of 1863 was the root of all the mayhem. This law made it possible for bank officials to lend large amounts of shareholders' and depositors' money to anyone and everyone, including the poor, wealthy and people with average incomes, but not in proportion to their financial situations or other obligations and without any caution or reasonable limits. Lakhs were given away on personal security that didn't even have a guarantee from a separate individual, which is the norm in places where cash credits are allowed. Again, these could be renewed indefinitely, or at least until the damage was done and couldn't be fixed. Accounts could be taken out of balance by lakhs of rupees. Premchand was at the centre of this trouble because of his web of companies and financial interests. The other shareholders and directors of the bank let him take out huge loans to pay for his numerous schemes. He took out, directly and indirectly, Rs 1.38 crore, which was a huge and unprecedented advance that constituted half of the Bank of Bombay's capital.

A century later, a Bengal-based bear cartel triggered the 1982 crash by primarily short-selling Reliance Company stock. Shorting approximately 1 million shares of Reliance Industries caused a rapid sell-off. As the value of shares dropped, the BSE was forced to shut down for three consecutive days.

In the wake of economic liberalization in India, the stock market saw several boom and bust cycles in 1991. A major crash occurred on 28 April 1992, caused by a man who can be considered a reincarnation of Premchand Roychand. His name was Harshad Mehta.

Like Premchand Roychand, Harshad Mehta was a successful stockbroker and a brilliant market manipulator. Besides, he was a cricket enthusiast who did not show much promise in school. He moved to Mumbai from Raipur after high school to study and look for work. After getting his B.Com. degree in 1976, Mehta worked odd jobs in Mumbai for the next eight years. These jobs often had something to do with sales, such as selling stockings, cement and diamonds.

Mehta began his career as a salesperson at the New India Assurance Company Limited (NIACL) in Mumbai. During this time, he became interested in the stock market, so he quit his job and joined a brokerage firm. In the early 1980s, he moved to a lower-level clerical job at the brokerage firm Harjivandas Nemidas Securities, where he worked as a jobber for the broker Prasann Pranjivandas Broker, whom he considered his 'Guru'.

He worked at several brokerage firms for the next ten years, taking on more responsibility with each successive job. By 1990, he had become a well-known figure in the Indian securities business. Popular magazines like *Business Today* called him the 'Amitabh Bachchan of the Stock Market'. Amitabh Bachchan is one of the most influential and successful actors in the history of Indian cinema.

In 1986, when the BSE sold a broker's card at auction, Mehta set up Grow More Research and Asset Management with the financial support of his partners. Then he began to trade actively in securities. By the beginning of 1990, many well-known people had invested in his business and were using his services. At this time, he started actively trading the shares of Associated Cement Company (ACC). The price of ACC shares went from Rs 200 to almost Rs 9000 after a group of brokers, including Mehta, bought a lot of them. Mehta explained the high volume of trading in ACC shares by simply stating that the stock was undervalued and that the market had just fixed it by revaluing the company at a price equal to what it would cost to build a similar business. He called this 'replacement cost theory', a theory of his own making.

But what Mehta did was deceptive, and he did it in two ways: fake bank receipts and stamp papers.

In India, banks were not permitted to invest in the equity markets until the early 1990s. However, they were required to turn a profit and keep a predetermined percentage (threshold) of their assets in fixed-interest government bonds. To meet this need, Mehta deftly extracted capital from the banking system and invested it in the stock market. He pretended to be buying securities for the banks from other banks by using phoney stamp papers to promise them higher rates of interest while requesting that they transfer the money into his personal account. At that time, purchasing securities and forward bonds from other banks required a bank to work through a broker. Mehta used this money in his account to buy shares, dramatically increasing demand for shares of certain reputable, well-established companies such as ACC, Sterlite Industries and Videocon. He sold them, gave the bank a portion of the proceeds and kept the rest for himself.

The bank receipt, also known as a BR, was another instrument that Mehta heavily utilized. Securities were not transferred back and forth in short-term bank-to-bank lending or ready-forward deals. Instead, the borrower—that is, the seller of the securities—gave a BR to the purchaser. In addition to acting as a receipt from the selling bank, the BR guarantees that the buyer will receive the securities they have paid for at the end of the term.

After Mehta realized this, he needed banks that could issue fake BRs, or BRs not backed by any government securities. Following the issuance of these phoney BRs, they were distributed to other banks, which then loaned money to Mehta while erroneously believing they were lending against government securities.

With this money, Mehta pushed up the stock prices in the market. When it was time to pay back the money, the shares were sold for a profit and the BR was retired. The money that was owed to the bank was given back. This kept happening as long as the stock prices went up, and nobody knew about Mehta's stock market operations.

Mehta was given a deified image by the media during this time, especially in 1990–1991 when they referred to him as 'The Big Bull', as he was said to have started the bull run in the stock market. Numerous publications, including the well-known economic magazine *Business Today*, featured him on the front cover. His extravagant lifestyle, which included a sea-facing, 15,000-square-foot penthouse in the upscale neighbourhood of Worli, complete with a mini golf course and swimming pool, as well as his collection of luxury vehicles, which included a Toyota Corolla, Lexus LS400 and Toyota Sera, were highlighted in an article titled 'Raging Bull' in *Business Today*.[8] These improved his reputation at a time when even India's wealthy lacked such luxurious things.

Mehta's life took a U-turn when the *Times of India* published a column on 23 April 1992, exposing his illegal tactics.[9] He was using the banking system improperly to fund his stock market manipulation. The Indian banking system had been defrauded of a staggering Rs 40 billion (equivalent to Rs 260 billion or $3.3 billion today), and many banks were left holding worthless BRs after the fraud was discovered. They were well aware that they would face accusations if it were discovered that they had been involved in writing checks to Mehta.

Later, it was revealed that several institutions and people had allegedly helped Mehta manipulate the market, including Citibank, brokers like Pallav Sheth and Ajay Kayan, businessmen like Aditya Birla and Hemendra Kothari and a few politicians, including the then governor of the Reserve Bank of India. All of this combined to make the Harshad Mehta scam the largest money market scam in India's history.

Since people first started buying and selling stocks 400 years ago, there have been numerous stock market bubbles. Share prices have gone up and down many times, reaching heights that cannot be sustained. The financial crisis that hit the Western world in the summer of 2007, which you can read about in the next chapter, was a good reminder of an enduring truth in financial history: every bubble eventually bursts. Sooner or later, sellers outnumber buyers and fear takes over from greed. What follows is a slow chain reaction that culminates in a catastrophe.

Still, the stock market has a life of its own. Since we don't know much about the future, we can't be sure how profitable companies will be in the future. If we were all computers, we would all look at the relevant information at the same time and come to the same conclusion. But we are humans, which means we can be short-sighted and suffer mood swings. When stock prices go up at the same time, as they often do, it seems like investors are in a state of collective euphoria, or what Alan Greenspan called 'irrational exuberance'.

When investors' 'animal spirits' change from greed to fear, on the other hand, the bubble of their earlier happiness can pop in a way that is hard to believe. Zoological metaphors are, of course, a big part of the culture of the stock market. Bulls are people who buy stocks with hope, and bears are people who sell stocks with fear. Investors today are like an electronic herd: they graze on the profits one moment and run for the farmyard gate the next. But the real point is that stock markets are a reflection of how people think. They can become depressed, just like Homo sapiens. They can even break down completely. Still, hope always seems to triumph over these pessimistic experiences.

# 3

# The Big Short

'It ain't what you don't know that gets you into trouble,
it is what you know for sure that just ain't so'

—Mark Twain

Lewis S. Ranieri was born in 1947 in the county of
Brooklyn, New York. Ranieri dreamed of becoming
an Italian chef, but he couldn't make it as his asthma
wouldn't let him work in a smoky kitchen. Ranieri got a
part-time job in the mail room at Salomon Brothers when
he was twenty-one years old. He worked his way up, and
by the late 1970s, he had joined the new mortgage trading
desk of this multinational investment bank, which was at
the time one of the largest investment banking enterprises
in the United States.

It is said that it was during the 1970s, when Ranieri
was in his twenties, that he came up with the word
'securitization', which was used to describe a new way

of trading mortgages. Securitization is the process of combining and repackaging different types of financial assets, such as mortgages, loans and credit card debt, into securities that are then sold to investors. In a legal process, the assets are turned into securities by creating a special purpose vehicle (SPV) that holds the assets and issues the securities. The SPV then pays the interest and principal on the securities with the cash flows that come from the underlying assets.

Securitization lets banks pass on the risk of the assets to investors. This frees up money that can be used to make new loans or investments. It also gives investors access to a wide range of assets that they might not have been able to invest in otherwise.

Ranieri was later known as the 'father' of mortgage-backed securities (MBSs) because he was one of the first people to create them in the 1970s. He was working at Salomon Brothers at the time and later rose to the position of vice chairman of the investment bank. *Business Week* called him 'one of the greatest innovators of the last 75 years' in 2004.[1]

## What Is an MBS?

An MBS is an asset-backed security (ABS), which is a type of financial instrument that is backed by a mortgage or bundle of mortgages. The mortgages are put together and sold to a group of people (a government agency or investment bank) that securitizes, or packages, the loans into a security that investors can buy.

The MBS may have a 'pass-through' structure, in which the interest and principal payments from the borrower or homebuyer go directly to the MBS holder, or it may have a more complicated structure made up of a pool of other MBSs. Collateralized mortgage obligations (CMOs), which are often set up as real estate mortgage investment conduits, and collateralized debt obligations (CDOs) are two other types of MBS.

Again, the CMO is believed to have been created by Ranieri in 1983.

MBS, the child of securitization, was running wild in the US housing market during the late twentieth century. The big banks were making billions from their 2 per cent fee from selling MBSs to institutional and retail investors. Rating agencies stamped them with AAA ratings, and pension funds stood in line to invest in them. All this took financial alchemy to a whole new level, making it look like lead was being turned into gold.

The key to this financial magic was that the people who took out mortgages in the US could be thousands of miles away from the people who got their interest payments. The risk was spread all over the world, from state pension funds in the US to public health networks in Australia and even to town councils north of the Arctic Circle. In Norway, for example, the cities of Rana, Hemnes, Hattjelldal and Narvik put about $120 million of their taxpayers' money into CDOs backed by American sub-prime mortgages.

All was well until 2003 when someone saw the lie that rested at the heart of the American economy. His name was Michael Burry, a physician turned hedge fund manager and the founder of the hedge fund Scion Capital.

By looking at how mortgages were given out in 2003 and 2004, he was able to spot the start of a real estate bubble that could burst in 2007. His research on the values of residential real estate led him to believe that sub-prime mortgages, especially those with 'teaser' rates, and the bonds based on these mortgages would start to lose value when the original interest rates were replaced by much higher interest rates, which often happened as soon as two years after the mortgages were issued.

When the banks ran out of mortgages to put in MBSs, they began to fill them with riskier sub-prime mortgages to keep the profit machine churning. They also offered no income, no job (NINJA) loans for higher commissions.

To the uninitiated, sub-prime lending, also called near-prime lending, subpar lending, non-prime lending or second-chance lending, is a practice in the US whereby loans are given to people who may have trouble paying them back on time. In order to make up for the higher credit risk, these loans have higher interest rates, less valuable collateral and less favourable terms. In other words, the term 'sub-prime' refers to the credit quality of some borrowers, who have bad credit histories and a higher chance of not paying back their loans than 'prime' borrowers.

This idea led Burry to short the sub-prime market. As there were no insurance contracts or options for MBSs, he persuaded Goldman Sachs and other investment firms to sell him credit default swaps (CDS) on sub-prime deals. CDS are contracts that would pay Burry if the underlying mortgages defaulted. By buying CDS on sub-prime deals, Michael Burry was creating a financial instrument to short not only MBSs but also the US housing market.

According to the popular wisdom of those days, betting against the housing market was a foolish idea. Burry's CDS positions would pay off only if the underlying bonds failed.

He also had to service those CDSs with monthly premiums that went up as the bond prices went up. Burry was on the wrong side—the bond prices were skyrocketing every passing day. 'The US housing market is strong.'[2] 'Bubbles, if any, are regional, and defaults are rare.'[3] These were the words of Alan Greenspan, the chairman of the Federal Reserve at the time.

Michael Burry was not foolish enough to buy into those words. When Goldman Sachs offered CDSs worth $5 million, he requested and bought CDSs worth $100 million from them. He also created a $200 million CDS position at Deutsche Bank and a similar mammoth short position at Bear Stearns. The size of his CDS short position reached $1.3 billion, taking up a larger portion of his hedge fund's liquidity.

Greg Lippmann, the executive in charge of global asset-backed security trading at Deutsche Bank, found out about Burry's gigantic short position. The news spread quickly within financial circles. Several prominent hedge fund managers, such as Steven Eisman and Ben Hockett, joined the shorting bandwagon.

## When Everything Fell Apart . . .

What Lewis S. Ranieri invented more than three decades ago was about to plunge the world into financial catastrophe.

'Is there a housing bubble?' 'If there is, how exposed are the banks?' These were the two critical questions that troubled Steven Eisman and his team. To find out the answers, they decided to visit Miami, one of the most overvalued and speculative housing markets in the US during the 2000s. They expected to see a booming real estate sector, but instead, they were shocked to discover empty houses and house owners who were defaulting on their mortgages. This confirmed their belief that the housing bubble was about to burst and that the banks were in big trouble.

Eisman realized that the big banks were obsessed with the fees and commissions on selling MBSs. These were financial instruments that pooled together thousands of mortgages and sold them to investors. However, nobody (including the banks) knew what was in the MBSs. They claimed that the MBSs comprised 65 per cent AAA-rated bonds, but in reality, all they held were sub-prime bonds with below-average credit ratings. The banks also repackaged them into CDOs with several B-rated mortgages, and credit rating agencies gave them AAA ratings in 92 to 93 per cent of the cases. Eisman also speculated that if the teaser rates, or low introductory interest rates, expired in 2007, the default rates would shoot up, and if they reached 8 per cent, Armageddon would ensue. Meanwhile, the market for synthetic CDOs, which were derivatives that bet on the performance of the underlying mortgages, grew twenty times faster than the market for actual CDO bonds.

The subprime mortgage crisis, which Eisman had anticipated, began to unfold in 2007. One of the first casualties was New Century Financial Corporation, which collapsed on 2 April 2007. It was a prominent real estate investment trust (REIT) that stood second only to HSBC Finance in issuing subprime mortgages. The trigger for its collapse was a surge in homeowner defaults, which made it unable to repay its creditors and investors. New

Century's bankruptcy was an early sign of the subprime meltdown, which soon spread to other lenders and banks. In March 2008, Morgan Stanley, which had significant losses due to its exposure to the subprime market, went down, followed by Bear Stearns, one of the biggest issuers and underwriters of MBSs and CDOs. The most dramatic event, however, was the failure of Lehman Brothers, which filed for Chapter 11 bankruptcy on 15 September 2008. This was the largest bankruptcy filing in US history, involving $639 billion in assets and $619 billion in debt. Lehman Brothers was a global investment bank that had been in operation for more than 160 years, so its failure was a significant event in the 2008 financial crisis. The bank was unable to prevent a crisis of confidence among its creditors and investors, despite its efforts to secure additional funding. The failure of Lehman Brothers contributed to the worst financial crisis since the Great Depression. It had far-reaching repercussions, including widespread job losses, the worsening of the global economy and the need for government intervention to stabilize the financial system. It also resulted in changes to regulations and policies intended to prevent similar occurrences in the future.

This terrible economic turmoil recalled the Dark Ages and anticipated the end of capitalism.

On the other side, Michael Burry made 489 per cent of his capital, or $69 billion, and closed his fund.

The sub-prime mortgage crisis was not the result of the speculation of a handful of hedge fund managers. A few factors added fuel to this financial wildfire.

Starting in 2004, several things pointed to the coming crisis, but few economists were ready for how big it would be. From June 2004 to June 2006, the Federal Reserve raised the federal funds rate from 1.25 per cent to 5.25 per cent. This led to more sub-prime borrowers with adjustable-rate mortgages (ARMs) going into default.

In 2005, home sales and prices started to go down, partly because interest rates went up and partly because the housing market had reached the saturation point. Many people with sub-prime mortgages couldn't get out of trouble by borrowing, refinancing or selling their homes because there were fewer buyers and because many mortgage holders now owed more on their loans than their homes were worth. In other words, they were 'underwater', which became more and more common as the crisis got worse.

As more and more sub-prime borrowers stopped paying back their loans and home prices continued to fall, MBSs based on sub-prime mortgages lost value, which hurt the portfolios of many banks and investment firms in terrible ways. In fact, because MBSs from the US housing market were also bought and sold in other countries (especially in Western Europe), many of which had their own housing bubbles, it quickly became clear that the problems in the US would affect the rest of the world. However, most experts insisted that the problems were not as bad as they seemed and that the damage to financial markets could be limited.

By 2007, the steep drop in the value of MBSs had caused many banks, hedge funds and mortgage lenders to lose a lot of money. Some large and well-known companies were even forced to liquidate hedge funds that had invested in MBSs, ask the government for loans, merge with healthier companies or declare bankruptcy.

# The Aftermath

In 2012, the Federal Reserve Bank of St Louis estimated that, when adjusted for inflation, the net worth of American households had dropped by about $17 trillion, or 26 per cent. The Federal Reserve Bank of San Francisco did a study in 2018 and found that ten years after the start of the financial crisis, the country's gross domestic product was about 7 per cent lower than it would have been had the crisis not happened. This means that every American lost $70,000 in lifetime income because of the crisis. Between 2007 and 2009, about 7.5 million jobs were lost. The unemployment rate doubled, reaching nearly 10 per cent in 2010. Even though the economy slowly added jobs after the recovery began in 2009 and brought the unemployment rate down to 3.9 per cent in 2018, many of the new jobs paid less and were less stable than the ones that had been lost.

Most Americans took a long time to get back on their feet after the financial crisis and the Great Recession. Those who had suffered the most—the millions of families who lost their homes, businesses or savings; the millions of workers who lost their jobs and faced long-term unemployment and the millions of people who fell into poverty—still struggled years after the worst of the trouble had passed.

But the lives of the bankers who had caused the crisis were very different from those of the common citizens. Some of these executives lost their jobs when shareholders and the public found out how badly they had managed their companies. However, those who quit often did so with big bonuses, also known as 'golden parachutes'. Also, no American CEO or other top executive went to jail or was even charged with a crime. This is in stark contrast to earlier financial scandals, such as the savings and loan crisis of the 1980s and the bankruptcy of Enron in 2001. In general, the top leaders of financial firms and other very wealthy Americans did not lose as much as people in the lower and middle classes. By 2010, they had mostly made up for their losses, while many ordinary Americans never did.

This obvious inequality caused a lot of anger in the public, which culminated in 2011 with the Occupy Wall Street movement. Taking aim at economic elites and a political and economic system that seemed to be set up to serve the interests of the very wealthy (the '1 per cent' as opposed to the '99 per cent'), the movement raised awareness of economic inequality in the US, a powerful issue that quickly became a theme of Democratic political rhetoric at both the federal and state levels. But the movement lacked a strong leader and clear goals, and it didn't lead to any specific changes, let alone a complete change of 'the system', as some of its members had hoped.

This is not the heroic story of a few smart hedge fund managers who made a fortune by betting against the American economy. This is a story that tries to expose the reality behind the centralized yet regulated global financial system.

# 4

# Our Troublesome Financial System

'I believe that banking institutions are more dangerous to our liberties than standing armies.'

—Thomas Jefferson

Money, in all its different forms and uses, has been an important part of human society for thousands of years. It has helped people trade and exchange goods and services. Everyone from land-owning elites and kings to dictators and democratic political systems has controlled and regulated these forms and functions of money. Today, our financial system has evolved into a complicated web of institutions, technologies, laws and regulations that make it possible for people all over the world to trade and conduct financial transactions.

The financial crises described in the last few chapters have illustrated some of the drawbacks, complexities and problems in our current financial system, such as taking too many risks, regulatory flaws and the growing gap between the rich and poor. All these boom-and-bust stories have revealed the frailty of our new economy's quadrilateral foundation: corporations, stock markets, banks and governments.

This chapter describes how our highly regulated financial institutions and systems contribute to problems such as inflation, uneven income distribution and economic regression, among others. We will also look to the future, where there is a lot of room to build a more resilient, inclusive and sustainable financial system that meets the needs of individuals, businesses and society as a whole. To understand the challenges and opportunities of the financial system, we need to examine its historical evolution and context.

One example of a country that has experienced dramatic changes in its financial system is Zimbabwe, formerly known as Rhodesia, a British colony. It was named after Cecil Rhodes, a British mining magnate whose British South Africa Company (BSAC) was created to take advantage of the mineral wealth of Mashonaland, a region in today's northern Zimbabwe that is home to nearly half of Zimbabwe's population. Rhodes University in South Africa is named after him. Rhodes also established the Rhodes Scholarship, which receives funding from his estate.

Rhodes became a member of the Cape Parliament in 1881 when he was only twenty-seven years old. The Cape Parliament was the legislature of the Cape Colony, a British territory in southern Africa that included present-day South Africa and Namibia.

In 1890, Rhodes became the prime minister of the Cape Colony and pursued his imperialist vision of expanding

British influence and control in the region. He used his political power to take land from black Africans, who were the majority of the population, to disenfranchise them. He passed the Glen Grey Act in 1894, which restricted the amount of land that black Africans could own and forced them to pay taxes and labour for white settlers. He also passed the Franchise and Ballot Act in 1892, which raised the property and income qualifications for voting, effectively excluding most black Africans and some poor whites from the electoral process. These acts were part of Rhodes's policy of segregation and discrimination, which aimed to secure white supremacy and economic interests in the colony. The situation did not improve for black Africans even after the colony of Rhodesia, named after Rhodes, declared its independence from Britain on 11 November 1965. Until 1980, a white minority government ruled Rhodesia that denied political and civil rights to the black majority.

The Lancaster House Agreement was signed in London on 21 December 1979, after months of negotiations between the British government, the Rhodesian government and the black nationalist parties, including the Robert Mugabe-led Zimbabwe African National Union (ZANU) and the Joshua Nkomo-led Zimbabwe African People's Union (ZAPU).

The agreement ended the Rhodesian Bush War, a violent conflict that started in 1965 when the white minority regime of Rhodesia declared its independence from Britain without the consent of the black majority population or the international community. The agreement restored British authority over Rhodesia, which was renamed Zimbabwe Rhodesia, and provided for a ceasefire, a new constitution and free and fair elections under British supervision. The agreement led to the country's first democratic elections and the creation of a new government in which black people had a voice.

Robert Mugabe won the elections, and on 17 April 1980, Zimbabwe became a sovereign, internationally recognized nation with its own government.

The Zimbabwean dollar replaced the Rhodesian dollar at par value. Officially, the newly introduced Zimbabwean dollar was initially more valuable than the US dollar. However, this did not reflect reality, as its purchasing power on the open and black markets was diminished, primarily due to Zimbabwe's higher inflation. Zimbabwe's early years were characterized by rapid growth and development. In drought-free years, wheat production was proportionally greater than in the past, and the tobacco industry was thriving. The nation's economic indicators were strong.

Mugabe instituted the Economic Structural Adjustment Programme (ESAP) in 1991 as a condition for receiving loans and aid from the International Monetary Fund (IMF) and the World Bank. The programme aimed to liberalize the economy, reduce government spending and promote exports. But it hurt the economy and society in big ways: rising inflation, unemployment, poverty and inequality.

In the late 1990s, Mugabe put in place land reforms as part of his political agenda. He claimed that land reforms were necessary to correct the historical injustice of colonial land dispossession and to empower the black majority. However, critics argued that land reforms were a way for Mugabe to reward his loyalists, punish his opponents and divert attention from the economic crisis. Land reforms involved the violent and chaotic seizure of white-owned farms, which disrupted the agricultural sector and reduced food production.

An unstable government, widespread corruption, bad economic management and high inflation, all played a role in the collapse of Zimbabwe's banking industry. The banks suffered from poor corporate governance, weak regulation, undercapitalization and low demand for credit. The banking crisis had severe consequences for the economy and society, such as cash shortages, loss of confidence, loss of employment and reduced access to finance. The collapse of the banking industry made it impossible for farmers to get loans for farming. In 2005, manufacturing output decreased by 29 per cent; in 2006, by 26 per cent; and in 2007, by 29 per cent. The unemployment rate increased to 80 per cent. Life expectancy decreased. Whites fled the country en masse, taking with them a large portion of the nation's capital.

Zimbabwe has been facing economic sanctions from the US, the IMF and the EU since the early 2000s when President Robert Mugabe was accused of violating human rights and undermining democracy. The sanctions mainly target individuals and entities linked to the Mugabe regime, imposing travel bans, asset freezes and trade restrictions. The Reserve Bank of Zimbabwe claims that the sanctions are the main cause of the country's hyperinflation and economic woes. However, the US, the IMF and the EU argue that the sanctions have no impact on the general population and that the real problem is the mismanagement and corruption of the Zimbabwean authorities.

The Zimbabwean government resorted to printing money to fund its military interventions in the Democratic

Republic of the Congo (DRC) from 1998 to 2002, which included the Second Congo War in 2000. These wars were costly and increased the demand for foreign currency, which the government did not have. To hide its financial troubles, the government underreported its war expenditures and debt levels to the IMF, which it was a member of. The IMF discovered the deception and suspended Zimbabwe's voting rights in 2003. The excessive money printing devalued the Zimbabwean dollar and caused hyperinflation, which touched its peak in 2008.

Self-dealing, which is the practice of using one's position or authority for personal gain, was another reason why the Zimbabwean government printed too much money. Many government officials and their cronies engaged in corruption and looted the country's resources while hiding their activities from the public and the international community. This eroded the trust and confidence of the people in the government and its policies, as well as in the Zimbabwean dollar, which became worthless due to hyperinflation.

Economic mistakes made by the government can lead to shortages that take workers' attention away from their jobs and force them to find workarounds. Widespread poverty and violence, such as when the government uses violence to suppress political opposition, also contribute to a lack of confidence in the future. The land reforms in Zimbabwe had hurt property rights and made farming less productive, especially in tobacco, which made up one-third of Zimbabwe's foreign exchange earnings. Also declining were manufacturing and mining.

In response to the falling value of the Zimbabwean dollar, the Reserve Bank of Zimbabwe kept ordering more banknotes to be printed, often at a high cost, from foreign companies like Giesecke & Devrient (G&D), based in Munich. Zimbabwe had to rely on foreign companies to print bank notes as it did not have the capacity or the resources to produce enough money domestically to meet the demand of its hyperinflationary economy. Overseas companies such as G&D also supplied high-denomination notes, such as the $100 trillion dollar bill, to the Reserve Bank of Zimbabwe. However, this only worsened the situation as the value of the currency continued to plummet and the cost of printing increased.

The government deemed inflation illegal in 2007! Anyone who increased the cost of goods and services faced arrest. This was essentially a price freeze, which is rarely successful in stopping inflation. Authorities detained numerous corporate executives after they changed the prices of their products and services.

On 13 July 2007, the Zimbabwean government said it would stop publishing inflation numbers for a while. This was seen as an attempt to draw attention away from the country's unprecedented economic collapse.

Zimbabwe experienced a period of hyperinflation from 2004 to 2009, which reached its peak in November 2008. The inflation rate fluctuated wildly, and at one point, the US ambassador to Zimbabwe said that it would reach 1.5 million per cent. By June 2008, the annual inflation rate was 11.2 million per cent, and by November 2008, it was estimated to be 79.6 billion per cent per month, or 89.7 sextillion per cent per year. The Zimbabwean dollar became virtually worthless, as one US dollar was equivalent to 2.6 billion Zimbabwean dollars. In fact, a piece of toilet paper was worth more than a Zimbabwean dollar.

As a result, the government banned the use of the local currency in January 2009 and allowed the use of foreign currencies, such as the US dollar, the South African rand and the Botswana pula. People also resorted to bartering goods and services or using commodities like gold, cigarettes and fuel as a medium of exchange. Street traders also offered better bargains than formal shops, as they accepted various forms of payment and sold cheaper imported goods.

The government did not make an effort to control inflation through monetary and fiscal policy. When Zimbabwe became independent in 1980, it introduced the Zimbabwean dollar in paper notes of 2, 5, 10 and 20 dollars and in coins of 1, 5, 10, 20 and 50 cents and one dollar. However, the Zimbabwean dollar lost its value due to hyperinflation. To cope with this, the Reserve Bank of Zimbabwe changed its currency three times, but without success. The first change was in August 2006, when the bank withdrew the old notes and issued new ones that had 1000 times less value. For example, a 10,000-dollar note became a 10-dollar note, with three zeros crossed out.

The Reserve Bank of Zimbabwe's governor, Gideon Gono, introduced a new Zimbabwean dollar in July 2008, which was the second redenomination of the currency. This new dollar had a value of 10 billion old dollars, which meant that ten zeros were removed from the old dollar. For example, a 100 trillion-dollar note became a 10,000-dollar note, with ten zeros crossed out. This change was meant to make the currency more manageable and to fight inflation, but it did not solve the underlying economic problems.

In February 2009, a third redenomination that resulted in the 'fourth Zimbabwe dollar' removed twelve more zeros from the currency. As a result, it was worth 10 trillion trillion original dollars because the combined effect of the three redenominations decreased the value of a dollar by $10^3$ x $10^{10}$ x $10^{12}$ = $10^{25}$. Bearer's checks had to be used instead of regular currency because computers couldn't handle the number of zeros. Banks were required to enter a lower amount on the deposit or withdrawal slip and then write a statement like 'multiply by 1,000,000 or add 10 zeros to your amount to get the real value'. The same applied to companies as well as all traders. In order to settle debts owed to the IMF, the Reserve Bank printed a bill worth 21 trillion Zimbabwean dollars.

Zimbabwe stopped printing its own currency in April 2009 after hyperinflation made it worthless. Instead, it adopted a multicurrency system, which allowed people to use different foreign currencies, such as the US dollar, the South African rand, the Botswana pula and the euro, as legal tender in the country. This solved the problem of low confidence in the Zimbabwean dollar and stabilized the economy. However, the US dollar became the most popular currency, as it was more stable and widely accepted.

The multicurrency system lasted until June 2019, when Zimbabwe reintroduced its local currency, the Zimbabwe dollar (ZWL), under the leadership of Mthuli Ncube, the country's new finance minister. The government hoped that this would ease the cash shortages and stimulate the economy. However, the new currency quickly lost value and triggered a surge in inflation. Inflation was anticipated to reach 500 per cent in 2019.[1] Zimbabwe's annual inflation rate in February 2020 was 540 per cent. In March 2020, the annual inflation rate had reached 676 per cent; the COVID-19 pandemic and the effects of the drought in

2019 had left the economy in a precarious state. Another period of high inflation struck the nation in 2022, rising to 131.7 per cent in May from 96.4 per cent in April.

Many Zimbabweans still prefer to use the US dollar or other foreign currencies, such as the South African rand or the Botswana pula, as they are more stable and widely accepted. The government has tried to control the exchange rate and the money supply, but the currency crisis persists.

Zimbabwe's hyperinflation devastated its economy and society. Political unrest, corruption and poor economic management were the root causes of it, and the government's tardy and ineffective response made it worse. All of this made the public doubt the government's competence and reliability in handling economic and monetary issues. Zimbabwe's hyperinflation serves as a warning not only for other vulnerable nations but also for our current financial systems, which are run by those who are greedy and fearful about losing their wealth and value.

The story of the legacy of inflation would be incomplete without the episode of massive inflation in Argentina. Argentina went from being the world's sixth richest country in the 1880s to an inflation-ridden basket case in the 1980s as a result of financial folly.

Argentina was once synonymous with prosperity. The country's very name means 'land of silver'. The Rio de la Plata, or Silver River, is the river on the banks of which the capital, Buenos Aires, is built. The name refers not to the river's colour, which is muddy brown, but to the silver deposits thought to lie upstream. Argentina was one of the world's ten richest countries in 1913 and its average income per person was higher than most of the English-speaking countries, such as the United States, Canada, Australia, New Zealand and Britain.

Argentina's economy grew faster than that of the United States and Germany between 1870 and 1913. Almost as much foreign capital was invested there as in Canada. It is no coincidence that there were once two Harrods stores in the world: one in London's Knightsbridge and the other in Buenos Aires' Avenida Flórida. Argentina could legitimately aspire to be the United Kingdom of the southern hemisphere, if not the United States.

When newly elected President General Juan Domingo Perón visited the central bank in Buenos Aires in February 1946, he was astounded by what he saw. 'There's so much gold,' he exclaimed, 'you can't even walk through the corridors.'

The history of Argentina's economy in the twentieth century shows that bad financial management has the power to destroy all of the world's resources. Particularly after the Second World War, the country consistently underperformed its neighbours and most of the world's other nations. It performed so poorly in the 1960s and 1970s, for example, that its per capita GDP in 1988 was the same as it had been in 1959. By 1998, it had fallen to 34 per cent of the US level, down from 72 per cent in 1913. Singapore, Japan, Taiwan and South Korea had all surpassed it, not to mention Chile, the neighbouring country, which was particularly painful to watch.

What went wrong?

The inflation rate, which peaked in 1989 at an annual rate of 5000 per cent, was in double digits until 1974. It was also in triple (or quadruple) digits between 1975 and 1990. Another answer to the question above is Argentina's default on debt. In 1982, 1989, 2002 and 2004, Argentina let down its international creditors.

However, these answers are not sufficient. Between 1870 and 1914, Argentina experienced double-digit inflation for at least eight years. In the same time frame, it defaulted on its debts at least twice. To comprehend Argentina's economic decline, it is essential to once more recognize that inflation is both a political and a monetary phenomenon.

An elite group of landowners tried to build Argentina's economy on exports of agricultural goods to the English-speaking world, which had failed miserably during the Great Depression. Large-scale immigration without making agricultural land available for settlement (as in North America) led to a large urban working class that was vulnerable to populist movements.

Argentina's political and economic turmoil began with the coup that brought General José F. Uriburu to power in 1930, ending the democratic rule of the Radical Civic Union (UCR). Italian fascism served as an inspiration for Uriburu and his successors, as they imposed a conservative and authoritarian regime that suppressed the opposition, rigged the elections and increased the national debt.

The UCR, along with other progressive and socialist parties, formed the Concordance, an alliance that demanded free and fair elections, civil liberties and social reforms. They also supported the workers' movements and strikes, which grew in the 1930s.

General Juan Domingo Perón emerged as the leader of the pro-fascist army officers who staged a coup in 1943. He gained the support of the workers, the unions and his wife, Eva Perón, and was elected president in 1946.

He seemed to offer something for everyone: higher wages better working conditions for workers and protective tariffs for industrialists.

Perón established a populist and nationalist regime, known as Peronism, that increased state intervention in the economy, social welfare and workers' rights. He also pursued an independent foreign policy, distancing himself from the United States and Britain and aligning himself with the Third World.

General Eduardo Lonardi, who proclaimed a "liberating revolution," led a military coup that ousted Perón in 1955. General Pedro Aramburu, who outlawed Peronism and changed many of Perón's policies, soon took over for Lonardi. A succession of civilian and military governments ruled Argentina between 1955 and 1966, trying to balance the interests of the agricultural and industrial sectors by devaluing the peso and enacting liberal economic reforms. However, these measures failed to stabilize the economy and resulted in high inflation, unemployment and social unrest.

In 1966, another military coup took place, headed by General Juan Carlos Onganía, who established an authoritarian regime known as the Argentine Revolution. Onganía promised to modernize the country and eliminate the political parties, but instead, he intensified the repression, the censorship and the wage freeze. He also devalued the peso again and increased the foreign debt, which worsened inflation and the economic crisis.

Perôn's return to power in 1973 was a disaster because it coincided with a worldwide price spike. Annual inflation had reached 444 per cent. Another military coup erupted in Argentina on 24 March 1976, sending thousands to arbitrary detention and 'disappearance'. General Jorge

Rafael Videla, Admiral Emilio Eduardo Massera and Brigadier Orlando Ramón Agosti formed a junta that was in charge of the coup. It initiated a period of state terrorism and human rights violations known as the Dirty War, which lasted until 1983.

In economic terms, the junta did nothing but make Argentina's external debt grow quickly. By 1984, it was more than 60 per cent of GDP, which was still lower than the early 1900s, when Argentina's external debt was over 120 per cent of its GDP. The ratio of external debt to GDP is a measure of how much a country owes to foreign creditors relative to its economic output. A higher ratio means a higher debt burden and a lower ability to repay. Argentina owed more than half of its annual income to foreign lenders when its external debt reached more than 60 per cent of GDP in 1984.

As is often the case with inflationary crises, war played a role, both inside Argentina against people who were thought to be subversives and outside against Britain over the Falkland Islands. But it would be wrong to see this as another case of a defeated government using inflation to pay off its debts. Argentina's inflation was out of control because of a combination of social forces, such as oligarchs, political leaders, military commanders, producer interest groups, trade unions and impoverished people.

Simply put, there was no significant group interested in price stability. Capitalists liked deficits and devaluation, and labourers became accustomed to a wage-price curve. Because of the gradual shift from paying for government deficits at home to paying for them abroad, bond holding had to be done elsewhere. With this in mind, it is easy to see why various attempts to stabilize the Argentine peso failed.

In 1985, Bernardo Grinspun, who was Argentina's minister of economy at the time and worked for President Raul Alfonsin, tried to reschedule debt and use Keynesian demand management. Grinspun resigned in September 1985 because he couldn't work out a new plan for Argentina's foreign debt or an economic policy on which he and the president could mutually agree. He didn't agree with the government's decision to put austerity measures in place to deal with the country's debt crisis.

The new minister of economy under President Raul Alfonsin, Juan Sourrouille, tried the Austral Plan in Argentina the same year. The Austral Plan was a broad economic stabilization plan that was made to fight hyperinflation and bring economic stability back to Argentina. The plan called for a new currency, the Austral, that was pegged to the US dollar. It also called for wage and price controls, limits on spending and taxes and a new way to pay off debt.

Even though the Austral Plan initially helped stabilize the economy and lower inflation, it ran into big problems due to shocks from the outside and political opposition from within. In the end, the plan didn't keep the economy stable, and hyperinflation returned to Argentina in the late 1980s.

Argentina experienced one of the hottest summers on record in February 1989. The hot summer increased the demand for electricity, which the state-owned utility company could not supply due to a lack of investment and maintenance. The power outages affected the production and distribution of goods and services, as well as the quality of life of the population.

The government's attempt to control the exchange rate by closing the banks and the foreign exchange houses was ineffective, as the black market and the speculation continued to devalue the austral. In just one month, the austral fell by 140 per cent against the US dollar. The loss of purchasing power and the shortage of basic products triggered riots and looting in several cities, especially in Rosario and Buenos Aires.

At the same time, the World Bank stopped lending money to Argentina because the government hadn't done anything to fix the country's huge public sector deficit. Lenders in the private sector were also less enthusiastic. Investors were unlikely to buy bonds with the threat of inflation wiping out the real value of their investments in a matter of days. Bond prices fell as fears grew that the central bank's reserves were running low. The desperate government had only one option: the printing press. But even that ultimately failed. Argentina literally ran out of money on Friday, 28 April 1989.

'It's a physical issue,' Central Bank Vice President Roberto Eilbaum said at a press conference. The mint was literally out of paper and printers were on strike. 'I'm not sure how we're going to do it, but the money has to be there on Monday,' he admitted.

By June, when the monthly inflation rate was over 100 per cent, the public's anger had peaked. When the manager of a Buenos Aires supermarket announced over the loudspeaker that all prices would immediately be going up by 30 per cent, customers turned over shopping carts full of goods. Crowds ran amok in Argentina's second-largest city, Rosario, for two days in June, resulting in rioting and looting that killed at least fourteen people as was the case in the Weimar Republic.

The Weimar Republic was the democratic government of Germany from 1919 to 1933. It faced many economic and political challenges, especially after the First World War and the Treaty of Versailles, which imposed harsh reparations on Germany. One of the most severe crises was the hyperinflation that occurred in 1922 and 1923,[2] when the German currency, the mark, lost almost all of its value. Numerous factors contributed to this, including the printing of money to pay off war debts, France and Belgium's occupation of the Ruhr region and speculation on the foreign exchange market. People lost their savings and pensions, wages and prices rose constantly, goods became scarce and expensive and social unrest and violence erupted. The social and economic chaos caused by the rapid rise in prices and loss of purchasing power sparked violent protests, strikes and clashes between various groups, including workers, communists, nationalists and Jews.

However, the main victims of Argentina's hyperinflation were not regular workers, who had a better chance of getting pay raises to match rising prices. Instead, it was people who earned fixed incomes such as civil servants, academics and retirees, who lived off the interest on their savings.

Similar to Germany in the 1920s, those who had a lot of debt wiped out by inflation were the ones who benefited the most. The government was among those who benefited because the money it owed was denominated in austral.

However, not all of Argentina's debts could be easily written off. In 1983, the country's foreign debt, denominated in US dollars, stood at $46 billion, or roughly 40 per cent of national output. Whatever happened to the Argentine peso, this dollar-denominated debt remained constant. Indeed, it grew as desperate governments borrowed even more money. By 1989, the country's foreign debt had risen to more than $65 billion. It would continue to grow over the next decade, eventually reaching $155 billion.

Inflation had already defrauded domestic creditors. However, only default could relieve Argentina's foreign debt burden. You have already seen that the Argentine government defaulted on its foreign debt in 1890. This debt default brought Baring Brothers to the verge of bankruptcy due to its investments in Argentine securities, notably a failed issue of bonds for the Buenos Aires Water Supply and Drainage Company.

By the end of the twentieth century, the IMF had to undertake the thankless job of trying to stop an Argentine default or at least lessen the damage it would cause. Once again, the remedy was a currency board, this time pegging the peso to the dollar. When Argentina's Finance Minister Domingo Cavallo introduced the new peso convertible in 1991, it was the country's sixth currency in a century. But this solution also didn't work.

Inflation had been reduced to zero by 1996, and it had even turned negative in 1999. However, unemployment was at 15 per cent, and income inequality was only marginally better than in Nigeria. Also, fiscal tightening was not done at the same time as monetary tightening. The public debt went from 35 per cent of GDP at the end of 1994 to 64 per cent at the end of 2001, as both the central government and provincial governments borrowed money on the international bond market instead of balancing their budgets.

In short, even though Cavallo pegged the currency to the US dollar and cut inflation, he did not change the social and institutional factors that had led to so many financial crises in the past. The stage was set for Argentina to default again and for the implementation of a new currency. The IMF did not offer a third bailout after giving $15 billion and $8 billion in January and May 2001, respectively. On 23 December 2001, at the end of a year in which GDP per person had dropped by a painful 12 per cent, the government announced a moratorium on all its foreign debt, including bonds worth $81 billion. This was the biggest debt default in history.

'Inflation is always and everywhere a monetary phenomenon, in the sense that it is and can be produced only by a more rapid increase in the quantity of money than in output,' is how American economist Milton Friedman,[3] who won the Nobel Prize, defined inflation. But he was slightly wrong. In most cases, inflation is a political phenomenon as well.

What happened during and after World War I in all the countries that fought the war demonstrates this quite well. Not only did the war make it hard to get goods, but it also forced governments to borrow money from the central bank on a short-term basis. This turned debt into cash. This increased the supply of money, which altered people's perceptions of how inflation would work by lowering the demand for cash and raising the price of goods.

Even today, we see the government as our saviour from day-to-day problems, offering us a stress-free life. We expect freebies, price control, subsidies, tax cuts, jobs and more from our government. The uncertain nature of our economy and markets makes us believe that government intervention will alleviate our present financial troubles and future economic problems. Subconsciously, we wish for our government to be our messiah.

Justifications for government interventions are aplenty. They may range from preventing corporations from making unreasonable profits and ensuring stable and affordable prices for consumers to ensuring producers get a 'fair' value for their products. We also want our government to protect our jobs and ensure high wages by preventing the exploitation of workers and guaranteeing welfare and social security for all.

We often forget that no messiah has ever really saved us from our struggles, and neither has our government. The vote bank matters for a democratic government, like military power matters for a totalitarian regime. So, the former always stands with the people, and the people believe that the government's intervention in their lives and economies is a democratic intervention.

But history shows that this isn't true. Every time a government stepped in to 'manage' the economy or markets, it was eventually forced to reverse the economic policies or fiscal measures it had put in place.

Suppose you try to treat a person with a fever by adjusting the temperature on the thermometer instead of giving them medicine or taking other steps. What would be the result? The fever remains despite the manipulation of the thermometer reading. On top of that, the person will not be able to determine the root cause of the fever, and neither will you. The case is the same when the government interferes with the economy or markets.

The recent Sri Lankan economic crisis is an example.

Following the end of the Sri Lankan civil war in 2009, the then president Mahinda Rajapaksa took out massive foreign loans to pay for war expenses and, more importantly, to begin flashy infrastructure projects to attract tourists and reward loyalists. Since the government didn't have enough foreign reserves, it had to borrow from other countries, like China, to pay its debts. Instead of focusing on economic reforms that could add financial reserves, Mahinda Rajapaksa and his younger brothers, President Gotabaya Rajapaksa and Basil Rajapaksa, then finance minister, cut taxes to boost political support.

Both the COVID-19 pandemic and the Easter bombings in 2019 harmed Sri Lanka's main source of foreign income, tourism. To make matters worse, Mahinda Rajapaksa's brother, President Gotabaya Rajapaksa, decided to ban chemical fertilizers in 2021 to make Sri Lankan farming 'all organic'. This seriously hurt Sri Lanka's main export crop, tea. The fertilizer ban (subsequently lifted) and global grain shortages caused by Ukraine's civil war, exacerbated the country's food insecurity. Gotabaya Rajapaksa's economic strategy proved to be a series of blunders that led to the demise of a once vibrant and economically promising South Asian nation.

Gotabaya was elected in 2019, and under the banner of populism and Sinhalese nationalism, his party, the Sri Lanka People's Front (SLPP), was able to keep its supermajority in parliament in 2020. By getting the 20th amendment to the Constitution passed, Gotabaya was able to give the executive president more power than ever before. Nepotism, corruption, the appointment of retired military officers to almost every level of government and serious allegations of human rights violations during the civil war all increased under his dictatorial tendencies. Poor governance and mismanagement of Sri Lanka's economy, particularly during the pandemic, by him and his family—including his brothers, former prime minister Mahinda Rajapaksa and former finance minister Basil Rajapaksa—ultimately led to the economic crisis in 2021.

President Gotabaya Rajapaksa left his country after months of mass protests over the economic crisis. This led to the government declaring a state of emergency. After protesters stormed his office, Prime Minister Ranil Wickremesinghe directed the country's military to do 'whatever is necessary' to restore order. However, the military intervention faced resistance from some of the protesters, who accused the government of using excessive force and violating human rights. The situation in the country remained tense and uncertain as the parliament awaited the official resignation of Rajapaksa and the election of a new president. Meanwhile, the international community expressed concern and urged for a peaceful and democratic transition of power.

If you think that government interventions bring trouble only to countries that face political instability and civil unrest, you are mistaken. Government interventions can also have negative consequences in the financial sector, especially when they distort market incentives and create moral hazards. For example, when the government bails out failing banks, it may encourage them to take excessive risks in the future, knowing that they will be rescued again. This can lead to more instability and inefficiency in the banking system.

Earlier we described how the Bank of England helped Overend, Gurney & Company, the biggest discount house in England at the time, when it failed in 1866. In 1890, the Bank of England saved Barings Bank from collapse. In 2008, the US government set up a $700 billion Troubled Asset Relief Program (TARP) after Lehman Brothers faced bankruptcy, leading to an international financial crisis.

The Silicon Valley Bank (SVB) in the US collapsed on 10 March 2023, while we were finishing this book. It was not a small bank; it was the country's sixteenth-largest bank, with $210 billion in assets. It was the second-largest bank failure in US history. The bank failed due to a combination of factors, including poor risk management and a bank run by investors from the tech industry.

Before we can understand what went wrong at SVB, we must first understand how banks work. A bank, in essence, accepts deposits from its customers. The deposits are then used to make loans to other customers, with the remainder invested elsewhere. This is done under the assumption that all depositors will not arrive at the bank's door at the same time to withdraw their funds.

SVB, like other banks, had invested its funds in safe instruments such as bonds. Interest rates in the US were extremely low following the 2008 recession. This resulted in lower-cost loans, and venture capitalists continued to pour money into start-ups. As a result, banks like SVB benefited because these start-ups trusted them with their deposits.

However, the US Federal Reserve began raising interest rates in 2023. The federal funds rate was raised from 0.25-0.50 per cent in March 2022 to 4.5-4.75 per cent in 2023. Interest rates could be raised to 5.75 per cent, according to Federal Reserve Chair Jerome Powell.

Bond returns were reduced as a result. It would not have been a big deal if the bank had waited for the bonds to mature, but higher interest rates have also slowed start-up funding. This slowed the deposit rate at SVB. On 8 March 2023, the bank announced that it had sold $21 billion in securities at a $1.8 billion loss to ensure liquidity. It also intended to sell $2.2 billion in stock.

Moody's lowered the bank's credit rating. On the same day, Peter Thiel's Founders Fund requested that its portfolio companies withdraw their funds from SVB. Several venture capital firms followed, including Union Square Ventures and Coatue Management.

SVB was unable to meet such a high withdrawal demand on such short notice. Customers attempted to withdraw $42 billion from the bank on Thursday, 9 March. This amounted to one-quarter of the bank's total deposits. The trading of the bank's stock was halted on Friday, and the bank attempted to sell itself. Regulators intervened and shut down the bank.

The Biden administration said on Sunday, 13 March 2023, that SVB's decision would not cost taxpayers any money.

Why does the government show up as a lender of last resort when banks fail? The answer is simple. When a bank fails, depositors or citizens of a country lose money. When citizens lose money, it can create civil unrest, mass protests and chaos. A democratic government doesn't like that because to win the next election, they need votes. For votes, they need to appease the masses. This motive led to the creation of measures such as the European Stability Mechanism (ESM), deposit insurance and TARP.

Where does the government get the money to support these measures? This question is as simple as asking: Where does a self-proclaimed messiah who lives on the donations of his followers get money? The answer is also as simple as the question: from his followers!

The case is the same with the government. The government gets money from citizens either through borrowing or taxes. The government can also print more money if needed. So, when a bank or a financial organization fails, the depositors lose money. Citizens are the losers in the first place. Then the government steps in and rescues the bank with the citizens' money, making them losers in the second place. If the government prints more money, it can lead to inflation in the long term. Inflation takes away people's purchasing power. It is akin to gradual robbery from the pockets of the citizens. Again, citizens are the losers in the third place.

In short, if a bank fails once, citizens lose thrice!

This phenomenon happens all over the world in economies with centralized yet regulated banking systems and democratic governments.

Now, let's look at another example to make the issue clearer.

Kerala, the state with the highest literacy rate in India, wakes up seeing the name 'Milma'. This is an abbreviation for the Kerala Co-operative Milk Marketing Federation, which delivers packaged milk to a larger number of the state's households. Besides their unique intellectual capacity, Keralites are known for their love of tea, coffee (and alcohol). So, milk is an indispensable item in every home in Kerala.

In November 2022, the Cabinet approved raising the price of Milma milk by Rs 6 per litre. The price of Milma's other milk products would also go up in tandem with the increase in milk prices. A two-member committee that had been formed to assess a price hike recommended that the price of milk be raised by Rs 8.57 rupees per litre. But, fearing that implementing a sharp increase all at once would enrage the public, the Cabinet limited the price increase to Rs 6 per litre. Individual milk suppliers in Kerala set their prices based on Milma's price revision.

The price hike of Milma milk and other milk products was the result of years of protests by dairy farmers. A democratic political system is based on appeasing the masses. The Kerala government wanted to appease the majority of Milma customers. So, it did not let dairy farmers (a minority) charge a price that covered their production costs, and that too for years. As a result, dairy farmers were forced to reduce quality to cut costs or exit the market entirely. These government measures hurt not only poor farmers but also the lowest-paid employees in the dairy sector, increasing the loss of potential jobs in the sector.

Though milk prices have now been raised on the grounds that dairy farmers are losing even their operating costs, it is claimed that the benefits of this hike are not reaching the farmers. Since the price of cattle feed and other inputs has nearly doubled, dairy farmers want the government to give them benefits directly.

In response to dairy farmers' demands, J. Chinchu Rani, Kerala's minister of animal husbandry, stated that for every rupee increase in the milk price, the farmer would receive 88 paise. She also said that the government would provide subsidies and incentives to the dairy sector to help them cope with the rising costs of production. However, some dairy farmers and cooperatives have expressed dissatisfaction with the minister's statement, saying that the hike is insufficient and the benefits are delayed. They have also accused the government of favouring Milma over the private players. The milk price hike has sparked a debate over the role of the government and the market in the dairy industry and its impact on consumers and producers.

Let's now look at yet another detrimental measure the government has taken to try and control prices, this time in

Mumbai, India's financial hub. The price control measure was known as the Rent Control Act, formally known as the Hotel and Lodging House Rates Control Act of 1947, and it was in effect until 1999 only for Mumbai and some other parts of Maharashtra, not for the whole country. It declared that the rents of residential and commercial premises that existed before 1947 were to remain fixed at the level they were at the time of Indian independence. This means that the landlords could not increase the rents beyond what they were charging in 1947, regardless of inflation, demand or property value. As of 2010, 17 per cent of dwelling units in Mumbai were under rent control, meaning that they were subject to the provisions of the Act.[4]

A person with common sense can see that with time and rising costs all around, low rents frequently fail to cover even the most basic upkeep of a building. The Act resulted in little to no building maintenance, pushing tenants into deplorable living conditions. Some owners lost interest and the capacity to maintain their buildings, which allowed them to crumble. The collapse of buildings not only costs money; it also costs the lives of innocent people.

In 2019, the Indian government enacted the Model Tenancy Act. The Ministry of Housing and Urban Affairs drafted this proposed law. Its goal was to regulate India's rental housing market and balance the interests of landlords and tenants by establishing a uniform set of rules for renting properties across the country.

Since the day the Indian government proposed this Act, Mumbai has seen a surge in protests. Around 6 lakh tenants living in old, dilapidated buildings and chawls (multi-dwelling buildings) have been fighting any amendments to the existing Rent Control Act.

Regional political parties joined forces. They stated that if the Model Tenant Act were to be passed, all existing Rent Control Acts would be deemed repealed; in other words, if the law is passed, more than 2.5 million people would become homeless. The state is free to reject or only partially implement the Act, and it is reluctant to take any action for fear of losing votes in the next election.

Assar Lindbeck, a prominent Swedish professor of economics at Stockholm University, once joked, 'In many cases, rent control appears to be the most efficient technique presently known to destroy a city—except for bombing.'[5]

As you have seen in the case of Sri Lanka, price control creates shortages of goods and services. It also has several other harmful effects. Artificially reducing prices increases demand for goods and services. It can disincentivize suppliers and reduce supply. Small suppliers cannot survive in a situation where the cost of production constantly rises. Price control creates protectionism and trade barriers, which eliminate incentives for new suppliers to enter the market.

'Price controls almost invariably produce black markets, where prices are not only higher than the legally permitted prices but also higher than they would be in a free-market since the legal risks must also be compensated. While small-scale black markets may function in secrecy, large-scale black markets usually require bribes to officials to look the other way,' said Thomas Sowell, an author, economist and one of the most influential black conservatives of our times.[6]

Hoarding is caused by uncertainty about the ability to find goods, particularly non-perishable goods, in the future. Then, buyers and sellers mutually agree to transact goods at prices higher than the legally permitted price, giving rise to the black market. Corruption and bribery follow.

A democratic government is an ineffective entity that survives on taxes and borrowing, both domestic and foreign. Have you ever thought about the source of funds for the government to deliver freebies or subsidies to its citizens? The source is the citizens who believe their government is a messiah. Freebies and subsidies do more harm than good. Freebies are a tool to appease the masses, which turns voters unproductive, just like the government.

Another tool for favouritism is subsidies for industries such as agriculture. In most cases, they create a lower price and less demand for the produce on the market. All these mass appeasement measures ultimately lead to increased taxation, borrowing or printing more money, a sure-shot way to higher inflation.

There is another popular 'welfare' measure by a democratic government known as the minimum wage. This is a government intervention in the labour market that is intended to address market failures that may result in low wages and poor working conditions, particularly for workers in low-skill jobs or industries with high levels of competition.

Does this economic policy benefit workers? No. Does it go down well with employers? Never.

We will show you how the vicious cycle of the minimum wage works. When the government sets the minimum wage, it increases the operating costs of businesses. Businesses pass on the increased cost to consumers, which can lead to higher prices for products and services. This creates higher inflation rates and lower purchasing power for consumers, particularly those with lower incomes.

Some employers may cut employees' working hours to compensate for the higher wages. This can result in lower income for workers.

In some cases, the minimum wage results in lower employment rates. Employers find it hard to afford to hire the required number of workers, or they may resort to substituting automation or other technology for workers. This is especially true for small businesses or those operating in low-profit industries. The higher the government raises the minimum wage, the higher the unemployment rate.

Higher minimum wage rates make it harder for employers, especially those with less skilled workers, to invest in their training and growth. This can make it harder for workers to learn new skills and move up the career ladder.

When there is a minimum wage, businesses may find it more difficult to adjust their workforce to adapt to changing market conditions. It is disheartening to see that small businesses are more likely to struggle to afford higher wages than larger firms with greater capacity to deal with increased wages.

On top of everything else, the minimum wage discourages young people with an entrepreneurial spirit from starting new businesses. This hinders job creation and wealth generation in a country.

The same negative impact is associated with a government-set 'floor price'. The floor price is the lowest price that can be charged for a good or service. Floor prices are often used in situations where there is concern about prices falling too low, such as in the case of commodities or agricultural products, where farmers or producers may be at risk of not being able to sell their goods at a profit. This price, which is set to provide a safety net for producers and ensure a stable supply of goods and services in the market, usually has disastrous effects. It reduces competition, distorts market signals and leads to inefficiencies in resource allocation.

The interference of a centralized agency like the government in its markets and economy fails most of the time. The government's plans for wealth creation result in wealth deterioration. The government's policies to create jobs ultimately create more jobless people. Milton Friedman once observed that the government's solution to a problem is usually as bad as the problem itself.

Why do government interventions fail miserably?

First, is a lack of in-depth knowledge. Most governments across the world don't have effective tools to understand the real issues of their citizens. Even if they do, they lack an efficient, skilled and unbiased workforce to put those tools to use. Only the citizens are intimately familiar with their problems, not the governments.

Politicians and bureaucrats need incentives to work effectively for the public good. Incentives can be rewards or punishments that depend on their performance and outcomes. For example, incentives can be higher salaries, promotions, recognition, sanctions, fines or dismissal. However, many politicians and bureaucrats lack such incentives, and they may act irresponsibly or inefficiently when implementing projects or policies. They may also face political pressure from interest groups that have different agendas or preferences than the general public. These interest groups can influence or manipulate politicians and bureaucrats through lobbying, donations, threats or violence. Moreover, politicians and bureaucrats may use force or coercion to impose their decisions or policies on the citizens, rather than seeking their consent or cooperation. This can lead to mass protests and civil unrest as citizens resist or oppose the actions of the government.

The issue our world faces today is not economics, politics, democracy or capitalism; it is the confluence of politics and economics. When these two independent productive forces overlap or converge, both lose their goodness and exert a dark power that ruins democracy, economic growth and human development.

You have already seen that the intertwining of politics and economics creates a greater risk of corruption. Politicians and bureaucrats may use their power to benefit themselves or their allies rather than the public. When politicians put short-term political gains ahead of long-term economic benefits, they make decisions that aren't as good as they could be.

Cronyism flourishes when politicians and bureaucrats get a chance to get their hands on various business interests. Some businesses may be given preferential treatment and government contracts in a crony capitalist setting, regardless of their qualifications or performance.

The politics-economics duo creates a lack of transparency and accountability. It may be difficult for the public to understand how economic policies are being implemented and who is benefiting from them. The joining of politics and economics creates fertile ground for politicians to manipulate economic policies to promote their own ideological beliefs, even if those policies are not based on sound economic principles or evidence.

However, there is no need to lose hope or be pessimistic. Surprisingly, politics and economics can work independently. In other words, markets and economies can operate freely and transparently without government intervention. The following chapters will illustrate how.

# 5

# Capitalism is Good

'Capitalism was the only system in history where wealth
was not acquired by looting, but by production, not by
force, but by trade, the only system that stood for man's
right to his own mind, to his work, to his life, to his
happiness, to himself.'

—Ayn Rand[1]

Capitalists and corporations have had a dreaded image for
generations. You have no doubt watched movies in which
the villains were greedy and ruthless corporate heads, who
were ultimately defeated by a socialist hero who destroyed
them and distributed their wealth to the impoverished people
who had been exploited by them. The tale of Robin Hood
is an excellent example of how capitalists, corporations
and the rich have been embedded in popular imaginations
for more than a century. Shakespeare's Antonio, one of the
central characters of his play *The Merchant of Venice*, also

thought the same. He believed every lender was just a leech that drained the lifeblood of poor debtors.

Loan sharks may act as Antonio believed, but banks have changed since the time of the Medici to make it easier for money to move from point A, where it is, to point B, where it is needed.

Nonetheless, people continue to think like the sixteenth-century Shakespearean character, largely due to their lack of financial education. Our thoughts and belief systems haven't been freed from colonialism, slavery, wars, imperialism, royal chartered companies and monopolies. You have already read about some of these barbaric trading and economic practices of the past.

When we mention capitalism in this book, we are not talking about state capitalism, crony capitalism or social market capitalism. We are talking about free-market capitalism. Colonialism, slavery, war, imperialism, royal chartered companies and monopolies are all products of mercantilism and statism, not capitalism.

Mercantilism is an economic theory and practice that was common in Europe from the sixteenth to the eighteenth centuries. It aimed to increase the wealth and power of a nation by regulating its trade and production. It favoured exporting more than importing, accumulating gold and silver, using colonies for resources and markets, and supporting domestic industries and populations.

Mercantilism is not taken seriously as an economic theory because it is based on a poor understanding of economics and doesn't take into account the benefits of free trade and comparative advantage.

Statism is a political philosophy or ideology that stresses the role of the state or government as the main authority and decision-maker in leading and controlling society and the economy. Statism has two major forms. First, there are socialist or communist systems where the state owns and controls the means of production and distribution. Second, there are moderate or mixed economies, in which the government regulates and influences economic activity through policies such as taxation, subsidies and social welfare programmes. As you have seen, excessive government intervention can stifle individual freedom and initiative, create inefficiencies and bureaucracy and lead to corruption and abuse of power.

While socialism and statism are not synonymous, they frequently overlap. We can also say that socialism is a milder form of statism because both involve the state playing a significant role in shaping economic and social policies. Socialism and fascism are at the extremes of the statist spectrum.

Capitalism is fundamentally based on private ownership of the means of production and the pursuit of profit. In a capitalist economy, businesses compete with one another to meet consumer demand for goods and services, and the market determines prices.

Capitalism with a focus on free-markets, private property rights and individual freedom is called 'free-market capitalism'. The government's role is limited in this type of capitalism, and the market is left to regulate itself through the forces of supply and demand.

Do corporations and their greed determine the prices in a free-market economy? No, never. This is a myth that has been mostly propagated by socialists and communists. The price in a free-market economy is set by the voluntary forces of demand and supply.

There is another popular myth: the rich get richer, and the poor get poorer. Is this possible in a free-market economy?

When the poor get poorer, the demand for the products or services of corporations or the rich goes down because the poor, as a majority, don't have the money to purchase them. As a result, the rich have to bring down the price of their products or services so the poor can afford to buy them.

To make this point clearer, let us take a look at historical estimates of poverty. According to these estimates, the vast majority of the world's population lived in extreme poverty in the early 1800s. Extreme poverty is defined as earning less than $1.90 per day (adjusted for inflation). However, poverty rates began to fall during the nineteenth and twentieth centuries. One widely cited estimate by economist Max Roser states that the global poverty rate fell from around 85 per cent in 1800 to 9.6 per cent in 2015.[2]

The expansion of capitalist economies, technological advancements and public policies aimed at reducing poverty are just a few of the factors that contributed to this drop in extreme poverty.

A capitalist system aims to provide everyone with enough money and an improved standard of living. Enough liquidity in everyone's purse creates demand, and this increased demand is a profit-making opportunity for entrepreneurs. This scenario, combined with healthy competition, creates better, more affordable prices for the masses.

Price is the amount of money that people pay or receive for goods and services in an economy. Price shows how much people want or need something, and how much of it is available. Price also helps people make decisions about what to buy or sell, and how to use their resources. Price is like a message that travels from buyers to sellers, and from sellers to buyers. In some cases, prices compel consumers to reduce their use of a product, resource or service. Producers and suppliers increase or reduce the supply of a product in accordance with the price change. Higher prices also force consumers to find alternatives. Prices incentivize an individual to act in such a way that society as a whole maximizes the benefits from scarce resources.

Adam Smith, in his book *The Wealth of Nations*, introduced the concept of the 'invisible hand'. The term refers to how the market mechanism, driven by self-interest and competition—in other words, demand and supply—can lead to efficient resource allocation and economic growth without the need for central planning or intervention.

The invisible hand refers to how the market determines prices, allocates resources and produces goods and services valued by consumers through the interactions of buyers and sellers. The market functions as an invisible hand, directing resources to their most productive uses, resulting in increased efficiency and economic growth.

The invisible hand is strong enough to crush deadweight loss in an economy. Deadweight loss in economics refers to the decline in economic efficiency as a result of inefficient resource allocation in a market. It specifically refers to the loss of consumer and producer surplus that occurs when a market is not operating at equilibrium.

The difference between the price consumers are willing to pay and the price they actually pay for a good or service is known as consumer surplus, whereas producer surplus is the difference between the price producers are willing to sell a good or service for and the price they actually receive.

For example, if a consumer is willing to pay Rs 10 for a product but can get it for Rs 8, their consumer surplus is Rs 2. If a producer is willing to sell a product for Rs 6 but is able to sell it for Rs 8, then their producer surplus is Rs 2.

On the other hand, the difference between what a consumer is willing to pay for a product and what they actually pay for it when the price is higher than their willingness to pay is called a consumer deficit, or deadweight loss. For example, if a consumer is willing to pay Rs 8 but can only get the product for Rs 10, then their consumer deficit is Rs 2.

The difference between the lowest price a producer is willing to accept and the actual price they receive for a product when the price is lower than their willingness to accept is called producer deficit or deadweight loss. For example, if a producer is willing to sell a product for Rs 10 but can only sell it for Rs 8, then their producer deficit is Rs 2.

A variety of factors, such as taxes, subsidies, price controls or market power, can cause deadweight loss. It is an important concept in economics because it helps calculate the costs of market distortions and inefficiencies.

Consumer surplus and producer surplus are important measures of economic welfare because they represent the benefits that consumers and producers receive from participating in a market. The total amount of consumer and producer surplus in a market is used as a benchmark for market efficiency. Higher levels of surplus indicate more efficient resource allocation.

The invisible hand concept has been central to the development of modern free-market economic theory and is frequently used to argue against government intervention in the economy. Individuals who pursue their own self-interest in the market will, according to Smith, unintentionally promote the well-being of society as a whole.

Imagine that there is no intervention by a centralized agency like our government in the current rise in fuel prices in India. Forget, for the moment, the fact that government intervention is playing a significant role in raising fuel prices. Ignore also the blame games between the government and the opposition over the rising fuel prices. Focus instead on the face-off between rising fuel prices and the people.

What will people do if petrol prices rise and there is no government intervention to artificially control them?

A large number of ordinary people and industries will reduce or optimize their use of non-renewable fuels like petrol. This will bring down the demand for petrol. A smaller number of people and industries will begin to use other alternatives for petrol. Those alternatives could be electric vehicles or solar panels. Optimized fuel usage and the shift from non-renewable to renewable fuel usage will further reduce the demand for non-renewable fuel.

This decreased demand for non-renewable fuel will make petrol suppliers drop the price to increase demand. On the other hand, the makers of electric vehicles and solar panels will increase their supply to tap the increasing demand for their products. The increased supply of renewable energy products will make them cheaper and more accessible to a larger number of people. Then, more people will start using renewable energy products in their daily lives. This is how the invisible hand of the market can free humans from our fossil fuel dependency.

Freedom is the politics of free-market capitalism. A free-market economy gives the freedom to set prices; freedom to buy, own, use and sell private property; freedom to choose one's work; freedom to be an investor; freedom to compete; freedom to make profits; freedom to raise capital and freedom to be an entrepreneur. Finally, it promotes a free, cooperative and peaceful process.

Contrary to what most people think, the main goal of corporations in a free-market economy is to make goods affordable for consumers. Market competition determines how much anyone can charge and still make a profit. On the other hand, price controls prevent the free-market from exploiting all mutually profitable trades.

Let's take a brief look at how transforming from a communist-socialist economy to a free-market economy helped China drastically develop its economy and increase its national income.

The Chinese Civil War, waged between the Nationalists (Kuomintang) and the Communists for control of China, ended on 1 October 1949 with the proclamation of the People's Republic of China (PRC) by the Chinese Communist Party (CCP). The CCP, under Mao Zedong's leadership, triumphed and created a new socialist state. Mao Zedong (also known as Mao Tse-tung) was also a political theorist and one of the founding members of the CCP.

Mao Zedong then became the country's first chairman, a position he held until his death in 1976. Mao is regarded as one of China's most influential figures, and his ideas and policies had a profound impact on the country and its people. He was a prolific writer and thinker whose ideas on guerrilla warfare, peasant mobilization and socialist revolution continue to influence leftist movements worldwide.

Mao's policies and leadership, on the other hand, caused significant human suffering and economic disruption, particularly during the Great Leap Forward and the Cultural Revolution.

The CCP launched the Great Leap Forward, a large-scale economic and social campaign, in 1958. The campaign's goal was to rapidly transform China from an agrarian to a modern industrial economy while also bolstering the country's international standing as a superpower. The Great Leap Forward brought about massive changes in China's agricultural and industrial sectors, including the collectivization of agriculture, the formation of rural communes and the construction of new factories and infrastructure.

Many of these changes, though, were badly planned and carried out, which led to widespread starvation, economic problems and social chaos. The Great Leap Forward was a disaster, with millions of people dying from starvation and disease between 1958 and 1962. A lot of social and political change happened because of the campaign, and many people criticized the government's policies and Mao's leadership. The Great Leap Forward was a key lesson in the importance of effective planning and management of economic development.

From 1966 to 1976, Mao Zedong embarked on another historical mission called the Cultural Revolution. The movement aimed to rid the country of what Mao perceived to be capitalist and traditional elements, as well as to strengthen his own political and ideological position.

During the Cultural Revolution, Mao mobilized young people known as the Red Guards to hunt down and attack anyone perceived to be opposed to his leadership or communist principles. Universities and schools were closed, and many intellectuals and artists were persecuted, imprisoned or killed. The movement was also responsible for the widespread destruction of cultural artefacts and sites, as well as social and economic upheaval. The Cultural Revolution had a profound impact on Chinese society and politics, resulting in social disorder and widespread suffering.

It also had a significant impact on the Chinese economy. Because of its policies and disruptions, the growth and development of the economy slowed down. The GDP growth rate fell from an average of around 6 per cent in the early 1960s to 2.7 per cent from 1966 to 1976. During this time, foreign investment and trade were severely limited.

The country's economic institutions were largely dismantled. The widespread social and political chaos disrupted industrial production and commerce. Many educated and skilled workers were persecuted or forced to work in the countryside, having a long-term impact on human capital development.

The Great Leap Forward and Cultural Revolution came to an end after Mao's death in 1976 and the arrest of the Gang of Four, a group of Mao's supporters who had been instrumental in carrying out the campaigns.

These two movements also helped Deng Xiaoping rise to power. Deng was a Chinese revolutionary leader, military commander and statesman. From December 1978 to November 1989, he was the most powerful person in the People's Republic of China.

Following Mao Zedong's death, Deng gradually ascended to power and guided China through a series of far-reaching market-economy reforms, earning him the title 'Architect of Modern China'. He helped China become the world's second-largest economy by nominal GDP in 2010.

By the late seventies, the incomes of ordinary Chinese were so low in comparison to incomes in other Asian economies that the Chinese state and communist regime's future would be in jeopardy unless something was done to raise living standards through economic growth. Realizing this, from the late 1970s through the 1980s, Deng Xiaoping initiated a series of economic reforms in China. These reforms were dubbed the 'Four Modernizations'. They sought to modernize and liberalize China's economy by increasing output and efficiency, attracting foreign investment and opening the country to the international market.

The Four Modernizations gave priority to four key areas: agriculture, industry, national defence and science and technology. Deng implemented several policies to achieve these objectives, including the creation of special economic zones (SEZs), the decentralization of economic decision-making and the implementation of market-oriented reforms.

SEZs were designated areas where foreign investment and trade were encouraged and investors were given special tax breaks and incentives. This contributed to the inflow of foreign capital and technology into China, thereby boosting the country's economic growth.

Decentralizing economic decision-making meant giving local governments and businesses more power to make economic decisions instead of letting the central government plan everything. This increased the economy's flexibility and responsiveness, as well as its efficiency and productivity.

Market-oriented reforms meant bringing elements of market competition into the economy, such as letting farmers sell their goods on the open market, encouraging small-scale private businesses and allowing foreign trade and investment. By making China's economy more dynamic and diverse, these reforms helped the country become an international economic powerhouse.

Overall, Deng's economic reforms transformed China from a centralized economy to a more market-oriented one, lifting millions out of poverty. The effect of these reforms continues to shape China's economy today. China became the first country to kiss capitalism behind the wall of communism-socialism and take a 'great leap forward' to become an invincible superpower.

China embarked on the journey of economic reforms much before India did. As a result, India remained far behind China in terms of economic development and growth. Because of its peculiar circumstances at the time of its independence, India chose a mixed economy model of economic development characterized by tight state control over key industries. However, faced with a severe balance of payment crisis, popularly known as the economic crisis of 1991, India initiated far-reaching economic reforms and liberalized its economy. Even though China is still far ahead, India is speedily catching up and has become the world's fifth-largest economy.

Mercantilism, statism and socialism are the remnants of the Middle Ages, while capitalism has more to offer modern people and societies. These relics from the past support tribal premises and collective rights, which are ideas or assumptions that are based on the cultural beliefs and practices of a tribe or indigenous community. A tribe or community can be a group of people who are rich, poor, citizens of a specific country or people who belong to a specific profession. We can call them Indians, Africans, socialists, communists, writers, fund managers, the proletariat or capitalists. These group classifications are imaginary, and these imaginary entities take our attention away from the entity that really exists: the individual.

Imaginary entities like societies, tribes, professions or even nations don't matter much in a modern society. What matters more are the individuals and their rights. An imaginary collective entity like a society or a nation doesn't have feelings or goals, but an individual who is a part of it does.

Capitalism is associated with individual rights and freedoms because it allows people to pursue their own interests while also achieving economic success. One of the most important ways that capitalism protects individual rights is through the idea of private property. Individuals have the right to own property in a capitalist economy, which means they can control how it is used and reap the benefits of its value. Individuals are able to make their own decisions about how to use their resources, which can lead to innovation, entrepreneurship and economic growth. Capitalism also encourages freedom of choice, which is an important aspect of individual rights and personal autonomy.

History and the previous chapters of this book have shown us that ideologies, theories and economies that gave importance to collective imaginary entities have failed. People must accept the idea of individual rights if they want to live in a peaceful, productive and logical society and deal with each other in a way that is beneficial for everyone. Without this idea, no moral or civilized society is possible.

The modern world rewards rational thinking and logical economic systems such as capitalism, which are based not on imaginary entities but on realistic representations such as facts, efficiency, balance sheets, graphs and figures. On top of everything else, capitalism gives importance to the 'life, liberty, and pursuit of happiness' of an individual.

# 6

# The Rise of Crypto Assets

'Bitcoin is a technological tour de force.'

—Bill Gates

It is now time to turn our attention to 2008. The year was a slow-motion nightmare for the financial world. You have already read about what went wrong in the chapter 'The Big Short'. But that historical event also acted as a catalyst for something innovative and disruptive that could change the course of the financial history of the world.

Bear Stearns, the first major Wall Street institution to succumb to its demons, did so in March 2008. It was dragged down by a slumping housing market after weathering every type of market for eighty-five years. JPMorgan Chase & Co. purchased it for $2 per share or about 1 per cent of the previous year's price of $170 per share. The Federal Reserve agreed to facilitate the purchase of $29 billion in distressed assets from Bear Stearns to help the deal move forward. A month after the buyout, John Mack and Lloyd Blankfein, the CEOs of Morgan Stanley and Goldman Sachs Group Inc., respectively, told shareholders that the housing market crisis would be brief and would soon be over.

Sub-prime loans—irresponsible lending to Americans who couldn't pay back their debts—were a major contributor to this crisis. Traditionally, when a bank made a loan, it was responsible for ensuring that the borrower repaid the funds. But once sub-prime loans were given to borrowers, they were put into complicated instruments called CDOs and CMOs. These financial instruments were then sold to other investors, who took on the risk and passed it on like a hot potato through the financial markets. The promise of high returns and low risk through diversification enticed buyers.

What many people, including Wall Street executives, did not realize was how complex and interconnected the risks posed by these complicated financial instruments were. The problem was made worse by the fact that CMOs and CDOs were supported by an old financial architecture that mixed analogue and digital systems. Because of the lack of seamless digital documentation, it was difficult, if not impossible, to quantify the risk and understand exactly what CMOs and CDOs were made of. Also, as these complicated financial instruments spread around the world, investors everywhere suddenly found themselves caught up in a web of American mortgages.

As a storm raged around Wall Street and executives didn't grasp what was going on, Satoshi Nakamoto was hard at work developing the idea of Bitcoin. Bitcoin.org was registered on 18 August 2008.

But who is Satoshi Nakamoto?

Satoshi Nakamoto can be referred to as 'he', 'she', 'it' or 'they', depending on your preference, because no one knows who or what Satoshi is. He, she, it or they are anonymous. On a profile page he created for the P2P Foundation, Satoshi stated that he was a thirty-seven-year-old male living in Japan. The P2P Foundation is a non-profit organization and global network that promotes commons-oriented peer-to-peer (P2P) solutions for social, economic and environmental justice. P2P is a way of organizing and relating that is based on mutual cooperation, collaboration and sharing among equals. The P2P Foundation studies, researches, documents and advocates for P2P practices in various fields, such as technology, culture, politics and ecology. Satoshi used this page to communicate with others as he developed Bitcoin.

However, fact-checking outside of Japan has led people to believe Satoshi lived in the United Kingdom, North America, Central America, South America or even the Caribbean. People say that his perfect written English and occasional use of British phrases show that he lives in the UK, while others state that the pattern of his posts indicates that he lives in the Eastern or Central time zones of the US or Canada.

There have also been a few fake Satoshis since the media is so eager to solve the interesting puzzle of who Satoshi is. In May 2016, an Australian named Craig Wright claimed that he was Satoshi. For a short time, publications like *The Economist* and *Wired* paid attention to him, but he was soon shown to be a fake.

Now, there are claims regarding Satoshi's background from five different continents. This brings us back to the idea that Satoshi might not be a single person, but a group of people. The theory that Satoshi is more than one person seems to be supported by the fact that Satoshi is proficient in a variety of subjects, such as cryptography, computer science, economics and psychology, and can explain the fundamental concepts of each.

Who would they be, though? Even if the mystery is never solved, Satoshi knew that Wall Street was getting more and more unstable.

In 2008, when Wall Street was on the brink of failure, Bitcoin rose like a phoenix from the ashes. From August to October 2008, several unprecedented events occurred: Bitcoin.org was set up, Lehman Brothers filed for bankruptcy, Bank of America bought Merrill Lynch for $50 billion, the US government started the $700 billion TARP and Satoshi Nakamoto published a paper that laid the groundwork for Bitcoin and blockchain technology.

Blockchain technology is a decentralized and transparent digital ledger system that records transactions. A network of computers is used to verify and record transactions, which are then bundled into blocks and added to a chain of other blocks to create a permanent and tamper-proof record.

Due to its decentralized nature, blockchain technology can never be controlled by a single entity or group. Instead, a network of computers keeps the ledger up to date. Each of these computers has a copy of the blockchain and works in concert with the other computers in the network to verify transactions and maintain the ledger's integrity.

Beyond its original use for digital currencies like Bitcoin, blockchain technology has a wide range of potential applications, which we will discuss later.

It's hard to ignore how the collapse of the financial system and the rise of Bitcoin are connected. The financial crisis cost the world economy trillions of dollars and destroyed trust between the public and our current financial system. Bitcoin, on the other hand, created a system for transferring value that didn't depend on people's morals but on the cold calculations of computers. This could make Wall Street less important in the future.

Whether Satoshi is a person or a group, it is now clear that he designed a technology that, had it existed earlier, would have likely made CMOs and CDOs less toxic and opaque. Because a blockchain is transparent and has an audit log that cannot be changed, each loan that was given out and put into different CMOs could have been recorded on a single blockchain. This would have let any buyer see a clear record of who owned the CMO and how each mortgage was doing. In 2008, the financial system was held together by digital strings that connected several different, expensive systems that didn't work well together.

On 31 October 2008, Satoshi Nakamoto published the Bitcoin white paper. This document serves as the foundation for every single blockchain implementation deployed today and in the future. This white paper is available for free download on the Internet.

In the concluding paragraph of his paper, Satoshi wrote, 'We have proposed a system for electronic transactions without relying on trust.'[1]

His words point to the fact that he had already coded the entire system at the time he published the paper: 'I had to write all the code before I could convince myself that I could solve every problem; then I wrote the paper.'[2]

Estimates show that Satoshi started putting the Bitcoin idea in writing around the end of 2006 and started coding it around the beginning of 2007. During the same period, many regulators began to believe that the US housing market was overstressed and headed for a rough ride. It's hard to believe that someone with Satoshi's depth and breadth of knowledge would work in isolation from what he was witnessing in international financial markets.

Satoshi sent an email to 'The Cryptography Mailing List' with a link to his white paper the day after it was published. The list was made up of subscribers who were interested in cryptography and its potential applications. Satoshi's email sparked endless, enthusiastic responses.

On Friday, 7 November 2008, he wrote in response to his growing number of ardent followers: 'You will not find a solution to political problems in cryptography . . . but we can win a major battle in the arms race and gain a new territory of freedom for several years. Governments are good at cutting off the heads of centrally controlled networks like Napster, but pure P2P networks like Gnutella and Tor seem to be holding their own.'[3] This quote makes it clear that Satoshi didn't make Bitcoin to fit into the current government and financial systems. Instead, he created an alternative system that the decentralized masses could run without the help of a central authority.

Decentralized autonomy was also very important in the early days of the Internet, when each node on the network was an autonomous agent that communicated with other agents via shared protocols.

The Bitcoin project was registered on SourceForge.net on 9 November. SourceForge.net is a website that helps with open-source software development. Satoshi then went silent for a few months as Wall Street continued to crumble.

The Emergency Economic Stabilization Act, which the US Congress passed and President George W. Bush signed on 3 October 2008, didn't do much to stop the stock market crash that happened after Lehman Brothers went bankrupt. The emergency act established the $700 billion TARP. As a result of TARP, the US government bought preferred stock in several banks and big companies such as AIG, General Motors and Chrysler. However, the stock did not come cheap. It took $550 billion in investments to bring those teetering behemoths back to life.

When Bitcoin first became a public network, Satoshi made it clear that he was aware of the problems with the world's financial system. Satoshi was the first person to write something on Bitcoin's blockchain: 'The Times, January 3, 2009, Chancellor on brink of second bailout of banks.'[4] This was a reference to an article in the British newspaper, *The Times*, about how the UK government might need to help more banks stay afloat.

People would realize several years later that one of the best ways to use blockchain technology was to record information, which was then open for everyone to see and could not be erased from digital history. When Satoshi used this feature for the first time, he wrote a note about bank bailouts. This showed that he didn't want us to forget how disastrous the 2008 financial crisis was.

This touching message was written nine days before the first Bitcoin transaction took place. It was between Satoshi Nakamoto and Hal Finney, an early supporter of Bitcoin and one of the people who helped build it. The first exchange rate for Bitcoin was set nine months later. It was eight-hundredths of a cent per coin or 1309 bitcoins to the dollar. A dollar invested then would be worth more than $1 million by the beginning of 2017. This shows how quickly this innovation was going to grow.

Satoshi wrote about Bitcoin after the network had been running for more than a month. 'It's completely decentralized, with no central server or trusted parties, because everything is based on cryptographic proof instead of trust . . . I think this is the first time we're trying a decentralized, non-trust-based system.'[5]

On 5 December 2010, Satoshi showed an unsettlingly human side when he asked WikiLeaks not to accept Bitcoin as a form of payment. This was after major credit card networks blocked users from giving money to the site. 'No, don't bring it on,' Satoshi wrote. 'The project needs to grow gradually so the software can be strengthened along the way. I make this appeal to WikiLeaks not to try to use Bitcoin. Bitcoin is a small beta community in its infancy. You would not stand to get more than pocket change, and the heat you would bring would likely destroy us at this stage.'[6]

Satoshi disappeared soon after that. Some people think it was for Bitcoin's good. After all, anyone who makes a technology that could replace a big part of the current financial system will eventually get in trouble with powerful government and business forces. By vanishing into thin air, Satoshi got rid of Bitcoin's head and, with it, a single point of failure. He left behind a network with millions of users and thousands of access points.

Wall Street, on the other hand, had numerous points of failure. When the dust settled, the US government had spent far more than the $700 billion originally set aside for TARP. In total, $2.5 trillion was injected into the system, not including the $12.2 trillion pledged to restore trust in financial institutions' fidelity.

While Wall Street, as we knew it, was dying, the birth of Bitcoin cost the world nothing. Many people lost faith in the traditional banking system at the time when Bitcoin entered the scene, ushering in an innovative way to exchange value online without relying on intermediaries or regulators. However, it was not widely used or accepted at first by the mainstream and was quickly abandoned, much like a motherless child in the world. This initial lack of popularity and value, even at the right time, has been good for Bitcoin's development. Bitcoin faced less competition, regulation and criticism from the established players. It got more time and space to grow and improve its technology and community, transforming into the strong and grumpy toddler that it is now.

Bitcoin has caused a tidal wave of disruption and rethinking of global financial and technological systems since Satoshi's disappearance. Many different versions of Bitcoin have been developed, such as Ethereum, Litecoin, Monero and Zcash. All these use blockchain technology, which Satoshi gave to the world. At the same time, many financial and technological incumbents have embraced the technology, creating confusion about all the innovation that is taking place and what is most relevant to the innovative investor.

This chapter tries to clear up the confusion and doubts about Bitcoin and the blockchain.

At first glance, this chapter may seem full of jargon, which could keep many readers from even trying to understand it. In reality, there are only a few foreign concepts that are wrapped up in words that were made up. Unfortunately, these words keep people out. People often use these words when talking about different ways to use Bitcoin or blockchain technology. This makes the chapter seem hard to understand, but it's not. All it takes is a concerted effort to understand the key ideas, which then serve as the mental framework for understanding the many ways blockchain technology can be used.

Bitcoin, with a capital letter 'B', refers to the software that facilitates the transfer and possession of bitcoin, the currency, which starts with a lowercase 'b'.

The blockchain movement started with Bitcoin. People often compare new blockchains to Bitcoin's blockchain because it has been around the longest. Because of this, it is important to know the basics of Bitcoin. But to really understand Bitcoin, you have to stop thinking of it as a digital Ponzi scheme or a mysterious system that criminals use. These are old stories that keep making the rounds in the media.

Certainly, some of the first Bitcoin users were criminals. However, this is true of most revolutionary technologies, as new technologies are frequently useful tools for those seeking to trick the law. It's clear that Bitcoin's story as a currency has progressed beyond being a means of payment for illegal goods and services. Over a hundred media articles have jumped at the chance to declare Bitcoin dead, only to be proven wrong each time.

When viewed in the context of how technology is evolving, Bitcoin falls right in the middle of the most important trends. For example, the world is becoming more real-time, with people connecting in peer-to-peer settings, which helps empower and connect people regardless of their geographic or socioeconomic background. Bitcoin fits into these thematic categories. It enables a global transaction to be settled in an hour rather than a few days. It operates on a peer-to-peer model, the same one that has propelled Uber, Airbnb and LendingClub to multibillion-dollar valuations. Bitcoin allows anyone to be their own bank, giving control to a grassroots movement and empowering the world's unbanked.

On the other hand, Bitcoin has done something that might be more impressive than what Uber, Airbnb and LendingClub have done. Those businesses decentralized services that were simple to understand and had a track record of being peer-to-peer. Everyone has had a friend drive them to the airport, stayed with a relative abroad or borrowed money from their parents. Without a central authority, decentralizing a currency means that people all over the world accept it as a common means of payment and store of value.

Currency was first made to make trade easier. It got rid of bartering and the 'double coincidence of wants'—a situation where two people have goods or services that they are both willing to exchange with each other. For example, if you have eggs and I have bread, and we both want what the other has, then we have a double coincidence of wants, and we can trade our goods. However, this is very rare and inefficient in a barter economy, where there is no money or common medium of exchange.

Money has evolved over time to make it easier to use, and now it is made of paper and various digital representations. The only reason that a piece of paper or digital entity has value is because everyone else thinks it does, and the government says it must be accepted to meet financial obligations. Thus, it is a useful way to show how much value is shared.

If you are a libertarian, you would say that it's a usefully 'shared illusion of value', going back to the idea that the paper itself isn't worth much. Bitcoin is also a shared representation of value, but it can't be seen or touched and isn't protected by a central authority. Even with these problems, the beautiful math that makes it work has helped it grow and store billions of dollars in value.

## Bitcoin's Blockchain: How It Really Works

The creation of Bitcoin's blockchain, which can be thought of as a digital ledger that keeps track of user balances via debits and credits, is a component of the Bitcoin software. In this sense, Bitcoin's blockchain is a database that records the movement of its native currency, bitcoin.

What distinguishes this digital ledger?

Bitcoin's blockchain is a distributed, cryptographic and immutable database that uses proof-of-work to keep the ecosystem synchronized. This definition may seem like technobabble, but we will make it clear for you.

### Distributed

The term distributed refers to how computers access and maintain Bitcoin's blockchain. Unlike most databases, which strictly limit who can access the information contained within, anyone in the world can access Bitcoin's blockchain. This feature is critical to the currency's global acceptance. Because anyone from anywhere can view the record of debits and credits between different accounts on

Bitcoin's blockchain, it creates a system of global trust. Because everything is transparent, everyone is on an equal playing field.

## Cryptographic

Before explaining the 'cryptographic' attribute of Bitcoin, we must first explore what cryptography is all about.

Cryptography, which used to be a scary word, is the science of secure communication. It involves presenting information in a way that only the person who is supposed to receive it can understand and use it for what it was meant for. Encryption is the process of making the message hard to read, and decryption is the process of making it easy to read again. Both processes use complex mathematical techniques.

Cryptography is the battleground where people who want to send information securely face off against people who want to decrypt or change the information. More recently, cryptography has grown to include ways to prove who owns information to a larger group of people, such as with public key cryptography. This is a big part of how cryptography is used in Bitcoin.

Encryption methods have been used for hundreds of years. Julius Caesar used a simple method of encryption to tell his generals what he was going to do at war. He employed a code whereby each letter of the alphabet was represented by the third letter after it. For example, A would be represented by D, B by E, C by F and so on. As they knew the key to the code, Caesar's generals were able to decipher the messages he sent to them. This type of encryption was not safe for very long, which makes sense.

In more recent times, a team of English cryptographers attempted to decipher the encrypted messages sent by Nazi Germany using the Enigma machine during World War II. This story was told in the movie *The Imitation Game*. Alan Turing was a British mathematician, computer scientist and cryptanalyst, widely regarded as one of the most influential figures in computer science and artificial intelligence. He was a key member of the team that helped break the Enigma code, which hurt German war plans and helped end the war.

Cryptography is now an important part of our everyday lives. When we type in a password, use a credit card to pay for something or use WhatsApp, we use cryptography. Without cryptography, it would be easy for criminals to steal sensitive information and use it against us. Cryptography makes sure that only the people who should be able to use the information can do so.

If you find cryptography fascinating, Simon Singh's *The Code Book: The Science of Secrecy from Ancient Egypt to Quantum Cryptography* is a good book to read to gain a better understanding of the concept.[7]

Now, let's take a look at the cryptographic feature of Bitcoin's blockchain.

Every transaction in Bitcoin's blockchain has to be cryptographically checked to ensure that the person sending Bitcoin really owns the Bitcoin they are sending. The way that groups of transactions are added to Bitcoin's blockchain is based on cryptography. Transactions are not added one at a time. Instead, they are added in groups called 'blocks' that are 'chained' together, hence the name 'blockchain'.

To put it another way, cryptography enables the computers that are creating Bitcoin's blockchain to work together in an automated system of mathematical trust. It is simply math, not subjective trust, that determines whether a transaction is confirmed in Bitcoin's blockchain.

People sometimes shudder when they hear the word 'crypto', possibly because they think it has something to do with illegal things. This is a bias that needs to be overcome. Crypto is just a nod to and shortening of cryptography, which is the key technology that makes these systems work. Cryptography is the study of sending information securely so that only the people who are supposed to get it can use it. Thus, cryptography is used to make sure that crypto assets are sent to the right people in a safe way. Crypto assets are a type of digital asset that uses encryption algorithms and distributed ledger technology to enable secure online transactions. They are not issued or controlled by any central authority and can be used as a form of payment, investment or utility. Some examples of crypto assets are Bitcoin, Ethereum and non-fungible tokens (NFTs).

In our digital world, where hacks are becoming more common, it is important that resources can be sent safely, and crypto assets possess this security in abundance.

## Immutable

The combination of globally distributed computers capable of cryptographically verifying transactions and the creation of Bitcoin's blockchain results in an immutable database. This implies that the computers responsible for the creation of Bitcoin's blockchain can only do so in an 'append-only' fashion. 'Append only' refers to the fact that information can be added to Bitcoin's blockchain over time but cannot be deleted. This is like a digital audit trail etched in steel.

Once information is confirmed in Bitcoin's blockchain, it is irreversible and cannot be erased. Immutability is a rare feature in a digital world where things can be easily erased, and it is likely to become a more valuable feature for Bitcoin over time.

## Proof-of-work

Even though the first three aspects are useful, none of them are inherently new. Proof-of-work (PoW) ties together the ideas of a distributed, cryptographic and immutable database. It is how the different computers agree on which group of transactions will be added to Bitcoin's blockchain next.

In other words, PoW is all about how Bitcoin transactions are put together into blocks and how those blocks are linked together to make the blockchain. The computers, referred to as 'miners', compete with one another for the right to add blocks of transactions to Bitcoin's blockchain using PoW. This is how transactions are confirmed. Miners get paid in Bitcoin every time they add a block. This is why they chose to compete in the first place.

Competition for monetary rewards is also what keeps Bitcoin's blockchain secure. If any malicious actors wanted to alter Bitcoin's blockchain, they would have to compete with all the other miners scattered around the world, who have collectively invested hundreds of millions of dollars in the machinery required to perform PoW.

Miners compete by solving a cryptographic puzzle that allows them to add a block of transactions to Bitcoin's blockchain. Combining four variables—the time, a summary of the proposed transactions, the name of the previous block and a variable known as the nonce—enables one to solve this cryptographic puzzle.

A nonce is a random number that, when combined with the other three variables using something called a cryptographic hash function, makes an output that fits a strict set of rules. A parameter that is changeable on the fly determines how difficult it will be to meet this requirement. About once every ten minutes, a miner finds a solution to this mathematical puzzle. If all of this seems like drinking from a fire hose, don't worry. That's how it is at first for everyone.

The most important part of the PoW process is that one of the four variables is the identity of the previous block, which includes when that block was made, its set of transactions, the identity of the previous block and the block's nonce. If smart investors keep using this line of reasoning, they will see that it connects every block in Bitcoin's blockchain. So, you can't change information in a block that came before it, even if it was made years ago, without changing all the blocks that came after it. The group of miners would reject this kind of change, which is what makes Bitcoin's blockchain and its transactions immutable.

Miners are financially rewarded when they make a new block. This is done through a transaction called a 'coinbase transaction', which gives them newly created bitcoins and fees for each transaction. The coinbase transaction is also how new bitcoins are added to the money supply over time.

An analogy that helps to understand the Bitcoin ecosystem is to think of the concepts as a stack of hardware, software, applications and users on a personal computer. The miners that use the PoW process to build Bitcoin's blockchain are the hardware, just like a MacBook Pro is the hardware for a computer.

An operating system (OS) runs on that hardware. In the case of Bitcoin, the OS is the open-source software that makes everything we've talked about so far possible. A group of volunteer developers created this software, just as a group of volunteer developers maintains Linux, the operating system that powers the majority of the cloud.

Applications run on top of this hardware and operating system combination, just as Safari is an application that runs on an Apple OS. The applications communicate with the Bitcoin OS, which pushes and pulls data to and from the Bitcoin blockchain as required.

Finally, end users interact with the applications, and someday they may have no idea about the hardware or software underneath because all they need to know is how to navigate the applications.

In general, two types of entities can own the hardware that supports blockchains: public and private. The difference between a public blockchain and a private one is like the difference between the Internet and intranets. The Internet is a free and open resource. There is no gatekeeper; anyone can access it. On the other hand, businesses or organizations use secure networks called intranets to transmit sensitive data.

Public blockchains are comparable to the Internet, whereas private blockchains are comparable to intranets. While both are useful today, the Internet has created orders of magnitude more value than intranets. This is despite incumbents' vociferous declarations in the 1980s and 1990s that the public Internet could never be trusted. History is on the side of the public networks, and while it does not repeat itself, it often rhymes.

Remember that a blockchain is a distributed system of computers that uses cryptography and a consensus process like PoW to keep the community members in sync. A blockchain is useless in isolation; a centralized database would suffice. The community of computers creating a blockchain can be public or private, also known as permissionless or permissioned.

Public systems, such as Bitcoin, allow anyone with the necessary hardware and software to connect to the network and access the information it contains. There is no bouncer at the door checking IDs. Rather, network participation creates an economic equilibrium in which entities will buy more hardware to participate in building Bitcoin's blockchain if they believe they can profit from it. Ethereum, Litecoin, Monero, Zcash and other public blockchains are examples.

On the other hand, a bouncer stands at the door of private systems. Entities can only join the network if they have the right to do so. After Bitcoin, when companies and businesses realized they liked the usefulness of Bitcoin's blockchain but didn't want or weren't allowed to be as open with the information they shared with the public, they made private systems.

These private blockchains are more suited to enterprises for reasons of performance, accountability and cost. The financial services industry has been the most open to adopting private blockchains as a way to modernize their IT infrastructure, which has been outdated since the Millennium Bug. In this industry, private blockchains are mostly used to streamline operations, enhance data integrity and simplify transactional processes. The big players, such as leading financial institutions and central banks, offer these solutions to their clients and partners, such as small and medium enterprises, asset managers and regulators. Some people say that the biggest benefit of private blockchains is not the technology itself but the collaboration and trust that it fosters among large, secretive organizations. This, they say, will reduce the cost and risk of services for the end consumer.

We think that the move towards open networks and the use of private blockchains will, over time, weaken the position of centralized powerhouses. In other words, it's a step towards more decentralization and the use of public blockchains.

Private blockchains have a wide range of potential uses outside of the financial services sector. Because it's easy to see how a system that specializes in securing transactions could be used, banks and other financial institutions have been the first to adopt it. The music industry, real estate, insurance, healthcare, networking, polling, supply chains, charities, gun tracking, law enforcement, governments and more are just a few of the sectors looking into the potential uses of blockchain technology.

We will concentrate on public blockchains and their native assets, which we will refer to as 'crypto assets', because we believe this is where the greatest opportunity for innovation, decentralization and investment exists.

Native assets are assets that are built into a blockchain or other decentralized platform. An asset is often used to make transactions easier or as a unit of value in the ecosystem of the platform. Native assets can also be used to pay transaction fees or as collateral for smart contracts or other services within the platform. Some native assets can also be staked or used to take part in the governance and decision-making processes of the platform.

Smart contracts are computer programmes that make sure that the terms of a contract are followed. They run on blockchain platforms and are automatically carried out when certain conditions are met, such as when a certain date or action is reached. Smart contracts try to get rid of the need for trusted middlemen like lawyers or banks, as well as arbitration costs, fraud and both intentional and accidental exceptions. Vending machines are the oldest thing that can be compared to smart contracts. They both use a predefined logic to execute transactions without the need for human intervention or intermediaries. For example, when you insert money and select a snack in a vending machine, you are making an offer to buy the snack, and the machine accepts your offer by dispensing the snack and returning any change. This is similar to how a smart contract can accept an offer from a user by transferring a digital asset or performing a service when certain conditions are met. Both vending machines and smart contracts rely on the code or hardware to enforce the terms of the exchange and make it difficult or costly for either party to breach the contract.

One of the smart contracts' key features is their ability to be programmed to enforce specific rules and conditions. This can help ensure that contracts are carried out fairly and transparently, as well as reduce the risk of fraud or errors.

Native assets are not needed for private blockchains. Access to the network is tightly controlled, which is a big part of how security is maintained. This means that the computers that support the blockchain have a different job. Since these computers are working behind a firewall and with known entities, they don't have to worry about being attacked from the outside. This removes the need for a native asset that encourages miners to build a strong network.

Most of the time, a private blockchain is used to speed up and improve existing processes, which rewards the people who made the software and keeps the computers running. In other words, the value comes from the savings in costs that are enjoyed by the entities that own the computers. As with public blockchains, the entities don't have to be paid in a native asset for their work.

On the other hand, Bitcoin relies on a network of global volunteers, called 'miners', who use their computers to verify and secure Bitcoin transactions. To incentivize the miners to do this work, they are rewarded with a native asset, which is Bitcoin itself. In this way, there is no central authority supporting the service; rather, it is the users who benefit from it. Public blockchains, such as Bitcoin, are not just databases but system architectures that enable the creation of decentralized digital services that can be accessed from anywhere in the world. As the number of bitcoins that can be created is limited, the miners will eventually receive fewer new bitcoins and more transaction fees, which are the payments that users make to send bitcoins to each other. Transaction fees ensure that the miners have a steady income by determining the supply and demand of the network. If Bitcoin becomes widely used, transaction fees will be sufficient to pay the miners for their work.

Crypto assets may have the same name as their parent blockchain but differ in capitalization. Sometimes the asset has a slightly different name. For example, bitcoin is the native asset of the Bitcoin blockchain, ether is the native asset of the Ethereum blockchain, litecoin is the native asset of the Litecoin blockchain, and so on.

## The Constantly Evolving Nature of Currencies

You have seen the evolution of money: from barter to gold to paper to digital money and everything in between. Decentralized, private and digital currencies were pursued for decades prior to bitcoin. Bitcoin and other digital currencies are just a small part of how money has changed over the centuries.

When they were first made, currencies were a way to make bartering less obscure. For hundreds of years, metal coins with real value were the most common form of currency. Fiat currency was an improvement over metal coins because it was much easier to move around, but it was worthless without the government's stamp of approval and an order that it be used as legal tender. We believe that money that doesn't exist in the real world is the next step in the evolution of currencies and that it will happen in our Internet-connected world.

As the ideas that made the Internet possible gained steam, it became clear that we would need a safe way to pay online. David Chaum, who is still one of the best-known cryptographers in the history of crypto assets, started DigiCash, which is one of Bitcoin's most notable ancestors. Before Marc Andreessen started Netscape in 1993, Chaum came up with an online payment system called eCash. This made it possible to send money over the Internet safely and anonymously, no matter the amount.

Clearly, Chaum couldn't have picked a better time to start his business than during the tech boom of the mid-to-late 1990s. His company, DigiCash, had several ways to grow, and any of them could have made it a household name. But even though Chaum was regarded by many as a technical genius, he wasn't a very good businessman. Bill Gates asked Chaum to add eCash to Windows 95, which would have made it instantly available all over the world, but Chaum said no. Similarly, Netscape approached Chaum about a partnership, but his attitude quickly killed the deal. Visa wanted to put $40 million into DigiCash in 1996, but Chaum's demand for $75 million stopped them. If these reports are true, it's clear that the potential price of Chaum's creation was going down.

If everything had gone well, DigiCash's eCash would have been built into all of our web browsers, making it the global way to pay on the Internet and possibly making credit cards obsolete. DigiCash failed in the end because of bad management, and it filed for bankruptcy in 1998.

DigiCash didn't become a household name, but some of the people who worked there, like Nick Szabo, invented 'smart contracts' in 1994, and Zooko Wilcox-O'Hearn founded Zcash in 2016. After eCash, other digital currencies, payment systems or value stores like e-gold and Karma were tried. The first one got into trouble with the FBI because it was used by criminals, while the second one was never widely used.

Although DigiCash didn't catch on, it paved the way for other digital payment systems, like Bitcoin, that use similar cryptographic principles. Chaum's work on eCash and digital privacy has also had a big impact on the development of online privacy and security technologies in general.

The potential of a new type of Internet currency drew the attention of modern-day tech titans such as Peter

Thiel and Elon Musk, both of whom were involved in the creation of PayPal. Except for Karma, the problem with all these attempts at digital money was that they weren't completely decentralized—they relied on a centralized entity in some way, which opened the door to corruption and attack points.

One of the most amazing aspects of Bitcoin is how it gained popularity in a decentralized manner. The significance and difficulty of being the first currency to do so cannot be overstated. People frequently argue that Bitcoin has no value as currency until they understand how it works because, unlike what they're used to, you can't see, touch or smell it.

Everyone agrees that paper money is worth something. When the government is involved, people are much more likely to agree to this. One of the most important things in the history of money is getting people all over the world to agree that something has value and can be used as money without government support or a physical form. When Bitcoin first came out, it had no value because it could not be used to buy anything. The first people to use and support Bitcoin did so because they thought it was an interesting experiment in computer science and game theory. As Bitcoin's blockchain proved to be a reliable way to handle money over the Internet protocol (MoIP), people started building use cases for it. Some of these use cases now include e-commerce, remittances and business-to-business payments across borders.

At the same time that early use cases were being made, investors began to guess what future use cases would look like and how much bitcoin they would need. Together, the current uses of Bitcoin and the fact that investors buy it because they think it will have even more uses in the future create market demand for Bitcoin. How much a buyer is willing to pay for something is called the 'bid', and how much a seller is willing to get for that item is called the 'ask'. As with any market, the price is set where the bid and the ask meet.

Bitcoin's issuance model was one of the pillars supporting its value. Each time a miner appends a block of transactions, they are compensated. Miners are the individuals who operate the computers that construct the Bitcoin blockchain. A coinbase transaction present in each block pays them in newly created bitcoin. During the first four years of Bitcoin's existence, a coinbase transaction would award the lucky miner 50 bitcoins. The difficulty of this proof-of-work process was automatically recalibrated every two weeks with the aim of maintaining an average time of ten minutes between blocks. In other words, 50 new bitcoins were released every ten minutes, and the Bitcoin software adjusted the level of difficulty to maintain this output schedule.

In Bitcoin's first year, 300 bitcoins were released every hour (sixty minutes, ten minutes per block, 50 bitcoins per block), 7200 bitcoins every day and 2.6 million bitcoins every year.

History shows that the scarcity of a resource is a big part of how valuable it is to humans. Satoshi understood that if he continued to issue bitcoins at a rate of 2.6 million per year, the currency would lose its scarcity value and cease to have any value. So, he decided that his programme would cut in half the number of bitcoins given out for coinbase transactions every 2,10,000 blocks. Since one block is made every ten minutes, this would take four years. This

occurrence is referred to as a 'block reward halving' or
'halving' for short. The block reward was halved from 50
bitcoins to 25 bitcoins on 28 November 2012, and again
from 25 bitcoins to 12.5 bitcoins on 9 July 2016. Four
years later, in July 2020, the third event occurred. Thus far,
the Bitcoin supply schedule has appeared relatively linear.

In fact, by the end of the 2020s, it will be getting close
to a horizontal asymptote, with less than 0.5 per cent
annual supply inflation. In other words, Satoshi gave the
most new bitcoins to early adopters to get their support. By
doing this, he created a large enough monetary base for the
network to use. He knew that if bitcoin was successful, its
dollar value would go up over time, so he could slow down
the rate of issuance while still giving rewards to those who
supported it.

We think that in the long run, bitcoin will become so
important to the world economy that no new bitcoins will
need to be made for it to keep gaining support. At that
point, miners will get paid through fees on high-volume
transactions for processing transactions and keeping the
network safe.

People often say that by 2140, there will be no more
bitcoins to make. This is because the supply units continue
to split by a factor of two every four years. As of 1 January
2017, 76.6 per cent of all bitcoins had already been made.
In 2020, when the next block reward halving happened,
87.5 per cent of all bitcoins that will ever be made were in
circulation. A few years after the year 2100, there will be
20,999,999 bitcoins or almost 21 million. Bitcoin is often
compared to digital gold because it is so difficult to obtain.

It is clear that Bitcoin is the first fully decentralized
currency that is widely used, but people still don't like

some things about it. For example, Bitcoin's ten-minute block time meant that depending on when a user hit 'send', it could take up to ten minutes, and sometimes even longer, for the transaction to be added to Bitcoin's blockchain. Often, this delay was more of a problem for the merchant than for the customer, since merchants needed to know they were getting paid before they could provide a good or service.

Others worried about Bitcoin's hash function in the proof-of-work process because hardware was being made that was especially good at this hash function. This would make the mining network more centralized. For a decentralized currency, the fact that the machines that processed its transactions were becoming more and more centralized was a cause for concern.

Fortunately, Bitcoin's protocol is open-source software, so developers could download the entire source code and tweak the parts they felt needed the most work. When the developers finished updating the software, they put it out to the public in the same way that Bitcoin was first released. The new software worked like Bitcoin, but it needed its own team of developers to keep it running, miners to provide the hardware and a separate blockchain to keep track of debits and credits for the new native asset.

Many other cryptocurrencies have been created as a result of the combination of open-source software and brilliant programmers. They are known as 'altcoins', which are cryptocurrencies that are only minor variations on Bitcoin.

Namecoin was the first digital offspring of Bitcoin. Surprisingly, it was less about creating a new currency and more about leveraging the blockchain's immutable nature.

A website created with Namecoin includes the '.bit' domain (rather than the '.com' domain) and provides security and censorship resistance to those sites that use it.

Namecoin started with an idea on the Bitcoin talk forum in 2010 that focused on BitDNS (DNS stands for domain naming service, which handles all web addresses). In 2013, a service called NameID came out. It uses the Namecoin blockchain to let people make websites with a Namecoin identity and give them access to them.

Namecoin is its own DNS service and gives users more privacy and control. Instead of using a government-run service like the Internet Corporation for Assigned Names and Numbers (ICANN), which is how most websites are registered, a Namecoin site is registered using a service that is on every computer in the Namecoin network. This makes things safer, more private and faster. To get a .bit site, you need namecoin, which is why the native asset is needed.

Ethereum, Litecoin, Ripple, Bitcoin Cash and Tether are some of the most well-known altcoins. We are not touching upon them as they would require a book in themselves. But we would like to discuss another altcoin whose unusual debut and life will likely pique your interest.

### Auroracoin

Auroracoin's creator, like Satoshi Nakamoto, used a fictitious name: Baldur Friggjar Óðinsson. Baldur created Auroracoin using Litecoin's code and decided to 'airdrop' the cryptocurrency to Icelanders, with the goal of providing them with 50 per cent of all Auroracoin in existence. His hope was that such a distribution would kick-start national cryptocurrency use.

When a cryptocurrency is airdropped, free tokens or coins are sent to a large number of cryptocurrency wallets or addresses. Most of the time, this is done as a way to market a new cryptocurrency or to thank people who already own a certain cryptocurrency.

Baldur's plan depended on him having access to the government's national identification system. This led speculators to believe that the Icelandic government was supporting Auroracoin, which was not true. Speculators put the value of Auroracoin's network at more than $1 billion before the airdrop.

By the time the airdrop started on 25 March 2014, people had calmed down a bit, and Auroracoin had a network value of just over $100 million. By the end of the month, it would be less than $20 million because people who got Auroracoin sold it on exchanges to make money.

Along with the price drop, people lost faith in and excitement about the new cryptocurrency. Auroracoin was not accepted by many stores, if any at all, and was soon called a 'failed experiment'. Some people also thought that the person who made it was pulling a scam.

To this day, Auroracoin is the cryptocurrency that has the most ambitious plan for wide use in one country. It still exists, and a few Icelandic developers are working to bring the idea and the technology back to life. In 2016, ads started popping up all over Reykjavik, the capital of Iceland, stating that Auroracoin was coming back. Because of this, people in Iceland started paying for beers with auroracoin, and many other stores started accepting it as well.

In 2016, a massive leak of 11.5 million documents from a Panama-based law firm exposed the offshore financial dealings of many powerful people and entities around the world. This scandal, known as the Panama Papers, led to the resignation of the prime minister of Iceland, who was among those implicated. As a result, people became interested in a political party called the Pirate Party, which liked cryptocurrencies. Suddenly, there were rumours that Iceland might think about Auroracoin again and how it could be used as a national cryptocurrency. As acceptance of the Icelandic cryptocurrency grows and politics change, it will be interesting to see what comes next for it.

Auroracoin is a lesson for both investors and developers about what not to do. What seemed like a strong and compelling use case for a crypto asset didn't work out because it couldn't help the people it was meant to help. Icelanders were given a digital currency, but they didn't know how to use it or how to learn how to use it.

Not surprisingly, the asset's value fell, and most people thought it was dead. Still, cryptocurrencies rarely die completely, and if Auroracoin's developers can find a way forward, its future could be interesting.

## Cryptocurrencies, Crypto Commodities and Crypto Tokens

Crypto assets have often been called cryptocurrencies in the past, which we think confuses new users and limits the conversation about the future of these assets. Most crypto assets are not currencies. Instead, they are either digital commodities (crypto commodities), which provide raw digital resources, or digital tokens (crypto tokens), which provide finished digital goods and services.

Cryptocurrencies are not to be confused with central bank digital currencies (CBDCs). CBDCs are intended to differ from cryptocurrencies, which are decentralized and not backed by a central authority. CBDCs, on the other hand, are issued by a central bank and are backed by the full faith and credit of the government.

CBDCs were created to rival cryptocurrencies, but they may not require blockchain technology or consensus mechanisms. CBDCs are meant to be a safe and stable form of digital money that can be used just like cash in everyday transactions.

A currency serves three distinct functions: it is a medium of exchange, a store of value and a unit of account. However, the currency itself has little intrinsic value. Paper bills in people's wallets, for example, have about the same value as the paper in their printers. Instead, they have the illusion of value, which, if widely shared by society and supported by the government, allows these monetary bills to be used to purchase goods and services, store value for future purchases and serve as a metric for pricing the value of other things.

On the other hand, commodities are very different. Most people think of them as raw materials that are used to make finished products. Oil, wheat and copper, to name a few, are all common commodities in our physical world.

But to think that a commodity must be physically present is to ignore the 'offline to online' shift that is happening in every part of the economy. In a world that is becoming more digital, it makes sense to have digital commodities such as computing power, storage space and network bandwidth. Even though computing power, storage and bandwidth aren't usually called commodities yet, they are building blocks that may be just as important as our physical commodities. When they are provided through a blockchain network, they are termed crypto commodities.

Crypto tokens make it possible to create 'finished products' like digital goods and services such as media, social networks, games and more, in addition to cryptocurrencies and crypto commodities. Blockchain networks also supply these things.

In the real world, currencies and commodities fuel an economy that makes finished goods and services. In the digital world, too, infrastructures made possible by cryptocurrencies and crypto commodities are coming together to support the digital goods and services mentioned above.

Crypto tokens are still in the early stages of development and are likely to be the last ones to catch on because they need a strong infrastructure for cryptocurrencies and crypto commodities to work reliably.

We believe that this brave new world of blockchain architecture includes cryptocurrencies, crypto commodities and crypto tokens, just as we have had currencies, commodities and finished goods and services for centuries. Whether it's a currency, a good or a service, blockchain architectures help make these digital resources available in a way that is decentralized, authentic and market-oriented.

In some ways, crypto commodities are more real than cryptocurrencies when it comes to their value. For example, Ethereum, the largest crypto commodity, is a decentralized world computer on which applications can be built that can be used anywhere in the world without being censored. It's easy to see how valuable it is to use a computer like this, so Ethereum gives us a real resource in digital form. Using Ethereum's world computer, which is also called the Ethereum Virtual Machine (EVM), is similar to when students use shared computers in schools and libraries. Someone can use a computer for a while and then move on. Then someone else will come and use it.

The EVM works a bit like a shared computer, except that it can be used on a global scale and more than one person can use it at the same time. Just like anyone can see Bitcoin transactions from anywhere in the world, anyone can see Ethereum programmes running from anywhere in the world.

Even though this book only talks about Ethereum as a crypto commodity, there are many other crypto commodities on the rise that provide decentralized resources like cloud storage, bandwidth, transcoding, proxy re-encryption and so on.

The founders of Ethereum and its native asset, ether, were not the first to envision globally distributed computer programmes, also known as smart contracts. For instance, Nick Szabo, a DigiCash employee and one of Chaum's students, has been discussing smart contracts and digital property since the early 1990s.

Szabo had the original idea for smart contracts, but the Ethereum team was the first to create a well-known and attention-grabbing platform for decentralized smart contract execution. Vitalik Buterin is at the centre of the team. Many people think of him as Ethereum's Satoshi. Buterin was born in Russia, but he spent his childhood in Canada. He was lucky to have a father who was a freethinker. In February 2011, when Buterin was seventeen years old, his father told him about Satoshi's work and

Bitcoin. At that time, Bitcoin had only been around for two years, and there were no major alternatives. Charlie Lee would not release Litecoin until October of that same year.

It didn't take long for Buterin to get caught up in Bitcoin. He quickly became one of the first well-known journalists to write about crypto assets. He even helped start Bitcoin Magazine, which remains one of the best sites for technical analysis of blockchain architectures. He used his math skills to think about how to improve the technology while he was writing articles that combined technical information with an upbeat and enthusiastic tone. We can't expect anything less from a bronze medal winner at the International Olympiad in Informatics at the age of just eighteen.

Many people were working hard to build a decentralized future on top of Bitcoin, but it wasn't easy. After all, Bitcoin was still a work in progress. Satoshi's holy grail was a decentralized currency, and he didn't have to swallow the entire world in one bite. Buterin, on the other hand, was dissatisfied with Bitcoin as it was and had grand goals for it. He desired a more flexible system that functioned more like a computer and less like a calculator for debits and credits on Bitcoin balances.

What makes Ethereum more intriguing is that the Ethereum protocol extends far beyond currency. Protocols based on decentralized file storage, decentralized computation and decentralized prediction markets, among several other concepts, have the potential to significantly increase computational efficiency and provide a massive boost to other peer-to-peer protocols by adding an economic layer for the first time.

Buterin did not want Ethereum and its native currency, ether, to be a small variation to Bitcoin's codebase. This made Ethereum different from a lot of the other altcoins that came before it. By not having the word 'coin' in its name, Ethereum moved past the idea of currency and into the world of crypto commodities.

While Bitcoin is mostly used to transfer money between people, Ethereum can be used to transfer data between programmes. It accomplishes this by constructing a decentralized world computer equipped with a Turing complete programming language. Developers can create programs or applications to run on top of this decentralized global computer. Ethereum thus promises to do the same in a distributed and global system that Apple does in the world of personal computing by building hardware and operating systems that allow developers to build applications on top of them.

Ether is the fuel that is needed for the distributed application platform Ethereum to work. It's a way for the people who use the platform to pay for the machines that do the work they have asked for. To put it another way, ether is the incentive that makes sure developers make good applications (because unwanted code costs more) and that the network stays healthy (people receive payment for the resources they have contributed).

Ethereum miners handle transactions that can send both ether and information between programmes. They receive ether in exchange for supporting the network, much like Bitcoin miners do, and a similar proof-of-work consensus mechanism underpins the process.

On 30 July 2015, the Ethereum network and its underlying blockchain went live. While much effort had gone into developing the Ethereum software, this was the first time that miners could participate because there was finally a blockchain for them to support. Ethereum was literally floating in the ether prior to this launch.

Ethereum's decentralization platform is now up and running, serving as the hardware and software foundation for decentralized applications (dApps). dApps are complex smart contracts that can be created by developers outside of the core Ethereum team, broadening the technology's reach.

As an example, we could use Etherisc, a decentralized application, for flight insurance. With Ethereum, developers can create insurance pools by stringing together conditional transactions. By open-sourcing this process and running it on top of Ethereum's world computer, ordinary investors can put their money into an insurance pool and earn returns from insurance premium buyers. Everyone can trust this system because it operates in the open and is controlled by computer codes.

Since Ethereum's inception, an almost infinite number of dApps have been released to run on it, many of which have their own native units. We refer to many of these native units as crypto tokens, while others refer to them as appcoins. A dApp with its own native crypto token will pay the Ethereum network in ether as a crypto commodity to process certain dApp transactions. While many dApps use a crypto token, the native units of some dApps should be classified as a crypto commodity layered on top of Ethereum. The distinction is whether the dApp is providing a raw digital resource (crypto commodity) or a consumer-centric finished digital good or service (crypto token).

The majority of crypto tokens do not have their own blockchain. These crypto tokens are frequently used in applications built on the blockchain of a crypto commodity, such as Ethereum. For instance, the applications in the Apple App Store do not need to develop their own operating systems; instead, they run on Apple's operating system.

As Ethereum grew so quickly, other decentralized world computers that can run their own dApps, like Dfinity, Lisk, Rootstock, Tezos, Waves and others, have sprung up. In the same way that many altcoins tried to make Bitcoin better, these platforms are crypto commodities that try to make Ethereum's design better. They do this by attracting their own dApps and crypto tokens.

A visit to www.ethereum.org, the website of Ethereum, will help you explore the full list of Ethereum dApps. There are several websites and online communities that share the codes of these dApps. Discussing how to invest in crypto assets and other aspects of crypto asset investing is beyond the scope of this book. We aim to introduce you to these new-age concepts, and we believe we have done it as simply as possible.

dApp development and the associated native units have been one of the most rapidly evolving areas in the crypto asset space, with new ones appearing every week while we were writing this book. So, you should spend some time after reading this chapter exploring them further, as we are only scratching the surface in this section.

## Non-Fungible Tokens

Another form of crypto token that began to gain popularity in 2017 was the non-fungible token (NFT). NFTs, like other crypto tokens, use cryptography to secure transactions and prove ownership, and they can be purchased, sold and traded on a variety of online marketplaces and platforms.

But unlike other fungible crypto tokens like Bitcoin and Ethereum, which can be traded for an equal unit of the same value, NFTs are unique and can't be traded for another token of the same value. NFTs are used to represent ownership or authenticity of a one-of-a-kind digital asset, such as artwork, music, videos or other types of content. When someone buys an NFT, they are basically buying a digital certificate of ownership that proves they are the only person who owns that particular item.

With several high-profile sales and auctions, NFTs gained mainstream attention and popularity. In February 2021, a digital artwork by the artist Beeple sold for $69 million at a Christie's auction, making it one of the first high-profile NFT sales. This sale put NFTs into the mainstream and sparked a surge of interest in the technology. Since then, there have been several notable NFT sales, including the $2.9 million sale of a tweet by Twitter CEO Jack Dorsey and the sale of a digital rock collection for more than $1.5 million.

Musicians, athletes and other celebrities have also used NFTs to sell exclusive digital content and merchandise. NFTs have already had a big effect on the art and entertainment industries, and their possible uses in other fields like gaming, virtual real estate and others are still being looked into.

Now that we have introduced you to the new world of crypto assets, we feel this chapter would not be complete without telling you how to participate in it.

To begin your journey into the world of dApps, NFTs, bitcoin and Ethereum, you must first create an Ethereum wallet to store your Ethereum and crypto tokens that you will use to participate in dApps and DeFi platforms. MetaMask, MyEtherWallet and Trust Wallet are some popular wallets.

Then you must purchase Ethereum. Ethereum can be purchased on a cryptocurrency exchange such as Coinbase, Binance or Kraken. To purchase Ethereum, you must first create an account, go through the verification process and deposit funds.

The next step is to utilize a dApp or DeFi platform. There are numerous dApps and DeFi platforms in which you can participate. Uniswap, Compound, Aave and MakerDAO are a few examples. Each platform has its own set of features and requirements, so do your research and select the one that best suits your needs.

After you have decided on a dApp or DeFi platform, you'll need to link your Ethereum wallet to it. This is typically accomplished through the use of a browser extension such as MetaMask, which allows you to interact with the platform directly from your wallet.

After connecting your wallet to the platform, you can select which activity you want to participate in. For example, if you use a decentralized exchange (DEX) such as Uniswap, you can trade Ethereum and other tokens with other platform users.

Remember that whenever you interact with a dApp or DeFi platform, you must pay a gas fee in Ethereum in order for the transaction to be processed on the Ethereum network. Gas prices can vary greatly depending on network congestion, so check the current gas prices before making any transactions.

It's important to remember that participating in dApps and DeFi platforms can be complicated and risky. Do your own research and consider consulting a financial advisor before you make any investment decisions.

Now we'll explain why cryptocurrency markets are so volatile. When compared to other global financial markets, crypto markets are infants. As a result, these are extremely thinly traded markets. A thin market refers to the size of the order book, which is the list of buys and sells on an exchange. In other words, it represents the number of people who want to buy and sell at any given time.

The thinness of the order book is also referred to as market liquidity. If the market is highly liquid, there will be many orders, many of which will be large. In this case, value can be easily traded. If the market is illiquid or thin, large price swings with low volume will occur because someone attempting to buy (or sell) a large quantity of the asset will fill all available sell (or buy) orders, causing the price to rise (or fall). As a result, when investors are bullish in thin or illiquid markets, they can drive massive swings to the upside, just as when investors turn bearish, strong selling volume can quickly drive the price down.

Despite the fact that crypto assets are gaining popularity among investors, the investor base is smaller at the moment, and trading is more irregular with small orders. This can lead to increased volatility in the price of crypto assets. This increased volatility can be seen as an initial hiccup associated with every innovative technology or market.

Before we conclude this chapter, we would like to tell you that the world of crypto assets and a massive shift to create a decentralized world are growing at a faster pace than we had ever imagined. We will explain the catalysts behind these grand developments in the following chapters.

# 7

# Welcome to the DeFi World

'DeFi is the future of finance.'

—Vitalik Buterin, co-founder
of Ethereum

## The Birth of the World Wide Web and the Information Age

The European Organization for Nuclear Research (CERN), is an intergovernmental organization that operates the world's largest particle physics laboratory. It was founded in 1954 and is headquartered in Meyrin, a north-western suburb of Geneva, on the France-Switzerland border.

CERN is also used to refer to the laboratory with the primary function of providing particle accelerators and other infrastructure required for high-energy physics research; as a result, numerous experiments have been built at CERN through international collaborations.

The Large Hadron Collider (LHC), the world's largest and highest-energy particle collider, is housed at CERN. The main site in Meyrin has a large computer centre that is mostly used to store and analyse data from experiments and to simulate events. Since researchers need remote access to these facilities, the lab has traditionally served as a major wide area network (WAN) hub.

Apart from all these golden feathers in its cap, CERN is internationally popular for another feat that changed the course of world history. The largest particle physics laboratory in the world is the birthplace of the World Wide Web and the Information Age.

Tim Berners-Lee graduated from Queen's College, Oxford, with a degree in physics. During his college years, he was fascinated by computers. This fascination inspired him to build a computer out of an old television set he bought from a repair shop while at university.

After graduating in 1976, Berners-Lee worked as an engineer for two telecommunications companies. Then he worked as an independent contractor at CERN from June to December 1980. While in Geneva, he proposed a project based on the concept of hypertext to help researchers share and update information. Hypertext is a technology that allows text, images and other content to be electronically linked together, allowing users to navigate through a document or collection of documents in a non-linear manner. He created a prototype system called ENQUIRE to demonstrate it.

After leaving CERN in late 1980, Berners-Lee went to work at John Poole's Image Computer Systems, Ltd. in Bournemouth, Dorset. For three years, he oversaw the company's technical operations. He worked on a 'real-time remote procedure call' project, which gave him experience with computer networking.

Berners-Lee returned to CERN as a fellow in 1984. At the time, CERN was the largest Internet node in Europe, and he saw an opportunity to connect hypertext to the Internet. Indeed, hypertext is the underlying technology that has enabled the creation of a vast, interconnected network of web pages and online resources.

In his book, *Weaving the Web*,[1] Berners-Lee describes his experience of creating the World Wide Web in his own words: 'Creating the Web was really an act of desperation because the situation without it was very difficult when I was working at CERN later. Most of the technology involved in the web, like the hypertext, the Internet and multifont text objects, had all been designed already. I just had to put them together. It was a step of generalizing, going to a higher level of abstraction, thinking about all the documentation systems out there as being possibly part of a larger imaginary documentation system.' He also added, 'I just had to take the hypertext idea and connect it to the TCP and DNS ideas, and—ta-da!—the World Wide Web.'

Berners-Lee wrote his proposal in March 1989 and redistributed it in 1990. His manager then gave his approval. Simultaneously, Robert Cailliau, a Belgian informatics engineer and computer scientist, proposed an independent project to develop a hypertext system at CERN. He then partnered with Berners-Lee in his efforts to get the web off the ground. They used ideas similar to those underlying the ENQUIRE system to create the world's first web browser, the World Wide Web, which Berners-Lee designed. The World Wide Web also served as an editor, which was run on the NeXTSTEP operating system and on the first web server, the CERN Hypertext Transfer Protocol daemon (HTTPd).

On 20 December 1990, Berners-Lee published the first website, which was accessible via the Internet through the CERN network. The website explained to the world what the World Wide Web was, how to use a browser and set up a web server and how to create one's own website. CERN made the web protocol and code royalty-free in 1993, triggering their widespread use.

In 2014, to commemorate their eightieth anniversary, the British Council published a list of '80 moments that shaped the world'. The World Wide Web was ranked first on the list, which was compiled by a panel of twenty-five eminent scientists, academics, writers and world leaders. According to the entry, 'The fastest growing communications medium of all time, the Internet, has changed the shape of modern life forever. We can connect with each other instantly, all over the world.'

What Tim Berners-Lee and Robert Cailliau created and gave to the world changed the way people work and play. It has also marked the beginning of a new era in human history. However, only a few have noticed that these two brilliant minds created the world's first technically decentralized system.

The World Wide Web facilitates a network of interconnected computers and servers that communicate with one another through standard protocols and routing algorithms. The network is not governed by a centralized authority but rather by a distributed system of nodes and routers that collaborate to facilitate communication and data exchange.

Today, a small number of large corporations and organizations control a sizable portion of the Internet's content and services. Those organizations include social media platforms, search engines and online marketplaces. These corporations wield significant influence over how people access and interact with information on the Internet.

Furthermore, some governments and regulatory bodies have control over specific aspects of the Internet, such as regulating access or content, which can concentrate power in the hands of a few authorities. The fact that a single group controls both content and access has raised concerns about censorship, privacy and monopolies.

Everything in this world, including man-made systems, evolves over time. The Internet is no exception. So far in its evolution, the World Wide Web has gone through three distinct phases.

Web 1.0 is a retronym for the first stage of the World Wide Web's evolution, which lasted roughly from 1989 to 2004. In Web 1.0, there were few content creators, with the vast majority of users simply acting as content consumers. Personal web pages were common, with static pages hosted on Internet service provider-managed web servers or on free web hosting services like Tripod and GeoCities.

These static pages were created only for information and not for interaction. So, the majority of interactions took place in comment sections and message boards. Web 1.0 introduced a new form of posting to a large audience. It also enabled people to buy online from a larger number of sellers. On the early Internet, email and instant messaging were the primary forms of one-on-one communication. In a nutshell, Web 1.0 was the era of information consumerism and one-on-one communication on the Internet.

The dawn of the twenty-first century also witnessed the advent of new technologies. Asynchronous JavaScript and XML (Ajax) allowed web applications to update content in real time without having to refresh the page. The Really Simple Syndication (RSS) protocol lets Internet users subscribe to website content and receive updates in a standardized format. Application Programming Interfaces (APIs) enable different software applications to communicate with one another, allowing mashups and other integrations to be created. Cloud computing creates a virtual space where anyone can access software and data via the Internet rather than installing it on their computers.

Since 2004, all these technological advancements have transformed the Internet from an interconnected web of web servers, hypertexts, hyperlinks and static web pages into a world of interactive social media platforms and user-generated content (UGC).

All Internet users began to have their own social network profiles, which began with MySpace and exploded in popularity with the likes of Facebook and Twitter. Personal blogs first gained popularity on sites like Blogger and Tumblr, and then bloggers began to create their own websites. YouTube provides a popular platform for content creators to reach the world through videos and be monetized. Podcasts enable creators to create their own audio platforms from which to communicate with the rest of the world.

This stage of Internet evolution is known as Web 2.0. It marked the beginning of two-way communication between content creators and consumers across various media platforms. Web 2.0 sparked the rise of platforms, such as Facebook, Twitter, YouTube, Google, Amazon, Etsy, Apple iTunes and others.

These massive platforms give us access to a global audience, and we can share our products, ideas and content with the world. In return, these virtual platforms collect our data to create algorithms that provide us with personalized content and hook us on their platform for as long as possible to display advertisements to us.

In 2014, Gavin Wood, co-founder of Ethereum and creator of Polkadot, a blockchain platform and cryptocurrency, coined the term 'Web 3.0'. This Web 3.0 is not to be confused with the Web 3.0 or the Semantic Web concept proposed by Tim Berners-Lee, the World Wide Web's inventor, in 1999.

The Semantic Web is based on the notion that web content should be structured in such a way that computers can comprehend the meaning of the information presented. Ontologies, which are formal descriptions of ideas and their relationships, are used to ensure that everyone understands the same things about web content.

The Semantic Web employs technologies such as the Resource Description Framework (RDF), Web Ontology Language (OWL), SPARQL Protocol and RDF Query Language to create and link machine-readable data across the web. This means that computers can not only get information from the web but can also analyse it.

The Semantic Web's goal is to enable new applications and services that can make more intelligent and efficient use of the vast amount of information available on the web. A search engine, for example, could use Semantic Web technologies to understand the relationships between various pieces of information on the web to provide more accurate and relevant search results.

Web 3.0, on the other hand, marks the beginning of the Internet's transition from being a big tech informational product to owning your own online ecosystem. Blockchain technology platforms are the main place where Web 3.0 is being built. Content can be monetized on these platforms, but it can't be removed or censored.

A decentralized autonomous organization (DAO) is one of the main tools being used. This is a community-led organization with no central authority. A DAO is a fully autonomous and transparent organization that uses smart contracts to lay the foundational rules and execute the agreed-upon parameters. These smart contracts, along with proposals, voting and the code that is used in the DAO, can be publicly audited.

In Web 3.0, your digital identity is not linked to your online identity. This is because blockchains are public and the wallets used for transactions are not linked to a personal identity, preventing algorithms from tracking your personal online actions. NFTs enable the sale of one-of-a-kind digital products to customers. Cryptocurrencies return value and monetary policy to currency owners while depriving central banks of power.

This DeFi world opens up a new financial world to everyone by providing replacement products to the monopolies that investment banks currently hold.

The ultimate goal of Web 3.0 is the metaverse: a decentralized virtual world with all the elements of the real world. Web 3.0 refers to the process of decentralizing the World Wide Web and removing the gatekeepers—the big tech virtual platforms.

## The Metaverse

Since the late nineteenth century, we have been developing various technologies to facilitate interactive communication and provide entertainment by tricking our senses. Televisions, audio speakers and more recent technological advances such as interactive video games, virtual reality (VR) and augmented reality (AR) all serve this purpose admirably. We may also develop highly advanced technological tools in the future to fool our other senses, such as smell and touch.

The metaverse is the most recent technological advancement towards that far-off goal.

The idea of the metaverse has caught people's attention, especially after the recent Covid-19 pandemic, when lockdowns and practices like work from home (WFH) forced more people to explore online virtual worlds for business and fun.

The word 'metaverse' comes from the words 'meta', which means 'beyond', and 'universe'. So, the metaverse refers to something 'beyond the universe'. Neal Stephenson, a science fiction author, used the word for the first time in his 1992 book *Snow Crash*.[2] Today, the term has far more than a romantic connotation.

The metaverse is a highly interactive virtual world where land, buildings and even personalized avatars can be traded, often with cryptocurrency. People can explore different places, make friends, build virtual assets, buy goods and services and attend virtual events in the metaverse's virtual environments.

In the blockchain-powered metaverse, users can create, own and trade decentralized digital assets using cryptocurrency and NFTs. Simply put, the metaverse connects our physical world to our fabricated extensions of reality: the virtual world.

The idea of the metaverse could help organize our societies or cause new political and cultural changes. All of this is done within the framework of shared standards and protocols that bring a variety of virtual world experiences and augmented realities into an open metaverse. It could help people interact, collaborate and reduce asset and skill duplication.

The metaverse is also an experiment to find new ways to solve societal problems and boost enterprise productivity by combining smartphones, 5G networks, AR, VR, cryptocurrencies and social media platforms.

The metaverse's rise is unavoidable. Apple, Facebook, Google and Microsoft are determined to embrace the metaverse well ahead of their competitors. It creates new markets, innovative social networks, cutting-edge devices, new consumer behavioural patterns and new patents. The only thing we should be concerned about is how we will fit into the future created by the metaverse.

The Internet has evolved beyond our imagination. It used to be an online world of hypertext and hyperlinks before becoming an interactive world of social media. In the next stage of evolution, are we really going to live in a virtual world? Or are we shifting from mere interaction to deep immersion in a virtual realm?

As of now, it is unclear how far the metaverse, which simulates real life, can go or how long it will take to develop. Many blockchain-based metaverse platforms are still working on AR and VR technology that will allow users to actively interact in virtual space.

So far in this chapter, we have talked about the evolution of the virtual world. But to make the picture clear, we must explore a revolution (not an evolution) that has been happening in our physical world.

This revolution started in the eighteenth century, mostly in Great Britain, continental Europe and the United States, and it lasted from the 1760s to the 1840s. This is the First Industrial Revolution or the first stage of the Industrial Revolution. The adoption of new manufacturing techniques set it apart. This transition included the transition from manual to machine production methods, new chemical manufacturing and iron production processes, increased use of steam power, the development of machine tools and the rise of the mechanized factory system.

Output increased dramatically, resulting in an unprecedented increase in population. Textiles were the first to use modern production methods, and they quickly became the dominant industry in terms of employment, output value and capital invested.

The United Kingdom was the epicentre of the Industrial Revolution, and many of the technological and architectural innovations were developed there. By the mid-eighteenth century, Britain was the world's leading commercial nation, commanding a global trading empire with colonies in North America and the Caribbean. Through the East India Company, Britain gained significant military and political power on the Indian subcontinent, especially in Mughal Bengal, which was just starting to become industrialized.

The Industrial Revolution was a watershed moment in history. In terms of material advancement, it was second only to humanity's adoption of agriculture. It influenced almost every aspect of daily life in some way. Average income and population, in particular, began to exhibit unprecedented sustained growth.

According to some economists, the most significant effect of the Industrial Revolution was that the standard of living in the Western world began to rise consistently for the first time in history. Prior to the Industrial Revolution and the emergence of the modern capitalist economy, GDP per capita was broadly stable, whereas the Industrial Revolution ushered in an era of per-capita economic growth in capitalist economies.

While the effects of the First Industrial Revolution are clear for all to see, the catalyst that triggered it is still a subject of debate among economists and historians.

To keep things short and simple, we would say it was the invention of the steam engine that triggered the Industrial Revolution. We will show you how.

Thomas Newcomen invented the first commercially successful steam engine capable of transmitting continuous power to a machine in 1712. In 1764, James Watt made a critical improvement by diverting spent steam to a separate vessel for condensation, significantly increasing the amount of work produced per unit of fuel consumed. Stationary steam engines have powered the factories of the Industrial Revolution ever since. Steam engines replaced sails on paddle steamers, and steam locomotives ran on railroads.

Historians still argue about when the first Industrial Revolution began and ended, as well as how quickly the economy and society changed. However, since the middle of the nineteenth century, the industrial environment had begun to change thanks to a technology that nineteenth-century scientists such as Thomas Edison, Michael Faraday,

Alessandro Volta and Benjamin Franklin developed: electricity.

Electricity is a type of energy that has always existed in the universe and has been known for thousands of years. So, electricity was never invented; rather, it was discovered. The significant discoveries and inventions of Benjamin Franklin, Alessandro Volta, Michael Faraday and Thomas Edison paved the way for modern electrical technology.

Modern electrical technology aided the rise of the Second Industrial Revolution, also known as the Technological Revolution or Industry 2.0. It was a period of rapid scientific discovery, standardization, mass production and industrialization that lasted from the late 1800s to the early 1900s.

Rapid industrialization was seen primarily in the United Kingdom, Germany and the United States, but also in France, the Low Countries, Italy and Japan. Manufacturing and production technology advancements enabled the widespread adoption of previously concentrated technological systems such as telegraph and railroad networks, gas and water supplies and sewage systems.

After 1870, the massive growth of rail and telegraph lines made it possible for people and ideas to move around in ways that had never been done before. This led to a new wave of globalization. At the same time, new technological systems, most notably electricity and telephones, were introduced.

While the First Industrial Revolution was characterized by the limited use of steam engines, interchangeable parts and mass production and was largely powered by water, Industry 2.0 was characterized by the construction of railroads, large-scale iron and steel production, widespread use of machinery in manufacturing, greatly increased use of steam power, widespread use of the telegraph, use of petroleum and the beginning of electrification. It was also the time when modern organizational methods for running large-scale businesses across broad areas became popular.

With early factory electrification and the production line, Industry 2.0 continued into the twentieth century; it ended at the start of World War I.

By the mid-twentieth century, another landmark disruption was on the horizon.

In 1945, John Mauchly and J. Presper Eckert of the University of Pennsylvania created the first electronic digital computer, known as the Electronic Numerical Integrator and Computer (ENIAC). During World War II, this machine did calculations with the help of vacuum tubes. It was primarily used by the military for tasks like figuring out how artillery would move.

After the invention of the personal computer, digital communication became economically feasible for widespread adoption. In his ground-breaking 1948 article,[3] 'A Mathematical Theory of Communication', Claude Shannon, a Bell Labs mathematician, is credited with laying the groundwork for digitization. He is also widely regarded as the father of digital circuit design theory and information theory.

Through digitization, technology was transformed from analogue to digital. This made it possible to create copies of the original that were exact replicas. For instance, reconfigurable hardware in digital communications was able to amplify the digital signal and transmit it while preserving all the signal's information. The ability to easily transfer digital information between media and to access or distribute it remotely was equally significant to the revolution.

The Digital Revolution, or Third Industrial Revolution, or Industry 3.0, brought massive disruption to the industrial ecosystem. It triggered the transition from mechanical and analogue electronic technology to digital electronics, which has continued to the present day, with the adoption and proliferation of digital computers and digital record-keeping. The term also implies the dramatic changes brought about by digital computing and communication technologies during this period.

Like the Agricultural Revolution, which began the Agricultural Age, and the First Industrial Revolution, which took the human race into the Industrial Age, the Digital Revolution ushered in the beginning of the Information Age.

It is often said that behind every successful man, there stands a woman. This statement may be right or wrong, but there are always some tremendous technologies that stand behind every revolution, evolution and 'age'. This technology is known as general purpose technology (GPT). Steam power and electricity were the GPTs of the Industrial Age, while electricity, digitization and computerization are the GPTs of the Information Age.

As technologies have transitioned from analogue to digital, they can mutate and transform into better technologies with ease, resulting in frequent disruptions.

Where do all these things point to?

They indicate that we have entered the fourth industrial revolution, or Industry 4.0.

The term 'Industry 4.0' was coined in 2015 by Klaus Schwab, founder and executive chairman of the

World Economic Forum. The term has since been used in numerous economic, political and scientific articles to refer to the current era of emerging high technology. According to Schwab, the changes seen are more than just efficiency improvements; they represent a significant shift in industrial capitalism.

The question now is: what is the GPT behind Industry 4.0?

A confluence of GPTs has sparked Industry 4.0. The first was electricity, the GPT of the Information Age and the previous two industrial revolutions. Then digitization and computerization—the GPTs of the Information Age—joined hands with electricity.

However, Industry 4.0 is not just a game of three GPTs. An army of GPTs stands behind this phase of the industrial revolution. These GPTs are artificial intelligence, machine learning, cloud computing, blockchain technology, gene editing and advanced robotics, which have the capability of blurring the lines between the physical, digital and biological worlds.

Industry 4.0 involves the automation of traditional manufacturing and industrial processes. Automation is made possible by the use of cutting-edge smart technology, high-speed connectivity, machine-to-machine communication (M2M) and the Internet of Things (IoT).

During this phase of the industrial revolution, there will be a big change in how global production and supply networks work. Increased automation, better communication and self-monitoring and the use of intelligent machines that can analyse and diagnose problems without human involvement are all outcomes of this integration.

Four key themes of Industry 4.0 are interconnection, information transparency, technical assistance and decentralized decisions. Industry 4.0 is the trend towards automation and data exchange in manufacturing technologies and processes, such as cyber-physical systems (CPS), the Industrial Internet of Things (IIoT) and cognitive computing.

Industry 4.0 connects the digital world, which is driven by information technology (IT), and the physical world, which is driven by operations technology (OT). Conventional factories are transforming into 'smart factories' or 'smart manufacturing' units. Advanced sensors are built into factory equipment and products so that data can be collected at different stages of the manufacturing process. Sensors are also used in the workplace to measure pressure, temperature, humidity and motion in real time. All these sensors send data to a centralized cloud platform, which analyses it to identify patterns, trends and anomalies.

Robotic arms, collaborative robots (cobots), automated guided vehicles (AGVs), autonomous mobile robots (AMRs) and automated storage and retrieval systems (AS/RS) are some of the most important automation systems in smart manufacturing.

Manufacturers in Industry 4.0 can create a 'digital twin', which is a virtual copy of a real product or process created using real-time data from sensors and other sources. Smart manufacturing uses digital twins, for example, to test and improve the layout and configuration of production lines and to simulate how a product or process will work in different situations.

Cloud computing and data analytics enable the collection, analysis and storage of massive amounts of data collected by connected devices, such as sensors, in the smart manufacturing environment.

Thanks to cloud computing, manufacturers can store and process data on remote servers rather than their own computers or servers. As their needs change, manufacturers will find it easier to expand their data storage and processing capabilities. The cloud's powerful processing capability allows manufacturers to analyse large data sets and gain deeper insights.

We as writers know the power of cloud technology. This book was not written with a pen on paper, or on our computers. We wrote this book on the cloud!

Writing on the cloud helped us in several ways. First, it provided a worry-free writing experience. We didn't need to worry as we were not writing on a Word file stored on our computers, which are vulnerable to crashes, hard disk failures and virus attacks. The content on the cloud is safe from these threats. Second, the cloud helped us collaborate on the book easily, especially as neither of us had met the other in real life and we lived far from each other. Third, a cloud platform like Google Docs utilizes artificial intelligence in addition to offering unlimited storage space. So, it helps identify and correct writing errors whenever they occur. We can also write without worrying about storage space.

If you are a 90s kid or a Millennial and got your first personal computer while you were studying in school, you would know how hard it was to store your favourite music in folders on your computer. Moreover, you had to 'write' it onto compact discs to keep it safe. You may have those compact discs even today, and you may keep them tomorrow for the sake of nostalgia. In reality, you won't need them today. They are just artefacts of the early days of the information age.

Today, most of us listen to music over applications such as Spotify and YouTube. Through these applications, you can access millions of songs and videos without storing them on your computer, smartphone, or writing them on to compact discs.

Furthermore, while using these cloud-based applications, they are also 'using' you. Artificial intelligence and machine learning algorithms run cloud-based applications like Spotify and YouTube. When you use these applications to listen to music or watch videos, they gain data on your favourite music, videos and your listening and watching patterns. They analyse this data on the cloud and recommend music, videos and advertisements as per your tastes and needs.

This is why listening to just two songs on an application like Spotify helps it create a personalized playlist for us, as a friend does.

One of our friends recently joked, 'Did you know that two guys know you better than your wife?' When we asked who these guys were, our friend replied: 'Google and Facebook!'

Your online searches, purchases, 'likes' and 'shares' on social media are generating data for big-tech social media platforms. They use this private data, which even your wife or friends may not have, to bombard you with advertisements and recommendations. They can even use that private data to manipulate your thoughts and actions.

The days are not far off when biometric devices in the form of smartwatches, smartphones and a human microchip implant will collect personal data, such as heartbeats, pulse rate, blood sugar levels and digital identities, and analyse it using algorithms on the cloud. This can help with faster and more effective personal identification and prevention of diseases, ailments and fraudulent activities.

We live in a physical world by leaving imprints in the virtual world. Although we exist in a material reality, we also create and interact with a digital reality through our online activities. We leave traces of our identity, preferences, opinions and emotions in the virtual world, such as social media posts, online purchases, search histories and digital art. These imprints can shape our self-image, influence our behaviour and affect our relationships with others. Others may also use them to find out more information about us, either for good or bad reasons. The physical and virtual worlds are not separate, but interconnected and interdependent.

Industry 4.0 is triggering a social, political and economic shift from the digital era of the late 1990s and early 2000s to an era of embedded connectivity. This era is marked by everyone using technology everywhere all the time. This changes how people see and understand the world around them. We have created and are entering an augmented social reality in comparison to mere human senses and industrial abilities.

Machines cannot replace deep expertise, but they are more efficient than humans at performing repetitive tasks. However, when machine learning is combined with computing power, machines can do very complicated tasks.

The Fourth Industrial Revolution brings new ways for humans and machines to interact, such as touch interfaces and virtual reality systems, as well as improvements in transferring digital instructions to the real world, such as robotics and 3D printing, which is also called 'additive manufacturing'.

You have already seen that Industry 4.0 is driven by 'big data', cloud computing and artificial intelligence-based systems. It is also characterized by increased adoption of off-grid or stand-alone renewable energy systems: solar, wind, wave, hydroelectric, lithium-ion renewable energy storage systems (ESS) and electric vehicles (EV).

The Fourth Industrial Revolution ushers in the Imagination Age.

In this age, creativity and imagination are the primary sources of economic value. On the other hand, analysis and thinking are significant skills in the Information Age. The Imagination Age theory says that technologies such as VR and user-generated content will change how people communicate with one another and how the economy and society work. Immersive virtual reality, or the metaverse, will become more popular. This will make the 'imagination work' of artists, designers and others more important than rational thinking as a cultural and economic foundation. Given that imagination is the most valued skill in our modern society, some argue that the Imagination Age has already begun.

The metaverse has the potential to take user experience to the next level. It will provide new diverse experiences in fields ranging from healthcare to the workplace to education and training. As Meta, the parent organization of Facebook, believes, 'The metaverse may be virtual, but the impact will be real'. It will help people learn and discover through 3D immersion. Just as the Internet is today, the metaverse will be a powerful storehouse of technologies, products and platforms. More importantly and uniquely, it won't be created, governed or operated by one organization or entity. In other words, it will be a completely decentralized system and give its users freedom of choice. However, as any technology is susceptible to misuse, so too is the metaverse. We therefore need to tread with care and ensure that the metaverse ecosystem is safe, transparent, secure and accessible and does not violate the privacy of its users.

The metaverse thus stands in the middle of our physical and virtual worlds as a stepping stone to our immersive virtual world life experiences.

One real-life story will help you understand how the metaverse opens up a world of limitless opportunities. The names of the characters have been changed for privacy.

Narendran was born in the 1960s, and he was a talented writer who dreamed of becoming a best-selling author. More than that, he deeply wished to make a living through his writing skills. He had written four books, but no publishers had accepted them for publication. Eventually, the manuscripts remained on his shelf.

Frustrated, Narendran began to work as a clerk at a finance company, his dream of becoming an author remaining unfulfilled. Later, he got married and became the father of a boy, Naresh.

Naresh was born in the 1980s, and he inherited his father's writing gene. He began to show an interest in writing at an early age. But his father, Narendran, discouraged him from pursuing writing and compelled him to pursue other professions that would offer him a well-paying job.

To Narendran, writing was a useless skill that would not get his son anywhere. He had learned that from his own experience, but what he failed to understand was that times had changed.

By the time Naresh completed his graduation in economics, Web 2.0 was rising, opening up a lot of opportunities for web content writers. Soon after graduation, he joined a content writing firm with a meagre salary.

Narendran opposed his son's career selection. But Naresh was determined because he saw what his father didn't: a world full of money-making opportunities for writers.

After gaining experience as a writer, Naresh began his career as a freelance writer. Within a few years, he began earning a six-figure income. In the meantime, he also published two books through self-publishing platforms, digitally marketed them over social media platforms and began to earn royalties from his work.

Narendran watched his son's rapid career growth with awe. He was immensely happy to see his son achieve things that he could only dream about.

We can generalize this story to apply to every person who makes a living out of Web 2.0, especially online entrepreneurs such as bloggers, vloggers and those in digital sales and marketing. It wouldn't be an exaggeration to say that today, the majority of us make a living one way or another through the Internet or cyberspace.

Naresh's story shows how Web 2.0 has transformed the lives of millions around the world. If interactive cyberspace can transform our lives in this tremendous way, can you imagine the extent to which an immersive virtual world like the metaverse could transform human lives? Sometimes, the opportunities put forward by the metaverse are beyond our imaginations, in the true sense.

Unlike our physical world, the virtual world is limitless. The physical and financial resources of our limited world won't be enough to deal with an immersive virtual realm like the metaverse. Like the real world, the virtual world has its own offerings, which people will want to enjoy. However, to enjoy those offerings one will have to buy them with money. Therefore, just as in the real world we spend money to fulfil our needs and wishes, in the virtual world too we need money to spend on the things we desire and cherish. This is where crypto assets like cryptocurrencies, crypto tokens like NFTs and crypto commodities like Ethereum play key roles. For example, in the metaverse, one can buy virtual assets like virtual land, virtual clothes and virtual educational products using a cryptocurrency. It is important to note that metaverse projects are mostly governed by crypto due to their fungibility and flexibility. Moreover, unlike a fiat currency, a cryptocurrency is not required to be converted into another currency while transacting. This is what makes crypto the metaverse currency or meta crypto. As more and more people start exploring the metaverse, the demand for various cryptocurrencies will surge.

Read more about the topic, gain more knowledge and reflect on it. That is the best way to align ourselves with the revolution that is happening right before our eyes. Take this book only as a beginner's guide to decentralized currencies and a world beyond the universe.

# 8

# Embarking on Your Crypto Investment Journey in India

Although investing in crypto assets is not illegal in India, the government heavily taxes and regulates it. The Finance Bill 2022 imposes a 30 per cent tax on crypto holdings and transfers, making it costly to trade crypto in India. The government has also expressed its intention to create a central bank digital currency (CBDC) and ban private cryptocurrencies.

However, despite these challenges, India is one of the fastest-growing crypto markets in the world, with over 100 million crypto owners. Some of the most popular crypto assets in India are Bitcoin, Ethereum, Dogecoin, Cardano and XRP.

The Indian crypto market is witnessing a surge of innovation and entrepreneurship as more and more crypto projects and platforms emerge and gain traction. Some examples include Polygon, a layer-2 scaling solution for Ethereum; WazirX, a leading crypto exchange and platform;

CoinDCX, a crypto investment app; and Instadapp, a DeFi aggregator and manager.

If you are a beginner and want to start investing in crypto assets in India, you need to follow five basic steps:

1. Choose a crypto exchange or broker that is registered with the Financial Intelligence Unit (FIU) and complies with the tax and regulatory requirements.

   An FIU is a national agency that collects, analyses and disseminates information on suspicious or unusual financial transactions that may be related to money laundering, terrorism financing or other crimes. FIUs also cooperate with other domestic and international agencies to combat financial crimes. The Financial Intelligence Unit-India (FIU-IND) reports directly to the finance minister-led Economic Intelligence Council.

   Some of the leading cryptocurrency exchanges in India are WazirX, CoinDCX, ZebPay and Unocoin. They allow users to buy, sell, trade and store various digital tokens, such as Bitcoin, Ethereum, Ripple and more. They also offer different features and services, such as crypto lending, margin trading, peer-to-peer (P2P) transactions and educational resources.

2. Create an account on the platform and verify your identity and address. You may need to provide your Permanent Account Number (PAN) card, Aadhaar card, bank account details and other documents.

3. Deposit funds into your account using your preferred payment method. You can use the Unified Payments Interface (UPI), bank transfers, debit cards or credit cards.

4. Start purchasing crypto assets of your choice. You can either buy them at the current market price or place a limit order to buy them at a specific price.
5. Store your crypto assets in a secure wallet. You can either use the platform's wallet or transfer your crypto to an external wallet, such as a hardware wallet or a software wallet.

As previously stated, there are two sorts of cryptocurrency wallets: software-based hot wallets and physical cold wallets. Hardware wallets, a sort of cold wallet, are one of the most secure methods of storing cryptocurrency. They function by keeping your private keys on a physical device (often a USB or Bluetooth device).

Some of the benefits of using a hard wallet are:

- Control: You have full ownership and control of your funds as you manage your private keys without relying on any third-party service.
- Security: Your private keys are kept offline at all times, which makes them immune to hacking, malware or phishing attacks.
- Compatibility: As long as the device supports them, you can store and access thousands of different cryptocurrencies with a single hard wallet.
- Convenience: You can easily connect your hard wallet to your computer or smartphone and make transactions with a simple click or tap.

Online platforms like TradingView can assist cryptocurrency traders and investors. They are platforms that provide advanced charting tools, market data and social features for traders and investors in various markets, including cryptocurrencies. They also support trading directly from the charts through various brokers and exchanges, such as Binance, Coinbase and Kraken.

Crypto investing offers a wide range of assets, pairs and derivatives to choose from. However, not all of them have the same performance and potential. Therefore, it is advisable to diversify the portfolio across different categories, such as Bitcoin, altcoins, stablecoins and tokens, as well as across different sectors, such as DeFi, NFTs, gaming and the metaverse. This way, one can reduce the correlation and dependency on a single asset or market and increase the chances of earning consistent returns.

If you are interested in crypto investing, there are a few things that you should be aware of.

The Finance Act 2022 introduced a new provision named Section 115BBH, which came into effect on 1 April 2023. It deals with the taxation of income from the transfer of any virtual digital asset (VDA), such as cryptocurrency or a non-fungible token (NFT).

According to Section 115BBH, the income from the transfer of any VDA is taxed at a flat rate of 30 per cent, irrespective of the holding period or the nature of the asset. This means that whether you sell your VDA after a day or a year, you will have to pay the same tax rate. Also, it does not matter if your VDA is a capital asset or not; the tax treatment is the same.

Moreover, Section 115BBH does not allow any deduction or allowance for any expenditure (other than the cost of acquisition) or the set off of any loss in computing the income from the transfer of VDA. This means that you cannot claim any expenses related to the transaction, such as fees, commissions, etc.

You cannot adjust the loss from one VDA against the gain from another VDA or any other income. For example, if you sell Bitcoin at a loss and Ethereum at a profit, you cannot reduce your taxable income by the amount of the loss from Bitcoin. Similarly, you cannot carry forward the loss from VDA to the next year.

The goal of Section 115BBH is to impose a high and uniform tax rate on the income from the transfer of any VDA without allowing any deduction or set-off of loss. It is also aimed at discouraging the use of VDA for financial transactions or investments and bringing them under the tax net.

Another important thing a crypto investor in India must know is how tax deducted at source (TDS) affects crypto investing in the country. TDS is a mechanism used to collect taxes from the source of income and record transaction information. It applies to all transfers of crypto assets that exceed Rs 50,000 (or Rs 10,000 in some cases) in the same financial year. According to the 2022 budget, crypto investors are subject to a 1 per cent TDS and 30 per cent tax on all crypto gains.

As a crypto investor, you may also face the possibility of losing money or value due to changes in the exchange rates of different cryptocurrencies or fiat currencies. Exchange risk can affect crypto investors who trade across different platforms, markets or countries, or who hold crypto assets for a long period of time.

Exchange risk can arise from various factors such as high price volatility, which crypto assets are famous for. Some cryptocurrencies may have low liquidity, which means they have fewer buyers and sellers, higher spreads and longer transaction times. This can make it difficult or costly for crypto investors to exchange their crypto assets at a favourable rate or in a timely manner.

Fake crypto exchanges and crypto wallets operate a scheme where the exchange or broker claims to have bought or sold crypto assets on behalf of the investor, but in reality, they have not. The exchange or broker may show fake transactions, balances or statements on the investor's account while pocketing the investor's money or using it for other purposes. This is a form of investment scam that is prevalent on social media. Investors should be wary of any offers that sound too good to be true, such as huge gains, low or no risk, or guaranteed returns.

Using hardware wallets can keep these fraudulent activities at bay to a great extent. As a crypto investor, you should also do your due diligence before choosing an exchange or broker and verify their credentials, reputation and security measures. If you suspect that you have been a victim of this sort of fraud, you should report it to the authorities as soon as possible.

Cryptocurrencies are subject to different and evolving regulations in different jurisdictions, which can affect their legal status, taxation and accessibility. Crypto investors may face challenges or risks when they need to comply with different rules or laws when exchanging their crypto assets across borders or platforms.

These challenges and risks are an inevitable part of crypto investing, but they can be managed and mitigated through hedging, diversification and in-depth research. Research involves gathering and analysing relevant and reliable information about the crypto market, the exchange rates, the regulations and the platforms in order to make informed and rational decisions. Crypto investors should always be aware of the potential risks and benefits of exchanging their crypto assets and seek professional advice if needed.

## Managing Crypto Assets in Your Portfolio

As previously stated, cryptocurrency investment provides a diverse choice of assets, pairs and derivatives to pick from. However, not all of them perform and have the same potential. Thus, it is prudent to diversify the portfolio across many categories and different sectors. This reduces correlation and dependency on a single asset or market, increasing the likelihood of obtaining consistent returns.

If you wish to add crypto assets to your diversified portfolio that already includes stocks, bonds or ETFs, it is recommended that you invest only 1–5 per cent of your total portfolio value in crypto assets. For example, if your portfolio is worth Rs 100,00,00, you should invest between Rs 10,000 and Rs 50,000 in crypto assets.

You can also implement core and satellite portfolio strategies in crypto investing. These investing strategies combine passive and active funds to achieve diversification, lower costs and higher returns. The core part of the portfolio should consist of well-established, stable and widely adopted cryptocurrencies, such as Bitcoin, Ethereum, Binance Coin, Cardano, Polkadot, Solana, etc. For the satellite part of your portfolio, you may want to allocate a smaller percentage of your capital to more speculative, risky and potentially rewarding crypto assets, such as DeFi tokens, NFTs, meme coins, gaming tokens, etc. The core part provides stability and reduces volatility, while the satellite part provides growth and enhances returns. A typical core and satellite portfolio may have an 80:20 or 70:30 ratio of core to satellite assets, depending on the investor's risk profile and investment goals.

## Continuous Learning Is the Key

Investing and trading, including crypto trading, requires constant learning and updating of knowledge and skills. Therefore, it is important to access reliable and relevant educational resources, such as books, blogs, podcasts, videos, courses and webinars, that can provide valuable insights and guidance on the crypto market. Moreover, you can also join crypto communities and groups, such as forums, chats, and social media, where you can interact with other traders and experts, and learn from their experiences and opinions.

Crypto trading involves high volatility and uncertainty, so it is important to manage your risk exposure and avoid losing more than you can afford. Some of the risk management techniques include setting clear stop-loss and take-profit orders, diversifying the portfolio across different assets and strategies, and using only a small percentage of the capital for each trade.

Apart from the risks of trading, crypto trading also involves security risks such as hacking, phishing and fraud. Therefore, it is essential to protect your funds and personal information by using reputable and regulated platforms, choosing strong passwords and encryption, enabling two-factor authentication, and storing the assets in secure hardware wallets.

Always remember that investing and trading are games of probabilities and risk-reward ratios. Crypto assets are highly volatile and speculative, and you may lose some or all of your investment.

# Afterword

The earliest forms of life on Earth are thought to have emerged in the oceans around 3.5 billion years ago. These life forms were most likely simple, single-celled organisms like bacteria and archaea that relied on the nutrients and energy sources found in the ocean.

We can distinguish living organisms from non-living ones by using a simple criterion: living organisms reproduce, while non-living entities do not. In the case of single-celled organisms, they reproduce by cell division. So, to produce offspring, a living organism must do one thing without fail: it must survive. To survive, it must adapt to various conditions on Earth.

Herbert Spencer, a British scientist and philosopher, came up with the phrase 'survival of the fittest' to explain how he thought Charles Darwin's theory of evolution by natural selection worked. The idea behind 'survival of the fittest' is that life forms that are best able to adapt to their environment are more likely to reproduce and pass on their positive traits to future generations.

In the evolutionary timeline, our aquatic ancestors came out of the ocean and began to adapt to life on land by surviving and reproducing. Eventually, they survived and reproduced enough to evolve into terrestrial animals, saying goodbye to aquatic life.

Evolution never stops. Our terrestrial ancestors evolved into a species called Homo sapiens that walked on their hind legs and had unique cognitive abilities that distinguished them from other species that survived on land, air and water. These unique cognitive abilities have helped us survive in an entirely different way than other species that have been surviving and reproducing on Earth for billions of years.

We can adequately describe different stages of human history based on the tools we use to survive. The Stone Age was a time in human history when most tools and weapons were made of stone, mostly flintstone (a hard form of stone). During this time, people also learned how to make fire, which allowed them to adapt to new environments and expand their territories.

Later, as populations gradually increased, hunting and gathering became more difficult. The only option was to grow and raise our own food. So we changed our survival tactics and tried our hand at agriculture, using simple tools such as digging sticks, hoes and sickles. In the process, we were developing the earliest form of automation. This period in human history is known as the Agricultural Age.

In those days, we didn't have much technology at our disposal, so we depended on natural resources like soil, water and climatic conditions. Eventually, we learned how to domesticate animals, another automation venture, enabling us to use them for flesh, milk, ploughs and transportation.

Although we had to face challenges like famine, heavy rains, floods, infectious diseases and other unfavourable environmental conditions, agriculture made our lives relatively easier and helped us settle as civilizations. We stopped constantly roaming in search of food and settled down to work in our fields. As a result, we had more time to relax in our homes, and we waited, praying for the day the farmland would produce food.

The next set of survival tools humans used were mechanized ones, giving birth to industries and leading to the Industrial Age. This was an era of mechanization and mass production, which removed physical labour from the manufacturing process. Mechanization increased agricultural output by removing labour from the field.

In the Information Age, people use tools such as computers, smartphones and the Internet to access, process and share information, which is the main source of economic value. In the Imagination Age, people will need tools, such as virtual reality, artificial intelligence and biotechnology to trade our creativity, innovation, collaboration and imagination for our survival.

The digital revolution and computerization have emerged in recent decades to ease our intellectual labour. Industry 4.0 is replete with technologies such as artificial intelligence and machine learning to simulate our cognitive abilities. Simply put, the revolutions and evolutions mentioned in this book are all about making our lives easier and our societies peaceful and transparent.

Have you ever wondered why humans frequently invent things that make our lives and livelihood easier? Are we a lazy lot?

Observing how wild animals behave can help answer this question. Let us take the lion, the king of the jungle, as an example. Do lions hunt from morning to night? No. Lions never get 'busy' like we do. They don't hunt unless they feel hungry. Moreover, while hunting, they always target the weakest prey in the vicinity. For instance, if a lion hunts a herd of gazelles, the king of the jungle always goes for the weakest gazelle in the herd.

Why does the lion do so? Isn't the king strong enough to chase and hunt down the strongest gazelle? Doesn't he have the endurance to hunt from morning to night? The lion is strong and energetic enough to go on countless hunts; he is also capable of hunting down the strongest gazelle in the herd. But the king is more concerned with one thing: conserving energy to survive. Energy conservation is a biological phenomenon that refers to how animals optimize their energy use to survive and thrive in their surroundings. Animals know they have limited energy resources, and they must balance their energy intake from food with their energy expenditure for things like hunting, physical growth and mating. Animals can use a variety of strategies to conserve energy, one of which is to reduce their physical activity levels. Energy conservation is written in the genetic code of every animal on earth, including humans.

'I choose a lazy person to do a hard job because a lazy person will find an easy way to do it.' This quote is frequently attributed to Bill Gates, Microsoft's co-founder. However, there is some disagreement about whether he actually said it, as there does not appear to be a verifiable source for the quote. Despite this, the sentiment expressed in the quote is frequently used to emphasize the importance of finding innovative and efficient solutions to our everyday challenges.

Man is not lazy; no animal is. We are very careful with how we spend our energy owing to the scarcity of energy resources. That is why we find it hard to work out at the gym, run a marathon or work for longer hours in the office.

Always keep in mind the term 'energy conservation' whenever a new technology is born. Technology is only innovative if it makes our lives and ways of making a living easier. It is common that some jobs become obsolete with the arrival of new technology, but on the other hand, it also opens the door for new opportunities.

What we are trying to say is that there is no need to be fearful and doubtful, and an open mind to embrace new technology is what is needed in these days of consistent technological disruptions.

In today's world, we have access to a lot of information, but we often fail to comprehend the events and issues that affect us. On top of that, financial illiteracy rules the world. It is a well-known fact that a large percentage of people in the English-speaking world don't know much about money. Bankrate did a survey[1] in 2022 and found that 40 per cent of Americans with credit card debt don't know what their interest rate is. Bankrate is an independent, ad-supported publisher and comparison service. ValuePenguin, a market research and analysis company, found out[2] recently that nearly 70 per cent of Americans don't know the concept of compound interest. This lack of knowledge is not limited to the US.

A recent survey[3] done by Opinium on behalf of the
Centre for Social Justice, a think tank, found that 44 per
cent of adults in the UK lack basic money management
skills, such as budgeting. Financial illiteracy is especially
acute among young people. More than two-thirds, 68 per
cent, cited a lack of money management skills as a major
contributor to their debt. The survey was conducted among
4000 adults in the UK.

The Asian Development Bank estimates[4] that only 27
per cent of Indian adults—and 24 per cent of women—
will meet the Reserve Bank of India's minimum level of
financial literacy in 2022. The Reserve Bank of India
defines the minimum level of financial literacy as the
ability to understand and use basic financial concepts,
such as interest rates, inflation, risk diversification and
compound interest.

Politicians, central bankers and businesspeople often
say that most people don't know much about money, and
they have a good reason to say this. A society that expects
most people to manage their income and expenditure
after taxes, that expects most adults to own their own
homes and that leaves it up to the individual to make
decisions on retirement savings and whether or not to get
health insurance is storing up trouble for the future by
not giving its citizens the tools they need to make sensible
financial decisions.

One of the tools that can help people improve their
financial literacy is historical knowledge. By learning about
the origins and evolution of the banks and financial terms
we use today, we can gain a better understanding of how
complex they are and how they affect our lives. If we know

where a financial institution or instrument came from, it will be much easier to understand what it does now and how to use it wisely.

Our nomadic forefathers survived in groups. These groups were led by strong and adaptable leaders. As time passed, these groups settled down to form civilizations, and their leaders became kings. Later, these civilizations developed into monarch-ruled nations. Monarchs led a luxurious life at the expense of their subjects for centuries until rebels entered the scene. Rebels overthrew these kings, and in some instances, the rebels grew in power to become dictators.

Many nations finally chose democracy after a long history of civil wars, rebellions, revolutions and two world wars. This system 'for the people, by the people, and of the people' changed the system of monarchs and dictators into one of elected political leaders who, unfortunately, still 'rule' the people.

We live in a paradoxical world. Democracy is all about leading and following, not ruling and yielding. You would have noticed that we and our media usually refer to the political party that won the elections as the 'ruling' party, not the 'leading' party. The elected politicians who are meant to serve the people live a king's life with high-level security and other fancy facilities. They introduce welfare measures as if the resources, including money, were taken from their pockets. They declare war, show favouritism and misuse public funds.

War, conquests and ruling over subjects are the relics of the Middle Ages. Alexander the Great and Napoleon Bonaparte both tried these. The East India Company tried

Afterword


it for centuries. History, however, was never on their side, and their miserable failures are etched in the annals of human history.

But why does this paradox happen in the twenty-first century? It happens because although we live in the twenty-first century, our mindset remains that of the Middle Ages.

Another paradox is that in a universe made up of energy and matter, we humans drill the earth and oceans to suck up crude oil, refine it and burn it for energy! This centuries-long process has led to air pollution, habitat destruction, water pollution, ecological imbalances, greenhouse gas emissions, climate change and health issues.

Throughout history, we transformed systems and technologies in the hope that things would change for the better. But we forgot the fact that things will change for the better only if we are daring enough to change the foundation of our current systems, that is, centralized control. You have no doubt seen how inefficient and corrupt the worldwide centralized systems are, including political systems, financial systems and companies.

We believe that the human race is going through an unlearning phase today. Unlearning is the process of letting go of old habits, systems, beliefs or ways of thinking that are no longer useful or can even be harmful. It entails actively seeking new information, technologies or perspectives, as well as engaging in critical self-reflection and challenging our own biases and assumptions.

When Klaus Schwab, founder and executive chairman of the World Economic Forum, came up with the term 'Industry 4.0', he said that the changes it brings are a significant shift in industrial capitalism rather than mere efficiency improvements. Industry 4.0 will take humans out of the production process, bring in decentralized decision-making and run everything on renewable energy sources. Simultaneously, blockchain technology will create decentralized financial, political and societal governance systems.

These innovative technologies are going to break down and rebuild the foundations of our new economy's quadrilateral foundation: corporations, stock markets, banks and governments. History was never on the side of centralized power. Time has taught us that only through peace and transparency can we trade and create value that benefits everyone.

After the world's third-largest crypto exchange, FTX, collapsed on 11 November 2022 under Sam Bankman-Fried's leadership, following a massive run on its funds, you might doubt the future of crypto assets. Let us make one thing clear. FTX built its business on risky trading options that are illegal in the US. Sam Bankman-Fried did it at a time when the crypto industry was increasingly becoming the target of regulatory scrutiny around the world. A complete breakdown in corporate control, which included the use of software to hide the misappropriation of customer funds, was the root cause of FTX's failure. This happens when a decentralized system is put under centralized leadership and has nothing to do with the underlying crypto assets based on blockchain technology.

The fault is not with the money but with the people who use it. Time has proven that the Victorian thought pattern was right. The fault is not with the systems we use today but with the people who use or control them. With blockchain, renewable energy and automation technologies, decentralization is around the corner.

It has never been more essential to comprehend the rise of money and technology than it is today, whether you are trying to make ends meet or want to be on top of the world. If this book helps break down the scary wall that has grown between financial literacy, technological knowledge and other kinds of knowledge, then we won't have worked for nothing.

The DeFi world has already opened its doors, and we would be happy if this book acts as a guide for your journey deep into the unexplored decentralized world.

# Recommended Reading

- Berners-Lee, Tim. 2000. *Weaving the Web: The Original Design and Ultimate Destiny of the World Wide Web*. New York: Harper Business.
- Burniske, Chris, and Jack Tatar. 2018. *Cryptoassets: The Innovative Investor's Guide to Bitcoin and Beyond*. New York: McGraw-Hill Education.
- Chancellor, Edward. 2000. *Devil Take the Hindmost: A History of Financial Speculation*. US: Plume.
- Dwivedi, Sharada. 2006. *Premchand Roychand: His Life and Times*. Mumbai: Eminence Designs.
- Ferguson, Niall. 2008. *The Ascent of Money: A Financial History of the World*. US: Penguin Press HC.
- Harari, Yuval Noah. 2016. *Homo Deus: A Brief History of Tomorrow*. London: Harvill Secker.
- Harari, Yuval Noah. 2014. *Sapiens: A Brief History of Humankind*. Trans. John Purcell and Haim Watzman. London: Harvill Secker.

- Mackay, Charles. 1980. *Extraordinary Popular Delusions and the Madness of Crowds*. Ed. Norman Cohn. New York: Harmony Books.
- Mallaby, Sebastian. 2011. *More Money Than God: Hedge Funds and the Making of a New Elite*. USA: Penguin Books.
- Rand, Ayn. 1967. *Capitalism: The Unknown Ideal*. New York: New American Library.
- Singh, Simon. 1999. *The Code Book: The Science of Secrecy from Ancient Egypt to Quantum Cryptography*. New York: Anchor Books.
- Smith, Adam. 1904. *An Inquiry into the Nature and Causes of the Wealth of Nations*. Ed. Edwin Cannan. London: Methuen & Co.

# Notes

## Preface

1. 'Jeff Bezos', *Forbes*, https://www.forbes.com/profile/jeff-bezos/?sh=4e6671ba1b23.

## Chapter 1: The Rise of Riches

1. Niall Ferguson, *The Ascent of Money: A Financial History of the World* (USA: Penguin, 2008), p. 23.
2. Ibid.
3. Ibid.
4. Ibid.
5. Ibid., p. 21.
6. Adam Smith, *An Inquiry into the Nature and Causes of the Wealth of Nations* (London: Methuen, 1776).
7. 'Money is the god of our time, and Rothschild is his prophet', AZ Quotes, https://www.wsj.com/public/resources/documents/mill-1-timeline-rothschild.htm.

8. Niall Ferguson, *The World's Banker: The History of the House of Rothschild* vols 1 and 2 (New York: Viking, 1998–1999); Niall Ferguson, *The House of Rothschild: Money's Prophets 1798–1848* Vol. 1 (New York: Viking, 1998); Niall Ferguson, *The House of Rothschild: The World's Banker, 1849–1999* Vol. 2 (New York: Viking, 1999).

9. Ibid.

10. Niall Ferguson, *The Ascent of Money: A Financial History of the World* (USA: Penguin, 2008), p. 184.

11. Thomas Bayes, 'An essay towards solving a problem in the doctrine of chances. By the late Rev. Mr. Bayes, F.R.S. communicated by Mr. Price, in a letter to John Canton, A.M.F.R.S.', *Philosophical Transactions of the Royal Society of London* 53 (1763), 370–418.

12. 'Edward Lloyd and his Coffee House', Lloyd's Register, https://www.lr.org/en/about-us/who-we-are/our-history/edward-lloyd-coffee-house/; James Thomas and Alexander Cherry, 'Coffee House 2.0: Innovation in Marine Insurance', Accenture, 3 June 2021, https://insuranceblog.accenture.com/coffee-house-2-0-innovation-in-marine-insurance; Robin Pearson, 'Lloyd's: Its History and Business Practices', *Delusions of Competence: The Near-Death of Lloyd's of London 1970–2002* (India: Palgrave Macmillan, 2022), https://link.springer.com/chapter/10.1007/978-3-030-94088-1_2; 'Lloyd's buildings', Lloyds, https://www.lloyds.com/about-lloyds/history/lloyds-buildings.

13. Robert Peel, 'Speech on the Bank Charter Act, House of Commons', 6 May 1844, *Speeches of the Late Right Honourable Sir Robert Peel, Bart., Delivered*

*in the House of Commons*, Vol. 4 (London: George Routledge and Co., 1853), p. 58.

14. 'The rise of the Gold Standard - records from 1660-1819', World Gold Council, https://www.gold.org/about-gold/history-of-gold/gold-as-money/history-of-gold-back-to-1600/the-rise-of-the-gold-standard, last accessed 29 January 2024;
'Gold Standard', Encyclopedia Britannica, 20 July 1998, https://www.britannica.com/money/topic/gold-standard.

15. 'How Britain gained an empire - economics and commerce', Bitesize BBC, https://www.bbc.co.uk/bitesize/guides/zwvqcwx/revision/3.

16. Niall Ferguson, *The Ascent of Money: A Financial History of the World* (USA: Penguin, 2008).

## Chapter 2: The Boom-and-Bust Stories

1. Lodewijk Petram, *The World's First Stock Exchange* (Columbia UP, 2014).

2. John Law, *Money and Trade Considered: With a Proposal for Supplying the Nation with Money*, (1705, reprint, Glasgow: R. & A. Foulis, 1750).

3. Niall Ferguson, *The Ascent of Money: A Financial History of the World* (London: Penguin, 2008), p. 150.

4. Bernard Wysocki Jr., 'Companies Chose to Rethink A Quaint Concept: Profits', *Wall Street Journal*, 3 December 1999, p. A1.

5. 'The Greatest Trades In Wall Street History', *Business Insider* India, 22 February 2013, https://www.businessinsider.in/finance/the-greatest-trades-in-wall-street-history/articleshow/21325520.cms.

6. Sharada Dwivedi, *Premchand Roychand: His Life and Times* (Eminence Designs, 2006).

7. Naresh Fernandes, *City Adrift: A Short Biography of Bombay* (Aleph Book Company, 2013), pp. 17–18

8. 'Raging Bull – Harshad Mehta', *Business Today*, April 1991; Yashwant Deshmukh and Sutana Guru, 'April Scam, and the Big Bull: Have Regulators Learnt From Harshad Mehta's Case?', Quint, 25 April 2023, https://www.thequint.com/opinion/april-scam-the-big-bull-have-regulators-learnt-from-harshad-mehta-case#read-more.

9. Sucheta Dalal, 'The Scam: From Harshad Mehta to Ketan Parekh', *Times of India*, 23 April 1992, p. 1.

## Chapter 3: The Big Short

1. 'Lewis S. Ranieri: Your Mortgage Was His Bond', *Bloomberg Businessweek*, 29 November 2004, https://www.bloomberg.com/news/articles/2004-11-28/lewis-s-dot-ranieri-your-mortgage-was-his-bond.

2. 'Greenspan: Housing Market Worst May Be Over', NBC News, 9 October 2006, https://www.nbcnews.com/id/wbna15198805.

3. Annette Haddad, 'Greenspan Sees Bubbles in Housing', *Los Angeles Times*, 2 March 2019, https://www.latimes.com/archives/la-xpm-2005-may-21-fi-green21-story.html.

## Chapter 4: Our Troublesome Financial System

1. 'Zim Inflation to Hit 500pc', *Business Times*, 13 September 2019, https://businesstimes.co.zw/zim-inflation-to-hit-500pc/.

2. 'Years of crisis (1920–23)', https://www.britannica.com/place/Weimar-Republic/Years-of-crisis-1920-23, last accessed 29 January 2024.
3. Milton Friedman, *Money Mischief: Episodes in Monetary History* (Boston: Mariner Books, 1994), p.63.
4. 'Act No. XIX of 1947', India Code, https://www.indiacode.nic.in/repealed-act/repealed_act_documents/A1947-19.pdf, last accessed 29 January 2024.
5. Assar Lindbeck, 'Rent Control as an Instrument of Housing Policy', *The Economic Problems of Housing*, ed. Adela Adam Nevitt (Palgrave Macmillan, 1967), pp. 39–54.
6. Thomas Sowell, *Basic Economics: A Common Sense Guide to the Economy* (4th ed.) (Basic Books, 2011), p. 28.

## Chapter 5: Capitalism is Good

1. Ayn Rand, *Capitalism: The Unknown Ideal* (New York: New American Library, 1966).
2. Max Roser, 'Poverty', Our World in Data, 2022, https://ourworldindata.org/poverty.

## Chapter 6: The Rise of Crypto Assets

1. Satoshi Nakamoto, 'Bitcoin: A Peer-to-Peer Electronic Cash System', SSRN, 21 August 2008, https://papers.ssrn.com/sol3/papers.cfm?abstract_id=3440802.
2. Satoshi Nakamoto, 'Bitcoin: A Peer-to-Peer Electronic Cash System', SSRN, 21 August 2008, https://papers.ssrn.com/sol3/papers.cfm?abstract_id=3440802.

3. Satoshi Nakamoto, 'Re: Bitcoin P2P e-cash paper', Cryptography Mailing List, 7 November 2008 https:// bitcoinik.com/quotes-by-satoshi-nakamoto/.

4. Chris Williams, 'Bitcoin's Birthday: Satoshi Nakamoto's Hidden Message Explained', Crypto Briefing, 3 January 2021,https://cryptobriefing.com/bitcoin-birthday-satoshi-hidden-message-explained/.

5. 'The Times 03 Jan 2009 Chancellor on Brink of Second Bailout for Banks', Genesis Block Newspaper, https://www.thetimes03jan2009.com, last accessed 29 January 2024.

6. Satoshi Nakamoto, 'Bitcoin open source implementation of P2P currency', P2P Foundation, 11 February 2009, last accessed 7 January 2024.

7. Satoshi Nakamoto, 'Re: Wikileaks contact info?', Bitcoin Forum, 5 December 2010, last accessed 7 January 2024.

8. Simon Singh, *The Code Book: The Science of Secrecy from Ancient Egypt to Quantum Cryptography* (Doubleday, 2000).

## Chapter 7: Welcome to the DeFi World

1. Tim Berners-Lee, *Weaving the Web: The Original Design and Ultimate Destiny of the World Wide Web* (Harper Business, 2000), p. 3.

2. Neal Stephenson, *Snow Crash* (Penguin Books Ltd, 2011).

3. C. E. Shannon, 'A Mathematical Theory of Communication', https://people.math.harvard.edu/~ctm/home/text/others/shannon/entropy/entropy.pdf

## Afterword

1. Michelle Fox, '40% of Americans with Credit Card Debt Don't Know Their Interest Rate, Survey Shows', CNBC, 10 January 2022, https://www.cnbc.com/2022/01/10/40percent-of-americans-with-credit-card-debt-dont-know-their-interest-rate.html.

2. Kathleen Elkins, 'Most Americans Don't Understand a Money Term That Can Help You Save Hundreds of Thousands of Dollars', CNBC, 12 February 2019, https://www.cnbc.com/2019/02/11/how-compound-interest-works-and-how-it-can-help-you-save-money.html.

3. 'On the Money: A roadmap for lifelong financial learning', Centre for Social Justice, June 2022, https://www.centreforsocialjustice.org.uk/wp-content/uploads/2022/06/CSJ-The_financial_education_initiative.pdf

4. 'In India, Financial Literacy Programs Are Lifting Families out of Debt and Fueling New Prosperity', Asian Development Bank, 8 March 2022, https://www.adb.org/results/india-financial-literacy-programs-lifting-families-out-debt-fueling-new-prosperity.

Scan QR code to access the
Penguin Random House India website